Crime and
Racial Constructions

Crime and Racial Constructions

Cultural Misinformation about African Americans in Media and Academia

Jeanette Covington

LEXINGTON BOOKS
A division of
ROWMAN & LITTLEFIELD PUBLISHERS, INC.
Lanham • Boulder • New York • Toronto • Plymouth, UK

Published by Lexington Books
A division of Rowman & Littlefield Publishers, Inc.
A wholly owned subsidiary of The Rowman & Littlefield Publishing Group, Inc.
4501 Forbes Boulevard, Suite 200, Lanham, Maryland 20706
http://www.lexingtonbooks.com

Estover Road, Plymouth PL6 7PY, United Kingdom

British Library Cataloguing in Publication Information Available

Library of Congress Cataloging-in-Publication Data

Covington, Jeanette, 1949–
  Crime and racial constructions : cultural misinformation about African Americans in
media and academia / Jeanette Covington.
      p.   cm.
  Includes bibliographical references and index.
  ISBN 978-0-7391-2591-5 (cloth : alk. paper) — ISBN 978-0-7391-4521-0 (electronic)
  1. African Americans in motion pictures. 2. African American women in motion
pictures. 3. Stereotypes (Social psychology) in motion pictures. 4. Violence in motion
pictures. 5. Motion pictures—Social aspects—United States. 6. United States—Race
relations. 7. Racism in popular culture—United States. 8. Crime and race—United
States. I. Title.
  PN1995.9.N4C625 2010
  791.43089'96073—dc22

                                                                    2009051200

Printed in the United States of America

*For my parents, who were absolutely delighted to have
a book on crime, violence and mayhem dedicated to them*

Contents

Introduction

Crime and Racial Constructions

These days, it sounds almost cliché to say that race is a social construction. Yet no matter how oft repeated the claim, it is important to begin by remarking on the socially constructed nature of race for several reasons.

For one thing, to argue that race is a social construction is to underscore the fact that much that is said about differences between blacks and whites has virtually no scientific merit. Rather than referring to some real or measurable difference, the concept of race has been used since America's founding to construct a sociopolitical hierarchy in which whites are defined as superior to blacks (Omi and Winant 1994; Vera and Gordon 2003; Healey 1997).[1]

Because they are the dominant group in American society, whites have traditionally had the power to construct race in ways that benefited them. Hence, they long ago selected an identifying characteristic like skin color to make racial distinctions and then proceeded to attach all manner of negative biological, physical, intellectual, emotional, psychological, cultural and spiritual traits to persons identifiable as black based on skin color.

Yet in saying that much of what has been constructed about race has no scientific merit is not to dismiss racial constructions as insignificant. Initially, racial constructions about white superiority and black inferiority were vital for justifying the exploitation of black labor during slavery. They continue to be important, even today, because they have been passed down from one generation to the next and as such are now part and parcel of American culture. Indeed, by now, the belief in racial categories has so much meaning to most Americans that they define themselves in terms of one racial category or another and proceed to interpret their existence and organize their lives around it. This is evidenced by the fact that racial identities figure in Americans' decisions on issues as basic as where they will live and where they will send their children to school. Indeed, because racial categories have so much

1

meaning to whites, they have long sought to exclude those in the "other" racial category (i.e., blacks) from their neighborhoods and their schools.

Because race is constructed in a way so that it justifies black exclusion and exploitation, there is a long history of blacks protesting these conditions. Hence, to maintain a racial hierarchy in which blacks can be exploited and excluded, it has been necessary for white elites to contain and control the black population. For that reason, they often construct blackness in such a way so that it seems to justify this kind of white domination. One of the best strategies for making white domination appear warranted is to represent blacks as dangerous and criminal. After all, if blacks can successfully be defined as a threat, all efforts to control them can be made to seem reasonable.

There is recent evidence of this from the 1960s when there was a good deal of black protest against racial exclusion and exploitation beginning with the civil rights movement followed closely by urban riots. In response to this wave of black protest, crime became even more important in white constructions of blackness. Hence, since the 1960s, Americans have been bombarded with images of dangerous blacks from all sides—film, television, political campaigns, news media and academia.

This book, then, is an examination of how crime has figured in racial representations of black folks in media (especially film) and academia in the post-civil rights era. In order to explain why black criminality has assumed such significance in the construction of racial categories in the past 40 years, it will be necessary to look at how defining blackness in terms of crime has served the conservative political agenda in that period. Therefore, in much of this introductory chapter, I examine crime and racial constructions against the backdrop of the post-1960s political climate.

But, before going on to examine how crime has figured in racial construction from the 1960s to the present, I will first take a look at an example of how crime influenced the construction of racial imagery in a bygone era—namely the 1890s. I begin with a look at the 1890s because, back then, white racial construction of the newly freed black slaves was still in its infancy. For that reason, this decade, in particular, provides an eye-opening look at how much significance the construction of blacks as criminal had for shoring up white racial identities and driving a wedge between blacks and whites.

CRIME AND RACIAL CONSTRUCTION IN THE 1890s

No matter how despicable it may seem to some, efforts to pit whites against blacks often have their intended effect of promoting white racial solidarity. After a campaign of racial polarization, whites may come to attach so much meaning to white racial solidarity that their racial concerns come to outweigh all other interests—including class or economic interests. There is ample evidence of this from history as white elites have repeatedly been able to divide black and white workers by race even in instances where black and white workingmen have had economic interests in common. For example, since black emancipation from slavery, the white working class has variously been urged to hate and even attack the black working class based on fears that black men would rape their women (i.e., white women), take their jobs, invade their neighborhoods, swim in their swimming pools and a host of other similar affronts (Spear 1967; Drake and Cayton 1945; Inverarity 1976).

In the 1890s, in particular, whites in the south were divided into two economic classes. In one class, there were white elites like the large planters, merchants and industrial entrepreneurs who had economic interests at odds with the other class that included the masses of working class or poor white southerners who were either small farmers, sharecroppers or laborers. Yet, white working class southerners were often less concerned about these class divisions than they were about their long-standing antipathy for blacks and their disagreements with the north. Indeed, their focus on racial and sectional divisions was generally sufficient to deflect their attention away from any disagreements they might have with white elites.

This tendency to focus on sectional and racial divisions only intensified after the Civil War with the temporary occupation of the south by federal troops during Reconstruction (1867–1876) along with the enfranchisement of black men and the election of a handful to public office in this period. Hence, in the years after Reconstruction and before black men were disenfranchised anew around 1900, the white working class and the white elite were increasingly united in their desire to react to what they saw as the twin external evils of dominance by the north (i.e., the federal government) and the potential for "Negro Rule." Racial interests, then, easily outweighed class interests for most whites, at least until the Populist revolt of the 1890s.

As agricultural prices (especially cotton prices) declined and credit became tighter in the 1890s, white small farmers increasingly found themselves supporting the Populist Party. Populist leaders were able to draw upon the support of the white working class because they promised to end the exploitation of white workers by the white elite. Because of their focus on class oppression, they even briefly urged white workers to move away from the false consciousness of racial solidarity and join with similarly situated black small farmers to pursue their economic interests against the white elites who exploited both races. Or, as one Populist leader succinctly put it, "The accident of color can make no possible difference in the interest of farmers, croppers and laborers" (Inverarity 1976; Beck and Tolnay 1990).

Obviously, the possibility of an interracial coalition of black and white small farmers, sharecroppers and laborers was anathema to the white elite as it threatened their ability to continue exploiting the working class. Hence, it was in their interest to stir up racial hostilities between black and white small farmers.

Lynchings provided the perfect solution for white elites seeking to prevent the formation of political coalitions between black and white workingmen as they motivated white laborers to join with white elites in racial solidarity in the ritual punishment of "dangerous" blacks. Many black lynchings did not even require that a crime be committed in order to stir up racial passions as an innocent black man could be strung up for crimes like rape or murder or breaches of racial etiquette (i.e., vagrancy, disobedience, making threats, etc.) on the basis of rumor and innuendo alone. Indeed most lynchings involved a mob of angry whites pulling a black man from his home or the local jail and stringing him up without actually waiting for a trial and the presentation of evidence.

That this kind of mob violence did indeed bring whites together in opposition to a common black enemy is indicated by the fact that a broad cross-section of the white community openly participated in these extralegal attacks on "dangerous" black men. Indeed the lynching of a black man met with so much community acceptance that some participants allowed their pictures to be taken with the lynched and often mutilated remains of their black victims. Even those whites who did not participate in the actual lynching expressed their approval of this brand of vigilante justice as white elites like newspaper editors or politicians publicly described lynchings as necessary to maintain law and order, protect white females and keep blacks in their place (Inverarity 1976).

Clearly, then, as white elites and white laborers stood side by side to vent their shared racial hatred, lynchings functioned to divert white workers' attention away from their economic interests and reaffirm white racial solidarity. Lynchings were also useful rituals for allowing poor whites to reflect on the psychological benefits of "being white." After all, when the price of cotton fell and economic conditions worsened for white small farmers, the differences between themselves and black small farmers must have seemed quite small. Under such conditions, their need to express their racial superiority to blacks in like economic circumstances would have become that much more pressing. Lynchings, then, became a way of highlighting racial difference in hard times.[2]

HOLLYWOOD AND THE CULTURAL
AFFIRMATION OF WHITE RACIAL VIOLENCE

Back in the 1890s, white elites were typically able to sow the seeds of racial division through their domination of traditional media like literature or newspapers. By the early years of the twentieth century, they were able to add the emerging medium of moving pictures as a platform from which to provoke racial conflict. Moving pictures represented an improvement over traditional media because they allowed the white solidarity rituals, then being played out in lynchings in small towns across the south, to be performed before a much larger, national audience.

So, for example, a few years after white elites and white workingmen joined together to execute their 1890s campaign of racial terror against blacks, white cultural elites in Hollywood released the 1915 movie classic, *Birth of a Nation. Birth* sought to justify the wave of black lynchings conducted by the Ku Klux Klan and other hate groups by appealing to white fears that black males would rape white women. In an act of self-defense, prominent blacks and the NAACP immediately protested *Birth* and its affirmation of white mob violence because black males (and some black females) were still being lynched (Beck and Tolnay 1990; Lerner 1972). Nonetheless, the film still received enormous amounts of media attention and enjoyed blockbuster ticket sales (Bogle 1994; Rocchio 2000).

To be certain, the kind of white mob violence celebrated in *Birth* is much discredited today; yet white aggression towards blacks on the silver screen continues. Today, however, many of the extralegal functions that were traditionally carried out by white mobs to control and contain the black population have been taken over on screen by legal bodies within the criminal justice system including the police, the courts and the prisons. Yet, even though the agents of white domination have changed, images of dangerous black males are still required to legitimize any criminal justice system aggression against blacks. Indeed the more savagely black males are depicted in media, the more license a white-male-dominated criminal justice system acquires to arrest, imprison or even kill them off on screen. This is perhaps best illustrated by two recent Oscar-winning films on race—namely *Crash* and *Monster's Ball.*

In 2006, *Crash* won the Oscar for Best Picture for what its writers and director called its ugly, but real, depiction of race relations in America. Apparently, in their eyes, a real picture of race relations in America today refers to the relationship between violent black criminals and a white-dominated criminal justice system as the movie opens with two black car thieves stealing a Lincoln Navigator from the white district attorney and his wife in a carjacking.

Because *Crash* depicts a couple of dangerous black males victimizing whites in an upscale white neighborhood, it can be expected to ignite fears of black criminals in white audiences, and hence with this opening scene, the filmmakers provide the police with the moral space to go to great lengths to try to allay those fears. Hence, during the course of the movie, one white police officer picks up a black hitchhiker walking alone in a white neighborhood and shoots him dead. Yet, despite this white police officer's summary execution of a black hitchhiker, the writers and directors of *Crash* manage to keep this killing from generating much audience sympathy because, unbeknownst to the white cop, the black hitchhiker he kills conveniently turns out to be one of the vicious carjackers who has taken the district attorney's Lincoln Navigator.

In another scene, two white police officers can be seen engaged in a man-hunt for the two black carjackers that have stolen the white district attorney's Navigator. Hence, in the film's moral calculus, the vicious acts of two dangerous black criminals provide the white police officers with a free hand to assign collective blame to the entire black community and stop any and all black motorists at will—both the law abiding and criminal alike. In the course of their random stops of black motorists, one white cop stops an innocent black couple, illegally searches them and molests the wife in front of her husband. And yet through a series of plot twists, *Crash* strives to make the illegal search and sexual assault appear unobjectionable by humanizing the selfsame white cop who has victimized this innocent black couple; in fact, the film's creators ultimately turn the abusive white cop into a hero. Hence, by constructing blacks as dangerous, *Crash* manages to make white domination and control of the black population seem reasonable.

Much like *Crash*, *Monster's Ball* also attempts to humanize the white males who work in a white-dominated criminal justice system by once again relying on images of the dangerous black man. It likewise won an Oscar as Halle Berry became the first black woman in the history of the motion picture industry to win the 2001 Academy Award for Best Actress for her performance in the film.

The movie title, *Monster's Ball*, refers to the old English custom of providing a dangerous convicted criminal or monster with a party or ball on the eve of his execution—hence the term "monster's ball" (*Monster's Ball* 2001). Berry's Oscar-winning performance casts her as Leticia Musgrove, the wife of the "monster" of the title—a black man on death row named Lawrence Musgrove. The movie opens by following two white executioners as they host the final ball for the black monster in question. However, this last ball for the convicted monster is not celebratory but rather refers to the white executioners' efforts to keep the condemned man calm as he faces his last hours on earth. Much of the film, then, is dedicated to trying to humanize the white executioners by examining the emotional toll it takes on them to execute a black "monster" like Lawrence Musgrove.

From Toms and Mammies to Civil Rights Protesters

To be sure, films like *Crash* and *Monster's Ball* represent a revival of black images first shown in *Birth of a Nation* in which the narrative requires the presence of a dangerous black man so that he can be controlled with white racial violence. Still, for much of the twentieth century, black men and black women alike were depicted as nonthreatening coons, toms and mammies who were loyal to their white masters and mistresses and content with their subordination first in slavery and then later in Jim Crow (Bogle 1994; Guerrero 1993; Watkins 1998; hooks 1981, 1992; Manatu 2003; Collins 1991; Jones 2005). Much of the changeover to the kinds of violent black male characters that cried out for control by the police and the prisons (as represented in *Crash* and *Monster's Ball*) came in the aftermath of the civil rights movement. Why this revival of violent black male characters, particularly in the years after the civil rights movement?

Back when the movement began, 1950s television audiences were still watching black female mammies fuss over their white employers on television (e.g., *Beulah*) or consuming television reruns of 1930s' Shirley Temple films (e.g., *The Littlest Rebel*) in which Bill "Bojangles" Robinson played an Uncle Tom character happily tap dancing his way through slavery alongside the young white moppet (Temple), who owned him (Bogle 1994). But, then some new disturbing images began to intrude into living rooms across America as television viewers also found themselves exposed to news accounts of blacks bravely and nonviolently organizing to secure their right to vote and end Jim Crow segregation that relegated them to separate and unequal public accommodations in the south. These real world images of black civil rights protesters challenging the racial caste system were remarkable because they were so greatly at odds with the fictionalized media images of loyal, happy-go-lucky black servants waiting on whites, content with their subordination in the racial order.

Television viewers in the 1950s and 1960s were also subjected to images of the southern white backlash to these protests as black churches were bombed, civil rights protesters were slain, and black students were stopped at the schoolhouse door (Meier and Rudwick 1970; Healey 1997; Watkins 1998). Often, the most visible face of this southern backlash was local white police forces that appeared on television screens clubbing black protesters, blasting them with water cannon or carting them off to jail.

Watching these events unfold, white audiences in and out of the south became increasingly aware of how southern state governments used their state legislatures and their police forces to abuse minorities and deny them their civil rights. And, for many white viewers, the violent white backlash to the demonstrators only served to make them more sympathetic to black protesters and more inclined to support them in their efforts to challenge long-standing southern institutions and cultural practices that treated them like an inferior social caste. Indeed, some 1960s television newscasts eventually showed images of whites marching in solidarity with black protesters to oppose Jim

Crow segregation. To say the least, these images of blacks and whites united in their opposition to racial inequality in the 1960s were directly at odds with earlier images from *Birth of a Nation* that showed whites lynching blacks in an orgy of white racial solidarity.

After watching these events unfold, many white viewers also found their faith in government authority and the police shaken by the violent southern backlash to the protesters. Such white misgivings regarding state authority and police legitimacy were only further reinforced a few years later when some encountered government opposition to their own protests for women's rights, gay rights and demonstrations against the Vietnam War. Then, when four white student antiwar protesters were slain by the state police at Kent State University in 1970, white doubts about the legitimacy of state authority soared.

Many northern blacks in the viewing audience were likewise watching the southern white backlash to the civil rights movement and grew angry as they saw nonviolent black protesters blasted with water cannon, clubbed, attacked by police dogs and arrested by southern police officers. As a consequence, some came to adopt a Black Power ideology which rejected integration with whites and the formation of interracial organizations to bring about social change. Instead of joining interracial organizations, many northern blacks began to talk in terms of bringing about racial change on their own in all-black organizations (Watkins 1998; Connor 1995; Healey 1997).

Racial change also took on different meanings in the north. Instead of referring to the need to dismantle Jim Crow segregation in the south, racial change in the north increasingly came to be equated with ridding blacks of the police bigotry and brutality which they routinely encountered in northern ghettos. As a consequence, many northern blacks proceeded to protest racism in the north by demanding a halt to police abuses of their civil liberties. By the mid-1960s, black anger at incidents of police brutality was so intense that it led to violent black protests in the form of urban riots (U.S. National Advisory Commission on Civil Disorders 1968).

Media coverage of these black urban uprisings and police brutality in the north exposed some of the other concerns of northern blacks including dire economic conditions in urban ghettos such as high levels of black male unemployment and large numbers of households headed by black women who were dependent on welfare to support their children. Because many white progressives were now suspect of state authority and its policing power, they were inclined to be more sympathetic to black protest and more willing to support economic change in black inner-city communities (Watkins 1998; U.S. National Advisory Commission on Civil Disorders 1968).

The 1960s, then, brought a good deal of racial change as the civil rights movement and the southern white backlash resulted in the extension of constitutional protections to blacks seeking to vote, the dismantling of Jim Crow segregation in public accommodations, and the institution of school busing to bring about racial integration in the schools. In the north, the Black Power movement, the urban uprisings and the publicizing of police brutality in northern ghettos led to calls for an expansion of Great Society programs that were meant to provide a social safety net for the poor (e.g., welfare, food stamps, affordable housing, job training, Medicaid, Medicare, etc.) and the establishment of affirmative action programs that were meant to end racial discrimination in universities and workplaces and increase opportunities for black social mobility (Watkins 1998; U.S. National Advisory Commission on Civil Disorders 1968).

THE WHITE BACKLASH AND THE REPUBLICAN PARTY

However, white sympathy for programs and policies meant to reduce racial inequalities was hardly universal. Many whites in the south and the north alike were not happy with what they saw as big government programs which handed out special privileges to blacks while simultaneously putting an end to white privilege and the system of racial stratification. Seeing an opportunity to expand their base, a number of Republican politicians immediately set about trying to turn this growing white resentment of government programs promoting racial equality into an attack on the Democratic Party. By linking these programs to the Democrats, they hoped to lure a number of white voters to their ranks who had previously voted Democratic.

Establishing links between the Democratic Party and programs to promote racial equality was not hard since civil rights legislation, Great Society antipoverty programs and affirmative action policies were all associated with the Democratic administration of President Lyndon B. Johnson. To attack the Democrats and appeal to white voters, then, Republicans described the establishment of these programs as evidence that the Democrats were too beholden to black civil rights organizations. They then presented themselves as the party that would not be intimidated by what, to their eyes, were outrageous demands by black protest organizations. Indeed, instead of constantly giving in to these minorities, they went out of their way to demonstrate their willingness to defend the rights of disgruntled white voters and uphold the old racial order.

Standing up for disgruntled white voters and restoring the traditional racial order came to mean that Great Society programs (which provided a social safety net for the poor of all races) would have to be gutted, constitutional protections for black voting rights would have to be reversed, school busing to create racially integrated schools would have to end and affirmative action policies that increased opportunities for black class mobility would have to be eliminated (Watkins 1998).

This turned out to be an extremely effective political strategy as Republicans have managed to secure a majority of the white vote in every presidential election from 1968 to 2008, in part, by broadcasting this message. Many of the white voters that they added to their base by promising to stand up for white voters were working class whites, who deserted the Democratic Party *en masse* despite its traditional support for higher pay and more benefits for workers. Hence, since the 1960s, white working class voters have once again allowed their economic interests to be outweighed by racial considerations.

Still, despite Republicans' capacity to win elections by dramatizing their opposition to minorities, they have had to be careful to avoid appearing to support racial discrimination and racial inequality. Hence they came up with a new narrative about the nature of race relations in America (Watkins 1998; Jones 2005). As they explained it, the United States was now a color-blind society that had overcome its racist past over the course of the civil rights movement. Because of the racial reconciliation that occurred in the 1960s, they claimed that special privileges (i.e., Great Society programs, affirmative action) for blacks were no longer needed. As evidence that blacks had overcome racial inequality in the aftermath of the civil rights movement, they pointed to the emergence of a small, but thriving, black middle class that they suggested had managed to be upwardly mobile without big government programs.

They have been quite successful in persuading many white Americans to adopt this view of America as a color blind nation as surveys conducted in the mid-1990s show that a majority of whites believe that institutional racism and discrimination have disappeared and been replaced with equal opportunity for all. Because so many whites feel that whites and blacks now operate on a level playing field, they can claim that blacks (and other minorities) have just as good a chance of securing desirable housing and employment and achieving social mobility as whites. Indeed, in some surveys, a majority of whites claim that blacks actually have an advantage over whites in finding desirable employment (Gallagher 2003).

The willingness of a majority of whites to believe that racial discrimination is a thing of the past is, in many ways, understandable as such beliefs come with a certain psychological payoff. After all, by subscribing to the notion that post-civil rights America has somehow been transformed into a color-blind utopia, whites can convince themselves that their continued higher status in the socioeconomic hierarchy (higher income, greater wealth, lower unemployment) is due to their own hard work and thrift rather than to a system of racial stratification which continues to privilege them over blacks (Gallagher 2003). This perception that America is now color-blind can also be the source of racial resentments, particularly when it emerges in reaction to black requests for the expansion of affirmative action. Because many whites have convinced themselves that America is now a color-blind nation in which they and everyone else can get ahead through hard work and talent, they tend to interpret black calls for enforcement of affirmative action policies as an appeal for "special favors."

Unfortunately, there are any number of inconvenient facts which challenge this rosy picture of American race relations. Because whites continue to exclude blacks from their neighborhoods—which typically have better funded schools and more access to blue collar jobs—ongoing racial segregation in housing has typically meant that blacks have far less access to living wage blue collar jobs or to schools that might prepare them to move up into the middle class (W. Wilson 1996; Massey and Denton 1993; Royster 2003). As a consequence, blacks, on average, continue to be poorer than whites and have less education and higher unemployment rates as well. However, a number of scholars in conservative think tanks have quickly stepped in to explain why persisting high rates of black poverty are not due to racial discrimination in housing. To accomplish this, they have made use of old style culture-of-poverty arguments (Watkins 1998).

Conservative Racial Constructions and the Culture of Poverty

Old-style culture of poverty arguments begin with the assumption that the poor have created their own value system that is separate and distinct from the middle-class value system. This perspective also suggests that the separate cultural values, beliefs and behaviors that the poor have created cause them to remain poor. Because these values, behaviors and beliefs are thought to be passed on from poor parents to their children, children born into low-income households are supposedly socialized to remain poor themselves (Banfield 1970; W. Miller 1958).

Critics of these arguments have suggested that the poor probably have the same cultural values as the middle class thereby raising doubts about the notion that the poor have a unique value system that causes their poverty. They also fault culture-of-poverty arguments for their tendency to blame the poor for their own poverty by ignoring how the low incomes of the poor alone may limit their opportunities to gain access to an education that will prepare them for a middle-class job—regardless of their cultural beliefs (Ryan 1976; Valentine 1968).

Yet, despite these long-standing critiques of culture-of-poverty arguments, conservatives in right-wing think tanks and academia have simply revived them to explain why black poverty was caused by black people themselves rather than by their racial segregation into resource-deprived black ghettos that limited opportunities for black upward mobility. So, for example, they claimed that so many blacks remained mired in poverty because they were held back by a cultural value system of their own creation that induced them to live in the moment going from one thrill to the next with no thought of bettering themselves or the lot of their children. To hear conservatives tell it, high levels of black unemployment and high rates of school dropout were explained by lazy undisciplined black males who shunned work and opportunities for social mobility. Presumably, because these black males had assimilated underclass cultural values, they had come to prefer the excitement of street life to the boring routines of work. Hence, they did not discipline themselves or make the necessary sacrifices to acquire an education that might have helped them to become socially mobile (W. Miller 1958; Banfield 1970).

The Political Uses of the Culture of Poverty

All this conservative emphasis on black underclass poverty in the post-civil rights era was not accidental. By focusing on the cultural dysfunctions of the black inner city, white political elites in the Republican Party were able to use this construction of blackness to divert working-class and lower-middle-class whites away from focusing on their economic concerns. That lower-middle-class and working-class whites had cause to be apprehensive about their economic circumstances had a lot to do with the fact that by the 1970s, more and more workers—black and white alike—began to see American corporations ship their living wage, blue-collar manufacturing jobs overseas to cheaper labor markets.

However, the Republican Party was not especially interested in addressing white working-class and lower-middle-class fears about the impact of deindustrialization on their economic futures. Rather they were more interested in rewarding the corporate elite who actually shipped these jobs overseas with more tax cuts for the wealthy, fewer regulations on business and industry and fewer environmental protections to cut into corporate profits. These were hardly the kinds of policies that were likely to have much appeal to an increasingly anxious white working class, and so Republicans had to find a way to appeal to these voters in terms of their noneconomic concerns—for example, their concerns about shifts in American culture.

A number of socially conservative voters, particularly those on the religious right, had become increasingly disturbed about American culture's shift leftward in the wake of liberal 1960s social movements like those orchestrated by feminists, gays and lesbians, the youth counterculture, antiwar protesters and, of course, blacks. As these groups demanded more rights and introduced new lifestyles into American society, a number of socially conservative voters began to feel that American culture was experiencing a moral decline. The Republican Party made its appeal to these socially conservative voters by talking about a return to an emphasis on traditional values like virtue, hard work, family (i.e., nuclear family), religion, individualism and patriotism. Consequently, rather than addressing the growing economic concerns of conservative working-class voters, they began waging a culture war against these liberal 1960s social movements instead. Waging a culture war meant opposing abortion rights for women or additional rights for gays and lesbians (e.g., gays in the military, marriage rights). This turned out to be an effective strategy for adding socially conservative "values voters" to their base.

The Culture War on Blacks

At least some Republican attacks on left-leaning 1960s social movements were directed at blacks. In the case of blacks, these attacks took the form of denunciations of what they described as black underclass culture. In reality, though, their vilification of the black underclass was meant to justify turning back some of the hard-won progress that blacks had made in the 1960s. By their incessant denunciations of black underclass culture they meant to incur white voter opposition to programs that would reduce inner-city blight, improve ghetto schools and provide jobs and job training. Instead of developing programs to empower these communities, conservatives were only interested in crafting a message that would justify more government control over the ghetto to make sure it did not explode in rage. Hence, they successfully persuaded the public that greater state surveillance over the black population was necessary by concocting a crisis over the spread of crack cocaine.

Among other things, they suggested that crack use was spreading across the land in leaps and bounds and they blamed violent drug-dealing black youth gangs for the spread of the crack menace (Reinarman and Levine 1997; Covington 1997; Maxson 1995). Neither claim was true as crack cocaine never became especially popular and was typically not sold by black youth gangs. Moreover, the crack epidemic was tiny by comparison with the much larger powder cocaine epidemic that had spread among whites a few years earlier. Yet conservatives chose to ignore the earlier and much larger powder cocaine epidemic among whites even as they clamped down on the tiny epidemic in crack use by blacks (Covington 1997, 2004a, 2004b).

Hence, the public was once again bombarded with images of the dangerous black male as television, political campaigns and newspapers all piled on to make a media spectacle of violent crack-dealing black youth gangs in the ghetto (Reinarman and Levine 1997). In the midst of this crisis atmosphere, conservative politicians were able to justify a crackdown on the black community by toughening the penalties for crack use and sales in the waning years of the Reagan administration.

Hence in 1986 and 1988, Congress passed legislation mandating minimum prison terms for minute amounts of crack cocaine. These laws had an immediate and devastating impact on the black community as more and more blacks were sent to prison for the nonviolent use and sale of small amounts of crack. Thus, conservative politicians succeeded in justifying a surge in black incarcerations by once again conjuring up images of the dangerous black male (Covington 1997, 2004a, 2004b).

Crime and Racial Imagery in Conservative Political Campaigns

Images of violent, criminal black men have not just been used to justify a prison buildup in the ghetto; they have also been used to explain why poverty rates have remained so high in black communities decade after decade. So, for example, a number of conservatives have suggested that crime is central in explaining the continued low socioeconomic status of underclass blacks as so many black men supposedly shun legitimate jobs to become violent criminals and drug dealers. They also make use of culture-of-poverty arguments to blame the black poor for their high crime rates by suggesting that many blacks willingly choose to rob and steal from others as a way of conforming to their own unique underclass cultural value system. Indeed some conservative scholars have even claimed that racial inequalities in socioeconomic status stem from moral inequalities between ghetto cultures and mainstream cultures. In other words, they argue that the high crime rates found in underclass neighborhoods reflect what they call the moral poverty of violent black criminals and drug dealers, while the low crime rates found in white neighborhoods reflect the moral superiority of middle-class, law-abiding whites (Bennett et al. 1996).

Conservatives have not just stopped at equating blackness with criminality as a way of signifying moral inequalities between the races; they have also used it to mobilize white voters in political campaigns. One of the best examples of conservative use of black crime to mobilize white voters comes from the 1988 presidential campaign. During the general election, Republican candidate George Herbert Walker Bush played on white fear of black crime with his repeated airing of a campaign ad that featured a black convicted murderer named Willie Horton, who raped a white woman while on furlough from a Massachusetts prison. By featuring Willie Horton, Bush meant to label his Democratic opponent, Michael Dukakis, as "soft on crime" because Dukakis had been governor of Massachusetts when Willie Horton was furloughed.

With his use of the Willie Horton ad in 1988, Bush managed to resurrect images from the 1915 movie classic *Birth of a Nation* that defined black males as sexual predators and polluters of white purity, privilege and nationhood. And, by his constant referencing of the dangerous, criminal black male, he was also able to imply that his Democratic opponent would not stand up to his black constituency and protect white America from violent black rapists like Willie Horton. While critics of Bush's tactics accused him of using racial polarization to drum up white support and faulted him for his distortion of prison furlough programs, he did manage to garner some 59 percent of the white vote, in part, by playing on white fears of black crime (S. Walker et al. 2004; D. M. Jones 2005; *New York Times* 2008).

Conservative Discourse on Black Women

Republican politicians did not just stop at conjuring up images of the dangerous black male to mobilize conservative white voters; they also demonized black women in their efforts to provoke voter resentment of big government programs like welfare. President Ronald Reagan set the tone for this debate early in his administration with the following comments about welfare queens: "The Chicago welfare queen has eighty names, thirty addresses, twelve social security cards and is collecting veteran's benefits on four non-existing deceased husbands. . . . Her tax-free cash income alone is over $150,000" (quoted in Albelda et al. 1996: 92).

By representing women on welfare as welfare queens or frauds seeking to manipulate the system, Reagan meant to depict this particular big government program as wasteful. His suggestion that taxpayer money was being wasted on welfare fraud helped to fuel conservative claims that it was time to call off the war on poverty, despite the fact that fewer than 4 percent of women on welfare were engaged in welfare fraud (Albelda et al. 1996; Associated Press 1994). Yet as conservatives waged a campaign against welfare in the 1980s and 1990s, they chose to represent welfare mothers in terms of the dishonest 4 percent, while ignoring the honest 96 percent who sincerely needed the program to support themselves and their families. Still, facts aside, the practice of vilifying all welfare mothers as welfare cheats served the larger conservative political agenda as such images helped to generate public repugnance for "big government" programs.

Conservatives also decided to make black mothers the public face of their war against welfare, despite the fact that there were slightly more white women on welfare than black women. By representing welfare mothers (and welfare queens) as black women, they were able to play on racial resentments in their campaign to rouse public anger at the program. Still, despite their best efforts, conservatives were not successful in dismantling welfare during the Reagan years; they only managed to eviscerate it in the mid-1990s when the Republicans took over Congress.

In the course of waging their campaign against welfare in the 1980s and 1990s, conservatives once again turned to old-style culture-of-poverty arguments that suggested that the cultures that the black poor created kept them poor despite the government's best efforts. So, for example, because welfare payments in the ghetto were typically made to fatherless households headed by black mothers supporting their children, conservatives applied old-style culture-of-poverty arguments to suggest that black women on welfare were responsible for creating these fatherless households.

One long-standing explanation implicating black women in the creation of so many fatherless, female-headed households in the ghetto suggested that they were such overbearing and domineering matriarchs that black men refused to marry them or ultimately abandoned them because they felt emasculated by these intimidating women (Rainwater and Yancey 1967; Wolfgang and Ferracuti 1967).

After blaming these women for the high rates of fatherless households among blacks, a number of conservatives went on to argue that the female-headed households that these emasculating black matriarchs formed had devastating consequences for inner-city neighborhoods. For one thing, they claimed that boys raised in these fatherless families were more prone to turn to crime and violence in their teen years (W. Miller 1958; Wolfgang and Ferracuti 1967). Moreover, they argued that because these women did not work, they tended to pass on their own lack of a work ethic to their children. By making such claims, conservatives essentially blamed black women on welfare for widespread intergenerational poverty in the ghetto.

Yet in relying on culture-of-poverty explanations to blame poor black women for fatherless households, crime and intergenerational poverty in the ghetto, conservatives never even considered the much greater impact that high rates of black male unemployment might have on these problems. However, it is widely believed that because of high unemployment rates, black men have traditionally been unable to support a family. Presumably, it is this inability to support a family that causes widespread divorce and separation in the ghetto and thereby the high rates of female-headed households (Albelda et al. 1996; Lubiano 1992; Watkins 1998). In other words, black women on welfare become the sole support of so many underclass households not because of their overbearing and domineering personalities, but because of black males' lack of access to living-wage work.

Critics of conservative culture-of-poverty explanations also claim that kids raised in these female-headed households in urban ghettos are likely to go on to attend poorly funded ghetto schools that do little to prepare them for white-collar jobs or funnel them into living-wage blue-collar work; it is these conditions, they suggest, which explain intergenerational poverty in the ghetto rather than underclass culture (W. Wilson 1996; Royster 2003). Finally when it comes to crime, a number of criminologists have long argued that high rates of poverty and unemployment among black males are sufficient to explain high crime rates in the ghetto, independent of female-headed households (S. Walker 1990). Nonetheless, conservatives have ignored these more likely explanations for persisting ghetto poverty and crime and instead have continued to blame black underclass culture.

The War on Welfare and the Culture Wars

To some degree, these conservative denunciations of black women on welfare have to be understood as part of the larger culture war that they have waged against a number of liberal 1960s and 1970s social movements. For example, they attacked the largely white middle-class women's liberation movement by blaming it for America's cultural decline. To hear them tell it, the America that existed before middle-class white women were liberated in the 1960s and 1970s was one in which divorce rates were low, father-headed two-parent families were supposedly the norm and illegitimate births were uncommon. Armed with this picture of traditional America, right-wing politicians made their appeal to socially conservative voters by promising to return society to the traditional family values that existed before women were liberated.

However, rather than attacking liberated white women directly, one of the conservatives' most frequently used strategies for defending this push for a return to traditional values has been to point to the cultural deficits of black women on welfare. By constantly berating black women for the spread of fatherless, female-headed households in the ghetto, they have been able to present poor black females as a threat to the traditional father-headed nuclear family. Moreover, by constantly making unsubstantiated claims that these female-headed households are the cause of intergenerational poverty and crime, they can appear to be offering up proof that a rise in households without a male presence will only further unravel American culture. Based on these misleading arguments, then, they claim that because welfare has paid for the formation and support of these supposedly dysfunctional fatherless black households, taxpayer dollars are being used to enable and promote values like black dependency and crime.

As if this were not enough, conservatives also blame welfare for subsidizing the immoral sexual behaviors of women in the black underclass. For example, they claim that poor black women on welfare are incentivized to have additional children out of wedlock so that they can collect larger welfare payments. Yet such efforts to blame welfare for the rise in births outside of marriage ignore the fact that illegitimate births have also risen among women who are not on welfare (Albelda et al. 1996; Gans 2005).

Conservatives have also linked welfare to black intergenerational poverty by suggesting that illegitimate births to black teen mothers prevent them from getting the kind of education they need to be upwardly mobile. They, then, go on to claim that reductions in intergenerational poverty among the poor might best be achieved by efforts to shame immoral black teenagers to stop sleeping around rather than wasting taxpayer dollars on providing them and their illegitimate children with welfare. Unfortunately, such arguments tend to exaggerate the impact of teen pregnancy on intergenerational poverty in the underclass as girls born into poor families who do not get pregnant as teenagers fare no better than those teenagers who do get pregnant (Albelda et al. 1996)

In conservative discourse, then, black women on welfare are a threat to the moral fiber of America because the underclass cultures that they have formed encourage high rates of teen pregnancies and out-of-wedlock births. By their constant belittling of these women as hedonistic and lacking in personal responsibility, conservatives have managed to revive old racial myths that have described black women as licentious and oversexed since slavery (Collins 1991; Manatu 2003; hooks 1981, 1992; Jewel 1993).

The rise in popularity of crack cocaine in the mid-1980s only gave conservatives additional opportunities to condemn underclass black women for their supposed hedonism and lack of personal responsibility. For example, they depicted them as bad mothers because their crack addictions presumably caused them to neglect their children or even pass on their addictions to their unborn babies. They also made constant reference to their involvement in trading sex for crack and pointed to this use of prostitution in order to support a drug habit as further evidence of their lax sexual morality (Morgan and Zimmer 1997; L. Siegel 1997; Lubiano 1992). Because crack use and prostitution are both crimes, the rising popularity of crack also gave conservatives an opportunity to label black women as criminals, who deserved to be punished for their immoral behaviors.[3]

The Political Uses of Conservative Discourse on Underclass Culture

By the mid-1990s, the debate over welfare was going on in a political climate where there were growing concerns about balancing the budget. Hence a number of conservative attacks on big government programs like welfare were made in terms of the need to cut government spending. Yet, far bigger cuts in government spending could have been achieved if conservatives had been willing to take the budget ax to the kinds of corporate welfare programs that benefited large businesses and wealthy individuals rather than trying to wring a few extra dollars from government resources extended to the poor (Albelda et al. 1996). The affluent, after all, got far more from the government than the poor in the form of tax breaks and exemptions for corporations and wealthy individuals as well as huge subsidies for business.

However, conservative condemnations of black women on welfare served to divert voters' attention away from these far costlier corporate welfare programs. Consequently, after years of discourse on the cultural deficits of the underclass the Republicans succeeded in passing legislation that gutted the social safety net for poor black mothers and their children without seeming mean-spirited.

By disparaging the black underclass, conservatives were also able to undermine any lingering sympathies that many whites had developed for the condition of ghetto blacks in the wake of the civil rights movement. As they explained it, big government programs were no match for inner-city blacks who were hell-bent on their own cultural self-destruction. Moreover, by claiming that America had become a color-blind society in which racial discrimination no longer limited black opportunities for advancement, conservatives were able to convince many voters that these programs were no longer necessary to bring about black social mobility (Albelda et al. 1996; Watkins 1998; D. Jones 2005).

The conservative chronicling of the supposed dysfunctions of black underclass culture also provided a number of white voters with a narrative for defending their opposition to school busing and the desegregation of their communities (Watkins 1998; D. Jones 2005). After exposure to relentless right-wing attacks on the violent and immoral black underclass, conservative white voters could claim that their own opposition to racial integration was not based on racial animus, but rather on their fear of an invasion of underclass lifestyles. From their perspective, it would have been cultural suicide to allow the violent, licentious and lazy underclass blacks depicted in media to integrate their neighborhoods and attend school with their children. Hence, Republican discourse on the underclass gave white Americans the space to oppose integrated neighborhoods not in terms of racial prejudice, but in terms of an opposition to the supposed criminality, violence, drugs and lax sexual moralities of the underclass.

The fear that black underclass violence might invade their neighborhoods also made it possible for a number of white voters to support law and order crackdowns by the police in black communities that ultimately violated the civil liberties of law-abiding African Americans. After all, conservative politicians routinely promoted the notion that such crackdowns enabled the police to contain underclass crime and violence in the black community and prevent its spillover into their own communities. Hence, after relentless Republican pronouncements on the violent black underclass, many whites who had previously been horrified by police excesses such as attacks on black protesters during the civil rights movement could now turn a blind eye to new violations of black civil rights in the form of racial profiling, police crackdowns and police killings of unarmed black civilians. Indeed in a 1999 poll taken after a spate of well-publicized police killings of unarmed black civilians in New York City, a majority of white New Yorkers (54 percent) saw it as a case of the police using necessary force in dangerous situations. By contrast, a majority of black New Yorkers (72 percent) in the same poll accused the police of using excessive force (Barry and Connelly 1999). It would seem, then, that for many whites, conservative discourse on underclass crime, drugs and violence justified a return to the bad old days for blacks when their legal rights could be openly violated by the police.

THE MEDIA AND RACIAL CONSTRUCTION

Clearly, over the past 40 years, conservative politicians have experienced some success in using a variety of racial myths and distortions about dangerous, violent black males and immoral black women on welfare to divide the races and mobilize white support. In many ways, it has been easy for them to represent blacks in such distorted terms because the United States is a racially segregated society where blacks and whites are typically not privy to intimate details about each other. Because blacks and whites do not live together, grow up together or go to school together—especially in K-12—they typically do not know each other well. Hence, much of what white Americans believe about blacks is based on what they can glean from movies, television dramas, newspapers, television newscasts, political campaigns, radio talk shows, blogs and other media. Because most whites cannot balance the images and messages that they get about blacks from films, political campaigns or the nightly news with their own constructions of blackness based on their interactions with living, breathing black folks, these media representations of blackness can come to serve as a substitute for actual knowledge of real black people (Manatu 2003).

Sadly, media elites may have some incentive to represent blacks in negative terms. After all, they may find that they can appeal to and entertain white viewers with images of blacks that justify white privilege and white domination of blacks—particularly those viewers who derive psychological benefits from "being white." Moreover, media elites, themselves, may not be adverse to circulating images of race that justify white privilege and white domination of blacks as whites—particularly white males—control the media.

For example, white males account for the vast majority of those in news management jobs like daily newspaper editors and television news directors (Chideya 1995). Because of their dominance in management positions in newspapers and television news, they are able to determine the tone and the content of the news. Unfortunately some of these white media elites seem inclined to use their control over the news to disseminate images that justify their hegemony.

Their dominance over news outlets also extends to entertainment media on television and in film. In the film industry, in particular, white males make up the vast majority of the writers, producers and directors in Hollywood. As such, they create most of the characters, structure most of the movie narratives and distribute most of the movies that Americans see. They are likewise the dominant force in the Academy of Motion Picture Arts and Sciences, which selects those pictures and performances that are deemed worthy of an Oscar (Chideya 1995; Mapp 2003). Consequently, they have the power to define what constitutes excellence in moviemaking. Indeed, because the cinema plays such an important role in shaping black images, this book will mainly focus on the kinds of racial myths that are disseminated by Hollywood and examine their origins in academia.

OUTLINE OF THE BOOK

By highlighting Hollywood's importance in constructing race, I do not mean to minimize the role of other media outlets in serving up negative stereotypes about black folks. However, there are a number of reasons for making cinematic representations of race the focal point of my analysis. For one thing, the film industry has the capacity to circulate racial constructions to a much wider audience than most other types of media. Film also has an enormous influence on American racial constructions because its effects are cumulative. After all, most Americans have watched films all their lives and hence they may have grown up watching first-run films or reruns from the 1930s that depict negative images of docile, loyal, happy-go-lucky black slaves or servants (e.g., *Gone with the Wind*). As they get older, they can see these negative black stereotypes updated in more recent films that take into account the sensitivities of a post-1960s color-blind nation (e.g., *Driving Miss Daisy*). Similarly, they can see images of the kinds of dangerous black men that required blatant expressions of white conquest and subordination in *Birth of a Nation* toned down and updated for twenty-first-century audiences that require more subtle expressions of white control of the black population (e.g., *Crash, Monster's Ball*).

To be sure, news media—both broadcast and print—are capable of disseminating myths about dangerous black males by selecting the one story out of the many that fits the stereotype and then repeating it over and over. The media frenzy that attended the arrest and trial of black ex-football player O. J. Simpson for the alleged murder of his white ex-wife and her white friend is probably the best, recent example of news media's capacity to create a crisis over the dangerous black male (D. Jones 2005).

News media similarly manufactured a crisis over the dangerous black male with reporting on the 1989 Central Park Jogger Rape in New York. In fact, media coverage of the story was so intense that several black teenagers were railroaded into confessing to the gang rape of the white female jogger and collective blame was assigned to all black youth with calls for a crackdown on ghetto teenagers. It was only several years later after the young men had served time for the crime and been released from prison and after public anger at black teenagers had subsided somewhat, that the media announced the innocence of the black teenagers with considerably less fanfare (D. Jones 2005). News outlets have likewise managed to turn a tiny little uptick in ghetto crack-cocaine use into a nationwide epidemic by repeating the same story over and over again about violent, crack-dealing black youth spreading crack use across the land (Reinarman and Levine 1997; Covington 1997, 2004a, 2004b).

Still, despite the news media's considerable abilities to circulate racial stereotypes and promote racial division, it is hemmed in by its stated goal of reporting the facts. Hence, it always risks having to reverse itself and admit that the black youth that it has demonized are innocent or that the crisis in drug addiction that it has announced has been grossly overstated. It also risks frustrating the very public demands for revenge that it stirs up, particularly, when juries in the real world refuse to convict the latest racial demon.

The film industry, however, faces no such limits. It is not hemmed in by the potential innocence of its black characters or by jury acquittals or by facts that contradict its exaggerations because its intention is not to present the facts, but to entertain. Thus movie narratives can proceed without any attention to the kinds of contradictions that can occur in the real world.

Moreover, in its efforts to entertain, film can appeal to the collective unconscious of the dominant society by speaking to those fears, desires and daydreams of an audience that cannot be publicly and verbally expressed (Manatu 2003). This is especially useful in a self-professed color-blind nation that claims to have conquered its problem with race. For, even though white dominance and white privilege are taboo subjects in polite company throughout much of America, they can be celebrated in visual images on film.

Hence, white males can openly flaunt their power and privilege on the silver screen, by engaging in acts of racial injustice and avoiding any punishment for it. For example, in a film like *Crash*, an openly racist white cop can stop an innocent black couple, illegally search the wife and molest her and avoid punishment for it. He can then just happen to save her life the next day thereby making him appear more human and less bigoted to audiences with post-civil rights era sensitivities. All the script writers have to do is simply write it into the story.

Because films are so important in disseminating stereotypes about violent black men, I devote chapters 1, 2, 3, 6 and 8 to an exploration of crime and racial constructions in the post-1960s cinema.

Cinematic Constructions of Black Males

A number of the chapters in the first section of the book on "Images of Black Male Criminality in Media and the Social Sciences" are devoted to a consideration of cinematic constructions of black men. I begin in chapter 1 by examining how images of the dangerous underclass black men, described in conservative political discourse, were brought to the silver screen. Because cinematic images of violent black males like those dramatized in recent films like *Crash* and *Monster's Ball* did not just spring up in the 2000s, chapter 1 will consider how Hollywood revived these images as far back as the late 1960s and early 1970s in blaxploitation films, marketed to black audiences. Coming in the immediate aftermath of black civil rights protest and urban rioting, blaxploitation films represented Hollywood's first attempt to entertain and attract black audiences newly politicized by the protests of the 1960s.

However, rather than accurately depicting the political reawakening that was going on in inner-city ghettos or showing the ongoing problems with racial discrimination that were the source of this new black activism, filmmakers chose instead to depict blacks as apolitical criminals. Hence, the real star of blaxploitation pictures was the black ghetto, which was invariably depicted as the site for the black culture of poverty then being described in news media, academia and government reports (U.S. National Advisory Commission on Civil Disorders 1968; Rainwater and Yancey 1967; Banfield 1970; Curtis 1975).

After examining the rise and rapid demise of blaxploitation films in chapter 1, in chapter 2, I go on to examine the revival of many of these images in action films based in the ghetto (i.e., ghetto action films) that emerged in the early 1990s and continued to be released in the 2000s. While ghetto action movies rolled out the same culturally self-destructive black criminals, hustlers, drug dealers, pimps and prostitutes that had been used to represent black life on screen in 1970s blaxploitation films, they placed more emphasis on the role of black violence in black cultural self-destruction than the earlier films.

The fact that they were released in the early 1990s probably explains this focus on black violence. After all, they came out in a time when President George Herbert Walker Bush had just successfully used images of dangerous black males to stir up racial divisions and mobilize white voter support in the 1988 presidential campaign. This was also a time when the media had just turned a tiny little outbreak in crack-cocaine use into a major crisis, in part, by exaggerating the role of violent, crack-dealing black youth gangs in spreading crack use. The early 1990s were also a time when criminal justice policymakers were using these images of dangerous, violent black males to justify a massive increase in the number of blacks being sent to prison—often for nonviolent crimes (Donziger 1996; J. Miller 1996). As if this was not enough, blacks rioted in Los Angeles in 1992.

Hence, chapters 1 and 2 examine how Hollywood produced more images of violent, criminal black men in the wake of urban revolts, beginning with the rise of blaxploitation films after the 1960s racial unrest followed by the rise in ghetto action films in the years after the 1992 Los Angeles riot. As such, these first two chapters show how violence was racialized in the aftermath of these urban revolts as violence increasingly became a way of constructing blackness on the big screen. On the other hand, violent white political protest that occurred in the 1970s and the 1990s (at about the same time as the black urban uprisings) did not lead to similar efforts to use violence to construct whiteness. In other words, incidents of white violent protest remained unraced on screen.

By comparing Hollywood's treatment of violent black uprisings to violent white uprisings (e.g., 1970s bombings by Weather Underground, 1995 Oklahoma City bombing) in chapter 2, it will be possible to examine how cinematic images of violent black protest were used to justify the domination and subordination of the black community even as equally violent protests in the white community were depicted in ways that did not seem to require such law-and-order crackdowns.

Hollywood's tendency to construct black violence as more threatening than white violence is not limited to the distinctions it makes between occasional violent protests by blacks and whites against the government. It likewise applies to its treatment of everyday acts of interpersonal violence that involve average citizens assaulting and killing each other over minor disputes. In a number of ghetto action films, black communities are depicted as lawless war zones where bands of violent black youth prey on each other and law-abiding residents of the community. And yet, the adults in the community are portrayed as powerless to control these young black superpredators. Indeed, in many of these pictures, the only organization capable of entering these lawless spaces and regaining control over neighborhood streets seems to be the local police force.

However, the film industry typically does not depict similar assaults and murders by white teens against the backdrop of a lawless community. For that reason, assaults and murders by white teens appear less threatening and do not seem to require turning the entire white community into a police state. In chapter 3, then, I examine the ways in which the film industry has made black interpersonal violence in the ghetto appear more threatening than interpersonal violence in white communities and how it proceeds to use its images of menacing black youth to justify a criminal justice takeover of the black community.

While Hollywood images of nonstop violence in the ghetto often exaggerate the amount of violence that actually goes on there, there is nothing exaggerated about cinematic images of police crackdowns on this violence. For just as *Crash* shows scenes of the police extending their manhunt for the one or two blacks who have actually committed a crime to include law-abiding blacks as well, such dragnets also occur in real life. In other words, the police can also stop and search law-abiding blacks in the real world in their quest to find one or two black criminals.

On screen, the black male criminals, who are the focus of ghetto action films, usually consent to these intrusions by the criminal justice system as they can reasonably expect to be stopped and searched because of their criminal behavior. However, in real life the masses of law-abiding blacks who also get drawn into police dragnets in the black community are understandably not inclined to consent to these repeated stops and searches. Indeed, some are even politicized by police round-ups and inclined to protest police violations of their rights as a result. In part, then, chapter 3 examines how Hollywood either ignores law-abiding blacks in the real world that protest police violations of their rights or how it actively seeks to discredit them on screen.

Hollywood and Cultural Misinformation about Black Women

With its fixation on scenes of black male teens revering the local drug dealers, pimps and violent criminals, Hollywood has managed to bring the culture of poverty to the silver screen. As such, it provides images to match the discourse on the culture of poverty coming out of conservative think tanks and academia. Across a whole range of media, then, the ghetto is depicted as a place in which the black poor can be held responsible for their own poverty and violence because their underclass value systems cause their self-defeating behaviors.

Even the black women characters in many films get implicated in the violence of the males, especially the black single mothers who raise their sons alone. Ghetto action movies, in particular, picture black women as incapable of raising their sons without a male presence as boys raised in these female-headed households seem more prone to turn to violence in their teen years. In chapter 3, then, I look at how these films depict black single mothers in ways that suggest that they cannot control their children, thereby blaming them for the poverty and violence that pervades underclass communities. I also examine how these films represent black women as hedonistic and oversexed by routinely casting them as drug addicts and prostitutes.

However, these images of black women as irresponsible mothers and prostitutes did not just emerge with the rise of ghetto action movies in the 1990s. They are actually quite old. Hence, I trace the origins of these stereotypical black female characters in a separate section on "Cinematic and Academic Images of Black Female Criminals and Victims." Beginning in chapter 6 of this second section, I consider how black women historically came to be represented in terms of these stereotypes and how these negative images have been updated for modern times.

By representing black women as irresponsible black single mothers or as hedonistic crack addicts and prostitutes in recent films, Hollywood has been able to disseminate images of a black female population that is undeserving of big government programs like welfare. After all, these cinematic images of underclass black women seem to offer visual proof for what political conservatives have been saying all along, namely that these women cause their own poverty with their dysfunctional and immoral lifestyles.

By blaming black women for their own poverty, conservative politicians have been able to claim that they were actually helping poor women when they dismantled the social safety net. So, for example, in 1995, when right-wing politicians succeeded in gutting welfare, then Republican Speaker of the House, Newt Gingrich, would claim:

> I'm trying to help people on welfare: I'm not hurting them. The government hurt them. The government took away something more important than this money. They took away their initiative, they took away a substantial measure of their freedom, they took away, in many cases, their morality, their drive, their pride. I want to help them get that back. . . . I want to do it because I love them, because I want them to be Americans. And their children and grandchildren will thank us. (quoted in Fischer et al. 2005, footnote 3)

Chapters 3, 6 and 7, then, will show how culture-of-poverty arguments, used by political conservatives, were matched by cinematic images and academic discourse on how poor black women caused their own poverty and criminal lifestyles. By implicating poor black women in their own poverty, these political, academic and cultural elites have been able to avoid any mention of the role that ongoing racial discrimination might play in high black poverty levels.

While citing culture-of-poverty arguments to blame poor blacks for their own poverty is the most common strategy that conservatives use to steer clear of considering the role that racial discrimination plays in the poverty of black women, political conservatives have employed other strategies as well. For example, they have claimed that government no longer needs to be in the business of providing "special favors" to blacks (e.g., social safety net programs, affirmative action), because post-1960s America is a color-blind society (Gallagher 2003). By claiming that blacks no longer need these "special favors" because they no longer experience racial discrimination, conservatives hope to avoid any accusations that they are heartless and prejudiced when they call for the elimination of these programs.

Maintaining the fiction of a color-blind America, however, takes some effort and, once again, Hollywood has stepped up to provide images that support this notion. One strategy for making America appear to be color-blind on the big screen is to construct racism as a problem of individual biases and prejudices. If racism is relegated to the biases of individuals, then it is possible to argue that blacks and whites alike can be racist. In other words, just as individual whites can express anti-black prejudices, individual blacks can similarly express anti-white prejudices (Blauner 2006; Gallagher 2003). By depicting white racism side-by side with black racism, Hollywood can make it seem as if blacks and whites in modern-day America operate on a level playing field.

Such images, of course, ignore the fact that white anti-black prejudices are often backed up by the policies and practices of major legal, social, cultural, and educational institutions. Because white racial hatred of blacks has long been buttressed by the policies and practices of major American institutions, this kind of institutional racism has resulted in blacks being excluded from desirable schools or living-wage jobs; hence, institutional racism has traditionally limited black life chances. By contrast, black anti-white prejudices are never buttressed by major American institutions and therefore, black prejudice towards whites does not affect white life chances.

Institutional racism, then, makes white racism a much more powerful and destructive force than what passes for black racism. Yet, for the most part, Hollywood has chosen to ignore institutional racism and define racism solely in terms of the individual prejudices of blacks and whites. For that reason, it has been able to preserve the fiction of America as a color-blind nation on the silver screen.

Chapter 8 examines how black female characters are constructed in ways that help to maintain this fiction of an American racial utopia in which blacks and whites operate on equal footing. However, the film industry's effort to avoid any mention of institutionalized racism has meant that black female characters have had to be presented as lacking in any political consciousness. After all, black women, who have been politicized, have long been inclined to protest the kinds of institutional racism that deny them privileges and opportunities that are only extended to whites. Hence, by depicting black women as apolitical, Hollywood can avoid all mention of institutional racism.

Racial Construction in the Social Sciences

Clearly, crime has increasingly become a way to talk about race difference in Hollywood, political campaigns, and news media. By depicting black males as dangerous, conservatives have managed to legitimize the militarization of black communities and the ensuing violations of black civil rights. And, by portraying black females as irresponsible, overbearing and hedonistic, they have also been able to justify the gutting of social programs that were meant to help lift single black mothers and their children out of poverty. While much of this negative discourse on blacks has come from right-wing politicians, at least some of it has come from conservative scholars in right-wing think tanks.

By relying on old culture-of-poverty arguments, conservative think tanks have succeeded in constructing race differences in terms of cultural differences that blame poor blacks for their poverty. Many of the culture-of-poverty arguments that they use to describe the black underclass were originally developed by social scientists in academia—particularly academic criminologists. Because criminological theories about the culture of poverty underlie the discourse used by conservative politicians and think tanks and shape many of the images found in blaxploitation and ghetto action films, I examine social scientific thinking on the culture of poverty in chapters 4, 5 and 7.

Beginning in the section on black males in chapter 4, I look at how culture-of-poverty arguments have traditionally been applied to explain not just how black men caused their own poverty, but also how they caused their own high rates of murder and assault as well. The thinking has been that because violence is such an important way of expressing masculinity in the underclass value system, black males are constantly assaulting or killing each other in gang fights or barroom brawls as a way of achieving manhood. Because black males have traditionally had much higher rates of violence than white males, criminologists have long assigned negative cultural predispositions to black males and black communities to explain this seemingly outsized need to use violence as a way of achieving manhood (Wolfgang and Ferracuti 1967; Silberman 1978; Curtis 1975). In chapter 4, then, I examine and critique the ways in which criminologists have used these culture-of-poverty arguments to blame black underclass culture for the high violent crime rates found in the ghetto.

One particular concern that I have with many of these theories is their tendency to describe an inclination to equate violence with masculinity as if it is unique to black males because it is supposedly rooted in a black psychological or cultural reaction to a peculiar set of structural conditions that are only found in black underclass neighborhoods. In chapter 5, then, I raise questions about this notion that black violence is a unique reaction to a peculiar set of circumstances found only in the black underclass by examining the much older problem of white violence.

Because white males traditionally used violence as a way of doing masculinity as far back as colonial times, I explore the possibility that the origins of modern black subcultures of violence may actually be found in the much older white subcultures of violence that formed in colonial America rather than in structural, psychological or cultural conditions that only emerged in the modern day black ghetto. I then examine some of the explanations for the origins of this much older white subculture of violence.

What is noteworthy about these explanations of white violence is that white assaults and homicides have traditionally been unraced. In other words, whiteness has not traditionally been one of the factors used to explain white male violence. Instead, those who would explain why violence originally came to be valued as an expression of masculinity among white males have relied on nonracial factors like region, social class or marital status. In suggesting that black subcultures of violence are the logical offspring of these much older violent white subcultures, I explore the possibility that nonracial factors like social class and marital status might explain high violent crime rates among black males as well. In so doing, I consider whether black violence should be unraced much like white violence. Or, to put it differently, I examine whether gender, social class, and marital status suffice to explain black violence, while questioning whether race has much impact at all.

Despite the flaws in criminological theories that racialize black male violence, the reasons for this approach are at least clear. Black males, after all, do have very high violent crime rates. On that basis alone, black females, presumably would be spared from such discussions because their violent crime rates are much lower than those of black males even though they live in the same culture of poverty. One explanation has been that black females are considerably less violent than black males because violence is a way of "doing masculinity" and as such violates feminine roles. Because violence is seen as a way of doing masculinity, explanations of female violence have long rested on the assumption that the handful of women who do turn violent are somehow masculinized (Klein 1995).

As it turns out, black women have long been represented as masculinized in media and academia. For example, black women who head single-parent households have been depicted as masculinized matriarchs that have usurped the traditional male roles of breadwinner and head of the household and emasculated black men in the process. Together, the black mother/matriarch and the absent black father she supplants as household head are said to form a kind of strong, masculinized black woman/weak, emasculated black male dyad (Collins 1991; Jewel 1993; hooks 1993; Lubiano 1992).

Supposedly, a similar sex role reversal also occurs with images of the stereotypical Sapphire character and her mate. Sapphires are talkative, headstrong black women who emasculate their black male mates with their barbs and constant put-downs. The black male mate, whose patriarchal authority the Sapphire character questions, is typically depicted as dishonest and inadequate. Hence, Sapphires and their mates also form a strong, masculinized black woman/weak, emasculated black male dyad (Jewel 1993; hooks 1993; Collins 1991, Lubiano 1992).

In the section on black women in chapter 6, I examine how Hollywood, in particular, has depicted black women as masculinized matriarchs and Sapphires. However, Hollywood is not alone in depicting black women in these stereotypical terms. Images of domineering black matriarchs and browbeating Sapphires can be found in news media, television, radio, government reports and the academic literature; indeed these stereotypes of emasculating black women are nearly as ubiquitous as images of the dangerous black male (Lubiano 1992; Collins 1991; hooks 1993; Jewel 1993; Rainwater and Yancey 1967; Wolfgang and Ferracuti 1968; Anderson 1994).[4] Therefore, in chapter 7, I consider how these images of emasculating black women have been used to explain black female violence in the academic literature, particularly in the context of violent domestic disputes between black women and black men.

Racial Construction: Is Change on the Way?

I began writing this book in the waning days of the administration of George W. Bush when conservative efforts to use black images to foment racial division were in full force in media, academia and political campaigns. However, as I finish the book, Barack Obama has recently been elected president. As the first black president, Obama is not likely to have much of a personal stake in stirring up racial hatreds. Moreover, he has no political interest in doing so because his election victory was secured by a racially and ethnically diverse coalition of blacks, whites and Latinos. Because only a minority of white voters supported him (43 percent), his fairly substantial victory was the result of the majority support of Latinos (67 percent) and nearly unanimous support (95 percent) from blacks (*New York Times* 2008). Because minority support was vital to his substantial election win, perhaps blacks can hope for a 4-year or even an 8-year reprieve from a president that uses the White House as a platform to stir up racial division.

Indeed in his first few months in office, President Obama has been focused on trying to grapple with an economic meltdown left over from the previous administration that has left millions of Americans—of all races—out of work. In that time, the President has shown himself to be totally unconcerned with waging a culture war against blacks (or any other 1960s liberal social movement) and more concerned with trying to wage a war on high unemployment (Stolberg and Nagourney 2009). Most of the discourse coming out of this new administration, then, has been about preserving jobs, providing states with the funds to shore up the social safety net in hard times (e.g., unemployment benefits) and creating new jobs in alternative energy—and not on what divides us as Americans.

As the economic crisis has meant rising unemployment levels among white males and white females, expanding big government programs like unemployment benefits, food stamps and health insurance has increasingly begun to seem like a necessary governmental response in a time of crisis rather than a way of wasting money on the undeserving poor. As more Americans have come to see government programs as a necessary backstop in these dire economic times, it has become more difficult for conservatives to single out the black poor for condemnation as a way of promoting racial division. It remains to be seen if constructions of blackness will change anew in the midst of this economic downturn.

Still, the legacy of years of conservative dominance of the discourse on race remains with us in media and academia. Even worse, it shows up in conditions brought about by that discourse in the form of high black imprisonment rates, high black unemployment rates, and too many black women unable to support themselves or their children. This book, then, is about how we got here.

NOTES

1. There is always a temptation to comment on a whole host of racial or ethnic minorities at once (e.g., blacks, Latinos, Asian Americans and Native Americans) when assessing how images of minorities are constructed. In this book, however, I focus

only on how crime affects constructions of blacks in media and the social sciences for a couple of reasons. For one thing, media have a long history of constructing blacks as more criminal than whites. This has been especially true of the cinema where blacks have been disproportionately represented as criminals since the 1960s. Crime also figures heavily in how race is constructed in the social sciences, largely because blacks have higher violent crime rates than whites. Because of the high crime rates among blacks, social scientists have developed a number of theories that construct blacks as more prone to violence than whites. For these reasons, racial constructions in this book will refer to constructions of blackness.

2. In fact, there is evidence that the number of blacks lynched rose and fell based on rises and falls in the price of cotton. In other words, when cotton prices rose, the number of blacks lynched fell and when the price of cotton fell — and white economic anxieties worsened — white mob violence against blacks increased. Interestingly enough, declining cotton prices had their greatest impact on a rise in black lynchings in the 1890s. While falling prices continued to translate into a rise in black lynchings from 1900 till 1930, the impact was much attenuated. Perhaps falling cotton prices had less of an effect on lynchings after 1900, in part, because a number of southern states had passed legislation successfully disfranchising black men between 1900 and 1910. As a consequence, white elites no longer had to fear a political coalition between poor whites and poor blacks since blacks could not vote. Furthermore, Populist efforts to unite poor blacks and poor whites against the white elite turned out to be short-lived as the Populists rather quickly reversed themselves and began to support black disfranchisement (Beck and Tolnay 1990; Inverarity 1976).

3. Pregnant women in some states were briefly prosecuted and imprisoned for using crack during pregnancy after being accused of addicting their babies to crack cocaine in the womb. It should come as no surprise that many of the women imprisoned for "addicting" their fetuses in this way were black. Critics of this policy questioned whether theses babies were actually physically addicted to crack. They also felt the policy was counterproductive because fetuses are likely to be healthier if their mothers seek prenatal care and with this policy in place, pregnant women might have avoided prenatal care out of fear that they would be arrested and prosecuted for passing crack on to their fetuses. Some also suggested that there was a double standard in place for crack as opposed to alcohol since drinking during pregnancy typically does not lead to arrest and prosecution. Yet, despite the fact that alcohol gets favorable treatment, it does far more damage to the fetus than crack cocaine (Morgan and Zimmer 1997; L. Siegel 1997).

4. Sapphire was originally a character on the radio program *Amos 'n' Andy* and then later in the television series of the same name. The black female Sapphire character was later resurrected in a number of 1980s black television sitcoms such as *Amen, Gimme a Break, What's Happening, That's My Momma* and *Family Matters* (Jewel 1993).

Section I

IMAGES OF BLACK MALE CRIMINALITY IN MEDIA AND THE SOCIAL SCIENCES

Chapter One

Black Images in the Post-Civil Rights Era

Racial constructions do not simply stand still. Rather they are subject to change, particularly in the face of major social upheavals. The decades of the 1950s, 1960s and 1970s were just such a time of dramatic social change and hence they mark a period when the images of blacks on the silver screen changed significantly.

Beginning with the civil rights movement in the 1950s and 1960s, African Americans protested racial injustice in the Jim Crow south. For the most part, they relied on strategies such as nonviolent civil disobedience, which meant deliberately violating Jim Crow laws that restricted their right to vote, prohibited them from sitting at lunch counters with whites or relegated them to separate hotels, separate restrooms, separate water fountains or separate seating at the back of the bus. By being arrested for deliberately violating these laws, the protesters called attention to racial injustice in the south and generated tremendous sympathy for their cause in regions outside the south.

While generally regarded as heroes today, back then southern governments depicted the civil rights protesters as anarchists and tools of the Communist Party. And because this interpretation of black protest was widely accepted in the south, southern governments felt entitled to unleash local and state police forces to attack the protesters with dogs, billy clubs and water hoses. White hate groups, such as the Ku Klux Klan, also joined in the attack by instituting a campaign of racial terror against blacks that included church bombings, murders, lynchings, mutilations and other forms of racial intimidation meant to silence the protesters. Meanwhile, white city and state governments in the south did little to prosecute the white hate groups behind this campaign of racial terror (Meier and Rudwick 1970; Healey 1997).

Ultimately the civil rights movement was successful in eliciting social and political reform as Jim Crow laws were abolished and voting rights laws were passed to insure blacks the franchise. The civil rights protesters also won the culture war as they came to be seen as heroes and martyrs to a just cause rather than as anarchists and Communist sympathizers. By contrast, southern governments were eventually vilified for having engaged in a kind of state terrorism because they used their police forces to repress their black citizenry and because they turned a blind eye to the violence of white vigilantes.

Mainstream America's eventual acceptance of the civil rights protesters had a lot to do with the fact that they had largely relied on nonviolent tactics to elicit social change. Moreover the civil rights movement was integrated as both blacks and whites alike protested racial conditions in the south. However, by the mid-1960s, black protest of racial injustice increasingly moved out of the south and the emphasis shifted to the needs of the urban poor in the north. Black protest also came to be dominated by black nationalists who excluded whites from the movement out of fear that they might compromise their agenda.

Most importantly of all, by 1965, black protest turned violent as blacks rioted in the Watts section of south central Los Angeles. Two years later, these black uprisings spread to cities across the country as there were 164 riots in 1967 alone (U.S. National Advisory Commission on Civil Disorders 1968). In the course of these disturbances, black rioters looted local businesses and set fires, and the government clamped down swiftly and severely by sending in National Guard troops armed with rifles and tanks to quell the disturbances.

A number of blacks died as the National Guard went about suppressing the rioters. Regrettably, many of those killed were little more than innocent bystanders (Gurr 1979). For example, in one of the more severe 1967 disturbances in Newark, New Jersey, some 23 people were killed as the New Jersey National Guard, the New Jersey state troopers and the Newark police attempted to put down the disturbance. Of those killed, 1 was a white policeman, another was a white fireman and the remaining 21 victims were black including 6 black females, 2 black children and one 73-year-old black man (U.S. National Advisory Commission on Civil Disorders 1968).

Many of the black victims were killed or injured as the police, the state troopers and the guard fired back at what they thought were black snipers. However, in later testimony before Congress, officials from the New Jersey National Guard and the Newark police department admitted that there was actually no sniper fire. Instead, they claimed guardsmen were mistakenly firing at the police when they heard their gunfire and misinterpreted it as sniper fire and the police were wrongly firing back at the guard mistaking them for black snipers. That the National Guard so frequently fired at nonexistent snipers was attributed to the fact that the guardsmen were for the most part young and very scared white males who had had little contact with blacks and thus were susceptible to rumors that they were under attack by black snipers when even one shot was heard.

As the police, state troopers and the guard mistakenly fired at each other or fired at fleeing looters, unarmed black bystanders were often caught in the crossfire. Hence, innocent blacks were killed or injured as they were sprayed with bullets while standing on the streets or on their porches, taking out the garbage, driving home in cars that came too close to a National Guard road-block or standing too close to the windows in their own homes (U.S. National Advisory Commission on Civil Disorders 1968). One young widow named Eloise Spellman ventured too close to her window in the projects and was killed by the guard right in front of her children as they sprayed the projects with bullets in the course of returning fire on their phantom black sniper.

The Kerner Commission was set up to identify the causes of this wide-spread rioting and for the most part, the Commission's 1968 report took a fairly sympathetic view of these black uprisings despite the fact that the Commission was largely made up of moderate to conservative white males (Wicker 1968). In the report's assessment of the causes of the major and seri-ous riots, the commissioners concluded that there was a widely shared and deeply held sense of injustice among blacks living in the riot-torn cities that typically preceded any unrest. Moreover they argued that this sense of injus-tice among blacks was deeply ingrained because it had been built up over the years as complaints to local governments about racial discrimination in jobs, job training, housing and education had repeatedly gone unanswered. In light of that, many of the commission members concluded that the riots were actu-ally a form of protest against these longstanding injustices.

In interviews with blacks in the riot-torn cities, the commission members found that blacks were especially outraged about racial injustice in the crimi-nal justice system, and over the years had amassed a backlog of complaints about police practices. For example, the blacks interviewed accused the police of physically and verbally abusing African Americans, of abusing blacks in police custody and of failing to respond to blacks victimized by crime. More-over when blacks complained to police departments about these abuses, they claimed that the mechanisms in place to respond to their complaints were in-effective as the police often ended up investigating themselves—particularly when complaints of murder and brutality were brought against them. Some of the blacks interviewed also described racial injustice in the courts as they accused judges of failing to punish police abuses (brutality, murders) in the black community and of automatically treating blacks as if they were guilty if the police testified against them in court. They also reported that the courts failed to punish private white citizens who attacked or intimidated them.

The commissioners suggested that black anger about this backlog of complaints typically simmered below the surface until tensions were raised in the weeks or months before a disturbance by new incidents of police abuse or unpunished white attacks on blacks. Indeed some 40 percent of the incidents that raised tensions in the months or weeks before the many 1967 disturbances involved discriminatory or abusive police practices. Another 17 percent of the incidents that intensified black anger involved instances in which the courts refused to punish private white citizens who had attacked and intimidated blacks (U.S. National Advisory Commission on Civil Disorders 1968).

Moreover, these cases of unpunished white intimidation of blacks were not confined to the south as some occurred in northern cities like Dayton, Ohio, and Bridgeton, New Jersey. Indeed, a case of largely unpunished white intimidation occurred about a month before the most serious of the 1967 disturbances, namely the disturbance in Detroit. In that case, a black man, who was trying to protect his pregnant wife from an attack by 7 white youths, was shot and killed. Yet the courts saw fit to charge only one of the white males involved, while the other six were released.

1960s PROTEST AND THE RISE
OF NEW BLACK MASCULINITIES

In the wake of all this racial ferment in the 1950s and 1960s, a number of black leaders, who were active in protesting racial injustice, could regularly be seen on the nightly news talking about racial conflict. Included among them were Malcolm X, Martin Luther King, Jr., Stokely Carmichael (later known as Kwame Toure) and other leaders in the civil rights movement, the Black Muslims, the Black Panthers and the Black Power movement. By their example, many of these leaders offered black men a new type of masculinity based on protest.

The new protest masculinities projected by these leaders in the movement presented black males with a new metric of manhood that was based on a man's capacity to survive racial injustice in America and to channel his anger and frustration at racial inequality into moving the black community forward (Connor 1995; Healey 1997). Because achieving black manhood in America was all about taking pride in oneself and the black race, many black men began to seek enlightenment about the race and its accomplishments. Supposedly, by learning about blacks' proud history in Africa and America, black men would reject the old sense of racial inferiority and self-hatred and acquire a new pride in themselves and the race.

The thinking back then was that much of this enlightenment would have to come from the black masses themselves as a white-dominated school system could not be trusted to teach blacks to be proud of themselves. Hence, blacks began raising each others' consciousness by talking and learning amongst themselves about their history and the never-ending struggle for justice (Connor 1995). Many black men also signaled their conversion into race men by adopting the styles of the Black Nationalist movement which meant donning dashikis, berets, and dark sunglasses, while displaying posters of revolutionary heroes and Black Nationalist flags. This newfound self-love and love of all things "black" also found its expression in the rising popularity of natural hairstyles (Afros, braids, dreadlocks, etc.). Moreover, as blacks went about moving the community forward by building a strong black nation, there was more talk of racial unity with one's black brothers and sisters.

At least some organizations involved in the movement also made an effort to try to lure blacks in prison away from a life of crime—particularly the Black Muslims. Indeed many black men who had pursued a criminal lifestyle suddenly found themselves trying to emulate Malcolm X. Malcolm X's life seemed to offer them a road map to the kind of racial enlightenment occurring among law-abiding blacks as Malcolm X had used Islam to convert from a violent and criminal lifestyle to a life marked by self-pride and the struggle for racial justice.

BLACK PROTEST OF THE FILM INDUSTRY

Not only did blacks protest racial inequalities in America, they also protested the racist images coming out of Hollywood. Black leaders and black protest organizations began calling for a change in the subservient black characters that had appeared on the silver screen prior to the civil rights movement and there were threats of audience boycotts if changes were not made. In addition, in 1963, the NAACP and the ACLU complained about hiring discrimination in Hollywood's craft unions. In 1969, there were even rumblings from the U.S. Justice Department as it announced plans to sue six film studios and two television networks over racial discrimination in hiring (Guerrero 1993).

In the wake of these protests, Hollywood images of black Americans began to change. Prior to the civil rights movement, blacks appearing on the big screen had largely been confined to the subservient roles of toms, coons, mammies and tragic mulattos. These characters were routinely trotted out in films about the antebellum south to justify slavery by displaying the obvious inferiority of the lazy, dim-witted or fiercely loyal black slaves, who were inevitably presented as content with the plantation system. These lazy, slow, dim-witted, loyal black characters also appeared in films set in the years after slavery as black actors were routinely cast as servants in wealthy white households, or as shoeshine boys and happy, but childlike, sidekicks to white performers (Bogle 1994).

However, by the late 1960s in response to the civil rights movement, black images increasingly came to be defined by the virtuous, nearly perfect, assimilationist black male characters that were frequently played by Sidney Poitier. 1967 turned out to be a banner year for these post-civil rights images as Poitier starred in two pictures that took home numerous Oscars—namely *Guess Who's Coming to Dinner* (1967) and *In the Heat of the Night* (1967). *Dinner* won for Best Actress (Katharine Hepburn), Best Story and Best Screenplay, while *Heat* won in most of the other major categories including Oscars for Best Picture and Best Actor (Rod Steiger). Because of Poitier's presence, some white reviewers even claimed that both these films addressed the race question. However, this was not a view shared by black audiences (Guerrero 1993).

By the late 1960s, black audiences had not only grown tired of the traditional toms, coons and mammies, but they were also a little weary of Poitier's assimilationist black characters as many regarded them as sexless and unassertive. Poitier's characters were also seen as inauthentic by black audiences because they were typically black men isolated in a predominantly white world. This meant that instead of focusing on problems that were of central concern to blacks, his characters frequently found themselves trying to make themselves acceptable to a white-dominated society or trying to help whites solve their problems (*Guess Who's Coming to Dinner, Lilies of the Field, To Sir with Love*). This had little appeal to black audiences, who increasingly wanted to see more assertive, more realistic black characters than those depicted in *Dinner*. And, given their recent experiences with the struggle for racial justice, they also wanted more politicized black characters, who were actively involved in the black social and political upheavals going on off-screen (Guerrero 1993).

Hence, in a backlash to Poitier's characters, his sexless black saint was replaced by a highly sexed, assertive, and arrogant black male hero in a series of blaxploitation films. Blaxploitation films were typically made in the action-adventure genre and featured black casts and black story lines that focused on the problems of blacks living in the ghetto. Between 1969 and 1974, Hollywood cranked out approximately 60 of these movies (Guerrero 1993).

In large part, the film industry was motivated to make these black-oriented pictures in the early 1970s because they were in dire economic straits and estimates suggested that blacks made up as much as 30 percent of the movie-going audience at that time. In deciding on how to appeal to this African American audience, the studios took into account that there had been a sea change in black social and political consciousness in the aftermath of the civil rights movement and the urban uprisings. For that reason, they were willing to forgo the traditional images of blacks that depicted them as subordinate to whites or as hell-bent on assimilation into white society.

The blaxploitation films they released did indeed help them to address their financial crisis as they were often so cheaply made that they managed to be fairly profitable despite their modest earnings. For example, *Sweet Sweetback's Badasssss Song* (1971) cost $500,000 to make and made $10 million by the end of its first year. *Shaft* (1971) cost $1.2 million to make and made $10.8 million in its first year, and *Superfly* (1972) cost less than $500,000 to make and brought in $11 million in its first 2 months. The modest successes of these blaxploitation classics spurred a number of low-cost copycat films that were marketed to young black male audiences in an effort to reap similar profits (Guerrero 1993).

To attract newly politicized black audiences, these movies typically included a black hero and an evil white villain and a story line that involved the black hero (or heroine) triumphing over the evil white villain or "sticking it to the man." "The man" referred to the white man, although in the vernacular of that time, "the man" was not really a person, but a system of racial stratification that was deliberately set up in ways to limit black opportunities to succeed (Boyd 2000). In other words, "the man" was really shorthand for a system that segregated blacks in ghettos where they lacked decent housing, high-quality schools, access to living-wage jobs and fair and courteous treatment by the police. As such "the man" referred to many of the grievances that had precipitated the riots of the 1960s.

BLAXPLOITATION FILMS AND AUTHENTIC BLACKNESS

The black male characters depicted in blaxploitation movies came to be equated with authentic blackness largely by acting in ways that were the opposite of the unreal black characters that had gone before them. For example, Poitier's character in *Dinner* had seemed unreal because he was an upper-middle-class black man, isolated in the upper reaches of white society, who was trying to adapt himself to its demands. Hence, his problems included gaining the acceptance of the upper-class white family that he sought to marry into. Because these problems were not the kinds of problems that concerned most blacks, the roles he played did not seem to depict genuine black men addressing genuine black problems.

Rather, the 1960s uprisings suggested that the problems of blacks in the ghetto ran more towards acquiring living-wage jobs, securing decent housing, sending their children to schools that could prepare them to make a living and ending police brutality in their communities. Hence, the efforts of Poitier's characters to be accepted by whites made no connection to the racial conflicts raging outside Hollywood, and therefore his characters' problems had little appeal to blacks striving for racial justice.

One way, then, in which the film industry sought to achieve an authenticity in blaxploitation movies that was absent in Poitier's assimilationist films was to situate many of their stories in the ghetto. The ghetto became the site of authentic blackness because it was the product of years of racial discrimination in jobs, housing, schools and policing. And because it was ghetto blacks who had rioted in reaction to these conditions, the heroes of blaxploitation movies were generally blacks raised in the ghetto who had grown up facing genuine ghetto problems. In that sense, then, the heroes of blaxploitation movies seemed more like real black men than Poitier's characters had because they were poor or had been raised in ghetto poverty and had thereby been forced to acquire street smarts in order to survive the ghetto. In addition, many of them had pulled themselves up from poverty by hustling and not by assimilating like Poitier's characters.

The ghetto was easily recognized in these films by its gritty streets and dilapidated buildings as well as its cast of desperate junkies, greedy pimps, and ubiquitous streetwalkers, all outfitted in the dramatic underworld fashions popular in the early 1970s. In an effort to further represent the realities of ghetto life, there were also repeated scenes of illegal drug use and casual, gratuitous sex.

THE INAUTHENTICITY OF BLAXPLOITATION FILMS

However, blaxploitation films were rather quickly faulted for also being inauthentic. In large part, their characters likewise appeared to be unreal because Hollywood shunned the authentic protest masculinities then being expressed in the real world off screen and substituted their own version of "authentic" black heroes in the form of sex show studs (*Sweetback*), dope dealers (*Superfly*) and black private detectives prone to pursuing their own self-interests rather than a program of empowerment in the black community (*Shaft*).

Indeed Guerrero (1993) suggests that it was never the film industry's intent to tell the stories of the real race men off screen who were then active in trying to improve the lot of black people. Rather, for him, their intent was to rewrite black male characters in ways so that long-standing racial hierarchies might be preserved. Commenting on the new black images depicted in blaxploitation films, he argues:

This did not mean, however, that the newly emergent black *macho* images . . . were able to escape the "tar baby," Hollywood's subtle entangling system of racial devaluation. For the racial ideology and stereotypes that are but part of dominant cinema's work are not fixed or static. Instead, they are a set of dynamic, lived relations and social transactions; the filmic conventions and codes of racial subordination are continually being reworked, shifting under the pressure of material, aesthetic and social conditions. *For all the new potent force, sexuality and assertiveness expressed in the images, bodies and portrayals of the macho men, their strength was almost always either at the service, or under the control, of white institutional power and authority.* (Guerrero 1993:79, emphasis mine)

However, even if Hollywood had no intention of allowing a black man to express himself in terms of social and political activism on screen, black audiences still had to be entertained if Hollywood was to reap any type of profit. Hence, some way had to be found to offer black audiences a semblance of the revolutionary spirit then being expressed in black ghettos without actually delivering. The film industry employed several strategies.

According to Guerrero, one strategy employed to prevent the black male heroes in blaxploitation films from triumphing over white institutional power and authority through social and political activism was to have the black male lead pursue an individualistic agenda rather than an activist agenda. Depicting an activist agenda on screen would have meant that the black male hero would be shown making plans on how to help whole communities of black people triumph over the system by empowering them to bring about community-wide improvements in housing, schools, jobs and treatment by the police. In place of black activists, blaxploitation films depicted black lead characters with an individualistic agenda in which a single black male hero took his revenge on the system and emerged triumphant.

Another way in which Hollywood sought to provide black audiences with the mere semblance of social and political activism without actually delivering was to prominently display the gestures and symbols of black activism (e.g., black power handshakes, Afros, etc.). These gestures and symbols, then, served as stand-ins for political and social changes that never actually took place. Among the many symbols used to simulate black protest was a black revolutionary presence. However, any militant presence in these films was typically neutralized by portraying the black militants as impotent and powerless.

By making use of these strategies, then, Hollywood was able to appeal to newly politicized black audiences and profit handily even as it contained black social and political aspirations on the silver screen. In the process, it was also able to update old stereotypes of blacks as dope dealers, sex show studs, prostitutes and pimps. Examples of these strategies abound in two classic blaxploitation films—namely *Shaft* (1971) and *Superfly* (1972).

DISCREDITING BLACK POLITICAL ACTIVISM IN *SHAFT*

In *Shaft*, the narrative itself precludes any expression of the black activist agenda as the story follows the black detective-hero, John Shaft, after he is hired by a black crime lord and heroin dealer. The black crime lord hires Shaft to rescue his daughter, who has been kidnapped by the white mafia in order to run him out of the heroin business. Hence, in *Shaft*, racial conflict is reduced to a conflict between a black crime boss and his white mafia competitors. As such, the film's narrative is completely divorced from the kind of racial conflicts that precipitated the black uprisings off screen.

Because *Shaft* reduces racial conflict to conflict between black and white criminals, it is able to avoid appealing to any activist impulses lurking in its black audiences. Instead, *Shaft* upholds the racial status quo by refusing to address the sentiments that are meant to change it. Because the story is centered on the planning and execution of the kidnapped woman's rescue, there is little room for the hero, John Shaft, to pursue the kinds of social and political changes that might mean empowering the black community.

The only concessions that the film makes to the activist zeal latent in its black audiences is to show Shaft, who does not live in the ghetto, regularly going to the ghetto to get information and engaging in solidarity handshakes and hand slaps with black residents in the ghetto. There is also a black activist presence in the movie as Shaft meets with the local black militants to get information about the whereabouts of the kidnapped woman on one of his trips to the ghetto. The audience can tell they are militants involved in the struggle for racial justice as they can be seen sitting under a picture of Malcolm X during their meeting.

Still, the presence of these black militants in the picture is no indicator that the struggle for racial justice will somehow be addressed in the film. In fact, it is doubtful that the black militants depicted in *Shaft* would be very effective in bringing about social and political change as five of them are killed—presumably by the white mafia—within minutes after Shaft finds them in their hideaway. As further evidence of their impotence, the black militant leader, Ben, is ultimately forced to give up on his principles because he needs money to get some of his fellow militants out of jail.

Hence, in one minute in a fit of revolutionary zeal, Ben can be seen accusing the black crime czar of undermining the black community by selling drugs and running a prostitution ring in the ghetto. In the next minute, he is shown trading the lives of his fallen men for $10,000 each in payment for going to work for the same black crime czar that he has just denounced. In these scenes, the lives of black activists come across as cheap and expendable, and their leaders seem to be open to violating their revolutionary principles by working with black criminals who exploit black people.

Shaft also fails to recognize the separatist impulses that characterized many protest organizations by the late 1960s as black nationalists increasingly separated from whites and set about pursuing racial equality in solidarity with other black men and black women (Healey 1997). Yet, no such opportunity exists for the expression of these separatist instincts in *Shaft*. In fact, the black detective-hero John Shaft, himself, seems to be lacking in these separatist instincts as he can be seen working hand in hand with white police officers to find the kidnapped woman and rescue her.

In the film at least, the white police officers have an incentive to work with this black private detective to insure that the kidnapped black woman is rescued from the white mafia in order to rid themselves of some white criminal organizations and avoid a bloodbath. Hence, instead of working in solidarity with his black brothers and sisters to solve the problems of the ghetto, John Shaft works hand in hand with white policemen to find the white mafia involved in the kidnapping. As such *Shaft* appeals more to the integrationist spirit rather than to black separatist sentiments.

Furthermore, while the elimination of police brutality was very much a concern in black ghettos that had recently rioted over abusive police forces, there is nothing in the film to suggest that blacks in the real world off screen might have been in conflict with the police. For example, there is no evidence of white police officers beating or abusing John Shaft or any other blacks in the film. Instead black audiences were only exposed to scenes depicting a cooperative relationship between Shaft and white police officers acting in solidarity against the white mob. At best, then, *Shaft* shows a black private detective, a black crime lord and some white policemen triumphing over the white mob rather than a black community triumphing over racism.

THWARTING BLACK ACTIVISM IN *SUPERFLY*

Because Shaft works hand in hand with white cops to rescue the black gangster's daughter, he cannot be said to be "sticking it to the man." However, *Superfly* (1972) is all about a black man taking his revenge on a racist white legal system that seeks to control him.

Superfly tells the story of a black cocaine dealer named Youngblood Priest, who sells a brand of cocaine that is extremely potent or "super-fly."

Unlike John Shaft, Priest and his crew of black cocaine sellers live in the ghetto and sell a lot of their drugs there; they also sell drugs to upper-class white Wall Street brokers, patriotic white construction workers and almost everyone else.[1]

In the opening scenes of the movie, it is clear that Priest has grown weary of the cocaine trade as he is fearful of being killed by someone seeking to rob him of his cocaine or his money. He also has reason to worry about being killed or turned in to the police by his crew of sellers as he is forced to constantly alienate them by threatening them and manipulating them in order to make sure that they pay him for his cocaine.

In an effort to get out of the cocaine business, Priest goes to his mentor, Scatter, who had previously fronted him with the cocaine that got him started in the business. He asks Scatter to provide him with 30 kilograms of cocaine to sell so he can retire. As Scatter has retired from the cocaine trade himself, he is forced to turn to his supplier to provide Priest with the 30 kilograms. Scatter's source for such large quantities of cocaine turns out to be a white deputy police commissioner named Riordan, who arranges to have his detectives meet with Priest and sell him the cocaine. Once the deputy commissioner arranges to have Priest and his crew sell cocaine for him, he no longer needs Scatter. Hence, he has Scatter killed by his white patrolmen because Scatter knows too much and wants to leave the drug business.

After Scatter's murder, Priest realizes that the deputy police commissioner will kill him too if he tries to retire after selling his 30 kilograms of cocaine. Nonetheless, after selling most of his cocaine for nearly a million dollars, he lets the deputy commissioner know that he plans to retire. When Deputy Commissioner Riordan and several other white policemen take him down to a deserted wharf to kill him, Priest single-handedly beats up the deputy commissioner's men and snorts cocaine right in front of Riordan as Riordan holds a gun on him. It is at this point that Priest "sticks it to the man" as he tells Riordan that he has taken out a contract on his life and that the deputy commissioner and his family will be killed by his white hit men in the event that Priest is harmed in any way. The movie ends as "the man" (i.e., the deputy commissioner) is forced to let Priest walk away and retire with his last big score.

This ending touched a nerve with black audiences as there was cheering in some theaters as black spectators saw a black man triumphing over the criminal justice system (Boyd 2000). Presumably, many black fans of this movie felt empowered because Priest beat up several white patrolmen and managed to outsmart the white deputy commissioner and thereby break free from a system that was designed to control him. After all, as the 1960s riots indicated, many blacks in the audience probably longed to tell off many of the police officers in their own communities and break free from a criminal justice system that exercised so much control over their lives.

In many ways, *Superfly* broke with long-standing movie traditions that painted cops as honest, upstanding heroes committed to upholding the law. Instead *Superfly* depicts them as corrupt underworld types intent on making money on the very vices (drugs, illegal gambling, prostitution, etc.) that they are supposed to police. And while other films with white casts and white narratives (*The Godfather*, *Serpico*) also portrayed the police as corrupt, it is likely that *Superfly* with its black hero, Priest, had particular resonance for black audiences who had recently rioted over the unpunished beatings and killings that the police meted out in the black community.

Nonetheless, *Superfly* undercuts this appeal to black anger at corrupt and brutal cops by making the instrument of revenge on "the man" an unsympathetic figure such as a dope dealer rather than a black male actively involved in the struggle for racial justice. In fact, the dope dealer-hero Priest is totally uninterested in joining with local black activists to bring about change in the black community. Hence, in one scene, he angrily refuses to give some of his drug money to three black militants who are soliciting funds for building the new black nation and goes on to dismiss them as all talk and no action.

Therefore, much as was the case in *Shaft* and other blaxploitation films, the activist agenda meant to bring about collective improvement in the lives of all blacks in the ghetto is given short shrift. In fact, in *Superfly*, the black militants come across as shakedown artists intent on taking some of Priest's drug money rather than as race men committed to empowering black communities. Furthermore, instead of focusing on black activism, *Superfly* focuses on the individualistic agenda of one apolitical dope dealer named Youngblood Priest whose means to triumphing over a racist system involves selling a lot of cocaine and retiring from the business. As much of that cocaine is sold to Priest's black brothers and sisters, Priest's eventual triumph over the system does nothing to improve the lives of his ghetto neighbors or further racial solidarity.

Hence, in both *Superfly* and *Shaft*, the penultimate expressions of black masculinity are the violent masculine expressions required of a dope dealer trying to maximize his profits or those necessary for a black private detective trying to make his way in the underworld in order to do a job for his drug lord-client. The protest masculinities that emerged off screen in the 1960s urban insurrections are simply shunted to the sidelines in blaxploitation movies as Hollywood assigns center stage to apolitical black male characters that pursue their own self-interested agendas.

THE DEMISE OF BLAXPLOITATION AND
THE RISE OF CROSSOVER FILMS

The blaxploitation film cycle turned out to be short-lived. By 1973, there was a significant decline in the number of blaxploitation films released, and by January of 1974, the death knell of blaxploitation was officially being sounded (Guerrero 1993). There are several reasons for the sudden demise of these films, including protests from black civil rights organizations. Beginning in 1972, various civil rights groups like Operation PUSH, the NAACP, Core and the SCLC started calling for an end to these movies as they accused them of exploiting black images and of feeding black youth vulgar, unreal images of ghetto life that encouraged the single-minded pursuit of materialism. Many of these organizations were especially outraged about *Superfly* as they argued that this film, in particular, glamorized drug consumption in the ghetto at a time when no other media were involved in promoting drug use.

For once, the film industry was in a mood to accommodate the civil rights organizations as their economic fortunes had improved with their absorption into multimedia conglomerates and therefore they no longer needed the modest profits they received from blaxploitation films. The film industry was also willing to stop releasing blaxploitation films because it realized that both black and white movie fans alike would attend films with black lead characters as long as themes of racial conflict were not addressed.

Hence the studios began to develop crossover films, which were films with black stars that could be expected to attract white moviegoers. However, in order to insure that white moviegoers would be willing to attend a movie with black lead characters, black images in these crossover films had to be adjusted to white tastes. This meant that the blaxploitation formula of a black hero triumphing over a white villain was no longer possible. And while blaxploitation films themselves had never really provided any serious treatment of black activist efforts to address racism in America, the rise of these crossover films made it even less likely that real race men and race women would be seen on the silver screen involved in the struggle for racial justice.

After all, white movie audiences could hardly be expected to sit through films which talked about ongoing racial injustice or black cultural nationalism. At the very least, such images would have been in conflict with the widespread belief that post-1960s America was a color-blind nation. Indeed, the only way that films showing black men and women struggling to rid America of white domination and white privilege could be seen as entertaining by white moviegoers would be if whites could somehow be depicted as the heroes of these pictures.

THE RISE OF INTERRACIAL BUDDY FILMS

The most common strategy for luring a white audience to a film with a black lead character was to make a movie about black and white buddies (*48 Hours, Beverly Hills Cop, Silver Streak, Lethal Weapon, Trading Places, The Negotiator*). In these biracial buddy films, the presence of the white buddy assured white audiences that nothing substantial would be said about white racism and its role in perpetuating racial inequalities. Instead the story line in many of these films often forced the black and white buddies into situations where they were required to cooperate to attain a goal, and thus racial harmony could be achieved on screen even as racial divisions persisted in the real world outside the theater (Guerrero 1993a).

In an effort to present images that would not make white spectators uncomfortable, some of the early biracial buddy films duplicated traditional racial hierarchies on screen by placing the black character in a subservient role to his white buddy. Hence, in *Silver Streak*, comedian Richard Pryor plays a meek train porter who serves white passengers on the train and Gene Wilder plays one of the white passengers. In *Trading Places*, Eddie Murphy plays a beggar while his eventual white buddy is a wealthy stockbroker played by Dan Ackroyd. And in *48 Hours*, Eddie Murphy is cast as an ex-con newly released from prison into the custody of his parole officer and soon-to-be white buddy played by Nick Nolte. As second bananas to the white male leads, these characters were often black males isolated in a white world helping whites to solve their problems (Guerrero 1993, 1993a).

Even when blacks played the lead character, they were still cast as blacks alone in a white world (*Beverly Hills Cop, Burglar, Jumpin' Jack Flash, Sister Act, The Associate, The Negotiator*). By removing their black characters from black culture and black communities, buddy pictures managed to strip them of any black identity. And because these lead characters were blacks surrounded by whites working together with them to solve problems that had nothing to do with race, there was no chance that they would get into a meaningful discussion with other blacks about racism in America.

THE INTERRACIAL BUDDY FORMULA IN *THE ASSOCIATE*

There is evidence of this in the 1996 Whoopi Goldberg comedy, *The Associate*. In it, Ms. Goldberg stars as a talented black female financial executive named Laurel Ayres. In the opening scenes, Laurel is turned down for a promotion by her white male employers at a Wall Street firm. Instead they give the promotion to Laurel's considerably less qualified white male coworker, who has relied on Laurel's accomplishments to win the promotion.

Angry about being passed over, Laurel quits the firm and strikes out on her own to form her own investment firm. Yet as she circulates investment proposals to a number of white male-owned businesses, she quickly comes to realize that no one will hire her because she is a woman. After a series of rejections, Laurel comes up with a new plan to lure clients to her business. She creates a fictional white male business partner and rather quickly persuades much of Wall Street that her new white male associate is a financial whiz. Hence, the film's message seems to be that a woman has to pretend to be a white male on Wall Street in order for her talents to be recognized.

Because Laurel is a black female, the audience might surmise that the discrimination she encounters on Wall Street reflects both racism and sexism. Nonetheless, the film skirts all mention of racial discrimination and focuses only on sex discrimination. It does this in several ways. First, it isolates Laurel in an all-white world, thereby eliminating any black friends who might define her missed promotion as evidence of racial discrimination in the workplace. Instead, only white friends come along to console her, and they define her problems in the workplace solely in terms of sex discrimination.

For example, early in the picture, one of Laurel's white subordinates at the firm named Sally (played by Dianne Wiest) accuses Laurel of looking down on her because she works for her. She goes on to warn Laurel that she is about to be passed over for a promotion and frames the problem totally in terms of sex discrimination against women. Because the racial hierarchy is reversed with Sally working for Laurel, Sally is even able to accuse Laurel of discriminating against her—in a kind of reverse discrimination. In this early scene then, the movie narrative minimizes any audience concerns about white racism in the workplace by giving Laurel white subordinates. This makes it that much easier to frame Laurel's lost promotion solely in terms of sexism.

Furthermore, the eventual success of Laurel's business depends upon the help and the talents of her white buddy, Sally, who eventually goes to work for Laurel in her new business and becomes her business partner. In the end, then, it is these two women working together in an interracial buddy pair, who manage to triumph over sexism and the old boy's network on Wall Street. By studiously avoiding any discussion of racial discrimination in the workplace, then, *The Associate* is able to maintain the fiction that America is a color-blind nation.

While *The Associate* was not especially popular, a number of crossover films have been successful at the box office. The ability of some to pull in profits is understandable because they can draw black and white audiences alike as long as they downplay racial conflict (Guerrero 1993, 1993a). In 1990, they also enjoyed some critical acclaim as Whoopi Goldberg became only the second black woman in history to win an Oscar for Best Supporting Actress for following the interracial buddy formula in *Ghost*. In *Ghost*, Ms. Goldberg plays a black con woman and spiritual medium helping the two white lead characters to solve their romantic problems.

HOLLYWOOD AND THE
THREAT TO WHITE MALE HEGEMONY

The move away from films in which blacks triumphed over whites—even the artificial triumphs of blaxploitation films—was also dictated by events occurring off screen. By the end of the 1970s, white male moviegoers were growing ever more conservative as white male dominance in America and abroad seemed to be under siege.

Threats to the white male sense of hegemony came with America's defeat in Vietnam, spiraling inflation, the Arab oil shocks, Watergate and increasing deindustrialization (Guerrero 1993, Watkins 1998). As events at home and abroad challenged their dominance, conservative white males became increasingly less willing to tolerate demands from the less powerful including women, gays and lesbians, or left-wing white antiwar protesters. In this atmosphere, they certainly were not in a frame of mind to tolerate demands for racial equality from blacks.

In fact, even during the blaxploitation wave of the early 1970s as Hollywood lured black audiences to the theaters with stories of black male heroes triumphing over white villains, they were simultaneously marketing films to white audiences which heroicized white vigilantes or aggressive white police forces for their involvement in the violent suppression of black men (e.g., *Dirty Harry* movies, *Death Wish* series).

For example, in *Death Wish* (1974), a law-abiding white everyman played by Charles Bronson is driven to a vigilante killing spree after his wife is brutally murdered by white criminals in the course of a home invasion. Thereafter, Bronson's character is on the lookout for criminals, and every criminal that he encounters—black and white alike—in deserted parks or on subway platforms is subjected to his brand of instant justice at the end of a gun barrel. The film also promotes the fanciful notion that Bronson's one-man killing spree somehow leads to a reduction in the crime rates as criminals presumably grow afraid to rob strangers on the street because they fear they might confront Bronson's vigilante killer. Hence, even when the police identify Bronson as the vigilante killer, they urge him to leave town rather than arresting him. And so with their blessing he takes his vigilante justice on the road in a series of sequels.

Coming near the end of a 20-year crime wave in America, it is likely that this 1974 film served to empower many moviegoers who felt intimidated by criminals—at least symbolically. Hence, in films like *Death Wish*, it is the law-abiding white everyman who triumphs over a menacing black population. The fact that all the black men that Bronson's character kills off are conveniently robbers and muggers justifies his one-man killing spree and provides him with the kind of moral cover he needs to mercilessly dispose of them. And because race relations in *Death Wish* are defined by this white vigilante killer dispatching menacing black muggers, the film plays to racial divisions and white fears of black criminals. Indeed there is little to distinguish Bronson's vigilante killer from organized hate groups like the Ku Klux Klan as both were fairly effective at ridding America of a black population that was regarded as dangerous.

Thus in *Death Wish* and a number of other 1980s films, there was often an effort to recuperate lost white male hegemony on screen. And as white male moviegoers felt more threatened and grew ever more conservative, the black characters in crossover films had to be beaten down and controlled so as to accommodate them.

RIGHT-WING POLITICIANS AND
THE APPEAL TO WHITE MALE DOMINANCE

Hollywood was by no means the only medium to appeal to white males who felt their hegemony had been threatened. Political elites likewise made an effort to speak to white male anxieties about their continued dominance during election campaigns. For example, Ronald Reagan's election to the presidency in 1980, in large part, stemmed from his successful appeal to the anxieties of white working-class men or the so-called Reagan Democrats. Traditionally these white blue-collar workers had voted for Democrats because the Democratic Party addressed their economic interests by supporting their labor unions. Yet, even though Reagan and the Republican Party offered little to these Reagan Democrats that furthered their economic interests, they managed to garner their support, in part, by appealing to their concerns about threats to their racial hegemony (Watkins 1998).

Initially white male racial hegemony had been threatened when blacks protested the old order during the civil rights movement. After all, blacks had achieved some gains as a result of their protests as Jim Crow segregation was dismantled, constitutional protections for black voting rights were established and some initial efforts were made to integrate the schools via court-mandated school busing. White male racial dominance was further imperiled when the Black Power Movement and the urban uprisings in the north publicized urban poverty and police brutality and led to the expansion of the social safety net to help the inner-city poor as well as the establishment of affirmative action programs to speed black upward mobility.

A number of conservative white politicians immediately saw an opportunity to appeal to those white voters who felt threatened as they saw the old racial order slipping away. They wooed these disgruntled voters by promising to restore the traditional racial order with policies that would limit black voting rights, dismantle the social safety net, end school busing and eliminate affirmative action programs. To hear conservatives tell it, these programs were no longer needed because the United States had overcome its racist past and transformed itself into a color-blind meritocracy over the course of the civil rights movement. In the new, post-1960s color-blind America that they talked about, blacks could make it on their own and no longer needed the "special privileges" that came with affirmative action or an expanded social safety net (Watkins 1998; Jones 2005; Gallagher 2003).

However, the fact that large numbers of blacks were still mired in poverty suggested that Great Society programs were still needed. Hence, conservative politicians had to find a way to say that persisting high levels of black poverty were not the fault of any lingering white racism, but rather that they were somehow the fault of the black poor themselves. In order to blame the poor for their own poverty, then, right-wing politicians revived traditional culture-of-poverty arguments that suggested that the dysfunctional values of black underclass culture promoted a whole host of misbehaviors that prevented inner-city blacks from rising out of poverty.

Culture-of-poverty arguments that blame black culture for persisting black poverty turned out to be the types of explanations that registered with many white voters because, among other things, they allowed them to openly speak of black inferiority once again. By contrast, traditional racial hierarchies provided whites with less and less leeway to openly express their superiority to blacks—particularly after the 1960s. The reason these traditional racial hierarchies were slowly losing legitimacy is because they were based on slavery or the class and race privileges of an employer-employee relationship in which white employers demanded deference from their loyal black servants.

Racial hierarchies, based on slavery or an employer/employee relationship, are almost always suspect in a democracy where all persons are presumably created equal. Hence, as the old rankings came to be perceived as more unjust in the wake of black protest during the 1960s, conservatives constructed a new, more acceptable racial hierarchy based on cultural difference rather than class and race privilege. What made this new construction of black inferiority especially appealing was the fact that it was no longer white oppression that was holding blacks back, but rather a cultural value system that blacks, themselves, had created that kept them mired in poverty.

Conservative politicians and academics alike offered any number of explanations for why black underclass culture kept blacks mired in poverty. For example, some argued that the present-oriented hedonistic lifestyles of the black underclass made them inclined to live in the moment, pursuing illicit sexual thrills (e.g., teen sex, premarital sex) or illegal drug use without any consideration for future consequences (illegitimate births, drug addiction). And because their lives were taken up with the excitements of street life, conservatives would claim that underclass blacks did not discipline themselves or make the necessary sacrifices to acquire an education that might have helped them to become socially mobile (Banfield 1970). Furthermore, because underclass males achieved status in the ghetto by bullying and beating each other up to establish dominance, the thinking was that blacks did far more harm to each other than whites ever did by killing each other off in an endless cycle of gang wars or fights over drug turf (Wolfgang and Ferracuti 1967; Curtis 1975). Indeed this endless cycle of black-on-black violence meant that young black males were infinitely more likely to die in a homicide than anyone else and that their killers were usually other black men.

By focusing on the black underclass, then, whites could openly speak of black inferiority by simply referring to their values and all the social problems associated with underclass lifestyles. In post-1960s conservative discourse, then, black inferiority was constructed as a black culture that actually encouraged black-on-black violence, dropping out of school, high unemployment rates, numerous teen pregnancies, widespread drug addiction, low marriage rates and high levels of illegitimacy. And because black social disadvantage was now seen as the result of ghetto culture—and not white oppression—it meant the end of white guilt and thereby any lingering white sympathy for the economic plight of blacks (Watkins 1998).

Because the thinking was that blacks in the ghetto would remain poor as long as they subscribed to this destructive value system, what seemed to be required to rid America of its black poverty problem was for the black poor to assimilate white middle-class values and turn away from the hedonistic cultural practices that kept them locked in the ghetto. Hence, with media representations of violent, unemployed black males, black female welfare queens and their dangerous illegitimate children coming at them from all sides (film, television, news media, political campaigns), whites could once again claim innocence as they supported the elimination of social programs to address racial inequalities.

RACIAL SEGREGATION AND
THE RISE OF THE JOBLESS BLACK GHETTO

Yet, by focusing on these sensationalized images of the pathological underclass culture that blacks had created, it was possible for whites to ignore how white racism continued to implicate itself in worsening structural conditions in the nation's ghettos in the years after the civil rights movement. In his discussion of at least some of these structural conditions, Wilson (1996) identifies the role of racial segregation in the further deterioration of black ghettos into a jobless underclass in the years between 1970 and 1990. He argues that joblessness skyrocketed in a number of black ghettos as white workingmen suburbanized in the 1960s and 1970s and manufacturing jobs suburbanized with them.

Wilson's focus on the loss of manufacturing jobs in the inner cities is understandable because they are the kinds of jobs that hire men with a high school education or less. Because many of these jobs were unionized back then, they represented one of the few types of occupations that provided a living wage to men with no more than a 12th grade education, thereby making it possible for them to support their families. To illustrate the extent of the exodus of these manufacturing jobs from the cities in the 1970s and 1980s, Wilson notes that Chicago lost 60 percent of its manufacturing jobs between 1967 and 1987, while Philadelphia lost 64 percent of its manufacturing jobs and New York and Detroit lost 58 percent and 51 percent of their manufacturing jobs respectively.

As these manufacturing jobs suburbanized, white privilege meant that low-skilled, less educated white males could suburbanize with them and continue to work at these living-wage jobs. However, because of racial discrimination in suburban housing, black males were not able to follow these jobs out to the suburbs and hence the kinds of jobs that had traditionally been available to low-skilled, less educated men were increasingly less available to low-skilled, less educated urban poor black men.

As jobs suburbanized, black male unemployment in the urban ghetto rose or even worse, many men ceased to look for work and left the labor force entirely. Furthermore, as work disappeared from these neighborhoods, ghetto schools failed to train inner-city males for alternative jobs as many of these schools were hobbled by poor facilities, overcrowded classrooms and teachers who lacked confidence in black students. Hence, while as many as 69 percent of black men had worked in 12 of Chicago's poorest ghettos in 1950, by 1990 only about one-third of working-age black men held a job in a typical week in these same inner-city ghettos.

The rise in joblessness among inner-city black males had a number of other devastating effects as it contributed to a decline in marriage rates in underclass neighborhoods as these chronically unemployed males were less able to support a family. Faced with fewer men who could help them support a family, more black women living in the ghetto either did not marry or divorced, and many were forced to turn to welfare to support themselves and their children.

As a result, the jobless ghettos that emerged in the 1970s and 1980s in cities across the country were characterized by high levels of unemployment, large numbers of households headed by women, high rates of school dropout and high levels of welfare dependency. They were also the communities with the highest crime rates in the city as many of these chronically unemployed males turned to crimes such as robbery, burglary or theft to support themselves as legal work increasingly became unavailable (Taylor and Covington 1988).

Furthermore, joblessness provided many of them with an incentive to sell drugs, which brought a new level of lawlessness to these communities as illegal drug markets attract crime and violence. Hence, many of these ghettos experienced even further deterioration as drugs were increasingly sold openly on ghetto streets, and drug-related murders rose as drug dealers fought over drug-selling turf—particularly during the years when crack cocaine experienced a rise in popularity between 1985 and 1992 (Goldstein et al. 1997; Golub and Johnson 1997).

Confronted with the poor schools and the high crime rates, any ghetto resident who could afford to leave these new jobless ghettos left. Hence, between 1970 and 1990, many of these communities were depopulated as middle-class blacks and working-class blacks left these ghettos in droves for other neighborhoods in the city and then eventually for the suburbs. As a result, poverty became even more concentrated in these jobless underclass communities as only the poorest of the poor, who could not afford to leave, remained. Consequently by the 1990s, there was a rise in the number of underclass communities in cities across the country where 40 percent or more of neighborhood residents were poor. And as employed blacks in the middle and working class left, the black poor left behind found themselves cut off from the kinds of informal job search networks that were typically needed to find work (W. Wilson 1996).

Before the exodus of manufacturing jobs from the inner city, ghetto males had relied on friends and neighbors to tell them about a job opening. But as work left the cities, such informal job-seeking networks deteriorated as many of their friends and neighbors no longer had access to manufacturing jobs. Increasingly, then, many residents of jobless underclass neighborhoods found themselves turning to less effective formal sources to find work, such as newspaper ads.

Yet, in a survey of employers in Chicago and its suburbs, conducted in 1988 and 1989, white employers reported that they often deliberately avoided hiring low-skilled inner-city black workers by refusing to advertise job openings in citywide newspapers that black job seekers might read (W. Wilson 1996). Instead they confined their job advertisements to suburban newspapers or those distributed in white ethnic communities, thereby assuring themselves of a mostly white job-applicant pool. They also relied on informal networks to fill job openings by asking their current employees to refer someone who might be looking for work. This practice also had the effect of screening out black job-seekers in workplaces that were predominantly white as white workers primarily referred other whites.

In explaining why they deliberately avoided hiring blacks from Chicago's urban ghettos, many of the white employers surveyed went to great lengths to argue that they were not guilty of racial discrimination. Consistent with the conservative mantra, they blamed the culture of the black poor by arguing that their dysfunctional value systems made them less desirable workers. So, for example, many said that they avoided hiring black workers because they lacked a work ethic and were in fact lazier than whites, Asians and Latinos. In explaining why blacks were more likely to be lazy than other racial or ethnic groups, some employers reasoned that blacks had never acquired a work ethic as so many had been raised in fatherless households where they had seen their mothers abandon work and force the state to support them by going on welfare. Because of this type of upbringing, some employers felt that blacks were simply culturally unprepared to show up at work every day on time. Moreover, some speculated that this cultural aversion to work, learned in childhood, might have been further reinforced in the adult years in something akin to a culture of idleness as the high levels of joblessness in urban ghettos meant that blacks were surrounded by and reinforced in their idleness by other people who did not work.

In short, many of these Chicago area employers blamed widespread black joblessness on the cultural deficiencies of inner-city blacks rather than on structural forces such as the suburbanization of manufacturing jobs in the 1970s and 1980s. Moreover, it was rare for these employers to consider how their own decisions to deliberately screen out black job-applicants on the basis of race might have contributed to widespread black unemployment. In fact, only 4 percent of the employers interviewed thought that racial discrimination in hiring was responsible for high levels of black unemployment.

When asked how they knew that black job-applicants subscribed to a cultural value system that made them undependable and averse to working hard, some employers claimed that they could discern the negative attitudes of black job-seekers in job interviews. However, as Wilson argues, work attitudes and behaviors such as dependability and commitment to the job are notoriously difficult to assess in a short, subjective job interview. And in fact one employer acknowledged that many negative employer perceptions of black workers were not based on actual evidence, but rather on unfavorable perceptions or feelings that they had developed about blacks over time. Hence, because these employers screened out black job-applicants based on their preconceived notions of what inner-city blacks were like in general, it meant that individual blacks suffered as they were never given an opportunity to prove their qualifications as workers because they had been eliminated based on their race and their residence in an urban poor ghetto.

For the most part, the employers surveyed stereotyped black males and black females alike as undesirable workers. However, some were even more reluctant to hire black males than black females. The tendency on the part of some employers to reject black male applicants stemmed from their fear that black male job-seekers might have a history of participating in inner-city gangs, crime or drug selling. They thereby deduced that if black males came from high crime neighborhoods where violent responses to arguments and conflicts were common, they might bring some of these violent subcultural practices to the workplace and be overly aggressive and inclined to intimidate other workers. Indeed one employer suggested that because black males felt so emasculated in the ghetto they might feel more of a need to assert themselves with their white employers so as to avoid any further threats to their manhood.

Because black male job-seekers resided in communities where crime and violence were rampant, some employers also reasoned that they could not hire black males because they feared that black males would come out to their suburban companies, find out about the security system and proceed to steal from the company. Some of the employers surveyed also claimed that they were forced to reject black applicants because urine testing during the application process indicated that so many had used drugs, while others claimed that they had had to fire blacks because of their stealing or drinking.

Hence rather than considering how persistently high levels of unemployment have historically caused high crime rates in black and white urban communities alike, the employers used the high crime rates in black ghettos to justify screening out black job-applicants.

BLACK CRIME, WHITE FEAR AND
THE RISE OF LAW-AND-ORDER POLITICS

Clearly, the perception on the part of these white Chicago area employers that individual black job-seekers were dangerous was not based on evidence, but rather on racial biases that they had developed over time. They were hardly alone in their thinking as white fears of violent and criminal black men were running quite high by the end of the 1980s. In part, this was because of the media focus on the rising popularity of crack cocaine.

As crack use spread to blacks and whites alike, both print and broadcast media fueled white fears of dangerous black men by focusing only on numerous sensationalized accounts of the crack trade in the black ghetto. Hence there were tales of crack selling by violent black juvenile gangs like the Bloods and the Crips that told of their involvement in spreading the crack trade from city to city or spoke of their involvement in drive-by shootings that led to the killings of innocent bystanders. Despite the fact that many of these accounts were exaggerated or simply untrue, they did draw in large audiences, thereby generating more advertising dollars for newspapers, magazines and television. It comes as no surprise, then, that these tales of drugs in the inner city were repeated over and over to fuel media profits (Reinarman and Levine 1997; Maxson 1995).

The sheer repetition of these stories about crack in the inner city was sufficient to convince many Americans that there was a crack epidemic afoot across the land despite the fact that crack cocaine was never that widely used (Covington 1997; Reinarman and Levine 1997). White fears of violent and criminal black men were also fueled during the 1988 presidential campaign, as Republican presidential candidate, George Herbert Walker Bush, invoked the specter of the dangerous black man in the form of Willie Horton in order to label his Democratic opponent, Massachusetts Governor Michael Dukakis, as soft on crime (D. Jones 2005).

With the media and political campaigns increasingly focused on gangs, drugs, and violence in the ghetto by the late 1980s, it became possible for conservative politicians to appeal to newly fearful whites who were anxious about black underclass violence spilling over and invading their neighborhoods. Hence, after successfully raising white fear levels, a number of right-wing politicians sought to turn around and allay the white fears that they had created by running law-and-order campaigns. In the course of these campaigns, conservative law-and-order politicians promised to institute more police crackdowns and more surveillance in black communities to contain crime and violence in the ghetto and insure that it did not spill over into white communities.

Hence while many whites had previously been horrified by the brutalities and violence that white police forces heaped upon civil rights protesters in the south and upon blacks living in northern ghettos, the constant stream of images of a violent black underclass now made it possible for more whites to turn a blind eye to police excesses that took the form of police violence against minorities (police brutality, killings) and the violation of their civil liberties (racial profiling).

Now, instead of arousing sympathy for the black victims of police brutality, police violence against blacks induced more and more whites to grudgingly support crackdowns in the ghetto as they increasingly came to seem like a necessity. That the cultural climate had changed so that black complaints about police brutality increasingly fell upon deaf ears is perhaps best illustrated by the social and cinematic reaction to the 1992 riot in Los Angeles.

NOTE

1. In fact, a good deal of research on drug users in the real world indicates that cocaine was quite popular among whites in the early 1970s (Waldorf et al. 1991; Adler 1993; Bachman et al. 1990). Because it was so expensive at the time, it was not nearly as popular among low-income blacks who had to await powder cocaine's conversion to the less expensive crack cocaine in the 1980s before increasing their levels of use.

Chapter Two

Hollywood and Black Protest

The Rise of Ghetto Action Movies

On April 29 and 30, 1992, there was yet another riot in Los Angeles that left 52 people dead and more than 2,000 injured (M. Oliver et al. 1993; *Newsweek* 1992). The local police proved to be fairly ineffective in quelling the violence as they did not successfully mobilize their forces until several hours after the disturbance began. Hence, by 10 p.m., 25 square blocks of Los Angeles were on fire, and by midnight, Governor Pete Wilson sent in the National Guard.

In terms of the events that led up to it, the 1992 Los Angeles riot looked remarkably similar to the riots of the 1960s. As the Kerner Commission had concluded some 24 years before, the 1960s riots began after a sequence of events that played out in 3 stages. By their account, the first stage began with years and years of unaddressed grievances in the black community followed by a second stage in which there was an incident to intensify black anger and frustration in the weeks and months before the outbreak of rioting. In the third and final stage, occurring in the hours before tensions exploded, there was a precipitating event that led directly to full scale unrest.

The urban uprising in Los Angeles in 1992 seemed to follow this same 3-stage sequence as consistent with the first stage, black Angelenos likewise had long-standing grievances with the police. For example, in the years before the 1992 uprising, the city of Los Angeles had had to pay out millions to black residents to settle complaints against the Los Angeles Police Department (LAPD). Prominent among these complaints were black protests of police chokeholds as some reports suggest that in the decade prior to the 1992 unrest, some 16 out of 18 citizens who died in police chokeholds were black (M. Oliver et al. 1993).

Consistent with the second stage, there was an event to raise black anger in the months before the 1992 disturbance in the form of a verdict over the murder of a black honor student named Latasha Harlins. Apparently, Ms. Harlins and a Korean shopkeeper had had a dispute over a carton of orange juice and the shopkeeper shot her in the back of her head. The fact that the court punished the shopkeeper with a slap on the wrist that included a six-month suspended sentence and six months of community service for the murder of this black female honor student only served to further intensify black anger in the months before the April disturbance (Oliver et al. 1993). Finally, consistent with the third step, there was a precipitating event that occurred a few hours before the riot in Los Angeles began, namely a largely white jury's refusal to punish police abuse of a black man named Rodney King.

A year before the disturbance, Rodney King had been beaten by four white police officers after they pursued him in a high-speed car chase for traffic violations. The beating received widespread publicity because it was caught on videotape. In the year before the trial, the videotape of the four white policemen administering some 56 blows to a black man lying helplessly in the street was shown over and over on television. Perhaps, because of these repeated viewings, many Americans were surprised when a jury of 10 whites, one Latino and one Asian in the white middle-class suburb of Simi Valley acquitted the four officers of the beating.

As might have been expected, 92 percent of blacks surveyed in the immediate aftermath of the Simi Valley verdict felt the acquittal of the 4 white police officers was not justified; they were joined by a majority of whites—fully 73 percent—who also felt the verdict was unjustified (*Newsweek* 1992). Moreover, polls showed that most Americans—91 percent of blacks and 77 percent of whites—felt that the federal government should pursue justice for Rodney King by trying the police under federal laws. It comes as no surprise, then, that even conservative President George Herbert Walker Bush attempted to appeal to the many Americans who were shocked by the verdict by immediately pressing federal civil rights charges against the acquitted police officers.

Much of the surprise about the jury verdict had a lot to do with the fact that the evidence against the four white police officers seemed to be overwhelming. After all, in addition to the videotape, transcripts indicated that the policemen used many racial and sexual slurs while subduing Mr. King. One of the officers was even recorded as saying, "I haven't beaten anyone this bad in a long time" (*Newsweek* 1992; Butler 1993). Yet while many Americans saw the police stepping outside the law to brutalize a black man, the mostly white jury in Simi Valley saw the police assault on a black man lying flat on his back in the street as the cost of protecting white suburbanites like them from urban blacks like Rodney King (*Newsweek* 1992).

Interviewed after the verdict, some of the Simi Valley jurors defended their acquittal of the four white officers by saying that they had been persuaded by defense attorneys who said that the police had to use that amount of force against this large black man who kept getting back up after they hit him (*Newsweek* 1992).

Because Rodney King kept getting back up, the defense essentially claimed that the police were forced to stun him with two Taser darts and beat him senseless. To explain why they continued to beat him even after he was lying flat on his back, they claimed that he moved about a little bit as if he planned to struggle to his knees again. And then when they beat him even after he stopped moving about, they claimed they beat him because he had a look of determination rather than an expression of fear. Hence, while many Americans saw white police officers beating a black man for speeding, what the mostly white jury saw was police officers using escalating degrees of force to subdue an especially resistant arrestee. According to the jurors, Rodney King could have controlled the situation at any time by simply assuming the position; hence, it was his "resistance" that had precipitated the unfortunate but, to their eyes, legal and appropriate beating.

In persuading the jurors of Rodney King's responsibility for his own beating, the defense attorneys basically invoked the strategy used by President George H. W. Bush some four years before during the 1988 election. As noted, during his campaign, President Bush had repeatedly invoked the specter of the dangerous, unpredictable and out-of-control black man in the form of Willie Horton to raise white racial fears and mobilize white support by proving he was tougher on crime than his opponent.

The defense attorneys in the Simi Valley courtroom played on these same white racial fears by describing Rodney King as the kind of dangerous black man who required a beat down by the police. Hence, by calling up longstanding racial myths about the violent black man, the defense attorneys succeeded in putting Rodney King on trial for lying helplessly in the street and being throttled by four white police officers (Oliver et al. 1993).

THE 1992 RIOT: URBAN REBELLION OR BREAKDOWN IN LAW AND ORDER?

A few hours after the Simi Valley acquittal of the four police officers, the rioting in Los Angeles began. Given that the unrest followed so quickly upon the verdict, it is understandable how many Americans saw the 1992 riot in Los Angeles as an instance of blacks rebelling against the racial injustice meted out by the legal system. In this way of thinking, blacks were protesting an oppressive criminal justice system, which allowed the police officers who beat Rodney King to go unpunished and allowed the shopkeeper who killed Latasha Harlins to get off with a slap on the wrist.

And in fact, in the immediate aftermath of the Simi Valley verdict, many angry Angelenos did protest by calling into newspapers, radio programs and television stations to voice their outrage at what they saw as a miscarriage of justice. In addition, a crowd of blacks, whites, and Latinos protested by attacking symbols of criminal justice authority by setting fires at the guardhouse outside police headquarters and at city hall and by trashing the criminal courts building.

However, riots are complex events in which riot participants have many motives. Hence, while some participants clearly meant to use the disturbance to protest prior injustices meted out by the criminal justice system, others sought to use the occasion to loot.

For those who claim that the riots are a form of black rebellion against government oppression, then, there is a tendency to focus on the precipitating events that caused the black community to explode and to examine reactions like those in which protesters directly attacked symbols of government authority. Conversely, for those for whom the riots are a simple breakdown in law and order, there is a tendency to focus on the looting. This enables them to describe the riot participants as dangerous apolitical criminals who are less concerned about protesting racial injustice than about using the opportunity to steal. And there were numerous scenes of looters shown on the evening news breaking though storefront security gates to take groceries, beer, clothes, televisions, stereo sets and a host of other items.

Naturally scenes of looters stealing could be expected to raise white fears that a race war between blacks and whites had begun. However, the fact that all race and ethnic groups—whites, blacks, Latinos and even a few Asians—were caught on camera looting tends to raise doubts that this disturbance marked the beginnings of a much dreaded race war. In fact, some reporters compared the multiracial crowds of looters they observed to participants in a carnival rather than to a bloodthirsty mob of blacks intent on attacking whites (*Newsweek* 1992).

Over and above the looting, there was also the much repeated story of a white truck driver named Reginald Denny being dragged from his truck and beaten by a crowd of blacks in South Central to give credence to the race war explanation. White journalists were also attacked by angry blacks in South Central, and one white journalist was even shot. The only thing detracting from this version of the race war narrative was the fact that African Americans were also among those who shielded Reginald Denny and the injured white journalists from the mob and smuggled them to the hospital for treatment (*Newsweek* 1992).

Other news accounts touched on black attacks on Asian Americans as more than 100 Asian-owned stores were burned. Such stories suggested that not only was there a race war going on between blacks and whites, but there was also one being waged between blacks and Asian Americans as well (*Newsweek* 1992). However, the fact that black businesses were also looted and burned during the riot raises doubts about explanations that would reduce this disturbance to a simple conflict between blacks and whites or blacks and Asians.

Moreover, stories that focus on the conflicts between Asian Americans and blacks to explain the burning and looting of so many Asian-owned stores ignore the fact that there may have been even more intense conflicts going on between Latinos and Asians than between blacks and Asians. The possibility that Latino-Asian conflicts may have explained much of the burning and looting is certainly worthy of consideration as more Latinos were arrested for looting than blacks (M. Oliver et al. 1993).

In truth, the racial and ethnic makeup of South Central in 1992 makes it almost impossible to describe the unrest as a race war between blacks and whites or between blacks and Asians. After all, by the time of the disturbance, South Central was a low-income community that was half black and half Latino with a number of Asian shopkeepers doing business there.

Yet despite the fact that the multi-ethnic nature of the looters and the multi-ethnic nature of those looted make it difficult to characterize this disturbance in terms of a race war, there can be little doubt that the unrest drove up white fear of blacks. Hence, all the way across the country in New York City, stores closed and whites left work early in the wake of the rioting in Los Angeles.

JUSTIFYING POLICE CRACKDOWNS:
LAW AND ORDER IN POST-RIOT LOS ANGELES

After widespread rioting in the 1960s, the Kerner Commission had recommended that efforts be made to address many long-standing black grievances about jobs, job training and a host of other complaints in an effort to prevent future disturbances. However, little was actually done to address the crisis in black unemployment after the 1960s unrest. Hence, by the time of the 1992 riot in Los Angeles, the job picture for blacks had grown progressively bleaker as South Central Los Angeles had fallen victim to deindustrialization like so many other cities across the country. This is evidenced by the fact that black unemployment levels in Los Angeles in the early 1990s stood at 50 percent.

Consequently, after the 1992 riot in Los Angeles, then-President George Herbert Walker Bush came up with a plan to rebuild the city that relied on tax cuts for businesses willing to locate in the inner city and employ local residents. However, as critics of these policies duly noted, these programs were a boon to businesses, but of little to no help for the unemployed as they failed to produce many jobs (M. Oliver et al. 1993). Even worse, rather than trying to address black grievances with the police and the courts that precipitated the rioting, the president proposed a program that would have translated into even more police crackdowns and mass incarcerations of black Angelenos.

The proposed program was called Weed and Seed. In part, Weed and Seed was geared towards seeding or building up inner-city neighborhoods by expanding Head Start and job-training programs. Unfortunately, 80 percent of the funding for the Weed and Seed program was to go towards weeding out dangerous blacks and putting them under criminal justice supervision (M. Oliver et al. 1993). While policies that weeded out dangerous black men would have been anathema to the black community, they would likely have had great appeal to many of the residents in white suburbs like Simi Valley where white fear of criminal blacks skyrocketed after the 1992 civil disturbance.

In fact, right-wing California politicians had for years successfully campaigned on the need for more police, more prisons and tougher punishment by appealing to white suburban voters who wanted more protection from crime. Because the riot brought some looting and fires to even affluent sections of Los Angeles, it presented an ideal opportunity for conservative political elites to exploit the disorder by talking about why black youth were so violent and crime prone in the first place. In so doing, they would remind white suburbanites why the police were needed to clamp down on the ghetto and protect them from the urban menace right on their doorstep.

Hence, some conservative politicians set about playing on white racial fears by identifying those blacks who were most likely to be in need of weeding out. One prominent example of this comes from California Governor Pete Wilson, who had been elected governor after running on a campaign of law and order. A few days after he sent in the National Guard to quell the rioting in Los Angeles, he went on *This Week with David Brinkley* on May 3, 1992, to discuss the riot (Watkins 1998).

However, he did not use the opportunity to talk about how deindustrialization and the loss of jobs had devastated black neighborhoods. Nor did he urge an expansion in job programs to revive black neighborhoods—as the Kerner Commission had suggested some 25 years earlier. He also did not use the opportunity to talk about ways for the legal system to grapple with police brutality in black communities, despite the fact that it was the acquittal of the four white policemen who beat Rodney King that had touched off the rioting. Rather, instead of talking about ongoing black grievances with racial injustice in the legal system, he urged viewers to see the movie *Boyz n the Hood*.

For him, the movie, *Boyz*, would give white audiences an understanding of the roots of black male violence in the ghetto that was in danger of spilling over into the white community and in so doing provide them with a sense of how to grapple with the black male threat on their doorstep. The explanation that *Boyz* seemed to offer for black male violence was that it was caused by so many black youth being raised by their mothers in fatherless households and not by staggering unemployment levels. Moreover, the movie offered a solution to the problem of dangerous black males by demonstrating that a strong father in the household could stop black youth from participating in the local cycle of black-on-black violence.

By recommending *Boyz* in the immediate aftermath of the riot, Governor Wilson responded to newly elevated fear levels among white Angelenos by playing up a film that repeated the conservative mantra that unduly generous welfare payments produced the female-headed households that churned out these young, violent, fatherless black males. By using *Boyz* to frame the riots, then, Governor Wilson managed to direct white anger and fear at the ghetto culture of poverty and at black women in the ghetto, who raised their sons alone.

THE RISE OF GHETTO ACTION MOVIES

Even more important than Governor Wilson's framing of the riots was the change in black images on the silver screen. Almost immediately after the 1992 Los Angeles riot, Hollywood released a whole cycle of movies about life in the ghetto that seemed to back up conservative arguments by reminding audiences how dangerous black neighborhoods actually were. These post-riot films likewise seemed to blame drugs and fatherless households for the roving gangs of out-of-control young black males who had rioted yet again in Los Angeles. As many of these movies were made in the action-adventure genre, they have been called ghetto action movies (Watkins 1998).

Much like the blaxploitation films of the early 1970s, ghetto action movies depicted life in the inner city and as such gave filmmakers an opportunity to represent the ghetto in terms of a whole host of pathologies. As these films were cranked out in the 1990s and on into the 2000s, moviegoers were, once again, subjected to a constant stream of images of violent black male criminals, black female welfare queens, black prostitutes, and illegitimate black children. For the most part, the lives of the dysfunctional black characters depicted in these movies were centered on sexual hedonism, drugs, crime and violence. And, while these movies varied in terms of their story lines, an ever-present element in them was at least one scene depicting the black-on-black cycle of violence in which roving bands of lawless black males routinely murdered or assaulted each other.

As these films showed scene after scene of violence, many also depicted an equally savage police force that seemed to be the only thing capable of thwarting the relentless criminal rampages and violence-ridden drug trades that characterized the film industry version of the ghetto. Indeed the more savagely young black males were depicted in these films, the more moral license the criminal justice system acquired to arrest, imprison or kill off the dangerous black youth depicted on screen, even if it meant violating their rights in the process.

These movies resembled the blaxploitation films of the early 1970s in other respects as well as they too relied on casts largely composed of black actors and black actresses to depict life in the ghetto. Yet, unlike many of the earlier blaxploitation films, which were often written and directed by whites, these new ghetto action films were typically written and directed by blacks. As such, they seemed to have greater authenticity than the earlier blaxploitation films, for it was now African American writers and directors who were shaping black images on the silver screen (Watkins 1998; Guerrero 1993).

This new wave of ghetto action films mirrored the earlier boom in blaxploitation films in other respects as well as once again these films were initially released as a means of boosting film industry profits in the aftermath of a 1991 slump at the box office. In reaction to the slump, Hollywood once again made some effort to attract a large black moviegoing audience—estimated at 25 to 30 percent in the early 1990s.

Following a formula that had been applied with some success some 20 years before with blaxploitation films, ghetto action movies were made with very low budgets on the premise that even if they only appealed to black audiences they would still turn a profit. So, for example, the 1991 ghetto action classic *New Jack City* was made for $8.5 million and earned $47 million. The film *Boyz n the Hood*, also made in 1991, cost $6 million to produce and grossed over $60 million by 1992. (By 1993, *Boyz* had become the most commercially successful black film ever made.) *Menace II Society*, another ghetto action classic, cost a mere $3 million to make and made $20 million in its first six weeks (Guerrero 1993; Watkins 1998).

However, unlike the blaxploitation films of the early 1970s, which drew almost exclusively black audiences, the ghetto action movies of the early 1990s managed to cross over and draw white audiences. Young white audiences were typically drawn to these movies by their rap music soundtracks and by the presence of rap musicians in these films (Watkins 1998).[1]

FRAMING URBAN UPRISINGS IN *MENACE II SOCIETY*

Released in 1993, *Menace II Society* was among the first of the ghetto action films to appear on movie screens in the aftermath of the 1992 Los Angeles riots. Much like other films in the ghetto action genre, *Menace* managed to piece together a movie version of an inner-city black community that was almost wholly peopled by residents whose lives were taken up with drugs, crime and violence. That drugs, crime and violence took center stage in *Menace* had a lot to do with the film's story line which, in essence, followed the escapades of a couple of young black male criminals.

Perhaps, because it was released so soon after the 1992 riot, *Menace* also manages to comment on the nature of black riots. In *Menace*, black riots are depicted as a breakdown in law and order rather than as a protest against police brutality. And because riots signal black lawlessness in *Menace*, they seem to justify harsh police crackdowns in the inner city, even if it requires the police to step outside the law. Furthermore, because the film represents young black males as not simply a threat to other blacks, but also as a danger to other races—most notably Asian Americans—it manages to conjure up links between black riots, black crime and the much feared race war, thereby making police suppression of lawless black males seem that much more urgent.

In the opening scene of *Menace*, the film's two vicious black lead characters, Caine and O-Dog, go into a liquor store where O-Dog proceeds to kill the Asian American storeowner in the course of a spat over malt liquor. He then brutally murders the owner's Asian American wife, who has witnessed the murder, and takes the security tape that records the murder.

In the next scene, the camera cuts to grainy videotape of the police beating black looters during the 1965 riot in the Watts section of Los Angeles. In this sequence that juxtaposes a fictional account of a 1990s liquor store murder by O-Dog with real-life footage from the 1965 unrest in Watts, the movie accomplishes several things.

First, scenes from the fictional account of the brutal murders of the Asian shopkeepers remind audiences of blacks looting Asian businesses the year before and call up images of a supposed race war between blacks and Asians that had been much in the news at that time. Furthermore, when the film shifts from the fictional account of the 1990s liquor store murder to the actual 1965 footage of white policemen beating black males in the midst of looting during the Watts riots, it demonstrates that the police are up to the task of restoring order with violent black males.

In films like *Menace*, then, the notion that black riots are a form of protest against racist conditions is thoroughly discredited by equating riots with black lawlessness and criminal behavior. Therefore, it is essential in *Menace* that the white racism that precipitated the riots totally disappears. In place of the police brutality that actually set off these disturbances, all moviegoers get to see is blacks on a rampage of burning and looting. In *Menace*, then, it is law-and-order governments that win the culture war while blacks angry about the steady stream of unpunished or lightly punished police attacks on blacks are the losers. Because viewers of *Menace* only get to see violent black looters, they are not likely to see the state as oppressive when it grants its police forces license to subdue a seemingly dangerous black population by any means necessary.

Indeed after watching this 1993 film, a viewer would be likely to conceive of the rioting that occurred in Los Angeles the year before as a breakdown in law and order rather than as a form of black protest against the police brutality so many witnessed in the Rodney King beating. Of course, the audience's failure to see black riots as a form of protest against an oppressive government has a lot to do with what *Menace* overlooks.

For one thing, what is missing from this film is any sense of why the majority of Americans—black and white alike—felt that the acquittal of the four police officers that beat Rodney King the year before was a miscarriage of justice. A viewer also will not be able to get any sense of why even conservative elected officials (including President George Herbert Walker Bush) condemned the verdict and initiated federal civil rights proceedings against the four officers.

This is largely because *Menace* has been stripped of any scenes that might have pointed to the ongoing grievances that eventually caused the black community to explode the year before. Instead of black outrage, the opening scene in *Menace* portrays a fictional character named O-Dog killing Asian shopkeepers in an almost complete reversal of the real-world Latasha Harlins case in which an Asian shopkeeper was punished with only a fine and a suspended sentence after shooting this black female honor student in the back of the head a few months before the 1992 rioting. Because there are no images of blacks complaining about the courts allowing the police or nonblack private citizens to attack or kill blacks with impunity, this movie offers viewers no explanations for why blacks felt the need to riot.

Instead, *Menace* manages to discredit rioting as a form of black protest by fashioning a link between black riots, black crime and black conflict with other races without alluding to the 1992 riot at all. It does so by only focusing on the earlier 1965 riot in Watts and directly linking that unrest to the violence of its fictional black gangbanger-heroes in 1990s Los Angeles. It establishes this link early on by rolling out grainy videotape of the 1960s riots that shows fires burning and blacks looting stores as a voiceover describes the scene as a "burning and looting Negro area" where the police are forced to confront "roving bands of rampaging Negroes." The narrator also describes police actions to put down these rampaging Negroes who have "attacked police with rocks, bricks and bottles" and quotes the Commander of the California National Guard ordering the guard to "use whatever force was necessary." This is followed by actual footage of tanks rolling through the streets of Watts while armed police officers fight with unarmed black men, hitting them with clubs and cuffing them. There is also an image of the police standing over the bullet ridden body of one black man.

This video of the 1965 riot in Watts is immediately followed by a scene in which Caine, the fictional black male criminal and lead character, begins to narrate by saying that "when the riots stopped, the drugs started . . ." In this scene, Caine, himself, makes a direct connection between the 1965 Watts riots and his own childhood socialization into a life of crime as immediately after videotape of the riots, the audience begins to see scenes of Caine as a little boy growing up in a household where his drug dealing father and his drug addicted mother can be seen giving parties for other underworld types. Hence, through their fictional lead character, Caine, the filmmakers set up a direct cause-and-effect relationship between the 1965 riots and black youth violence in the 1990s as Caine's criminal parents can be seen passing on the culture of poverty to him.

Yet, while *Menace* manages to convey a cause-and-effect relationship between the 1965 riots and the black youth violence of Caine's generation in the 1990s, it makes no mention of the simmering black anger over police brutality that existed in Los Angeles and other cities in the 1960s that actually caused the 1965 riot in Watts. This omission occurs despite the fact that surveys of black opinion in 1966 showed that 79 percent of black males in Watts believed the police lacked respect for Negroes and 74 percent believed that the police used unnecessary force (U.S. National Advisory Commission on Civil Disorders 1968). Because *Menace* fails to consider how police brutality may have sparked the 1965 riots in Watts, it is able to define black riots as a cause and symptom of ghetto lawlessness rather than as a protest against racial injustice in the legal system.

In directly linking the 1965 Watts riot to a teen-aged Caine's criminal behavior in 1990s Los Angeles, *Menace* also does not allude to any role that high levels of black unemployment in 1960s Los Angeles (and other cities) might have played in the criminality of black youth in the 1990s. This omission occurs despite the fact that conditions for inner-city blacks in Los Angeles and other cities around the country deteriorated even further between the 1960s riots and the 1992 riot in Los Angeles as manufacturing jobs left the inner city and black male unemployment rates climbed. Yet, the film makes no effort to link spiraling unemployment in the inner city to its high crime rates despite research on unemployment and crime suggesting otherwise (S. Walker 1990).

Instead, the film seems to support conservative assertions that the riots somehow led to drug use and the breakdown of black families and black communities and to visualize this as the cause of high black crime rates in 1990s Los Angeles. In order to make this point, the movie fast-forwards from videotape of the 1965 riots to 1993 where we see a fully grown Caine in his senior year of high school embarking on a crime spree in his Los Angeles neighborhood.

FRAMING URBAN UPRISINGS IN *SOUTH CENTRAL*

Links between the 1965 riot in Watts and black youth violence in the 1990s are also made in the 1992 ghetto action film *South Central*. *South Central* is loosely based on a story of the infamous black street gang called the Crips, who are dubbed the Deuces in the movie. The film follows the escapades of two Deuce leaders named Bobby and Ray-Ray. During a gang meeting as Bobby and Ray-Ray plan how to expand Deuce membership and turn their gang into the strongest force on the streets of Los Angeles, Ray-Ray turns to Bobby and mentions that both their fathers went to prison because of their participation in the 1965 Watts riots.

By the end of the movie, after Bobby is newly released from prison for his gang crimes, he realizes that because he was raised in a household made fatherless by the 1965 riots, he became immersed in the violent gang culture. Consequently, he goes on a quest to try to save his own son from the violent, criminal lifestyle that awaits him after having grown up without Bobby in a fatherless household. Hence, the 1965 riots are once again tied to the criminality of future generations of young black men because they deprived the 1992 gangster-hero, Bobby, of a father who might otherwise have saved him from a life of crime.

With these and numerous other ghetto action movies being cranked out in the 1990s, conservatives found themselves with any number of images of poorly parented, violent black males to back up their arguments about the drawbacks of female-headed families. Images from these films seemed to offer graphic proof that fatherless households had produced roving bands of dangerous black youth and thereby suggested that until the ghetto reformed itself into father-headed nuclear families, the violence would continue.

Moreover, the fact that law-abiding adults in the ghetto were not able to control their own kids and were seemingly defenseless against the vicious black youths in their midst was evidence to some that an equally vicious outside force would be needed to come in and take back ghetto streets—namely the police. In short, two-parent families and a law-and-order campaign by the police seemed to be the only solution to the problem of underclass violence depicted in these movies—and not jobs, better schools and better housing.

INAUTHENTICITY IN GHETTO ACTION MOVIES

By the mid-1990s, some conservative politicians were arguing that things were about to get much worse as they predicted that there was going to be an increase in the numbers of the violent black superpredators then routinely being portrayed on the silver screen (Bennett et al. 1996). They used this predicted surge in youth violence to argue for even more law and order crackdowns in the ghetto. Their predictions could not have been more wrong.

Just as they were forecasting that increases in the ranks of young, black superpredators would bring a new crime wave to urban America, crime rates plummeted. In city after city, homicide rates went into free fall. And, in no age group was the downturn in crime more dramatic than among the selfsame young black males that were then appearing in ghetto action movies. Moreover, this dramatic decline in black youth violence occurred without a corresponding drop in fatherless households in underclass neighborhoods, which suggests that conservatives may have been wrong about the importance of fatherlessness in producing violent black youth.

Yet, despite the remarkable crime drop occurring in the real world off screen, the murderous rampages of black youth continued in ghetto action movies throughout the 1990s and on into the opening years of the twenty-first century. Hence, a certain amount of inauthenticity crept into these films as the crime wave persisted in full force on the silver screen even as black youth in the real world off screen seemed to be turning away from drugs, crime and violence in droves.

Despite the fact that their warnings of an imminent crime wave had turned out to be wholly inaccurate, conservatives continued to call for more crackdowns in the ghetto—even in the face of plummeting murder rates. They simply shifted gears and began to argue that more police efforts to rein in the inner cities were still needed because tough policing had brought down the crime rates. So, for example, some proclaimed that crime rates declined in New York City because the police showed zero tolerance for even minor infractions in the ghetto (J. Wilson and Kelling 1982).

Among other things, zero tolerance policing was based on the premise that law-abiding adults in the ghetto could not control their streets. As a consequence, neighborhood teens supposedly felt emboldened to engage in acts of social disorder like spray painting buildings, turnstile jumping, public drinking, public use of illegal drugs and public urination (Wilson and Kelling 1982). Traditionally, minor infractions like these had simply caused the police to tell those involved to desist. However, with zero tolerance policing, these minor infractions became occasions for the police to respond with stop-and-frisk searches, identity checks, summonses and even arrests.

Zero tolerance proponents argued that if the police showed zero tolerance even for trifling offenses like these, it would lead to a reduction in more serious crimes (e.g., robberies, burglaries, auto theft, etc.). In other words, by casting such a wide net over citizens in high-crime underclass neighborhoods by stopping them for even minor violations, the police would inadvertently also catch more serious criminals (e.g., robbers, burglars) with outstanding warrants or parole violations or those carrying illegal drugs or guns obtained illegally (Wynn 2001).[2]

The only downside to this practice was that by casting such a wide net, the police also ended up harassing a lot of law-abiding people in high-crime black neighborhoods in order to catch a mere handful of serious criminals. This is indicated by the fact that the rise in zero tolerance policing in New York was accompanied by a rise in citizens' complaints to the Civilian Complaint Review Board. Furthermore, despite the fact that zero tolerance policing led to more citizen complaints against the police, there is no evidence that it actually led to a reduction in crime in New York (Karmen 2000; Conklin 2003).

For example, critics claimed that if zero tolerance policing had actually reduced crime, then such policies should have been in place in cities around the country as crime rates fell nationwide. However, a number of cities that did not practice zero tolerance policing also experienced a significant drop in their crime rates. For example, in San Diego, the police actually made *fewer* arrests for minor infractions like turnstile jumping, and yet the murder rates still plummeted.

Nowhere were arguments about the effectiveness of zero tolerance policing more in doubt than in Los Angeles itself—the setting for so many ghetto action movies. In Los Angeles, murder rates fell by a whopping 61 percent between 1992 and 1998, and yet this dramatic decline was decidedly *not* due to zero tolerance policing (Karmen 2000). In those years, the LAPD was suffering from low morale as *exposés* of their prior involvement in police brutality (e.g., Rodney King case) or in the mishandling of evidence in criminal investigations had caused the department to be widely discredited. Many police officers in the LAPD even complained that they felt abandoned by the city and by the top brass in the department.

Because they felt like they were on their own, a number of officers decided to protect themselves from any possible prosecution for overzealous policing by looking the other way when they saw minor crimes occurring. And, yet despite the fact that the police refused to engage in any zero-tolerance-style crackdowns, murder rates in Los Angeles continued to fall. Further, many cities other than Los Angeles and San Diego also experienced dramatic declines in their murder rates without this kind of hardball policing, leading some observers to conclude that zero tolerance policing did not reduce crime (Butterfield 2000; Moran 1997).

However, Hollywood continued to release pictures that were totally divorced from this reality. On one hand, they released more and more ghetto action films that represented black youth as violent and dangerous—despite their plummeting murder rates. They also continued to visualize police crackdowns in the ghetto without once questioning the effectiveness of these practices. Moreover, because these films continued to represent black youth as violent and criminal gangbangers, they failed to tell the stories of the hordes of black youth, who were deserting criminal subcultures in the 1990s and the early 2000s en masse.

It is regrettable that they did not examine this transformation in the black youth population as criminologists have argued that the dramatic downturn in murders in the 1990s had a lot to do with black youth reforming themselves (Covington 2004a, 2004b). In other words, as more and more black youth grew tired of crack cocaine, demand declined in the ghetto and the crack market contracted. As the market contracted, there was less crack-related violence to fuel the homicide rates. For example, with market contraction, there would have been fewer disputes among crack dealers competing over drug selling territory to cause drug-related murders (Goldstein et al. 1997). Hence, the dramatic declines in murder were due not to a stepped-up law-and-order campaign but rather to whole cohorts of black youth reforming themselves by turning away from crack use and crack-related violence (Golub and Johnson 1997). By continuing to focus on the ghetto crime wave, then, these films missed an opportunity to examine this transformation.[3]

BLACK PROTEST, WHITE PROTEST: HOLLYWOOD AND THE VIETNAM WAR

If nothing else, previous commentary on blaxploitation and ghetto action films indicates that filmmakers have been all too eager to discredit black uprisings against police brutality—particularly the disturbances that occurred in the 1960s and in 1992. Typically, they accomplish this by equating black protests against police excesses with black criminality. They then use this construction of black uprisings to justify turning the ghetto into a police state rather than addressing the grievances of black citizens that actually precipitate rioting.

Certainly, it could be argued that the film industry's decision to impugn black uprisings against overzealous policing has a lot to do with the fact that riots are violent and destructive forms of protest. However, if this were the case, then, one would expect Hollywood's willingness to disparage citizen protests against government oppression to apply to blacks and whites alike. This would mean that the film industry would be every bit as inclined to discredit violent white uprisings by equating them with breakdowns in law and order. However, a couple of examples may suffice to suggest that white protest against the government comes in for far better treatment on the silver screen than black protest, even when it turns violent. The first example of this can be seen in the film industry's treatment of white protest of the war in Vietnam.

Just about the time that blacks were rioting in the late 1960s to protest police excesses in their neighborhoods, a number of white Americans were starting to demonstrate against the Vietnam War. White antiwar protesters were vehemently opposed to the war because many young males feared being drafted and sent off to fight in an unwinnable war where they felt they would be treated like little more than cannon fodder. Further when many veterans of the war returned to the United States, they were not welcomed as heroes. Instead the government abandoned them to unemployment, homelessness and untreated physical and mental health problems caused by the war.

Many of those protesting the Vietnam War were white college students, who were not simply angry about the war itself, but also about the U.S. government's involvement in persecuting and exploiting a number of third world nations more generally (Brooks 1970). Through their protests, many of these students hoped to bring about an end to the war and to U.S. involvement in exploitation, death and destruction around the world. Hence, much like the black rioters of the 1960s, many of these student antiwar protesters turned to acts of property destruction to dramatize their opposition to the war, including setting bonfires, attempting to destroy army induction centers or rampaging through the streets smashing the windows of department stores, apartment buildings and cars (Kifner 1970).

Some of the student protesters even turned to methods that were far more violent than those employed by black protesters during the 1960s riots. This was especially true of a more militant faction of the student antiwar protesters called the Weathermen (later Weather Underground). The Weathermen went underground in 1970 and became involved in a string of bombings in the early 1970s as a means of waging their war against the government (Mitchell 2003; McGrath 2004). In taking a stand against the U.S. government and its war-making machine, the Weather Underground often chose symbols of government authority as their targets (Dwyer 2007; Greene 1970). Hence they set off explosions at ROTC offices as well as bombing draft and army induction centers, police stations, banks, federal buildings (e.g., the U.S. Capitol) and various corporate headquarters (Brooks 1970; *New York Times* 1975; Eder 1976; Greene 1970.

In their eyes, the drama of the bombing itself and the subsequent property destruction were sufficient to call attention to their causes and to symbolize that something had been done to the authorities who continued to wage an unpopular war. Setting off explosions was also seen as a last resort against a powerful and repressive government. After all, many of the more militant antiwar protesters realized they were no match for government crackdowns, especially after the National Guard killed four student antiwar protesters at Kent State University in 1970.

Bombing government targets, then, became a kind of guerilla tactic that enabled the Weather Underground to continue to call attention to their vehement opposition to the war even as they eluded the authorities. Moreover, the bombings were meant to bring the war home to an American public that had grown complacent about their government's repeated bombings overseas. And, to some degree, the resort to an extreme form of protest such as exploding bombs may also have reflected the Weather Underground's frustration with the failure of more peaceful marches and demonstrations to end the war (Greene 1970).

For the most part, the Weather Underground used these explosions to destroy property while going out of their way to avoid targeting humans; hence there were few injuries or deaths associated with their explosions. Still, because of their potential for ending in the death or injury of innocent civilians, these bombings were described by some as terrorist acts.

By the mid-1970s, after the Vietnam War had ended, the Weather Underground splintered even further as some decided to surface and turn themselves in while others remained fugitives. Those who surfaced in the late 1970s and the early 1980s typically received mild punishments for their acts of property destruction and went on to lead conventional lives (Dwyer 2007; Wakin 2003; D. Smith 2001).[4]

Yet, despite the fact that white student antiwar protest turned violent, the film industry remained sympathetic to the causes of the student protesters as evidenced by their release of a number of critically acclaimed antiwar films showcasing the events that precipitated the student demonstrations. These antiwar pictures about white soldiers in Vietnam (e.g., *Deer Hunter, Coming Home, Apocalypse Now*) played up the illegitimacy of the war by graphically depicting soldiers dying on the battlefield and by focusing on the atrocities American soldiers committed against the Vietnamese as well as those they witnessed in Vietnam. Because the war was depicted as brutal and ultimately futile, audiences could be expected to sympathize with the soldiers when they became disenchanted with the war.

These movies likewise showed how a number of white soldiers were eventually abandoned by their government as many of them came home to face permanent physical disabilities and untreated mental health problems that stemmed from the war (depression, suicide attempts, drug addiction). Movie audiences, then, could be expected to cheer for these disillusioned soldiers because of these powerful depictions of the war's toll on their lives.

Because these antiwar films urged audiences to sympathize with the many disillusioned fighting men, they may also have inadvertently encouraged them to root for the white college students who protested the war. In part, this was because white antiwar protesters were instrumental in convincing the public to see the government's involvement in an unwinnable war and its abandonment of its war veterans as crimes committed by the state (the U.S. government) against its citizens. When seen in that context, the student protesters' acts of civil disobedience seemed like legitimate responses to state oppression.

Further, because the protesters were instrumental in getting many Americans to see the war as illegitimate, their protests were crucial in bringing about an end to the fighting. In that sense, then, the student protesters emerged as heroes. And, in a context where antiwar protest came to be seen as at least legitimate, if not heroic, there was more tolerance shown even when antiwar protest turned violent as it did with groups like the Weather Underground. This meant that there was more leniency accorded to white antiwar protesters on screen—even violent antiwar protesters—than had been extended to black protesters during the 1960s uprisings.

As evidence of Hollywood's willingness to indulge even violent antiwar protest, there was a small, unsung documentary made about the violent protests of the Weather Underground called *Underground*. Initially the government sought to prevent the release of the film by subpoenaing the filmmakers and their materials in an effort to get information about fugitives in the Weather Underground. However, some well-known members of the film community, including prominent directors and actors, voiced their support of the film, and the government's subpoena was withdrawn (*New York Times* 1975).

Released in 1976, the film showed actual fugitives in the Weather Underground giving their account of their 1971 bombing of the U.S. Capitol. Yet, despite the fact that they protested the war by exploding a bomb, the filmmaker seems to have taken a fairly sympathetic view of their protest. Hence, in his interviews with actual members of the Weather Underground, he tries to get them to explain how white middle- and upper-class young adults like themselves had come to be involved in this type of violent revolutionary protest in 1970s America (Eder 1976; *New York Times* 1975).[5]

Yet, even as Hollywood was calling attention to the causes of white students protesting the war in its antiwar films and in its 1976 documentary on violent antiwar protesters, it was giving short shrift to the racist conditions endured by blacks that induced them to rebel against state oppression during the riots of the 1960s. Instead of releasing films that explored the state's role in segregating blacks into resource-poor ghettos and subjecting them to police brutality, they released a number of blaxploitation films between 1969 and 1973 which ultimately avoided talking about the government oppression that fueled these violent protests altogether. For the most part, these films managed to sidestep the issue of government repression of black communities by refusing to heroicize those black activists who protested the state's maltreatment of their neighborhoods.

Rather than celebrating black political activists, blaxploitation films assigned hero status to apolitical black criminals and hustlers instead. In so doing, they showcased links between black protest and crime rather than examining how government oppression fueled black protest. And, as a result of their focus on black criminals rather than black political activists, blaxploitation films turned an era of 1960s and 1970s black protest of racial oppression by the government into films about black criminality and the need for crime control.

Moreover, by giving leading roles to black criminals rather than black activists, these films succeeded in discrediting black political protest. After all, black criminals are likely to be the most apolitical members of the black community. Thus, by representing black communities in terms of their robbers, burglars and dope dealers, the film industry was able to direct audience attention to those persons in the ghetto who were least likely to protest ongoing racial inequalities. That the criminal-heroes represented in these movies were so apolitical has a lot to do with the fact that criminals on screen and in real life are the residents of the community who are least able to protest police brutality as so many of them spend their time making deals with the police and plea bargaining with the courts to avoid prosecution for their crimes.

They are also the persons who are least likely to be interested in joining with other blacks in a collective struggle against racial injustice because so many of them spend their time pursuing an individualistic agenda of using criminal activity to make money for themselves. Indeed, in their single-minded pursuit of their own self-interests, they usually turn against their black neighbors by stealing from them or selling them drugs. As such, they typically act in ways to thwart the kind of racial solidarity that is required for the struggle against racial injustice. Hence, because the early blaxploitation films as well as the more recent ghetto action films focus on black criminals, they tend to equate or confuse violent black protest against racial oppression with black criminality. By confounding the two, these films succeed in discrediting black protest of racist conditions. One example of a film that confuses black criminality and black protest is *Dead Presidents*.

CONFUSING CRIME AND PROTEST IN *DEAD PRESIDENTS*

Much like young white males, black males in the 1960s and 1970s were subject to be drafted and sent to fight in the Vietnam War where they were treated like little more than cannon fodder (*Apocalypse Now*). Furthermore, much like their white counterparts, their return to the states was typically marked not with a hero's welcome but rather with physical and mental health problems, homelessness and unemployment. A number of black veterans were actually quite angry about being drafted to fight in a war imposed upon them by a racist government and then find themselves returning home to find the same racial injustice that they had experienced before the war. In fact, such sentiments were expressed in the real world off screen by black Vietnam veterans as they stood by watching the indiscriminate shootings of black by-standers during the 1967 Newark riots (U.S. National Advisory Commission on Civil Disorders 1968).

In the film *Dead Presidents*, the audience follows three such black soldiers as they witness and commit various atrocities while fighting in Vietnam and then watches them as they return to the states. One soldier named Cleon has apparently been so emotionally damaged in the course of fighting the war that he starts carrying around the severed head of a Vietnamese soldier as a lucky charm during reconnaissance missions. He returns home and begins preaching in his father's church perhaps achieving some kind of redemption as a result. Anthony, the star of the film, supports the war from the beginning and voluntarily enlists. He returns to the ghetto with medals on his chest only to find himself being forced to take a low-paying job from which he is quickly laid off. His unemployment is made all the worse because he has to help support his girlfriend and their child. Finally, Anthony's boyhood friend, Skip (Chris Tucker), returns home with physical health problems and a drug addiction—both acquired in Vietnam. The audience looks on as he brags about all the disability checks he collects from the government due to his war-related injuries even as he passively sits on the corner blocking out his problems by getting high on heroin. Because of his obvious heroin addiction, other residents of the community are inclined to look at him with pity and disdain rather than looking up to him as some kind of war hero.

In a manner akin to white veterans and white student protesters, many of the black characters in *Dead Presidents* also express their opposition to the war. Much of this disenchantment with the war is expressed to Anthony by other characters in the film because Anthony has volunteered for the war and is proud of his service. Skip, by contrast, opposes the war from the very beginning, denouncing it as a white man's war and saying that the Viet Cong have never done anything to him. In fact, he seeks to avoid the draft by enrolling in college, and it is only after he flunks out that he is drafted and joins Anthony's unit in Vietnam.

In Anthony's estimation, Skip is a poor soldier who is not serious about fighting and is inclined to waste much of his time trying to find heroin and sex to avoid thinking about their brutal reconnaissance missions. By contrast, Skip accuses Anthony of having been brainwashed by the military to support the war and insists that they should both be back home in the states rather than fighting in Vietnam. In fact, Skip is so anxious to go back home that he claims to be envious of another soldier whose severe injuries have enabled him to return to the states.

Skip is not alone in accusing Anthony of having been brainwashed. When Anthony finally returns home, he is derided by a pool hustler, who did not fight, for thinking of himself as a war hero. The pool hustler goes on to call him a fool for fighting in Vietnam and reminds him that he has nothing to show for his medals as he is faced with low-paying jobs and layoffs—much like all those black men who never served. The pool hustler then taunts him by telling him that a local crime lord, who also did not serve, was dating his girlfriend and helping to support their daughter while he was in Vietnam. When Anthony confronts his girlfriend about these accusations, she admits they are true and acknowledges that she still dates the crime lord and takes money from him.

While the audience might initially be inclined to feel sympathy for Anthony and Skip in light of their mistreatment by the government, the filmmakers manage to quash any such sentiments. They do so in time-honored fashion by confounding black disgruntlement with an oppressive government with black criminality. Hence, instead of this being a movie about black outrage at the war and at a government which would exploit black veterans and then abandon them to unemployment and war-related illnesses, it becomes little more than another ghetto action movie in which black men react to any and all forms of adversity by turning to crime. In this case, Anthony and Skip join with Cleon and several other war veterans to rob an armored truck.

In and of itself, the robbery is not enough to divert audience attention away from their mistreatment by the U.S. government. In fact, their robbery could easily have been seen as a protest of their exploitation and abandonment by the government. After all audiences are still likely to sympathize with the hero who pulls off an armored truck robbery or a bank robbery provided no one is killed. Indeed bank robbers have even been depicted as heroes in comedies like *The In-Laws, Quick Change,* and *Raising Arizona.* However, it is clear that the audience is not meant to sympathize with these black Vietnam veterans and their abandonment by the U.S. government on their return as their armored truck robbery ends in a violent shootout with the white security guards on the truck and the white security guards end up being killed. A black policeman who happens to witness their shootout with the guards is also killed. After the deaths of the white security guards and the black policeman, *Dead Presidents* changes course as it ceases to be a picture about the government's racist oppression of black Vietnam veterans and instead becomes a film that makes the same government oppression seem justified as the black veterans depicted in the picture turn out to be little more than criminals.

After the changeover, *Dead Presidents* becomes little more than just another film showcasing the need for state control of violent and criminal black males. At that point, law-and-order government, once again, achieves the moral high ground as the legal authorities can be seen pursuing these black veterans in the wake of their botched robbery. First, the authorities quickly arrest Cleon, who proceeds to snitch on the others. Realizing that he too will soon be arrested, Skip dies in a heroin overdose thereby avoiding capture. Finally, Anthony is actually captured, arrested, tried, convicted and sentenced to a term of 15 years to life for his role in the robbery.

The movie ends as Anthony's lawyer tries to get the judge to give him a reduced sentence by mentioning the medals Anthony has earned for his service in Vietnam. The judge responds by alluding to his own service in World War II and saying that the Vietnam War is no excuse for Anthony's criminal behavior. In the final scene, the filmmakers make one last effort to equate black disenchantment with the war and black criminality, as Anthony can be seen getting on the prison bus with all the other black criminals headed to jail.

Because *Dead Presidents* focuses on black males adapting to their return with criminal behavior, the audience does not get to see more sympathetic treatment of the many law-abiding black veterans who were alienated, disabled, suicidal, depressed or suffering from other war-induced problems. *Dead Presidents* simply does not tell their stories. Instead of calling attention to black veterans involved in legitimate protest of an illegitimate war, the black Vietnam veterans in *Dead Presidents* are reduced to nothing more than unsympathetic criminal characters. Hence, their anger at the war and their poor treatment upon their return is never fully addressed in the movie as the audience is forced to focus on their crimes and their eventual punishment instead.

Dead Presidents, then, creates a moral divide between black Vietnam veterans and the white Vietnam veterans that appeared in a number of antiwar movies when it casts the 3 black veterans killing innocent white security guards. At that point, any sense of commonality between disgruntled white Vietnam veterans and disgruntled black Vietnam veterans ends. For while audiences can be expected to feel for and cheer on the white veterans depicted in antiwar movies, they cannot be expected to feel for or cheer on these black veterans in *Dead Presidents* once they descend into crime. Because *Dead Presidents* ultimately confuses or equates the antiwar protests of its black veteran lead characters with crime, it successfully discredits black protest of the Vietnam War.

Dead Presidents does not stop at simply discrediting the antiwar protest of its veteran lead characters; it likewise seeks to undercut black militant organizations who had also taken a principled stance against the war. Continuing in a tradition established with blaxploitation movies, black militants and the causes they fight for such as improved conditions for the black community are, once again, given short shrift in the movie.

Viewers first encounter the black militant presence in *Dead Presidents* when Anthony goes to a meeting of one of the local black revolutionary organizations to persuade one of his childhood friends to go in on the armored truck heist with him. The black militant presence in *Dead Presidents* is represented by Anthony's childhood friend, Delilah, who can be seen speaking at the meeting of black militants urging her fellow activists to engage in revolutionary struggle against a racist system. In the course of her speech, Delilah notes that so many black males were sent off to Vietnam only to return to this country and still be unable to find jobs.

Yet after this fleeting criticism of the war, Delilah rapidly descends into criminal violence as she joins with Anthony, Cleon and Skip in the botched armored truck robbery. She convinces Anthony that she is capable of the violence required for the armored truck heist—presumably to make money for the revolution—by telling him of her capacity to handle guns. However, once they begin planning the robbery, the audience hears nothing more of the ends of the revolution that Delilah is fighting for or of her frustrations regarding the black Vietnam veterans who have served a country that continues to discriminate against them.

Hence, even though Delilah participates in the robbery, seemingly for some unspecified noble revolutionary objectives, her male accomplices are all in on it for the traditional criminal motivations of making money for themselves rather than for the revolution. Consequently, legitimate black protest is, once again, confounded with criminality as Delilah, the revolutionary, works hand in hand with her apolitical criminal accomplices on the armored truck robbery. And, once the robbery takes center stage, viewers are diverted from pondering Delilah's high-minded opposition to the war to musing about the escapades of a gang of black robbers involved in a heist on an armored truck. Hence, the audience, once again, does not get to contemplate how black revolutionaries might have felt about the Vietnam War or the draft or service to a country that continues to oppress them.

Finally, in a tradition consistent with blaxploitation films, viewers are reminded of how futile and impotent black militants can be in waging revolution as Delilah, the revolutionary, is one of the first to be gunned down by the white security guards in the course of the shootout even as the criminal black veteran lead characters manage to make their temporary escape.

WHITE PROTEST AND THE OKLAHOMA CITY BOMBING

Of course, Hollywood may have released films sympathetic to white antiwar demonstrators as a way of appealing to the many young white moviegoers who opposed the Vietnam War; although the film industry's sympathies clearly did not extend to young black audiences angry about similar issues. Perhaps, then, the willingness to show white outrage at the U.S. government in a more favorable light was predicated on the popularity of antiwar protest in the larger society. Yet, even when white uprisings are not especially popular, they come in for far better treatment than black uprisings. This is indicated by cinematic and societal reaction to one of the more unpopular white uprisings in recent years, namely the Oklahoma City bombing.

On April 19, 1995, the Federal Building in Oklahoma City was bombed, and 169 people were killed in the explosion (Barkan 2001). The bombers turned out to be two white males named Timothy McVeigh and Terry Nichols. Ultimately Timothy McVeigh was executed for the bombing, while Terry Nichols received a life sentence. Both men were members of a militia group that defined itself as at war with the federal government, and therefore when McVeigh and Nichols bombed the federal government building, they saw it as an act of protest directed at the federal government. For both McVeigh and Nichols, the bombing was a way of avenging the federal government's siege on the Branch Davidian compound at Waco, Texas.

Described by terrorism experts as extremist paramilitary groups, the militias, which spawned McVeigh and Nichols, specialize in survivalism, outdoor skills and guerilla training. They also espouse white supremacist ideologies, as in their view, the United States is the Promised Land for whites only, while blacks and other people of color are regarded as the children of Satan (Hoffman 1993; Barkan 2001). Because these militias only use violence in support of their cause, they resemble groups like the student antiwar protesters and the Weather Underground as both movements see their antigovernment protests as justified. However, unlike the student protesters and the Weather Underground that represent the radical left, the militia movement represents the radical right.

In the course of waging their war on the government, these right-wing militias have become expert in the use of firearms and explosives. Hence Michael Moore interviews members of the militias in his award-winning documentary, *Bowling for Columbine*, because the film's overarching theme is an examination of Americans' love affair with weapons and violence. In his look at this topic, Moore considers how this infatuation with weapons and violence has resulted in incidents as diverse as students massacring their fellow students at Columbine High School or America's high murder rates due to gun violence. Thus, Moore treats the militia movement and the Oklahoma City bombing as just another example of the American love affair with violence, and in that context, he interviews members of the Michigan Militia as both McVeigh and Nichols had attended their meetings before the bombing.

Many of the Michigan Militia members that Moore interviews go to some pains to describe themselves as not anything like Timothy McVeigh and Terry Nichols, despite the fact that both men had attended their meetings. Instead they describe themselves as normal people, claiming that they are neither extremists nor terrorists nor racists. Like many other Americans, the Michigan Militia members are avid gunowners and in their way of thinking, Americans who do not own guns are in "dereliction of duty." They believe it is a patriotic duty to own a gun since, as they say, Americans have to defend themselves because the cops and the federal government cannot protect them. Hence, they defend their militias, their obsession with survivalism and their antigovernment stance by saying that they are only trying to defend the people of this country.

Moore also interviewed Terry Nichols' brother, James Nichols, on his Michigan farm. Moore's interest in James Nichols was based on the fact that Terry Nichols had practiced his bombing on James' farm and Timothy McVeigh had stayed on the farm for a few months. In fact, James Nichols had at one time been a suspect in the government's investigation of the Oklahoma City bombing.

While James Nichols grudgingly admits to Moore that blowing up the Federal Building in Oklahoma City was wrong, like any other antigovernment protester, he also tries to get Moore to at least think about the justness of his cause. In defense of the militia's antigovernment stance, he explains to Moore that "when the government turns tyrannical, it is a citizen's duty to revolt." And he adds that once other Americans realize how they have been ripped off and enslaved by the government, they will also revolt with merciless anger.

It seems doubtful that the interviews with the Michigan militia members and James Nichols will win many converts to the militia cause. After all, unlike earlier violent protests by left-wing militants like the Weather Underground, the Oklahoma City bombing was meant to result in mass loss of life.

Hence, in the case of the Oklahoma City bombing, it is safe to say that the government has won the culture war given the level of public horror and outrage over this extremely lethal explosion. Indeed, in the eyes of many Americans, the Oklahoma City bombing constitutes an act of terrorism because so many innocent American civilians were killed that day.

Still, Moore makes it clear that the Michigan Militias have at least one thing in common with many of their fellow Americans—namely a distinct fondness for guns. Hence, Moore shows James Nichols proudly brandishing his guns and bragging that the federal agents and police that came to search his farm were very much afraid of him because they feared he might have guns stowed everywhere. Moore also demonstrates that the love of guns and bomb-making is hardly limited to the militias as young white males at the local high school in Oscoda, Michigan, near James' farm also share this love of guns and bomb-making.

For example, Moore interviews one high school student, who has been expelled for a semester for drawing an assault weapon on another student. And in another interview, a student brags about being perceived as a threat by school authorities because he owns *The Anarchist's Cookbook* and has made a tiny bomb and some napalm. Even more interesting, Moore notes that Eric Harris, who would eventually move to Littleton, Colorado, and massacre his classmates and a teacher at Columbine High School, also grew up on the Air Force base in Oscoda and attended the same high school.

Yet, despite the fact that the little community of Oscoda seems to have provided an environment that furthered crimes as heinous as the Oklahoma City bombing and the massacre at Columbine High School, Moore makes no effort to disconnect the Michigan Militia members or the Oscoda high school students from the larger American culture's love affair with guns. On a larger scale, Hollywood also did not indict white militias in the wake of the 1995 bombing by embarking on a cycle of militia movement movies that identified cultural deficiencies in the white working-class communities that produced this movement to explain their violence. Nor did academics suddenly start applying culture-of-poverty arguments to the white working-class communities that spawned the militias.

Moreover, in the real world off screen, federal, state and local governments did not conduct a war against the militias or their surrounding communities despite the heinous nature of the crimes. Rather the government simply tried, convicted and punished the two men that they could prove committed the crime. And, because the white working-class communities that produced the right-wing militia movement were not subjected to wholesale indictment because of the crimes of a few, there was no law-and-order campaign waged against these communities. In other words, there were no widespread police crackdowns, stepped-up surveillance or mass incarcerations of white working-class men in communities like Oscoda in an effort to prevent future bombings. Furthermore, white students at the high school in Oscoda were not stopped at random, thrown up against police cars with legs spread and hands locked in handcuffs.

However, black violent protest against government oppression during the Los Angeles riots—and the 1960s riots before them—did induce the government to step up its law-and-order campaigns against the black community. Moreover, after the 1992 riot, Hollywood released a whole host of movies about violent black ghettos that seemed to justify these crackdowns.

NOTES

1. Rap and hip hop musicians have been cast in a number of films in the 1990s and 2000s in the hopes of luring their fans to a film. For example, rapper, Ice Cube, appeared in the 1991 ghetto action classic, *Boyz n the Hood*. Not only do rap and hip hop musicians appear in ghetto action movies, but they appear in films marketed to white audiences as well—including some Oscar winners. So, for example, Sean Combs and Mos Def appeared in *Monster's Ball* for which Halle Berry was awarded the Oscar for Best Actress in 2001. Denzel Washington became only the second black man to win an Oscar for Best Actor in *Training Day* in that same year and hip hop musicians Dr. Dre, Snoop Dogg and Macy Gray all appeared in the film. A few years later, hip hop musician, Ludacris, was cast as one of the vicious carjackers in *Crash*, which won the 2005 Oscar for Best Picture for its supposedly realistic depiction of race in America.

Not only do rap and hip hop musicians appear in these Oscar winners, they also appear in lesser known movies like *Juice* (1992) which starred Tupac Shakur and included an appearance by Queen Latifah as well as *Baby Boy* (2001), which starred musician Tyrese Gibson. Queen Latifah also starred in the 1996 ghetto action film, *Set It Off*.

For the most part, these musicians are cast in stereotypical roles as criminals including murderers, robbers, crack dealers, and carjackers. In a slight change of stereotypes, Tyrese Gibson in *Baby Boy* plays an unemployed black male and unmarried father of 2 children by 2 different girlfriends, who is financially dependent on his mother and his girlfriend.

2. It is not certain that the police actually caught many serious criminals with zero tolerance crackdowns on minor offenders as they offered only anecdotes to support this assertion rather than statistical data on the number and percentage of serious offenders actually apprehended by zero tolerance policing (Wynn 2001, Karmen 2000).

3. In fact, such transformations have occurred before with earlier drug crazes in the 1950s and the 1960s as young blacks first took up heroin use and then grew tired of it after they recognized its risks. Furthermore, similar patterns apply to youthful white

drug users as they have also taken up the use of a number of drugs only to drop them after a few years when they come to perceive them as risky. Yet these movies say nothing about the faddish nature of drugs or the common practice of whole cohorts of black youth desisting from the use of a particular drug after a few years—a practice that is also common among white youth.

Not only is the significant decline in black drug use and drug-related murders not reflected in films of the 1990s and 2000s, it is also not reflected in real-world criminal justice policy. For even though black drug use (and drug-related violence) rather predictably declined in the 1990s as black youth reformed themselves, blacks continue to go to prison at extremely high rates for nonviolent drug use and drug sales. This trend began in the late 1980s when tough laws were passed mandating tougher penalties for crack cocaine than powder cocaine. And because these laws have not been repealed, blacks continue to go to prison at high rates for nonviolent drug crimes. Because white youth have never been punished in equal numbers for their numerous drug crazes over the years, blacks now make up a disproportionate number of those in prison for nonviolent drug use and drug selling.

4. Bill Ayers was one of the Weathermen involved in some of the early 1970s bombings in which no one was killed; he went on to become a college professor. Because he once hosted a fund-raiser for Barack Obama, the Republicans made an attempt to connect candidate Obama to the violent antiwar protests of the Weather Underground during the 2008 election. This strategy turned out to be fairly ineffective, in part, because Obama was only 9 years old at the time of the bombing (Sinker 2008).

5. In a much later 2003 documentary on the Weathermen called *The Weather Underground*, they once again come in for sympathetic treatment as persons so committed to ending the war that they were willing to consider violence (Mitchell 2003).

Chapter Three

Black Violence, White Violence
Cinematic Images of the Urban Underclass

In chapter 2, I considered how Hollywood treats violent black protest against government oppression as if it is more threatening and dangerous than equally violent protest by whites. Yet, the lion's share of violence does not involve angry citizens protesting an oppressive government by bombing buildings, killing innocent civilians, looting or destroying property. Instead most violence involves average American citizens assaulting and killing other persons in the course of trivial disputes.

For the most part, such violence between persons occurs between males who are attempting to assert or defend their masculine honor. This kind of interpersonal violence also tends to be intraracial as white males generally assault and kill other white males, while black males mainly assault and kill black males. Yet even here, Hollywood treats violence differently based on race as interpersonal violence between black males is typically depicted as more dangerous than interpersonal violence between white males. It is possible to see evidence of this when Hollywood's characterization of black male violence in ghetto action movies is compared to its characterization of white male violence.

In his film *Bowling for Columbine*, Michael Moore provides the audience with some sense of how Hollywood treats interpersonal violence among white males. *Bowling for Columbine* won the 2002 Oscar for Best Documentary for its examination of the 1999 school shooting in Littleton, Colorado, in which two seniors at Columbine High School named Eric Harris and Dylan Klebold shot 12 other students and 1 teacher before killing themselves. Despite the heinous nature of their crimes, Moore is dismissive of any explanations that suggest that this massacre was somehow the outgrowth of a separate and excessively violent white youth culture that created mass murderers like Eric and Dylan. Instead he suggests that this school shooting was nothing more than the youthful manifestation of a larger American culture of violence.

In making his case that the American cultural mainstream is sufficiently violent to allow for a crime this monstrous, he implicates everyone and everything up to and including the U.S. government itself. He also takes note of the role of gun markets in making assault weapons all too available to the two young white male Columbine killers. In fact, by placing so much emphasis on adolescents' easy access to guns, he ultimately promotes the notion that gun control may be an appropriate response to the type of white youth violence that occurred at Columbine rather than a police crackdown on violent white youth cultures.

However, when the killers are black rather than white, their shootings are seen as the product of a separate and distinct ghetto-based subculture of violence rather than as just another reflection of the larger American culture of violence. Ghetto action movies, in particular, routinely depict black-on-black shootings as the product of a distinct ghetto-based subculture that is clearly divorced from the American cultural mainstream. As a consequence, these films typically urge the larger society to wage a war on black youth cultures because they are deemed to be so dangerous. Hence, police crackdowns in black communities that take the form of more targeting, surveillance and arrests of black males can come to be seen as appropriate responses to ghetto violence as opposed to simple gun-control measures.

That incidents of white youth violence do not require a similar war against the entire white community has a lot to do with differences in the way white communities and black communities are depicted on the silver screen. In ghetto action films, black neighborhoods are typically portrayed as disorderly places where adult residents cannot control local youth. And because lawless local teens have presumably taken over these neighborhoods, the police are needed to come in and wage a war against black teenagers in order to take back their streets.

By contrast, cinematic renditions of white youth violence typically occur against the backdrop of an orderly community where the adults in the community have full control over neighborhood streets. Therefore, even when individual white youth disrupt their communities with violence, crime or delinquency, there is no need for the police to come in and take back their streets as white adults never lose control.

WHITE COMMUNITIES ON THE SILVER SCREEN

One reason that white neighborhoods on screen can control local youth and maintain order on their streets has a lot to do with the characteristics of the residents.[1] On screen, white communities are depicted as largely composed of law-abiding nuclear families and homeowners. As such, residents of these communities can be seen as collections of people who share an interest in maintaining their families and improving their schools and their neighborhoods. Because residents are attached to their homes and committed to neighborhood upkeep, these communities seem to be occupied by fairly permanent populations. Furthermore, because residents of white communities are depicted as interested in maintaining their nuclear families, they also seem to be guided by a strong work ethic as they go about providing for their family's needs.

However, the focus on family support and the upkeep of schools and the community are goals that are largely confined to the adults in the neighborhood—particularly those who are parents. Their adolescent children, by contrast, typically belong to a youth subculture that exists apart from and in opposition to the adult community. Indeed youth subcultures typically bring disorder to the security of the community, local schools and the parental home thereby forcing adult members of the community to constantly restore order to their homes, schools and neighborhoods (Thornton 1997).

One reason that adolescents conflict with their parents is because they are dependent. Hence they tend to be rebellious, alienated and disaffected when their parents attempt to order them around and supervise their activities, particularly when they reach their teen years. Adolescents can also be a source of disorder in their families and their communities because they are transient with less attachment to the nuclear family or the local neighborhood than their parents as many will leave for college, jobs, family formation or the military when they turn eighteen. They are also considerably less likely to have a strong work ethic than their parents as they do not yet have permanent jobs or family responsibilities (Greenberg 1977).

Indeed compulsory schooling dictates that they spend most of their waking hours with other youth who are also not working and supporting families. Hence the youth subcultures that they form with their fellow students tend to be leisure cultures in which the emphasis is on the values and goals that typically govern leisure activities including the search for pleasure, excitement and thrills (Young 1997; Matza 1964). Adolescents also use their considerable leisure time to find, develop and express an identity and to join with cliques of their peers who express similar identities. For young males, in particular, the expression of a masculine identity may require them to use violence to express their dominance over other males (Messerschmidt 1993; W. Miller 1958)

Hence, in their quest for excitement and identity, young white males can be seen on screen engaging in crime and violence even as local adults never seem to lose control over their neighborhoods. Consequently, when white youth turn to crime and violence, it is typically depicted as the failure of the individual youth or their parents and not as evidence of a disorganized or chaotic community. And since the adults in white neighborhoods can control local youth, it is often not necessary to lock them up.

AMERICANIZING WHITE YOUTH
VIOLENCE IN *BOWLING FOR COLUMBINE*

Michael Moore's film *Bowling for Columbine* illustrates much of this as he examines how white middle-class suburban adults in Littleton, Colorado, control white youth violence in the wake of the Columbine High School shooting. In depicting adult reaction to the crime, he begins by reviewing the litany of reasons given for this tragedy by media, politicians, police and school officials across the country. He then goes on to dismiss most of these explanations, particularly those which suggest that the shootings somehow require the adults to respond by waging a war against white youth and white youth cultures.

For example, he accuses adult officials like school principals and superintendents of overkill when they react to the Columbine shooting by instituting zero tolerance policies in their own schools. As evidence that some of their reactions may be excessive, he points to police and school officials who take it to be a warning sign of imminent violence when students in their local elementary school take simulated guns made out of chicken strips or folded paper and aim them at fellow students or teachers and go "bang, bang." He lampoons other official reactions to the Columbine shootings as well, including an incident in which one young white male gets suspended for dyeing his hair blue while another white honor student is threatened with expulsion for wearing a Scottish bagpiper's outfit to his prom, complete with kilt and dagger. He likewise derides those schools which seek to prevent a Columbine-like tragedy by banning baggy pants and gang colors based on the far-fetched notion that a change in the dress code can somehow deter a school shooting.

He also condemns the efforts of politicians and media to blame various elements of white youth culture for the violence including heavy metal music, violent movies, and violent cartoons. In particular, he notes how the music of rock musician Marilyn Manson gets singled out by politicians, media and the religious right as an explanation for the shooting because the two white male shooters were fans of Manson. To demonstrate the excessive reaction to Manson's music, he shows the religious right holding a rally in Denver to protest a Manson concert two years after the shootings at which they accuse

Manson of promoting youth violence, hate, drug use, suicide and death. In another scene where Moore interviews Manson, Manson himself suggests that the religious right and political elites may have focused on his music to divert attention from the possibility that their own violence might be fueling youth violence.

Moore expands on this theme by suggesting that violence by the U.S. government against other nations may drive white youth to violence. To demonstrate, he shows footage of U.S. involvement in the overthrow of democratically elected regimes in other nations, as well as referring to its funding of brutal dictators in other countries and its involvement in the killing of civilians in other nations. He then ties violence by the U.S. government directly to the Columbine shooting by noting that Lockheed Martin, which makes the weapons used in these wars, also employs a number of the parents of Columbine's students. To further explore the possibility that government-sponsored violence might trickle down to youth at the local high school, he asks one Lockheed spokesman if the fact that the parents of students at Columbine High School work at a missile-making facility might make the students more prone to violence.

In these segments, Moore seems to be suggesting that the Columbine massacre was not the product of a youth subculture in conflict with the American mainstream. Rather, for him, the school killings seem to be nothing more than the youthful manifestation of a larger American love affair with guns and violence.

In order to demonstrate that mainstream American culture reveres guns and violence, he shows law-abiding men, women, little kids, and senior citizens clutching their guns; he even shows a blind man at target practice and a dog accidentally shooting his owner, who has given him a gun. As further proof that Americans love their guns, Moore shows how readily accessible guns are as he points to a bank that gives them out as gifts for opening a checking account or a Utah town where the residents are required to own guns.

In order to question official assertions that suggest that the violent music and videos of American youth cultures explain violence in this country, he notes that youth in other nations such as Canada, Germany, Japan, France, Australia and the United Kingdom are likewise alienated, listen to Marilyn Manson and heavy metal music, watch violent movies and play violent video games and yet they have only a tiny fraction of our gun killings. Moore also makes the case that easy gun access alone may not explain white youth violence in the United States as guns are also readily available in some of these other nations with low gun homicide rates. For example, Canadians own a lot of guns because of a strong hunting tradition, and yet they had 165 gun killings in a year in which there were 11,127 gun killings in the United States.

For him, then, Americans are violent because easy access to guns—especially assault weapons—is coupled with the U.S. government's frequent involvement in violence against other nations. Because the U.S. government is routinely involved in wars, coups and the sponsoring of brutal dictatorships around the world, Moore argues that Americans—young and old alike—are routinely socialized to hate and fear some enemy and to take up arms to defend themselves. And when they are not being urged to hate some enemy abroad, politicians and media are urging white Americans to hate and fear black Americans.

By contrast, he argues Canadian media and politicians talk about using diplomacy and avoiding wars and hence they are not constantly creating new enemies and pumping their citizens full of fear. Not only do they refrain from creating enemies abroad, but they do not drum up divisions and fear between white and nonwhite Canadians. Instead they seek to provide free health care and day care to all of their citizens while making quality housing available even to the poor.

Putting aside the validity of Moore's arguments, it is important that he suggests that a love of guns and violence are not products of white youth culture, but rather mainstream American culture. In so doing, he discourages white audiences from turning on their own youth. Instead, he seems to suggest that anger over the Columbine shootings should be directed at the National Rifle Association (NRA) and the gun industry which promote gun ownership and make it all too easy for youth to get guns—especially assault rifles. After all, as he notes, the Columbine killers, Eric and Dylan, had no trouble buying their guns at a local gun show. Moreover, he suggests that white middle-class citizens seem to recognize that the real responsibility for white youth violence lies with these pro-gun groups as he shows white residents of Littleton, Colorado, demonstrating against the NRA because of their insensitivity in holding a pro-gun rally in nearby Denver 10 days after the Columbine shootings.

That white middle-class citizens in Littleton recognize the real culprit as teenagers' easy access to guns is most graphically illustrated when a father of one of the 12 students killed at Columbine High School stands up to address the crowd at the anti-NRA rally. Despite his grief over the slaying of his son, this white middle-class father does not use the opportunity to condemn Eric and Dylan who killed his son nor does he rail against white youth or white youth cultures more generally. Instead he labels Eric and Dylan as "children" and condemns the gun industry for making it too easy for a child like Eric or Dylan to grab an assault weapon and shoot another child like his son in the face. Moreover, he notes that the Tech 9 that Eric and Dylan used to kill his son is not used for hunting, but rather is only used to kill humans. He concludes by saying that something has to be done about the problem of gun access. Thus, even for this father who has lost his son, the solution to the problem is gun control rather than controlling white-on-white violence.

The theme that the free and easy flow of guns to youth was the driving force behind the Columbine shooting—and not wayward white youth—is further explored in a scene where Moore interviews 2 white male victims who managed to survive the shooting at Columbine. One young man was paralyzed as a result of the shooting, while the other victim walks around with bullets from the shooting lodged near his heart. Because the shooters purchased their bullets at the local K-Mart, Moore convinces these 2 survivors to go to K-Mart headquarters in Troy, Michigan, in order to try to persuade this large retailer to stop selling bullets. With the media following the event, a K-Mart vice president announces that K-Mart will phase out its handgun ammunition over the next 90 days.

In this scene, then, the source of the problem is, once again, attributed to easy access to guns and ammunition and not violence-prone white youth cultures. Indeed by enlisting these white male victims in the fight for more gun control, Moore discourages the audience from demonizing all members of white youth culture because of the actions of a few as these two survivors make it very clear that some white youth are just as opposed to violence as the adults. Moore even manages to urge audiences to empathize with the two shooters, Eric and Dylan, as he speculates that they slaughtered their classmates and a teacher because they were repeatedly bullied and taunted by other students.

Hence, despite the fact that the youth subcultures in their midst have brought violence and disorder into their schools, the white middle-class parents depicted in Moore's *Bowling for Columbine* are not tempted to turn against their own children. Instead, they seem to identify gun control as the solution and mobilize to try to limit the flow of guns and restore order to their neighborhoods. Because the solution to their problems with school violence and disorder are defined in terms of gun control and the reduction of bullying—and not violent white youth cultures—the police are not needed to wage a law-and-order campaign against their children in order to restore peace to the neighborhood.

However, in the ghetto action films that emerged in the early 1990s, no one stands up for gun-toting ghetto youth to depict them as part of a larger American love affair with guns and violence. Instead these pictures portray gun violence in black youth cultures in ways that suggest that police crackdowns and the mass incarceration of black youth are the only ways to restore peace to inner-city neighborhoods. How then are blacks and black neighborhoods constructed on screen so that police crackdowns and widespread incarceration seem to be the only way to restore peace in these communities?

HOLLYWOOD'S BLACK GHETTOS AND
CONSERVATIVE POLITICAL IDEOLOGY

From the outset, it should be noted that there are similarities between the gun violence that occurred at Columbine and the gun violence pictured in ghetto action films. Much like *Bowling for Columbine*, ghetto action movies, such as *Boyz n the Hood*, show young black males being bullied by other young black males only to return the violence. Indeed the signature element in films in the ghetto action genre is a scene depicting an endless cycle of black male violence in which one violent gang member or drug dealer attacks a rival, who retaliates with additional violence and on and on and on.

This formula has been repeated so often that these films may well have succeeded in reducing urban poor black youths to a stereotype. Indeed, because these movies box black males into the role of ghetto action killer, they may have far more impact on the cultural images of young black males than *Bowling for Columbine* has had on the image of young white males. After all, movie spectators who saw two white males shoot up Columbine High School in *Bowling for Columbine* can also see young white males playing nerds, geeks, geniuses, wizards and a whole host of other non-threatening characters.

Yet, because so many ghetto action films have narrowly cast young black actors into the role of ghetto action thug, they have done much to reinforce notions that black males are universally dangerous. Hence, given the different ways in which Hollywood represents young white males and young black males, it is easier to talk about violence prevention programs to reduce bullying for violent middle-class white males like the Columbine killers even as the violence perpetrated by black teenagers in ghetto action movies seems to cry out for the militarization of entire black neighborhoods.

Understandably, the biggest fans of ghetto action movies have been young black males who thrill to their on-screen depictions of violence, easy sex, car chases and money being flashed around by teenagers like themselves. Yet strangely enough, some older conservative white males also include themselves among the fans of these movies. For example, conservative columnist, George Will, described the ghetto action movie *Menace II Society* as "therapeutic" and "relentlessly realistic." Presumably Will's praise for *Menace* was based on his thinking that such films document what he and other conservatives have said all along—namely that the black family is the cause of crime and persistent poverty in the urban underclass (Watkins 1998).

Certainly, *Menace* provides ample visual support for such conservative dogma as the film follows the escapades of two black underclass high school seniors named Caine and O-Dog as they go about stealing cars, making and selling crack cocaine, robbing liquor stores and bullying, assaulting and killing other neighborhood youth, local shopkeepers and anyone else unlucky enough to venture across their path. In the movie's early scenes, the audience gets some sense of how Caine came to acquire his penchant for violence as he is shown being socialized into the ghetto culture of poverty as a tiny child by his murderous drug-dealing father, his irresponsible drug-addicted mother and some local teenage thugs who teach him about guns and give him his first drink. After his father is killed and his mother dies from a drug overdose, his grandparents are forced to step in and raise him. It is scenes such as these that do much to bolster George Will's claim that it is the parent-to child transmission of violent lifestyles that explains the viciousness of ghetto adolescents like Caine.

Menace II Society was not alone in offering visual support for the conservative mantra as a number of other ghetto action films have also reinforced long-standing right-wing assertions that a morally deficient underclass culture of poverty explains why murders, rapes, robberies, assaults and thefts persist in black urban poor neighborhoods decade after decade. Because a defective culture has presumably been transmitted from parent to child, often in households headed by black women, the supposed intergenerational transmission of this defective culture has also been the basis for conservative claims that welfare and other social programs should be cut because they perpetuate the formation of these dysfunctional households (Albelda et al. 1996).

What these films do not do, however, is consider the possibility that the exodus of jobs from these communities might provide a better explanation for their persistently high crime rates. A number of liberal academics, however, have argued that deindustrialization and the exit of so many manufacturing jobs has left so many inner-city black men unemployed, underemployed or out of the labor force entirely that they have not been able to support a family (W. Wilson 1996). As a consequence, many of these men never marry or ultimately abandon their families. And because they lack a legal source of income and the stake in conformity that comes with involvement in the support and socialization of their children, many of these males presumably turn to crime as a means of support. Based on this understanding of the roots of ghetto crime, many liberals have concluded that only programs that provide jobs and job training can draw these males away from crime and violence (S. Walker 1990).

That said, the image of underclass life routinely trotted out in ghetto action movies offers more support for conservative claims that hold the poor responsible for their own poverty, crime and violence. Political conservatives have long held that the poor can be blamed for these problems because they subscribe to the values of an underclass culture that compels these self-destructive behaviors. Black single mothers are important in this analysis because they are held responsible for passing on these underclass values to their children thereby causing them to remain poor and to become involved in crime and violence.

These denunciations of black women on welfare by conservative political elites were also part of a larger culture war in which they sought to return Americans of all races to more traditional family values. By incessantly attacking poor black women, then, they were also able to engage in indirect attacks on middle- and upper-class white women who chose to have children outside of wedlock after the women's movement and the sexual revolution of the 1960s and 1970s.

Because affluent white females, who had been liberated by these movements, were financially independent, they were able to dismiss these conservative attacks on single motherhood as backwards and sexist (Gans 2005). However, poor black women on welfare were in no position to ignore these conservative attacks as they depended on government money to support themselves and their children. Hence, in the course of taking government money, they also had to subject themselves to constant public scrutiny and condemnation of their lifestyles, their values and their morals as well as being forced to submit to well-publicized campaigns to make them conform to the traditional values preached by political conservatives.

HOLLYWOOD AND THE BLACK SINGLE MOM

Hollywood has offered its own contribution to these conservative campaigns as film after film in the 1990s and early 2000s has shown the dire consequences that supposedly follow when young black males are raised in single parent households headed by poor black women. In part, poor black mothers in fatherless households are characterized as poor parents because they seem to be preparing their children for a life of poverty and dependence as they can be seen on screen shunning work and relying on a variety of government handouts (welfare, food stamps, Medicaid) to support themselves and their families.

Presumably, because they lack a work ethic, intergenerational poverty in these households can be explained by their tendency to pass on this absence of a work ethic to their offspring. On screen, then, poverty seems to persist in urban poor neighborhoods because of poor family socialization and not because of the exodus of living-wage jobs.

In fact, because they have neither jobs nor a work ethic, the black single mothers in these films bear more resemblance to irresponsible, dependent white teenagers in white youth subcultures than they do to the responsible white middle-class parents portrayed on screen in movies about white youth violence. After all, much like the members of a disruptive white youth subculture, Hollywood's black single mothers are free to pursue leisure activities as they are not hemmed in by work responsibilities. Hence, film after film shows them pursuing pleasure, excitement and thrills in the form of drug addictions and promiscuous sex (e.g., teen pregnancies and out-of-wedlock births). Thus, despite the fact that these women are adults who head families, their sexual excesses, lack of a work ethic and irresponsibility make it seem as if there are no adults in charge in female-headed households.

Much of this is illustrated in the 1991 ghetto action classic *Boyz n the Hood*, which received a nod from Hollywood in the form of Oscar nominations for Best Director (John Singleton) and Best Screenplay. *Boyz* compares two families living right across the street from each other in an inner-city neighborhood.

In one family, headed by a black single mother, the mother, Brenda, has two sons by two different fathers and is not married to either one of them. The audience can see that she has passed on her "lax" sexual attitudes to her children as one of her sons, Rick, has a baby outside of marriage before graduating from high school. Brenda's other son, Doughboy, begins stealing at a young age and has been in and out of jail by his teen years. Neither of Brenda's sons works and neither son seems to have a particularly bright future as Doughboy is chronically unemployed and Rick is having a difficult time doing well enough on his college entrance exams so that he can get into college on a football scholarship. By contrast, in the other family across the street, a single working father named Furious Styles is raising his son, Trey, alone. Trey has grown up to be a law-abiding young man who works part time and is headed for college.

Clearly, then, with its comparison of these two families, *Boyz* suggests that despite the fact that the sons from both of these families are exposed to the same daunting conditions—poverty, constant threats from violent black males in the community—Trey manages to avoid being drawn into the local cycle of black-on-black violence or teen fatherhood. The only reason that the college-bound Trey seems to have been spared from the violence and promiscuity of underclass life is due to the presence of a strong black father. By contrast, his neighbor Doughboy's absorption into the local cycle of violence that eventually kills him seems to stem from the fact that he was raised in a female-headed household.

There is even more graphic evidence that black single mothers make poor parents with a cameo appearance by another single mom in *Boyz*. This single mother comes on screen only long enough to be condemned by other ghetto residents for being a crack addict, who trades her body for crack and lets her baby run around wild in the streets in dirty diapers as she pursues her crack addiction. *Boyz* is not alone in characterizing black underclass females in these terms as a number of other ghetto action movies have linked black single motherhood to drugs, promiscuity and poor parenting.

FATHERLESS HOUSEHOLDS
AND CRIME IN *SOUTH CENTRAL*

That the promiscuity and drug addiction of a black single mother can somehow lead to the criminality of her son is perhaps best illustrated in the ghetto action movie *South Central*. In *South Central*, the audience is introduced to Carole who has had to go on welfare to have her baby because her boyfriend, Bobby, the father of the baby, is incarcerated. Carole's single motherhood is linked to drugs and promiscuity in the opening scenes of the movie as Carole is already addicted to drugs and beginning to use prostitution to support her addiction when Bobby is released from juvenile hall. While Bobby makes some effort to support Carole and their son Jimmie, he is eventually sent away to prison for a long time because he kills a local drug dealer. Bobby's imprisonment leaves Carole alone to raise little Jimmie on her own in a female-headed household. She, of course, botches it as she continues with her drug addiction and uses prostitution to support it.

Several scenes later, it becomes clear to the audience that Carole has passed on her criminal subcultural values to her son as we see Jimmie, at age 10, stealing money out of her purse as she lays in bed with one of her johns. Because Carole is so absorbed with her prostitution and drug addiction, she does not fix Jimmie meals or make him go to school. Hence, he spends his days out on the streets trying to impress the adult criminals and make money by stealing. When Jimmie is shot by a local man after trying to steal his car stereo, Carole comes to visit him at the hospital in a tight fitting red dress. The hospital visit only provides additional evidence that the drug addict/prostitute/single mom Carole is a bad mother as she refuses to sit with Jimmie and leaves after only a moment despite the fact that he is in serious condition. Her parting line as she abandons this mere 10-year-old to recuperate from a gunshot wound alone and then face criminal charges for his theft of the car stereo is to tell him that he got himself "caught stealing someone else's stuff" and that he is just going to end up in prison like his father. The audience can see little Jimmie's hurt reaction after his mother abandons him.

What *South Central* and a host of other recent ghetto action movies routinely depict, then, is black single moms in fatherless households who cannot cope with the responsibilities of motherhood and who throw up their hands when forced to deal with the penchant for criminal behavior that they inevitably pass on to their sons. The black single mothers pictured on screen also cannot be expected to have the kind of moral authority necessary to socialize their children properly because their own flawed lives (promiscuity, drug addiction, criminal behavior) prevent them from serving as role models. Indeed, consistent with the assertions of a number of conservatives, many of the violent black males that appear in Hollywood's underclass communities seem to have been passively socialized into a life of crime and violence by observing the deviance of their mothers. Unlike the white middle-class nuclear families depicted on screen in which the parents strive to control their children's antisocial behaviors, the black single mothers in ghetto action movies actually seem to be preparing their children for a life of crime rather than trying to prevent it.

HOLLYWOOD AND THE ABSENT BLACK FATHER

Young black fathers in ghetto action movies are not in any position to control the violence of their sons either as many have deserted their families, while others are separated from them due to imprisonment. Because many of them are neither working nor supporting their families, they, too, act more like members of a disruptive white youth subculture rather than members of an adult community. Much like Hollywood's black single mothers, they also pursue momentary thrills and excitement by using illegal drugs and forming temporary sexual liaisons with the women in their neighborhood only to abandon them when they become pregnant. As conservatives argue that a strong father is necessary to keep a young underclass male away from the cycle of black-on-black violence, the absence of a strong black father in the home typically has tragic results on screen.

Once again, this is illustrated in *South Central* after Carole's boyfriend, Bobby, is sent away to prison for a long time leaving their son Jimmie without a father. While he is in prison, Bobby hears that little 10-year-old Jimmie is being drawn into the street life, and yet, he is powerless to stop it because he is locked up. Indeed, the fatherless boy Jimmie's descent into the street life becomes the central dilemma of the film as evidenced by the fact that the second half of the movie is devoted to following Bobby after his release from prison as he goes on a crusade to rescue little Jimmie from a life of crime.

PARENTLESS BLACK HOUSEHOLDS
AND LAWLESS BLACK YOUTH

Not only do these films portray underclass parents as incapable of controlling their young, but other law-abiding adults in the community cannot control them either. In fact, the black neighborhoods pictured in ghetto action films are not controlled by law-abiding adults at all. Instead criminal black youth raised in fatherless homes seem to have run roughshod over law-abiding adults and taken over control of neighborhood streets. The notion that no law- abiding adults are in charge in these neighborhoods is also expressed in news media as *Newsweek* columnist Tom Morganthau describes the real South Central neighborhood in the following terms in the days after the 1992 Los Angeles riot:

> South Central is a vast residential cage in which most of the population is held prisoner by an armed and dangerous minority—an estimated 100,000 "gang-bangers" many of whom are still in their teens. To ride through South Central on a busy Saturday night is to watch the real-life version of "Blade Runner." The cops rush back and forth in their black and whites, sirens blaring, while helicopters clatter through the night sky to pinpoint the sources of intermittent gunfire with their searchlights. Law-abiding citizens cower behind locked doors and barred windows, fearful of going outside. It has been this way for years. . . . The kids (some of them, anyway) are out of control and seemingly beyond the reach of any form of family, community or societal authority. It is not so much a rebellion against the majority (white) culture as a rebellion against *any* adult culture, white or black. . . . (T)he values of work, love, growth and even survival—seem to be breaking down. Cocaine provides the money, guns provide the means and gangbangers provide the leadership in a war of all against all. (*Newsweek* May 11, 1992:54)

Presumably, with so many unsupervised young black males in underclass neighborhoods, gangs can take over these communities by acting like substitute families and socializing neighborhood youth into a life of crime. The process by which these gangs step into the vacuum left by morally inadequate single mothers and absent fathers is depicted in the movie version of *South Central*.

In the on-screen story of *South Central*, older teenagers and young adult members of a gang called the Deuces can be seen recruiting local youth to steal for them. One Deuce leader recruits Bobby's unsupervised 10-year-old son Jimmie and his friends to steal car stereos for the Deuces. The audience also witnesses the Deuces planning to expand membership in their gang for a complete takeover of neighborhood streets by recruiting at the local high schools and in the prisons. To mark their expansion, they claim they will

brand members with gang tattoos and spray paint local streets they have conquered with gang graffiti.

Images of law-abiding adult residents of the neighborhood being held prisoner by these gangbangers also appear, particularly in one scene where the
Deuce gang leaders retaliate against one local law-abiding black man after he
shoots little Jimmie in the back when he catches him stealing his car stereo.
The Deuces proceed to kidnap this law-abiding adult, tie him up and give 10-
year-old Jimmie an opportunity to kill him in retaliation for shooting him.

This theme of violent youth subcultures usurping adult authority in the
ghetto is also depicted in *Paid in Full* (2002) where three successful teenaged
drug dealers have surpassed the adults by earning more than much older men
in the neighborhood who work at legal jobs or those involved in petty crimes.
Hence, one successful violent drug dealer in his teens can be seen listening to
constant pleas from his mother's older unemployed drug-addicted boyfriend
to let him work for the youngster in the underground economy as a drug
dealer. And in another scene, when one teenaged drug dealer goes to have
dinner with his girlfriend and her family, he lays down a huge wad of money
on the table for "groceries." Because the family is obviously quite poor, the
girl's mother gratefully accepts the money from this teenaged drug dealer.

Even when underclass adults are not depicted as dependent on violent drug-
dealing teenagers for work or for handouts, they are clearly unable to stop
them from fighting. Hence in *Menace*, even though the violent thug Caine is
supported by his grandparents, he refuses to listen when his grandfather tries
to get him to stop fighting and committing crimes. Eventually his grandparents are forced to make Caine leave their home when he brings violence to
their very doorstep by getting in a fight right in their front yard. In these communities, then, where there is no adult in charge, presumably only the police
are capable of coming in and restoring order to neighborhood streets.

HOLLYWOOD TURNS ON BLACK YOUTH

Because the black teenagers depicted in these ghetto action films seem to
cry out for aggressive police tactics, they justify police aggression towards
blacks. Moreover, many of these images of lawless, out-of-control black
youth appear in films marketed to white audiences, seemingly for just that
purpose. Indeed, Hollywood has even seen fit to award its highest honors to
films that depict the police going so far as to abuse their authority in their
quest to control young black males.

As noted, *Crash* won the Oscar for Best Picture of 2005 for what movie
reviewers described as its realistic depiction of race in America. Much of the

praise heaped upon *Crash* stemmed from the belief that the movie would promote greater tolerance between the races by discouraging blacks and whites
in the audience from making snap judgments about each other that only led to
greater racial hostility. In fact, this notion was taken so seriously that *Crash*
was actually screened in diversity training programs around the country in an
effort to discourage either race from making prejudgments about the other.
Crash was also endorsed by a number of influential people including the
Police Chief of Los Angeles, William Bratton. Chief Bratton, who is in a
position to shape how the Los Angeles public is policed, saw the film three
times and urged his deputy chief of professional standards to distribute copies
around the department (Hsu 2006).

Yet, despite these endorsements, *Crash* may actually do more to further
racial polarization rather than racial harmony as it trades in some of the same
stereotypes of dangerous black youth that are found in ghetto action films. In
so doing, it justifies police aggression against blacks rather than promoting
racial tolerance.

For example, *Crash* opens with two black ghetto action-type thugs stealing
the SUV of the white district attorney in a carjacking thereby setting the stage
for white police aggression against blacks. Indeed because the carjackers
are black and the victims are white, this crime could easily appeal to white
viewers' fear of black crime and thereby make the police aggression that
follows seem justified. Predictably, this carjacking is followed by scenes of
white police aggression against blacks as one white police officer picks up
and then kills a black hitchhiker after a trivial dispute over country music. In
yet another scene a white police officer kills a fellow police officer who also
happens to be black.

Police aggression against blacks is also depicted in the Oscar-winning
movie *Training Day*. Perhaps, in an effort to appeal to its largely black audience, the policeman who bullies black citizens in this film is a black cop
named Alonzo Harris. Cast as Officer Harris, Denzel Washington became
only the second black man in the Academy's history to win the Oscar for best
actor for his portrayal of the abusive black cop. And Officer Harris' abuses
of his authority are many as he searches a ghetto female's house without a
warrant and steals her money. In another scene, he holds a gun to the head of
a ghetto man confined to a wheelchair. And in still another scene, he is shown
beating up another black male and stealing $60 from him.

In each of these cases of police excess, it helps that the ghetto blacks killed,
beaten up, threatened at gunpoint and subjected to warrantless searches are
guilty of some crime. For example, the black woman whose house is searched
without a warrant in *Training Day* is conveniently involved in the drug trade
and the money Officer Harris steals from her is drug money. The black man

in the wheelchair that Officer Harris threatens at gunpoint just happens to be a crack dealer and the black man that he beats up has just attempted to rape a young girl and is carrying crack. The blacks subjected to police aggression in *Crash* are likewise criminal as the seemingly innocent black hitchhiker killed by the white policeman is, unbeknownst to the police officer, actually one of the vicious carjackers who has stolen the white district attorney's SUV. And, just by happenstance, the black policeman killed by the white policeman in *Crash* seems to be taking bribes.

Because the blacks subjected to these police abuses of their civil rights are all criminal, they cannot be expected to inspire much audience sympathy. Rather, it is the white police officers who end up as heroes, despite their excesses, because their murders and intimidation of these black characters inadvertently net them real criminals—at least, on-screen.

Still, it is important to remember that these police actions constitute violations of their authority. As well, many of these police abuses do not really seem to be necessary as in each of these cases, the officers involved could lawfully have read these criminal suspects their rights and arrested them. Instead, in each of these cases, the police choose to go outside the law and administer their own form of justice, thereby depriving the blacks involved of their rights.

Yet, because these films represent black neighborhoods as if they were almost entirely comprised of criminals, it provides filmmakers with the space to camouflage white aggression against black populations as justifiable police crackdowns on a dangerous population. As such these films go a long way towards justifying police excesses in the black community that would never be tolerated in the white community.

ROUNDUPS IN THE 'HOOD

Obviously, these police excesses are easiest to justify if the blacks targeted are actually criminal. Unfortunately, at least some of the police abuses depicted on screen involve the wholesale roundup of blacks which can result in the police netting innocent, law-abiding blacks in their dragnets right alongside the real criminals. For example, in *Boyz n the Hood*, the police are seen stopping young black males at will in their effort to crack down on the roving bands of violent black males that keep the cycle of violence going in black neighborhoods. In the course of one of these dragnets, one black cop wrongfully stops and holds the law-abiding, nonviolent college-bound teenager, Trey. While holding a gun to Trey's head, the cop boasts of his power over the local youth, as he explains to Trey that his ability to stop and humiliate black teens in the ghetto is one reason why he took the job of a police officer. Hence, what *Boyz* makes clear is that not only are law-abiding black teenagers subject to assault and humiliation by their fellow black teens, but they are also subject to assault and humiliation at the hands of power-hungry police officers.

Still, because ghetto action movies stereotype black males as violent gang-bangers, they indict whole communities and thereby legitimize such dragnets in which the police are allowed to treat every young black male in the black community as a suspect. Because the police are allowed to treat anyone black as dangerous or criminal, there is no need for them to distinguish between the violent black gangbangers who actually initiate violence and the law-abiding black teenagers in the neighborhood who fall victim to these gangbangers. In many of these films, then, the black presence on screen seems to have become an excuse for police violence.

Moreover, the police can extend these dragnets beyond adolescent black males in the ghetto to law-abiding black adults and middle-class blacks as well. For example, in *Crash*, the power of armed police officers to stop, hold and humiliate law-abiding, middle-class black adults is depicted in a pivotal scene which opens with two white policemen named Ryan and Hanson looking for the two young black male carjackers who have stolen the white district attorney's Lincoln Navigator. In the course of this search, Ryan decides to pull over a black couple driving a Lincoln Navigator. His white partner, Hanson, urges him not to stop the couple as he claims that they are obviously innocent and that stopping them will make them guilty of racial profiling.

Yet, despite Officer Hanson's protest, Officer Ryan still insists on making the illegal stop because he is angry at black people that day and wishes to throw his weight around (Hsu 2006). Then, even after the black man proves his Lincoln Navigator is not stolen, Ryan proceeds to bully and humiliate him by first searching him and then subjecting him to a sobriety check. He then goes on to search the man's wife and molest her. The next day, Officer Hanson complains about Ryan's racial profiling to their black commanding officer, who refuses to pursue the complaint. Hence, Ryan's abuse of his authority goes unpunished.

Because *Crash* goes on to transform Ryan into a hero after this unpunished abuse of his authority, it is not certain that all viewers—particularly black viewers—will conclude that *Crash* promotes the racial tolerance described in some early reviews of the movie. Still, even though *Crash* does little to promote racial tolerance, it does achieve a certain amount of realism in these scenes because in the real world off screen, racial profiling can mean that the police net innocent law-abiding blacks in the course of their search for criminals.

RACIAL PROFILING IN THE REAL WORLD: DRIVING WHILE BLACK

A few years before *Crash* won an Oscar for its depiction of white police officers stopping innocent black motorists at will, there was a fair amount of controversy about the police stopping a broad cross section of black motorists in the real world off screen.

In the late 1990s, the police stepped up their stops and searches of black motorists because of heightened fears about the spread of the ghetto crack trade. In their effort to single out motorists who might be transporting drug shipments, federal, state and local police forces drew up drug courier profiles that helped them to identify any motorists that looked suspicious as they drove by on the highways. Race figured heavily in the drug courier profiles the police developed to identify suspicious looking motorists as state troopers in informal interviews, court testimony and police manuals claimed that they were inclined to regard black motorists as potential drug couriers if they were driving old cars or alternatively if they were driving new, expensive cars (Russell 1998; Cole 1999; Covington 2001; Meeks 2000). Black motorists were also seen as suspect if they had crosses or other religious items hanging from their rearview mirrors as the police took this to mean that they might really be drug couriers trying to pass themselves off as religious in order to divert suspicion. Moreover, in training videos, some state troopers were taught that drugs were primarily transported by violent Jamaican gangs and that these gang members might disguise themselves by wearing the conservative garb of the black middle class.

Critics of these profiles have described them as a hodgepodge of characteristics that are so expansive that they justify stopping anyone and everyone (Cole 1999). As such, they claim these profiles function to give police forces cover to search anyone they want to search. And because drug courier profiles specify that blacks can be stopped if they are driving old cars or new cars or if they are dressed in gang clothing or business suits, it is clear that almost any one black can qualify as a suspect. It comes as no surprise, then, that black motorists are more likely to be stopped and searched for drugs.

Angry about being stopped, many law-abiding blacks searched on the basis of these questionable racial profiles complained that the only crime they had committed was "driving while black." To determine the validity of their claims, some research was conducted on traffic stops. In one study of traffic stops in Maryland, blacks made up 17.5 percent of those driving on the highways, but fully 75 percent of those stopped and searched for drugs. And, in a study of New Jersey highway stops, blacks were found to make up 15 percent of motorists, but as many as 53 percent of those searched (Verniero and Zoubek 1999; Leadership Conference on Civil Rights 2000; Cole 1999; Covington 2001; Meeks 2000). That race was a poor basis for identifying a motorist as a potential drug courier is indicated by the fact that the black motorists searched were no more likely to carry drugs than the whites searched. Yet even though these racial profiles were not effective in helping the police to find motorists carrying drugs, the police continued to single out black motorists until some black motorists sued.

RACIAL PROFILING IN THE REAL WORLD: GANG PROFILES

While racial profiling in *Crash* is treated in such a way so that police searches of broad cross sections of the black driving public seem justified, in ghetto action films, it is black youth who are singled out for stops and searches by the police. A similar practice exists in the real world off screen as well as the police often use gang profiles to sweep through a neighborhood and stop youth identified as gang members at will. Unfortunately, instead of identifying teenagers as gang members based on their actual gang-related criminal or fighting behavior, these gang profiles define gang membership based on a teenager's clothing or on whether the teenager has friends who are gang members (Bass 2001). For that reason, gang profiles can mistakenly identify nonviolent, law-abiding youth as gang members since many teenagers have adopted gang clothing styles (baggy pants, scarves, etc.) even if they are not affiliated with a gang. Merely having friends who are gang members is also no indicator of gang membership as law-abiding teenagers' friendships with gang members may be quite casual and subject to constant turnover.

Even the process of identifying which groups of young males qualify as gangs in the first place turns out to be racially biased as groups of young white males involved in crime and violence may not be defined as a problem by the community and thus not be labeled as gangs (Bass 2001; Kim 1996). By contrast, groups of minority youth are more likely to be defined as gangs.

Once a community is defined as being infested with groups of young males that have been defined as gangs, the broad, vague criteria used in many gang profiles kick in to include many of the teenagers living in these "gang-infested" neighborhoods as gang members. Hence, in Denver, white males rarely made the gang list while as many as two-thirds of all young black males in Denver were identified as gang members. And, in Los Angeles County (CA), half of all teenaged black males were included on the gang list. Other minorities also figured heavily on gang lists in Orange County (CA), where 75 percent of the young men on the gang list are Latino and most of the remaining 25 percent are Asian (Kim 1996).

That so many young black males have been identified as gang members using gang profiles makes it very likely that these all-encompassing gang lists include large numbers of law-abiding black males mixed in with the criminals. Yet despite the inaccuracies of gang lists, being identified as a gang member has real consequences as it gives the police license to keep tabs on wide swaths of the youth population. Indeed some cities have used gang civil injunctions to keep youth identified as gang members from loitering in public or being seen in public with other persons identified as gang members. For example, in Chicago between 1992 and 1995, young black males could be stopped by the police for loitering in any one place in the presence of a suspected gang member. If black males engaged in this crime—derisively referred to as "standing while black"—failed to disperse, they could be arrested (Covington 2001).

Black males, who made the gang list, were also more likely to be arrested for disorderly conduct, wearing gang clothing, making noise, blocking the free passage of streets and littering (Bass 2001). Clearly, then, the police have enormous power over those that they have identified as gang members as youth included on their list will find that they have to restrict their movements, limit their affiliations and change their style of dress to avoid getting caught up in police sweeps.

One 20-year-old black man in Charlotte, North Carolina, named Jamal Reid illustrates the problems associated with using clothing or gang associates as a measure of gang membership (Moore 2007). While Mr. Reid is not a member of a gang, his fashion tastes run to gang clothing styles as he has the tattoos and the baggy jeans that signal gang membership in black neighborhoods. He has also befriended some of the local gangbangers in his gang-infested neighborhood—with good reason. As he describes it, "It's better to be their friend than their enemy."

Yet, even though he is not a member of a gang, the Charlotte police can apparently stop him at will. He describes an incident in which an officer stopped in front of his house and ordered him to come over to the car. Mr. Reid refused and ran. The officers gave chase, caught him and forced him to lay face down in the dirt. When interviewed, an officer on the police force openly admitted that they confronted anyone who associated with gang members in high crime (read black) neighborhoods, even if they were not gang members themselves and even if they were not involved in any crimes. Yet, the officer defended the practice as legitimate despite the occasional complaint of harassment (Moore 2007).

To the extent that the police follow practices such as these, it is clear that a number of black teenagers who are not in gangs will find that they can be stopped and even arrested for living in a neighborhood where there is gang activity. This suggests that the scene in *Boyz n the Hood* where the police wrongfully stop the law-abiding black teenager, Trey, may accurately reflect reality for all too many black youth living in neighborhoods that have been identified as "gang-infested."

Moreover, if one of the young men on the gang list gets involved in an act of minor delinquency, they will be punished more severely than delinquents who are not on the list as their gang membership turns their delinquent acts into gang-related offenses that receive enhanced penalties. As if this is not enough, police control over the comings and goings of young men in gang-infested neighborhoods can go on indefinitely as there are no provisions for purging the names of those appearing on gang lists.

This is especially problematic as even the young men who are most active in gangs tend to stay for only a year, while other more marginal members merely drift in and out of gang activities (Moore 2007; Yablonsky 1970). Furthermore, even those teenagers who are the most committed to the gang tend to age out of them by their late teens as they come to see street fights with rival gangs as childish (Steffensmeier and Allan 2000). Yet, these wildly inaccurate gang lists give police the power to continue to keep tabs on a neighborhood's young men even after they have left their violent and criminal lifestyles behind them.

In fact, because names are not purged from gang lists, it is conceivable that the police might suspect even middle-aged black men of gang membership. Perhaps that explains why the police stopped a 38-year-old black reporter for the *New York Times* when he went to interview gang members in a gang-infested neighborhood in Salisbury, NC. While he was standing in this high crime neighborhood talking to gang members, the police drove up, ordered him over to their car, shoved his face into the hood of the car and handcuffed him—all without asking him for his name or why he was in the neighborhood.

They claimed they were arresting him for loitering and only unlocked the handcuffs after they found his *New York Times* identification and checked for warrants. And yet as he angrily protested his rights as an American citizen, the police defended stopping him and cuffing him by reminding him that it was a dangerous neighborhood. Apparently then, even adult black males, who are innocent bystanders, can be subjected to the same police treatment as adolescent gang members simply for standing on the same street corners.

PROFILING A NEIGHBORHOOD: ZERO TOLERANCE POLICING

Policies that allow for similar police overreaching can also be instituted under the guise of zero tolerance policing. For example, in New York, after Rudolph Giuliani was elected mayor during a law-and-order campaign, he appointed

William Bratton as the police commissioner to crack down in minority neighborhoods. Commissioner Bratton proceeded to practice zero tolerance policing in minority neighborhoods which meant that, in the 1990s, the New York Police Department (NYPD) had greater license to go after black youth for such minor infractions as spray painting graffiti, turnstile jumping, spitting or riding their bicycles on the sidewalk (Barstow 2000; Wynn 2001). While these minor infractions had previously led the police to tell the teenagers involved to desist, the police during the Giuliani administration were urged to conduct stop-and-frisk searches, make identity checks, issue summonses and even make arrests. Obviously such policies risked raising the level of conflict between the police and local teens as law-abiding black teenagers were as likely to be caught up in these crackdowns as criminal youth (Wynn 2001).

Moreover, these zero tolerance policies were not simply directed at black adolescents. In an effort to curtail the drug trade, the police also went after black adults. So, for example in the 1990s, the NYPD circled minority neighborhoods in unmarked cars and surveillance vans and watched local residents from rooftops (Barstow 2000). They also secured agreements from landlords to conduct trespassing sweeps in which they roamed apartment buildings and arrested anyone that did not live in the building for trespassing. They also tailed, stopped and frisked anyone they suspected of drug dealing and then, for good measure, they tailed, stopped and frisked the friends and relatives of anyone they suspected. In some instances, they would saturate a block with officers and set up barricades to block traffic and then question anyone coming on the block; in some cases, these police barricades would stay up for months at a time (Roane 1999).

If they could not ticket black New Yorkers for these minor infractions, some police officers would just issue a summons to suspicious looking people even if they were not doing anything. Even though the police knew that these bogus charges would have to be dismissed if those ticketed went to court, they knew that most people would not bother to go to court to contest the charges. And yet, if those ticketed did not go to court, a warrant was issued for their arrest which then enabled the police to sweep through the community later and arrest all those with outstanding warrants (Wynn 2001).

These wholesale crackdowns on minorities were also applied to the gun problem in New York. Unlike the white communities depicted in *Bowling for Columbine*, where gun control meant crackdowns on the gun shows that supplied the teen-aged Columbine shooters, in New York it meant that the police had license to stop and search citizens on the street to see if they were carrying guns illegally. Research conducted by the State Attorney General's Office in 2000 indicated that the NYPD searched some 45,000 people for guns and drugs and yet only arrested 9,500 of those searched. This means that 35,000 people were needlessly stopped and searched as they were not carrying contraband. Blacks figured heavily among those searched as black New Yorkers were 6 times as likely to be stopped and searched as white New Yorkers. And yet, these stops and searches of blacks were actually less likely to turn up contraband than searches of whites since for every 16 blacks stopped, only 1 was arrested, while for every 10 whites stopped, 1 was arrested. In other words, the police were more likely to needlessly stop law-abiding blacks than law-abiding whites (Barry 2000).

DEVALUING BLACK MALES IN GHETTO ACTION FILMS

Clearly what these incidents indicate is that relationships between the black community and the police in the real world off screen are quite different from the police/community relationships depicted in movie theaters. In the real world outside Hollywood, racial profiling and roundups of black youth can look like police abuse of their authority to many ghetto residents. Hence, the police may not look like heroes who keep the lid on crime in black neighborhoods. Instead, all too often, they may be seen as an outside force that is involved in needlessly violating the civil rights of black citizens—both law abiding and criminal alike.

It is only in the Hollywood-inspired ghettos that appear on screen where all the young black males are criminals that the roundups and dragnets that target all black youth seem to be warranted. Yet one effect of allowing these police excesses to go unchallenged on screen is that black youth in these pictures are consigned to a kind of second class citizenship much like the second-class citizenship of blacks living in the Jim Crow south in the pre-Civil Rights era.

This time, however, instead of being relegated to separate and unequal public accommodations because of their race, the black characters in these movies are treated like second-class citizens because they are people who can be stopped, handcuffed and harassed by the police just because they are black. Ghetto action films go a long way towards naturalizing the second-class citizenship of their black characters by representing so many of them as vicious gangbangers, petty criminals, prostitutes, drug users or negligent parents who deserve to be subjected to constant scrutiny, violation of their rights and arrest just because of the color of their skin. And because skin color alone is enough to qualify blacks as suspects, even law-abiding blacks and affluent blacks on the silver screen are depicted as second-class citizens whose rights can be violated (e.g., *Crash, Boyz n the Hood*).

In large part, many of the young black male lead characters in ghetto action movies appear to be drawn to the violent and criminal lifestyles that justify these searches because violence and crime seem to be the only way to achieve manhood in these movies. Part of the allure of the criminal life in these films stems from the fact that violent and criminal masculinities are glamorized on screen as the teenaged black criminals, who dominate these pictures, are routinely shown earning more money and experiencing more excitement than law-abiding adults in the ghetto confined to menial jobs.

In fairness, these movies are meant to be fictionalized accounts of ghetto life that entertain an audience, and therefore all the violence, money, car chases and easy sex may be needed to transform them into escapist fare. Yet, even when these films are evaluated narrowly as a form of escapism, they fail. After all, the heroes of ghetto action movies typically do not emerge triumphant at the end of the picture by "sticking it to the man" as they once did in blaxploitation films. Instead these gangbangers usually lose out by the end of the picture as many are killed off by their fellow gang members, while others go to prison. This is in stark contrast to action movies with white characters where the lead character is typically celebrated by the end of the movie often for saving the innocent or the weak from the movie's villain (e.g., *Die Hard* series).

Not only do the stars of ghetto action movies fail to triumph in the end, in some ways, many of them end up confined to roles that are every bit as submissive and emasculating as the subservient roles meted out to black actors in the years before the civil rights movement. However, this time, instead of a submission based on their status as a slave or manservant or eyeball-rolling sidekick to whites, the submission and emasculation of the modern ghetto action thug is usually based on his subjugation and emasculation by the legal system as large portions of these pictures show black men being arrested, cuffed, jailed, locked up in prison or placed under police surveillance. Hence, in many ways, racial hierarchies are just as clearly drawn in ghetto action movies as in the films of the pre-civil rights era.

For example, there are numerous images of black males knuckling under to the legal system in *South Central* as the gang leader, Bobby, who heads the Deuces, spends much of the movie in prison for killing a local drug dealer. Racial hierarchies can be more clearly visualized in the prison scenes in *South Central* than in the scenes based in the ghetto. After all, it is Bobby and his fellow gangbangers, who rule the streets of the ghetto; by contrast, in prison, it is white authority figures that are clearly in charge. Hence, in one of the prison scenes, after Bobby gets in a fight with another inmate, two white prison guards come along to cart him off to solitary confinement as punishment. Bobby's submission to their control is clearly indicated as he is forced to strip naked in front of these guards before they place him into solitary.

In a later scene, Bobby has to appeal to white authority figures on the parole board to get out of prison and apparently goes before the parole board several times before they agree to release him after he has served his time. It is only when Bobby follows the advice of a fellow black inmate and learns to appear less threatening to the white parole board that they agree to release him.

In *South Central*, then, the filmic codes of a bygone era are simply reworked as black rule over ghetto streets ends at the prison house door. However, this time instead of pre-civil rights era slaves, manservants or eyeball-rolling side-kicks showing deference to their white owners or employers, the macho black gangbangers from the streets of *South Central* find themselves held in captivity and forced to defer to the white institutional power structure in prison.

As inmate populations are often divided into racially based gangs that protect their members from assaults and rapes by rival gangs, the prison setting in *South Central* provides additional opportunities for stripping these macho black gang-bangers of their manhood. For example, in one scene in *South Central*, Bobby breaks with his own gang, the Deuces, while in prison and as a consequence loses the protection of the prison chapter of his gang. Once it becomes known around the prison that Bobby is no longer protected by any gang, the rival white prison gang called the Aryan Nation realizes that they can assault him and rape him at will without fear of retaliation from the Deuces. Hence, one member of the Aryan Nation comes up to Bobby in the lunchroom to pick a fight by calling him a darkie and dropping something in his food. Bobby proceeds to beat him up, thereby prompting the Aryan Nation to retaliate. Later when they get an opportunity, several members of the Aryan Nation pull Bobby into a closet where they proceed to try to beat him up and rape him. He is saved by several Black Muslim inmates who come along, stop the assault and negotiate some payment to the Aryan Nation for Bobby's earlier assault on one of their members. Then, in a scene all too reminiscent of the racially submissive roles assigned to black men in the pre-civil rights era, all parties agree that Bobby's payment to the Aryan Nation will require him to shine the shoes of white Aryan Nation members, do their laundry and give them his dessert and 15 packs of cigarettes as tribute. In turn, this white prison gang agrees to desist from trying to turn him into a "punk" by sexually assaulting him.

Themes of black emasculation also drive the plot in *Juice*. *Juice* follows the escapades of four black male teenagers who are not in a gang. One of them named Bishop (played by late rapper Tupac Shakur) finds himself routinely subjected to taunts by a local Latino gang as he walks through the streets of his own neighborhood. He decides that the only way to stop these taunts and intimidation is by acquiring some "juice" or a reputation as someone who is so violent and dangerous that he will kill anyone who insults him. To that end, Bishop buys a gun and plans to rob a local grocery store to acquire the needed juice. He insists that his three nonviolent black friends go in with him on the robbery and they reluctantly go along with him until he kills the store's owner in the course of the robbery simply so that he can further enhance his reputation for being violent, unpredictable and dangerous.

Having acquired his juice or respect behind the barrel of a gun, Bishop kills one of his friends simply because the friend tries to take the gun away from him. Then, fearful that his remaining two black friends will snitch about the robbery and murder, Bishop tries to kill them and is ultimately killed by one of them in self-defense.

What drives Bishop's tragic desire for juice is not simply the daily taunts and intimidation from the local Latino gangbangers. He is also driven to his quest for juice when the Latino gang members imply that his father was raped repeatedly while he was in prison. And, in fact, in earlier scenes, there is evidence that Bishop suspects as much as he can be seen slipping money into the pocket of his unemployed father who acts like he has been traumatized by a sexual assault as he sits listlessly in front of the television, apparently still dazed from his prison ordeal. The possibility that his father has been emasculated in prison, then, seems to drive Bishop to robbery, murder and ultimately to his own tragic demise in his quest for *Juice*.

APOLITICAL BLACK CRIMINALS
AND LAW-ABIDING RACE MEN

In many ways it is understandable why the underclass black characters in these films do not resist being treated like second-class citizens by the criminal justice system. Because so many of them are depicted as criminals they are in no position to put up much of a fight against legal authorities. Instead, much like criminals in the real world, they spend much of their time attempting to negotiate with the criminal justice system to try to avoid punishment for their crimes or trying to secure a release from prison.

Because their criminal behavior causes these lead characters to consent to their domination by the legal system, they end up being little more than throwbacks to the coons and toms that appeared in films before the 1960s. Back then, these stereotypical black characters' consent and seeming contentment with white dominance was used to justify slavery and Jim Crow. In the more recent ghetto action films, the criminality of the film's black characters is used to justify their submissiveness to a white male-dominated criminal justice system. However, the apolitical black characters depicted in these recent films are very much at odds with blacks in real life as blacks in the real world do resist abuses by the legal system.

For example, during the 1990s when the NYPD was practicing zero toler-ance policing in black neighborhoods in New York, there was a significant rise in the number of citizens complaining about the police to the Civilian Complaint Review Board (Conklin 2003). Polls conducted with black New Yorkers at the time indicated that fully two-thirds of them felt that the zero tolerance policing practices instituted during the 1990s Giuliani administra-tion had resulted in an increase in police brutality. And, even though the police defended these crackdowns in black neighborhoods by saying that they made the city safer, only 33 percent of blacks felt that the law-and-order policies of the mayor had actually made their communities safer (Barry and Connelly 1999).

Since zero tolerance policing meant a rise in police stops and searches of black citizens, it comes as no surprise that at least some of these police encounters with law-abiding black citizens might turn deadly. One such in-cident involved the killing of an unarmed street vendor from Guinea named Amadou Diallo as he was stopped by the police on the steps of his own home in February of 1999. Four white NYPD police officers fired 41 bullets at Mr. Diallo when they mistook his wallet for a gun, killing him instantly.

Once again, blacks in the real world protested these police abuses. In the wake of the Diallo killing, the Reverend Al Sharpton, a black minister and civil rights leader, was arrested for staging a sit-in on Wall Street to protest the shooting. Upon his release from jail, Reverend Sharpton vowed to con-tinue to protest until the four officers involved in the shooting were arrested, and in the weeks that followed, he organized the demonstrations and arrests of a number of other people protesting the Diallo killing and police brutality including civil rights leaders and actors such as Jesse Jackson, Ossie Davis, Ruby Dee and Susan Sarandon.

A number of Democratic politicians were also arrested as part of this ongoing protest including the former mayor of New York, David Dinkins. Eventually some 1,200 people were arrested for demonstrating against police brutality in New York City. Yet, despite these protests, the four officers who shot Mr. Diallo were acquitted in February of 2000 resulting in even more protests. The protests finally ended with a march on Washington that drew 25,000 people in April of 2000. (Hsaio 2001; McArdle 2001; Cooper 1999).

RACE MEN AND VIOLENT
BLACK MASCULINITIES ON SCREEN

Clearly, these recent incidents indicate that the black population is still highly politicized and inclined to unite with other blacks to protest racial injustice much as it did during the civil rights movement and the urban uprisings of the 1960s and 1970s. The fact that ghetto action films fail to represent this politically conscious black population has a lot to do with their almost single-minded focus on ghetto action criminals. Because they stereotype so many black males as apolitical ghetto action thugs, these films crowd out alternative masculinities promoted in the ghetto in which black manhood is actually achieved through resistance to racial injustice.

In the real world, black men who protest racist conditions typically define themselves in terms of a race man identity rather than in terms of the violent and criminal masculinities promoted in these films. And, because race men tend to be law abiding, they are in a better position to protest racial injustice at the hands of the criminal justice system than the black criminals on screen as they are not subject to the legal system's control.

More important, the very fact that they are law abiding makes them inclined to condemn the kind of black-on-black violence that defines black masculinity on screen rather than celebrating it. Indeed in the real world outside Hollywood studios, race men denounce black-on-black violence as the very antithesis of true masculinity, in part, because it does not promote black unity.

While black men have long protested racial injustice, these race man identities were given quite a boost with the rise of black protest movements in the 1950s, 1960s and 1970s. A number of black-dominated organizations blossomed back then to protest racial inequalities including the Black Muslims, the Black Panthers and various black civil rights groups (e.g., NAACP, Urban League, black churches, etc.). While these groups varied enormously in terms of their ideologies and the strategies they employed to confront racism, they all urged blacks to join with other blacks in racial solidarity in order to bring about social change.

Leaders of these groups were especially important in raising black consciousness of racial injustice and with this newly raised consciousness, black-on-black crime came in for special condemnation because it was equated with genocide, racist conspiracies and self-hatred. Indeed, many of these protest organizations blamed white racism for encouraging blacks to hate themselves and other blacks and to act on that self-hatred by engaging in black-on-black crime.

For these groups, achieving black manhood in the face of white racism meant taking pride in one's self as a black man. They believed that black men could acquire pride in themselves and the race through a process of enlightenment that required them to reject the old sense of racial inferiority and self-hatred, acquire a new pride in themselves and black people by learning about black history in America and Africa and by gaining some understanding of how blacks had struggled against racial injustice and survived centuries of racism.

Presumably, with this newfound pride in self and the race, black men would come to realize that the enemy was not other black people like rival gang members; instead enlightenment for a newly transformed race man meant realizing that the enemy was an American system of racial domination, which segregated blacks into resource-poor ghettos. Much of this consciousness-raising came from other blacks as most blacks had little faith that they could acquire such knowledge from the formal educational system (Connor 1995).

As noted previously, some of the organizations promoting these new race man identities made a special effort to reach out to criminal black males and enlighten them—particularly the Black Muslims. Hence, many black males who had made a career out of crime suddenly found themselves trying to emulate Malcolm X, who joined the Nation of Islam to convert from a violent and criminal masculinity to a life marked by black pride and the struggle for racial justice. For many black ex-convicts, then, Malcolm's life provided them with a road map to a new masculinity based on the struggle for racial justice. Yet, in ghetto action movies, the race man identities promoted by Malcolm X and other black protest organizations seem to have little to no impact on black male socialization.

RACE MAN IDENTITIES IN GHETTO ACTION MOVIES

In fairness, some ghetto action movies do acknowledge the presence of race men in the ghetto, but only long enough to show how they are dismissed by the violent gangbangers and drug dealers who are the central focus of these films. For example, in *Boyz n the Hood*, the race man ideology is voiced by the patriarch, Furious Styles, who has successfully raised his son, Trey, alone in a father-headed household. In one scene, Furious can be seen lecturing to a crowd that includes his son and some of the local neighborhood gangbangers. He tells the gang members that by shooting at other black people, they are doing just what the white man wants them to do, and then to back up his claims that whites want black people to kill themselves, he argues that whites are helping to fuel the local cycle of black-on-black violence, by placing so many liquor stores, gun shops and illegal drugs in black neighborhoods. As he explains it, that is the reason why the crack trade flourishes in black neighborhoods and not in Beverly Hills.

Yet despite Furious' efforts to raise the race consciousness of the local gangbangers by making them see how destructive their violence is to racial solidarity, one gang member simply dismisses him by implying that he will shoot back if someone tries to shoot him regardless of the damage it does to racial solidarity.

In *Menace II Society*, notions of racial solidarity are voiced by Sharif, who is a friend of the ghetto action thugs Caine and O-Dog. While Sharif was formerly immersed in the local violent subculture like Caine and O-Dog, he has turned away from it as a result of his conversion to Islam and is trying to persuade Caine to leave the 'hood and go to college with him in Kansas. Once again, Sharif's efforts to raise the race consciousness of his violent friends fall on deaf ears as the ghetto action thugs, Caine and O-Dog, dismiss Sharif as nothing more than a "knucklehead turned Muslim." They also deride him for preaching against the use of alcohol because of his religious beliefs and for thinking that Allah can save black people.

In *South Central*, the race man is played by Bobby's prison cellmate, Ali. Ali functions as an older father figure for Bobby as he keeps Bobby from being raped in prison and proceeds to try to enlighten him. To raise Bobby's race consciousness, Ali sends him to the prison library to read about heroes in the struggle for racial justice like Malcolm X, Martin Luther King, Jr., Jesse Jackson and Adam Clayton Powell, Jr. Under Ali's tutelage, Bobby covers over his old gang tattoos and promises to opt out of the cycle of black-on-black violence when he is released from prison. Hence, unlike some other ghetto action movies, in *South Central*, the ghetto action thug, Bobby, does not reject the race man identity but rather embraces it and is changed by it.

The problem, here, lies in how Ali represents the race man identity to Bobby in his effort to convert him. Unlike the aforementioned heroes of the struggle for racial justice that he quotes, Ali does not urge Bobby to go out and join with other blacks in racial solidarity to try to improve conditions in the black community. Instead of collective struggle, Ali urges Bobby to pursue the individualistic agenda of saving his son from violence. Hence, when Ali quotes these heroes in the struggle, he does not focus on what they have said about the need for blacks to join together to protest for more jobs, decent schools, better housing, recognition of their civil rights and putting an end to police brutality. Instead he seems to suggest that the problems of the black community will be solved through responsible fatherhood, more harmonious relationships with whites and forgoing drugs—solutions that seem remarkably similar to the conservative agenda.

South Central also manages to tarnish black heroes in the struggle for racial justice by representing them in terms of the flawed character of Ali. Because Ali is in prison for life for having killed three black men, he is in no position to actually go out in the community and try to promote racial unity by condemning the endless cycle of black-on-black violence. Hence, black political leaders are, once again, represented as impotent.

MALIGNING RACE MEN IN *TALK TO ME*

This strategy of discrediting black protest by misrepresenting leaders in the struggle for racial justice also seems to be the main focus of the 2007 movie *Talk to Me*. Set in the late 1960s when Washington, D.C., and a number of other cities exploded in rioting after the 1968 assassination of Martin Luther King, Jr., it follows the escapades of one of Washington, D.C.'s black leaders in that period named Petey Green. Petey achieves much of his leadership status as a local radio talk show host, who, in conjunction with his black program director Dewey Hughes, is credited with having helped to quell the 1968 Washington, D.C. riots.

In the standard Hollywood treatment of black riots, *Talk to Me* exposes viewers to scenes of breaking store windows, burning buildings, overturned police cars and, of course, angry black rioters chasing innocent white bystanders, who happen to be out on the streets. In one scene, Petey and Dewey even manage to rescue one innocent white male bystander from the angry black rioters.

In keeping with other films that touch on the 1960s riots (e.g., *Menace*), *Talk to Me* presents the usual one-sided picture of these disturbances by showing only the lawlessness and disorder and avoiding any mention of the black frustrations about racial inequities in jobs, housing, schools and treatment by the police that actually precipitated the unrest. Furthermore, despite the fact that the movie makes much of Petey's supposed capacity to say things that more diplomatic middle-class blacks like Dewey are afraid to say, Petey is never seen speaking out about the sources of black anger and frustration that actually caused the disturbance.

While Petey achieves much of his leadership status by helping to bring the riots to an end, he was hardly alone. When the police and the National Guard found themselves unable to stop the disturbances in a number of other cities, they often turned to local black leaders who stepped in to soothe angry blacks (U.S. National Advisory Commission on Civil Disorders 1968). Many of these black leaders, then, proceeded to use the opportunity to persuade white elected officials to address some of the concerns of their black constituencies who were frustrated about ongoing racial injustice. As a consequence, many white elected officials, who had previously ignored appeals from their black constituencies, suddenly found themselves willing to address ghetto concerns for the first time in an attempt to restore order. However, in *Talk to Me*, Petey Green never makes an effort to have elected officials address the concerns of his black listeners. Instead, he responds to his listeners' anger and frustration by inviting them to a free concert where he introduces rhythm and blues musician James Brown.

As one of the pioneers of the radio talk show format, Petey has the capacity to communicate the concerns of his black listeners to a larger audience. And, as he and other characters in the movie repeatedly note, Petey is not afraid to "tell it like it is" when it comes to voicing black concerns. Yet, over the course of the movie, it becomes clear that Petey equates "telling it like it is" with calling black record producer Berry Gordy and some black elected officials hustlers and pimps on his radio show. Apparently, "telling it like it is" also means referring to blacks and whites in terms of racial slurs on television talk shows. However, for Petey, speaking out clearly does not mean speaking truth to power. Hence, despite his access to a public platform to protest for racial change, Petey is never seen talking to his listeners about empowering their communities.

That Petey never acts like a race man promoting community empowerment has a lot to do with the fact that he is more of a shock jock than a black activist. As such, he considers it a triumph when his name-calling, insults and racial slurs violate Federal Communications Commission rulings about what can and cannot be said on the air.

Another reason why Petey does not promote community empowerment is because he seems to be totally lacking in the kind of race consciousness that is generally associated with black activist leaders, who define ghetto problems in terms of racial injustice and try to address them. Instead, Petey acts more like a self-interested con man and charlatan, who is more concerned about using the struggle against racial injustice to empower himself rather than the community. There is some evidence of Petey's skills as a con man in the opening scenes of the movie when Petey, who is serving time in prison, manages to manipulate the prison warden into releasing him early.

Thereafter, when he gets on the air, he proceeds to manipulate his listeners not by promising to broadcast their concerns about racial injustice, but rather by promoting himself as an authentic son of the ghetto. According to Petey, his "authenticity" rests on the fact that he is a recovering alcoholic and an ex-heroin addict with only an 8th grade education, who has been incarcerated over half of his life and whose best friends are pimps, whores and gamblers.

Certainly, Malcolm X managed to emerge as a leader in the struggle for racial justice after spending time in prison for his many crimes. However, Malcolm X transformed himself from a criminal into a black leader by pursuing empowerment of the black community once he left prison. The Petey Green character in *Talk to Me* seems never to have made that transformation and so he pursues his own advancement instead.

For example, early in the picture, Petey manages to mobilize some blacks in the community to form a picket line. However, these protesters are not picketing racial injustice in their community; instead, they are picketing the local radio station because they have refused to hire Petey. Petey's ability to mobilize these black supporters quickly pays off as he immediately gets hired.

Then, later, after he helps to quell the riots, he uses his celebrity to expand from his radio talk show format to standup comedy and then eventually to his own television talk show. In each of these formats, he uses shock jock tactics to expand his audience, even inviting white shock jock, Howard Stern, on his television talk show in blackface. Sadly, such antics do little to further black empowerment.

By repeatedly confusing Petey Green, the popular shock jock, with Petey Green, the black political leader, *Talk to Me* manages to disparage genuine race men by equating them with self-interested con men like Petey Green.

PUTTING GHETTO ACTION VIOLENCE IN CONTEXT

That Hollywood repeatedly ignores, dismisses or misrepresents real race men means that little consideration is given to alternative masculine identities in the ghetto that condemn the black-on-black violence depicted on screen. And yet, more exploration of these race man identities might explain why the overwhelming majority of black males in the real world are not involved in the nonstop violence portrayed in ghetto action movies.

For example, in 2006, estimates suggest that some 7,210 black males murdered someone. In that same year, there were 17,497,000 black males. This means that 17,489,790 black males managed not to kill anyone that year.[2] However, because ghetto action films focus on that handful of black males who commit murder, they give short shrift to the vast majority of black males who have not killed anyone. As a consequence, fans of these movies end up knowing little about how manhood is defined by most black males (U.S. Census Bureau 2004; Puzzanchera and Kang 2008).

All viewers see is scene after scene of violent black males who are too concerned with pursuing an individualistic agenda that requires the dominance and humiliation of their fellow black males to concern themselves with organizing in a collective struggle to oppose such violence and defeat racism. Instead of becoming race men who seek to turn back years of racial inequality, the black men who appear in these films appear to be so atomized and pathologized by mainstream society's disinvestment in their communities that they have been reduced to victimizing their black neighbors in an endless cycle of robberies, burglaries, drug deals and shootings.

Yet because homicide is such a rare event, it cannot be used to define whole communities of young men as dangerous and prone to homicidal rages. This fact is recognized in *Bowling for Columbine* where the murderous rampage of 2 young white males is not treated as if it represented white youth or white youth cultures in general. However, it is not recognized in ghetto action films where the violent black males on screen seem to be the sole representatives of black youth cultures.

That there are so few race men in ghetto action films stems from the fact that most of the black lead characters in these films are criminals and hence incapable of the kind of race consciousness that would be required to identify their problem as high unemployment and collectively go about trying to change it. Even many of the adults in these films seem not to have been enlightened. In fact, there seem to be so few rational and responsible black adult citizens of any kind in these movies that are capable of exercising much influence over their communities. Instead, many of the adults are depicted as desperate, irrational and even violent. This seems to provide all the more reason for a takeover by outside institutions that are seemingly capable of bringing order and security to these communities—namely the police.

Off screen, however, black citizens seem to be quite capable of joining in solidarity with their fellow citizens to try to solve problems that plague their communities. Yet, because these films depict the ghetto as if it were dominated by oppositional criminal subcultures, they fail to see the adults in these communities as a body of rational and responsible citizens who are capable of forming their own thoughts and mobilizing to bring about change. This is somewhat surprising given the level of black activism during the 1950s, 1960s and 1970s. And, while one could argue that black protest ended with these earlier generations, it is at least possible that the generations who protested racial injustice back then might have managed to pass on the same determination to resist racism to their children. There is evidence of this in recent black protest against the legal system's treatment of six black teenagers known as the Jena 6.

RACE MEN AND RECENT BLACK PROTEST

The Jena 6 case refers to an incident that began in September 2006 when a black student at Jena High School in Louisiana asked the school administration for permission to sit under a tree that had traditionally been reserved for white students only. When the school authorities said he could sit wherever he pleased, the youth sat under the formerly all-white tree. The next day there were nooses hanging from the tree, presumably, to intimidate black students and discourage them from sitting in this all-white gathering place. When the school principal identified the three white youths responsible for hanging the nooses, he expelled them. However, they were never referred to the local police or charged with any crime. Even their expulsion was quickly overturned by the superintendent of schools who reduced their punishment to a three-day suspension based on his belief that these acts of racial intimidation were little more than a "youthful stunt."

Yet, even though the superintendent clearly did not see racial intimidation by the white students as a serious offense, black students at Jena High School continued to take it seriously and hence racial tensions remained high throughout the fall semester. On December 4, 2006, a white student, who supported the hanging of the nooses, was allegedly taunting some of the black students about it and they proceeded to beat him up. While the white student was hospitalized after the fight, his injuries were not that severe as he was able to attend a public function later that evening. Yet, despite the fact that his injuries were not serious, the six black Jena High School students involved in the fight—the Jena 6—were expelled from school and charged with attempted second-degree murder. One of them, a 16-year-old minor named Mychal Bell, was charged as an adult and locked up.

On the morning of the trial, the prosecutor reduced the charges to second degree aggravated battery and conspiracy, which brings with it a maximum sentence of 22 years in prison. Aggravated battery, charges usually mean that a dangerous weapon is used in the course of the battery and hence the prosecutor justified charging these young black males with such a serious crime by defining Mychal Bell's tennis shoes as a "dangerous weapon." An all-white jury agreed and after three hours of deliberation found Mychal Bell guilty of these serious charges. After Mr. Bell sat in jail for nearly a year, an appeals court decided that he should be retried as a minor rather than as an adult, and in September of 2007, his case was transferred to juvenile court (Associated Press, 2007).

On September 20, 2007, more than 10,000 black college students from around the country took buses to the town of Jena, Louisiana, to protest the harsh punishments meted out to the Jena 6. They were joined by civil rights leaders from an earlier generation, who helped to organize the march, including the Reverend Al Sharpton and the Reverend Jesse Jackson (Foster 2007).

Interviews with the protesters indicated that many were outraged at the disparate treatment of the 6 black students as compared to the treatment of the white students who started the whole incident by hanging the nooses. Many of those interviewed said they were marching in Jena because the white students were never charged with any criminal offenses and received a mere three-day suspension from the school system, even as the black teenagers in the Jena 6 were taken before the criminal justice system and slapped with charges for serious crimes that eventually had to be reduced (R. Jones 2007; Newman 2007).

In the eyes of many of the protesters, the original hanging of the nooses was a hate crime that should have been criminally prosecuted rather than dismissed by white school authorities as just a mere prank or youthful stunt (*The Crisis*-Digital Edition 2007). Some demonstrators also suggested that the Jena school administrators should at the very least establish a curriculum that taught cultural sensitivity and understanding. Other demonstrators also expressed concern that Mychal Bell—the only one of the six to be jailed—had been tried and convicted by an all-white jury rather than a jury that reflected the racial demographics of Jena (Jones 2007; *The Crisis*—Digital Edition 2007). And still others were surprised and outraged that black students would still have to ask permission to sit under a "whites-only tree" as they thought that such practices had ended during the civil rights era (Newman 2007).

In the months before the demonstration, concern about this injustice became the focus of a nationwide campaign as word about the case was circulated by black radio stations, YouTube, Internet, e-mail and text-messaging. These same channels were then used to mobilize thousands to come to Jena for the rally.

What is perhaps most surprising about this demonstration is that so many of the marchers were very young African Americans. While many were college students, some were mere high school students. For example, one 16-year-old black male rode on the bus all day and all night from Philadelphia to participate in the march. Indeed, many of the protesters were about the same age as the apolitical gangbangers that routinely appear in ghetto action films. However, unlike the black youth represented in these films, the young people that protested in Jena were very much interested in promoting racial solidarity and clearly were quite capable of mobilizing other African American youth like themselves to protest racist conditions. Moreover, their protests had some effect as the fact that the case became a *cause célèbre* among so many young blacks in the months before the demonstration prompted the prosecutors to reduce some of the charges (Jones 2007).

Evidence that this desire to rally against racism had been passed on from previous generations to this generation of adolescents comes from a black couple who brought their 17-year-old daughter to participate in the march. Moreover, other middle-aged black protesters in their 40s claimed that they had marched in earlier demonstrations in their youth and had come to Jena to show solidarity with this younger generation of marchers (Newman 2007).

RACE WOMEN AND GHETTO ACTION MOVIES

The fact that ghetto action films represent most young black males as apolitical thugs who prey on the black community probably explains why audiences for these movies might not have been able to foresee the show of racial solidarity demonstrated by the young black males protesting in Jena. Viewers of these movies might also have had trouble recognizing the many young black women who protested in Jena that day as these films likewise give short shrift to racially conscious black women.

However, as the Jena rally demonstrates, black women are just as politically conscious as black men. After all, black women have long participated in the struggle for racial justice as many were actively involved in protests during the civil rights movement and the black power movement. And, just like black men during the racial upheavals of the 1950s, 1960s, and 1970s, they too were involved in enlightening themselves and other blacks about their history. Back then, black women likewise expressed their newfound pride in themselves, their race and their history by adopting natural hairstyles (Afros, braids, dreadlocks, etc.) and African clothing—just like black males.

Yet, the black females depicted on screen in ghetto action films seem to have little of the self-love and love for their people manifested by their participation in these protests. Instead, many of the black female characters represented on screen seem to hate themselves as they are invariably cast as prostitutes, drug addicts and negligent mothers. As such, these characters seem to care little about the struggle for racial justice.

Instead, they only seem to be motivated to make more money through welfare or criminal behavior, feed their drug addictions and struggle to establish relationships with their leading men who are typically violent gangbangers or drug dealers. These black female characters certainly express no pride in their race nor do they seek to join in collective solidarity with other blacks. Many of them are not even motivated to care for their own children.

Indeed, these films never miss an opportunity to show how the poor parenting skills of their black female characters are implicated in the violent and criminal behavior of their sons. As such these films support the conservative orthodoxy, which suggests that black male violence is, in part, the product of their internalization of culture-of-poverty values that are passed on to them by their mothers.

Yet, even this turns out to be wrong as research done on black families in the real world shows that children raised in single-parent households are no more likely to become involved in crime than those raised in some two-parent households. Specifically, studies comparing teenagers raised in single-parent families and those raised in two-parent families with a stepparent (stepfather or stepmother) consistently show that the teens raised in the patriarchal two-parent families with a stepparent actually have higher crime rates than those raised in a single-parent family (Rebellon 2002).

SUMMARY

Clearly violence by black youth and white youth is depicted very differently by the film industry and other media. Because violent white youth subcultures are connected to a mainstream American culture that loves violence and guns, the public is urged to turn its anger at white gun crimes like the Columbine shootings on the NRA and the gun industry rather than directing it at violent white youth cultures. Hence the solution to white youth violence becomes gun control.

Moreover, by turning his camera on crowds of law-abiding, mainstream white Americans calling for gun control after the Columbine school shooting, director Michael Moore manages to depict the white middle-class parents in his documentary as a self-interested public that is capable of forming an opinion about the conditions that have harmed their communities and organizing a protest to bring about changes in these conditions. Hence, despite the fact that the youth subcultures in their midst have brought violence and disorder into their schools, these white middle-class parents are not tempted to turn on their own children. And, because the solution to their problems with school violence and disorder is defined in terms of gun control and the reduction of bullying—and not violent white youth cultures—the police are not called in to wage a law-and-order campaign against their children in order to restore peace to the neighborhood.

By contrast, Hollywood constructs black youth violence as if it is disconnected from the white cultural mainstream. On screen, black gun violence is depicted as an outgrowth of conditions peculiar to black underclass neighborhoods where boys raised in single-parent families left unattended by their mothers are raised by violent and criminal gangs that prey on the community. Moreover, these roving bands of violent criminal youth are portrayed as having brought law-abiding adults in the black community to their knees.

This is because the black adults seen on screen seem to be incapable of forming a self-interested public that can identify the roles that racism and joblessness play in encouraging youth violence in their midst and mobilizing to bring about changes in these conditions. Indeed, it is because of their inaction that the police are needed to use crackdowns, arrests and incarceration to take back the streets from underclass black youth.

Instead of turning their anger on the gun industry, then, law-abiding black adults on screen can be seen turning their anger on the violent black youth in their midst and the black female-headed households that presumably produce all this youth violence. In place of simple gun control measures, then, solutions to gun violence in these Hollywood-inspired ghettos require the police to come in and take charge of the underclass.

However, as real-world incidents like recent black protests against the police slaying of Amadou Diallo or against the treatment of the Jena 6 indicate, black mothers and fathers have not turned against their children but rather have turned against many of the police crackdowns on their sons and daughters. These recent demonstrations indicate that much like their white counterparts, blacks in the real world can form a racially conscious, self-interested public that is capable of identifying the conditions that have harmed their communities and organizing a protest to bring about changes in these conditions.

NOTES

1. In talking about how adults in a neighborhood control youth, I draw upon Thornton's (1997) discussion of the neighborhood conditions that enable adults to exercise these controls.

2. Murder is also extremely rare even when one considers the most murder-prone age group of 18–24 year olds in isolation. Some 2,887 black males, aged 18–24, killed someone in 2006 out of a total population of approximately 1.6 million black males aged 18–24. Given that murder is so rare, some might argue that a count of serious (aggravated) assaults might provide a better measure of black violence. However, I chose murder over assaults because murder is better defined, more accurately counted and more accurately recorded than assaults. Moreover, ghetto action films often represent black males in terms of their homicides.

Chapter Four

Making Race Matter

How Criminologists Look at African Americans and Violence

In previous chapters, I considered how Hollywood depicts violent protests and interpersonal violence very differently based on race. Generally violence by blacks is treated as much more threatening than violence by whites. So, for example, the young black males who kill each other in ghetto action films to assert and defend their masculine honor are depicted as more dangerous than the two young white males at Columbine High School, who massacred their fellow students for similar reasons. This, despite the fact that one could make a case that the white violence at Columbine was actually much worse than the black violence portrayed in ghetto action movies.

Nevertheless, Hollywood and news media treat the Columbine shooting as simply a youthful manifestation of the larger American culture's love affair with guns and violence. Consequently, the violent acts of the two young white males at Columbine who slaughtered their classmates remains *unraced* In other words, the fact that they are white is rightfully treated as if it had nothing to do with their crimes.

By contrast, the black violence depicted in ghetto action films is *raced*. That is, the fact that the males involved in violence in these films are black is treated as if it has everything to do with their crimes as these movies make it seem as if only black males are capable of the kind of nonstop violence pictured on screen. The race of the young black males in ghetto action films is made to matter because the black violence dramatized for movie audiences is characterized as the outgrowth of an experience that is unique to blacks.

For the film industry, the most important experience in making blacks more prone to violence seems to be living in a lawless black ghetto. By treating the lawless ghetto as if it is another country that is separate and foreign from the American cultural mainstream, Hollywood has managed to convey the impression that a uniquely black psyche develops with an upbringing

129

in an underclass neighborhood. Consequently, black crime gets racialized in these films as separate black-specific motives, cultures and experiences get assigned to black criminals that set them apart from the larger American society.

The race of black criminals is also made to matter in other media as well since political campaigns and nightly news reports on crime also routinely type black males as criminals and black ghettos as the source of their criminality. In so doing, these media end up telling their audiences what it means to "be black" even as these same sources refrain from using crime to define what it means to "be white."

Of course, media outlets have their reasons for racializing black crime. Hollywood creates fictionalized accounts of black crime, not with an eye to accuracy, but with an eye to appealing to and entertaining the largest possible audience. Similarly, news organizations select the most sensational black crimes to report on as they seek to broaden their readership or increase their viewing audience. Politicians likewise focus on those crimes committed by blacks that are most likely to incite fear in the white voting public so that they can mobilize white supporters during election campaigns (D. Jones 2005; Reinarman and Levine 1997; Watkins 1998). Consequently, black criminality has increasingly become a way to talk about "race differences" in popular culture.

In explaining what sets blacks apart and makes them more prone to crime and violence than whites, most of these media outlets have relied on old fashioned culture-of-poverty arguments. Many of the culture-of-poverty arguments that underlie these popular cultural images of violent black males were originally developed by academics—specifically academic social scientists.

Social scientists have long used the culture of poverty to claim, first and foremost, that the poor are responsible for their own poverty because they have developed a culture that keeps them poor (Banfield 1970). In similar vein, social scientists—particularly criminologists—have also argued that the black poor have formed a black subculture of violence in which assaults and murders have become a legitimate cultural expression of black masculinity (Wolfgang and Ferracuti 1967; Luckenbill and Doyle 1989; Anderson 1990, 1994, Curtis 1975, Silberman 1978).[1]

Traditionally, criminologists have felt it was necessary to construct a black subculture of violence, because black males have such high violent crime rates. At this writing, black males have murder rates that are over seven times as high of those of white males and this huge race gap in homicides has existed for years (Bureau of Justice Statistics 2009).

Because blacks are more likely to commit violent crimes than whites, a number of criminologists assume that black violence is somehow different-in-kind from white violence. Therefore, in order to explain this long-standing race gap in violence, many criminologists racialize black violence by assigning separate motives, separate cultural value systems and separate experiences to black males that set them apart from other Americans. Yet when it comes to similar violent behavior by white males, criminologists typically do not consider race to be important at all.

Because criminologists only consider race to be important when explaining black violence, they end up doing a whole lot more than just offering explanations for why blacks have higher violent crime rates than whites. They, too, much like other media, also end up defining what it means to be black and explaining why "being black" makes a person more prone to violence. In this chapter, then, I examine how criminologists construct blackness in ways so as to give meaning to observed "race differences" in violence.

THE RACIAL ANALYSIS OF CRIME

Criminologists typically begin with the assumption that if black males are currently more than 7 times as likely to commit homicides as white males, then any theory that would explain this race gap must explain why blacks are 7 times as likely to be disposed to turn violent as whites. For the most part, then, theories explaining the race gap in crime have been *dispositional* theories as observed differences in crime have come to be equated with race differences in dispositions.

To construct a race difference in dispositions, black males first have to be lumped together on some character trait or set of conditions that somehow explains their increased propensity for violence. Furthermore any character trait or set of conditions selected to lump all blacks together must simultaneously distinguish blacks from whites in ways that make blacks more prone to violence than whites (Covington 1995, 1999; Covington 2003).

Clearly blacks can be lumped together and distinguished from whites based on their collective experience with a history of slavery and Jim Crow. A number of low-income blacks can also be lumped together and distinguished from whites based on their current experience with being segregated into socially isolated ghettos characterized by high unemployment, poorly funded schools and substandard housing.

Such historical and contemporary conditions allow blacks to be grouped together because blacks are the only ones to experience these conditions or they experience them disproportionately. These same sets of conditions also allow blacks to be distinguished from whites because whites have never experienced these historical and contemporary conditions or are far less likely to have done so than blacks.

Furthermore, these conditions have the advantage of being real, objective and measurable. For example, there are any number of historical accounts that document the separate and unequal treatment that blacks received under slavery and Jim Crow. Moreover, a number of social scientists routinely measure the extent to which blacks are currently isolated into ghettos with high unemployment, poor schools and substandard housing (Comer 1985; Curtis 1975; Silberman 1978; Wilson 1996; Massey and Denton 1993).

However, a problem lies in explaining how these macrolevel, anonymous social forces penetrate the hearts and minds of individual blacks and cause them to be predisposed to violence. In other words, it is not immediately apparent why a history of living with slavery and Jim Crow conditions or the experience of living in one of today's resource-poor ghettos might alter the black psyche in ways so as to predispose blacks to violent behaviors. One way that criminologists speculate that these anonymous historical and current social forces can insinuate themselves into the hearts and minds of individual blacks and incite them to turn violent is to argue that blacks have coped with these conditions by forming a black subculture of violence.

THE BLACK SUBCULTURE OF VIOLENCE

The black subculture of violence refers to a black culture within the larger culture that distinguishes itself by its members' predisposition to resort to violence. The black males, who make up these subcultures, subscribe to a set of values that make them more likely to assault or kill others over trivial matters such as threats to their masculine honor, insults aimed at their mothers ("playing the dozens") or being stared at too long (Wolfgang and Ferracuti 1967; Luckenbill and Doyle 1989; Anderson 1990).

A theoretical device like the black subculture of violence is useful for showing how large-scale anonymous social forces can insinuate themselves into the black mind-set and alter the value systems of individual blacks because the assumption is that blacks have created these uniquely violent subcultures as a way of adjusting to historical and contemporary racism. Because whites have not had to cope with racism and because most whites—especially middle-class whites—would presumably not assault or kill someone over such trivial provocations, subscribing to the values of a black subculture of violence not only lumps blacks together, it also distinguishes them from most whites.

Researchers who study the black subculture of violence claim that these subcultures tend to be located in black urban ghettos where male residents see violence as an appropriate response to trifling affronts (Wolfgang and Ferracuti 1967; Oliver 1994). Moreover, they argue that violent responses to trivial insults are typically reinforced by other males in the neighborhood as friends and by-standers in the ghetto routinely express admiration and respect for a man who is willing to assault or even kill someone who stares too long or jostles them or plays the dozens. They have also observed that black males who are willing to fight over any untoward gesture, stare or minor insult are typically proud of their reputations for fighting and experience no moral qualms about injuring or even killing someone who has offended them. Conversely, those males who fail to respond violently to trivial insults are subject to ostracism and constant bullying by other males in the community as they are likely to be seen as cowardly.

Luckenbill and Doyle (1989) sum it all up by arguing that the characteristic that most distinguishes this black subculture of violence from the white cultural mainstream is its disputatiousness. They claim that the black subculture of violence is disputatious because members of the subculture are more likely to see stares, jostles and insults as an injury to self and so "name" them. And, then, because of their increased tendency to name these trivial affronts as a basis for grievance, members of the subculture are more likely to "claim" reparations that typically require the person who has stared too long or jostled the claimant to apologize or back down. As both parties typically refuse to back down in a subculture of violence, these disputes generally escalate until they end in an assault or even a homicide.

However, none of these theorists means to imply that a disputatious subculture of violence is only found in black ghettos. There is ample evidence that there are white subcultures of violence where white males likewise get involved in "naming" trivial insults as injurious and "claiming" reparations for them. Historically, gunfights between the cowboys in the Old West followed this ritual of naming and claiming, and southern white males have long been known to be prone to such disputes over trivia as well (Gastil1971; Nisbett 1993). Still, it is commonly assumed that the personality trait of disputatiousness is most pronounced among black males in urban ghettos because males in these communities have traditionally had the highest rates of assaults and homicides in the country (Bureau of Justice Statistics 2009).

As a consequence, a number of theorists have taken on the task of trying to explain why black subcultures of violence have come to be more disputatious than even white subcultures of violence. One such explanation comes from Lynn Curtis.

Lynn Curtis and the Origins of the Black Subculture of Violence

Curtis (1975) argues that a greater desire to "name and claim" has penetrated the hearts and minds of black men in today's ghettos due to certain historical and contemporary social conditions.

Historically, he argues, black males had little personal autonomy during slavery and as a consequence, they developed a heightened sensitivity to any threats to their autonomy. This heightened sensitivity, then, became a part of the African American subculture and was passed on from one generation of blacks to the next as the personal autonomy of black males continued to be threatened during the Jim Crow era.

He suggests that black males also developed a heightened sensitivity to any threats to their personal autonomy because of their exposure to the white southern subculture of violence. First as slaves and then later during Jim Crow, he claims that the masses of blacks living in the south assimilated white southern traditions that defined masculinity in terms of a militaristic or warrior mentality, an exaggerated sense of honor, a strong weapons-carrying tradition and a willingness to pursue vigilante justice (Nisbett 1993; Gastil 1971).

As blacks migrated to northern urban ghettos—particularly during the massive black migration of the 1950s—Curtis argues that they took these slave and southern subcultural predilections for violence with them. Moreover, these violent cultural traditions did not simply die out in the urban north as conditions in the ghetto conspired to reinforce the need for the heightened sensitivities that had animated black male violence in the past. After all, as early as the 1950s, a number of inner-city black males in the north found themselves limited to menial, low-wage service jobs that required them to be docile.

According to Curtis, a number of black males in the ghetto rejected these jobs because they threatened their personal autonomy in ways reminiscent of slavery, resulting in high rates of black unemployment. Since the 1950s, these conditions have only worsened with deindustrialization as the exodus of manufacturing jobs has increasingly meant that menial service jobs are the only jobs left in the inner city (W. Wilson 1996).

For Curtis, then, black males limited to these jobs find that the only way that they can assert their personal autonomy and express their masculinity is through violence. Hence the kinds of exaggerated masculinities that are expressed in the black subculture of violence supposedly function to help black males collectively cope with their wounded egos when they cannot express the traditional male roles associated with being an employee in a high-paying job or a patriarchal head of household. Denied the authority, autonomy and respect that come with these mainstream masculine roles, black men seek to assert their masculinity by acquiring a violent reputation through the process of "naming and claiming." In so doing, they deflect attention from their failure in traditional masculine roles.

On its face, Curtis' theory does not seem to racialize as white males in the white subculture of violence can be said to express the same kinds of violent masculinities when they are confined to menial jobs that limit their personal autonomy. However, Curtis begins to racialize when he argues that the need for these violent masculine displays takes on a more exaggerated quality among black males than similarly placed white males, in part, because black males are far more likely to find themselves excluded from traditional masculine roles such as that of breadwinner or employee in a high-paying job. And, in fact, there is evidence to support this notion that black males have limited access to these traditional masculine roles as black male unemployment rates have usually been double those of white males since the 1950s (S. Walker 1990).

Unemployed black males are also said to be more inclined to be overly sensitive to slights than even unemployed white males because of the defensiveness they have acquired due to their slave history and their roots in the white southern subculture of violence. In addition, since the 1950s, inner-city black males have been concentrated in urban ghettos where they are surrounded by other black males who are likewise unemployed. Because ghettos have increasingly become places where a critical mass of black men are clustered together with other unemployed black men who are likely to name and claim, it is all too easy for the inclination to name and claim to receive constant reinforcement. Thus, it is this critical mass of compulsively masculine black males, all packed together in the ghetto, which is said to make the black subculture of violence even more disputatious than the white subculture of violence (see also Bernard 1990).

For these reasons, Curtis argues that black males socialized into these highly disputatious black subcultures of violence will be even more violent than white males socialized into a white subculture of violence. In short, he racializes violence by assigning a separate and more intense predisposition to violent black males than violent white males because of the additive effects of blacks' historical experiences with slave culture and the southern subculture of violence as well as their current experiences with high unemployment and living in ghettos where they are surrounded by a critical mass of other compulsively masculine black males.

Black Masculinity and the Black Subculture of Violence

In many ways, Curtis' theory serves as the template for a number of later theories on the black subculture of violence (see Covington 2003 for review of these theories.) For example, William Oliver (1994) likewise racializes black violence by suggesting that black males are more inclined than white males to express a compulsive masculinity that defines manhood in terms of toughness and autonomy.

For him, this black-specific tendency to equate masculinity with autonomy once again finds its roots in slavery when black males, supposedly, first acquired the desire to be free from any external controls. Having been passed on from one generation of black males to the next, this long-standing tendency to equate masculinity with autonomy today is said to find its expression in fights between black men who now equate trivial insults and efforts to provoke them with the age-old effort to control them. It is through their violent retaliations to trivial insults, then, that they signal their refusal to be ordered about like children and in so doing, assert their autonomy and masculinity.

However, Oliver goes on to suggest that the current black male experience with high levels of unemployment has had even more impact on shaping a ghetto-based compulsive masculinity than the slave past. Because widespread joblessness has made many black males incapable of meeting mainstream conceptions of appropriate masculine roles, Oliver surmises that they are forced to focus on the male roles that are available to them—namely, violent masculine roles. And, even though these violent masculinities can be expressed in acts of assault and homicide, Oliver rightly notes that such acts are rare. Instead, he suggests that black males more frequently express their commitment to the norms of toughness and autonomy through a "cool pose" that announces their fearlessness to would-be opponents (Majors and Mancini-Billson 1992).

This cool pose is typically demonstrated with facial gestures, a certain posture and a certain style of walking. By affecting this stance, black males are able to display a public masculinity that indicates that they are aloof, emotionally detached and in control. Black males are also said to conform to compulsive masculinity norms like toughness and autonomy by woofing or seeming to dare other men to fight them. Such dares and instigation also allow them to demonstrate their own toughness while intimidating any would-be opponents.

Oliver bases these notions on his observations of a sample of 41 black men affecting this cool pose in a black bar where trivial insults frequently escalate into fairly severe assaults. Over the course of his research, he estimates that the black men in his small sample were involved in 86 violent confrontations and an additional 30 violent arguments. And while he confines his observations of the black subculture of violence to this bar, he notes that the violent posturing, fights and intimidation that he describes are also common in other informal bar-like settings in the ghetto. Other bar-like settings include places such as after-hours joints, greasy spoon restaurants, gambling parlors, streetcorners, bar parking lots, crackhouses, heroin-shooting galleries, schools, and schoolyards (Roncek and Maier 1991; Goldstein et al. 1997; Anderson 1990).

Further, while Oliver acknowledges that white males likewise assault each other over trivial insults in white bars and bar-like settings (see, e.g., Katz

1988; Felson et al. 1986; Campbell 1986), he suggests that black males are more inclined to turn to violence because they take the talk and the gestures in a leisure-time setting like a bar a lot more seriously than whites.

For him, the fact that black males take the woofing, the dares and the intimidation that occur in black bars more seriously is because these gestures have more reputational implications for them than they do for whites. Unlike white males, who have more access to alternative settings like the family or the job to express masculine roles, black males frequently find that the bar is practically the only place where a masculine reputation can be won, sustained or lost. Moreover, the reputations that black males establish in bars and other leisure-time settings theoretically assume more significance for them because they have more impact on how a man is perceived outside the bar. For these reasons, then, the jockeying for masculine status is said to be much more intense in the black subculture of violence.

Anderson (1994) would seem to agree as he likewise claims that violent masculinities assume special significance for black males. Based on his observations in the ghetto, he argues that black men seem to compete in a zero sum game where one either wins or loses by the code of the streets by violently humiliating others or being violently humiliated. That he reduces black manhood to being a violent aggressor or a victim of violence has much to do with the fact that he describes few desirable masculinities for black men living in the ghetto other than those which involve bullying and assaulting others.

CRITIQUE: CONTRADICTORY FINDINGS IN BLACK SUBCULTURE OF VIOLENCE RESEARCH

In varying degree, these subculture-of-violence theorists suggest that black males are more inclined towards violence than white males because threats, assaults and murders are one of the only ways for them to express masculinity. However, there are a number of contradictory findings in their work that suggest that black males may not be nearly as obsessed with violent masculine expressions as these theorists claim.

For example, while the 41 black men in Oliver's ethnographic study were routinely involved in the fights and the woofing that are a hallmark of this subculture, he also found that the most violent males in the bar where he conducted his study had only been involved in 6 acts of violence. Given the constant intimidation and jockeying for masculine status going on in this bar, this figure seems low as it means that even the most violent of black men in his sample did not always retaliate with violence. And, in fact, some of these men reported that while they had been involved in fights over trivial insults in some instances, at other times they had been willing to walk away or simply smooth over the situation when confronted with the same trivial insults. If these violent black men were as preoccupied with defending their masculine reputations as this research suggests, it would seem that they would have consistently responded with violence to any and all provocations.

Furthermore, even when they did fight, the black men in his sample described their opponents as immature, insecure or resentful for starting a fight over what they themselves deemed to be trivial insults. The fact that even violent black men could suggest that fighting over trivia was an indicator of immaturity, insecurity or resentment also raises doubts about whether violent retaliation in the face of provocation is always seen as a desirable expression of masculinity.

Finally, even when two men were willing to pummel each other over trivial insults, third parties often stepped in, defused the tensions and stopped the fight. The fact that third parties were able to stop fights coupled with the fact that some of the same men who fought were also able to walk away from some fights suggests that a refusal to fight might not necessarily have condemned these men to certain ostracism and future bullying from other men in the neighborhood as the black subculture of violence theorists argue. At the very least, such findings point to the need to determine how these black men retained their masculine honor after refusing a fight.

The Problem of Incomplete Cultures

Taken together, these contradictory findings certainly raise the possibility that there might be other nonviolent definitions of masculinity that directly compete with violent conceptions of maleness in the ghetto. Yet, the possibility that black males might be equally preoccupied with competing nonviolent definitions of masculinity is not considered in this research because the black-subculture-of-violence theorists only define masculinity in terms of the values, attitudes and beliefs that encourage violent behaviors.

However, men in the ghetto do not simply get involved in barroom brawls; they also work, vote, have families, go to school, worship and become involved in a variety of other activities. Hence, a complete description of ghetto culture should consider the values and norms that ghetto residents have developed to govern these other activities. At the very least, a complete description of ghetto-based subcultures should include some mention of men's values towards work as conceptions of masculinity are, in part, shaped by a man's work. Yet the subculture-of-violence theorists fail to consider the kinds of masculinities that black males develop in work environments.

Furthermore, a complete description of ghetto-based definitions of manhood should also consider the political values of black males. After all, as noted in previous chapters, black males have increasingly developed a masculinity based on resistance to racism, particularly since the 1960s (Connor 1995). Yet the woefully incomplete picture of ghetto culture presented by these subculture-of-violence theorists also does not consider political beliefs in the ghetto and any role they might play in shaping notions of black masculinity.

For these reasons, then, the role of work values and political values in shaping black masculinity will be considered in the following sections in an effort to determine whether these values somehow complement or compete with the values and norms of the black subculture of violence.

Ghetto-Based Masculinities and Work Values

One reason that black-subculture-of-violence theorists have long minimized the significance of any masculinities that black males might develop as workers is because they claim that black males in the ghetto do not find that the menial low-paying jobs available to them can enhance their masculine reputations. Indeed, Curtis (1975) goes so far as to suggest that many black males find these jobs to be reminiscent of slavery because they threaten their personal autonomy.

However, in her research, Katherine Newman (1999) speaks to the potential importance of black work values in Harlem, where as many as 69 percent of the adults were working at the time of her study. Just the fact that so many people worked in this ghetto-based study suggests that work values might play a more important role in shaping black masculinities than the subculture-of-violence theorists have suggested.

To determine how blacks in Harlem felt about work, Newman interviewed employees at a local fast-food restaurant that she called Burger Barn. Working at Burger Barn meant employment in the very types of menial, low-wage jobs that subculture-of-violence theorists claim that black males reject. Hence, it comes as no surprise that Newman was able to confirm that Burger Barn jobs were, in fact, stigmatized in the community because they were seen as dead-end jobs with low pay that required workers to defer to Burger Barn customers. The fact that Burger Barn workers had to work around grease and wear uniforms and hairnets rather than the latest fashion styles made these jobs seem undesirable as well.

Consistent with the claims of the subculture-of-violence theorists, a number of the local hustlers and drug dealers, who were probably members of Harlem's black subculture of violence, routinely reminded Burger Barn employees of their servile positions whenever they patronized the restaurant. However, in reaction to these insults, Newman argues that the Burger Barn workers formed a rebuttal culture amongst themselves in which they defined being a worker—even if it meant menial work—as far preferable to being a nonworker like the hustlers and drug dealers who came into the restaurant. While they did not have wads of cash to flash like the criminals, many Burger Barn workers saw themselves as morally superior to the nonworkers in the criminal underworld because they equated work—even low-wage work—with noneconomic, moral virtues such as dignity, self-discipline, maturity and responsibility.

Many of these workers also looked upon the nonworkers in the criminal underworld with contempt because they felt that no one deserved a free ride. Because they worked, they felt that they deserved respect and deference from the nonworking hustlers and drug dealers, who were trying to get something for nothing.

Because there were so many fast-food workers around, they were able to provide the critical mass needed to sustain these rebuttal work cultures in the ghetto. In other words, men who worked at Burger Barn were able to surround themselves with other Burger Barn workers, who reinforced them in their rejection of violent criminal lifestyles and provided them with an alternative nonviolent definition of manhood. Such worker-based rebuttal cultures also made it possible for local juveniles to choose menial jobs over violent criminal lifestyles by maturing into these rebuttal cultures as they aged out of the violent delinquency of their teen years. Hence, the fact that there were a number of ghetto males employed in these competing nonviolent work cultures suggests that socialization into manhood in the ghetto did not necessarily require the assimilation of definitions of masculinity that require fighting and a penchant for intimidation.

Black Masculinity and Political Beliefs

With their incomplete picture of ghetto subcultures, black-subculture-of-violence theorists also fail to examine the kinds of masculinities that black males have developed in the course of acquiring their political beliefs. However, particularly since the 1960s, black men have developed political beliefs that define masculinity in terms of protest against the racist conditions that surround them (Connor 1995).

The process of adopting such protest masculinities typically begins when black men become conscious of the role of white oppression in limiting their employment opportunities and in segregating them into dilapidated, resource-poor ghettos. Once racism is recognized as the source of many ghetto problems, achieving black manhood comes to be equated with joining with other blacks in racial solidarity to protest for better jobs, better housing and other improvements in black communities.

Because men who define masculinity in terms of political protest regard the kind of black-on-black violence that is revered in the black subculture of violence as anathema to the black community, assimilating a protest masculinity would likely motivate black men to condemn the kinds of violence they see in ghetto bars and on street corners as undermining racial solidarity. Perhaps this explains some of the contradictory findings from Oliver's (1994) research that show that some black males are able to stop a fight even in a bar where the violent defense of masculine reputations is common and accepted.

Because black masculinity can be defined by these competing nonviolent definitions of manhood, the ghetto-based subcultures described by Anderson (1990, 1994) likewise seem to be simplistic and incomplete. According to him, the ghetto-based code of the streets, defines a man as a winner if he is routinely violent or as a loser if he is nonviolent and backs down from a fight. However, by suggesting that black males rank each other solely in terms of this violent code of the streets, he ignores these other nonviolent definitions of masculinity in which black males appraise each other in terms of their willingness to reject such black-on-black violence.

In short, because the subculture-of-violence theories assume that masculine reputations rise or fall based on violence, they ignore the contribution that work values and political values make in shaping black masculinities. And, because they present readers with such limited conceptions of how black masculinity is constructed, the black males in their theories are presented with only one choice, namely choosing violent masculinities.

Because they overlook other nonviolent forms of masculinity, these theorists manage to make the violent masculinities shaped by the black subculture of violence seem much more compelling than they really are. Apparently, though, black males have managed to develop competing definitions of manhood that carry equal or greater weight.

VIOLENCE AND THE PSYCHOLOGICALLY DAMAGED BLACK MALE

Clearly, the subculture-of-violence theorists bridge the gap between anonymous, macrolevel historical and contemporary forces and the individual black male's disposition to violence by describing a black subculture of violence that shapes blacks' fundamental values, attitudes and beliefs about the nature of masculinity.

Another set of theories which shows how these anonymous, macrolevel historical and contemporary social forces can somehow penetrate the hearts and minds of individual blacks are those that claim that black men have coped

with historical and contemporary racism by developing psychological characteristics that predispose them to a self-destructive cycle of black-on-black
violence. Hence, such theories lump blacks together into a black psychological monolith based on their shared emotional reactions to racism. In so doing,
these theories also distinguish them from whites.

Racial Self-Hatred and the Damaged Black Psyche

Poussaint (1983) offers one explanation for why the exaggerated disputatiousness found in the ghetto subculture of violence might lie in the unique psychology of the black experience. He suggests that one unfortunate condition of living in a racially stratified society is the enduring exposure to negative images of
blackness. He surmises that blacks react by internalizing these negative images
and as a consequence are inclined to hate themselves because they are black.
This black self-hatred is also accompanied by group hatred in which blacks also
hate and denigrate other blacks because of their blackness.

Experiencing emotions such as racial self-hatred and racial hatred of other
blacks is, then, said to lower the threshold for violence among blacks thereby
enabling them to lash out at each other over even the most trivial of insults.
Hence, black racial hatred directed at other blacks presumably allows blacks
to injure other blacks without guilt because by assaulting or even killing each
other, blacks are able to project their own self-hatred onto other blacks.

Clearly, then, for Poussaint, racial oppression has scarred blacks emotionally and psychologically in ways that make them more prone to violence than
whites. This means that even when blacks and whites assault and kill others
in similar ways, for Poussaint at least, the blacks who commit these violent
acts are motivated by different underlying emotions than whites—despite
any surface similarities. Because, he suggests that only blacks lash out with
violence to grapple with their feelings of racial self-hatred and racial group
hatred, black violence is raced. In other words, only blacks can be said to be
"doing race" when they assault and kill each other because it is their way
of coping with feelings of racial self-hatred. By contrast, white-on-white
violence is not raced because it is not a manifestation of underlying feelings
regarding white racial identity.

Racial Inequality and the Damaged Black Psyche

Poussaint is not alone in explaining black violence in terms of a unique black
psychological makeup. Blau and Blau (1982) also argue that the black psyche
has been damaged by its exposure to conditions of racial inequality. By racial
inequality, they mean that, on average, blacks make less money than whites,

have less education, live in poorer housing and experience inequalities in other aspects of their lives relative to whites as well.

In and of themselves, such inequalities do not distinguish blacks from working-class and low-income whites who have less education, lower income and less desirable housing than middle- and upper-income whites. And, in fact, a number of criminologists argue that all working-class and low-income persons—black and white alike—are likely to become angry and frustrated in the face of all the wealth that surrounds them and turn to property crimes and violence to cope with their frustrations. However, racial inequality theorists argue that racial inequality is more likely to lead to a perception of injustice than class inequality and is thus better suited to generate the feelings of anger, frustration and resentment that lead to violent aggression (Blau and Blau 1982; Balkwell 1990).

In part, racial inequalities are believed to have a more profound impact on the psyche than class inequalities because class inequalities are more easily defended in societies that define themselves as egalitarian such as the United States. In egalitarian societies, it is assumed that everyone can achieve wealth because the public school system provides children from all social classes with the skills required for high-paying, prestigious occupations.

Presumably, because many Americans believe that high incomes are achieved due to individual effort, it is possible for them to accept the notion that middle- and upper-class persons deserve their higher incomes, better housing and higher class status because they made the individual effort to acquire the necessary skills. If high-status persons are believed to be deserving of their status due to effort, then low-income and working-class people may not be resentful of their wealth. Instead, low income and working class people could conceivably hold themselves responsible for their lower class status because they failed to acquire the educational skills needed to obtain high-powered jobs and higher incomes.

However, in contrast to class status which is presumably based on achievement, race (also gender) is an ascribed status. In other words, one is defined as black or white at conception and no amount of achievement changes the racial status assigned to one at birth. For that reason, racial inequalities are likely to be seen as the product of a system of racial discrimination that doles out income, housing, political rights and a host of other goods not on the basis of skills or achievements, but on the basis of an ascribed inferior social status like race.

In a democracy, where all persons are presumably created equal, depriving one group based on ascribed inferiority like race is generally seen as illegitimate. For that reason, racial inequality theorists lump blacks together and distinguish them from whites—even working-class and low-income whites—based on blacks' unique experience with racial inequalities that have been widely discredited.

In fact, there is some evidence that majorities of the black population see a system of racial stratification in place and perceive the racial inequalities that flow from it as illegitimate. For example, a survey conducted in the 1980s showed that fully 64 percent to 70 percent of the black population felt that blacks had worse jobs, income and housing than whites due to racial discrimination (Sigelman and Welch 1994). Moreover, as many as three-quarters of the African Americans surveyed felt that blacks were not achieving as fast as they could because many whites did not want them to get ahead.

However, the fact that blacks see racial inequalities as illegitimate presents racial inequality theorists with a dilemma. If blacks commit crimes because they are angry over racial oppression and the limits it places on their life chances, it is unclear why they would commit violent crimes like assaults and murders which do not improve their life chances. It is likewise unclear why they would attack other blacks instead of whites whom they see as the source of their problems.

To resolve these problems, racial inequality theorists have treated blacks as if they were part of a psychically damaged monolith. They suggest that blacks uniformly cope with racism by displacing their rage at distant and powerful whites into acts of violent aggression acted out against proximate and powerless blacks. Without this notion of displaced aggression, it would be difficult to see how black-on-black violence had much to do with black perceptions of racial inequality.

Hence, racial inequality theorists racialize crime by arguing that blacks' unique experience with living under racist conditions—conditions which they share with other blacks and which distinguish them from whites—has altered them emotionally making them more prone to violence. Blau and Blau (1982:119) describe the black emotional reaction to racial inequality in the following fashion:

> A realistic reaction of the underprivileged (i.e., blacks) would be to organize collective violence to overthrow the existing order and redistribute resources . . . However, the very differences manifested in great inequalities tend to deprive the lower strata of the strength and resources to organize successful collective action. . . . Coser (1968) notes that the conflict of interest that cannot find realistic expression in striving to achieve desired goals frequently finds expression as "nonrealistic conflict" by which he means diffuse aggression, with people being more driven by hostile impulses than governed by rational pursuit of their interests. It is such diffuse hostility that ascriptive inequalities engender and that criminal violence manifest . . . Ascriptive socioeconomic inequalities undermine the social integration of a community.

In short, they claim that because blacks lack the strength and resources to target the actual sources of the racial inequalities they experience (i.e., whites, white power elite), they become angry and hostile and lash out at other blacks. Blacks are also said to turn on other blacks rather than whites because so many live in racially segregated neighborhoods where white targets are not available. Furthermore, they are likely to target other blacks rather than whites because they realize that if they were to strike out at whites, they would be punished more severely. Balkwell (1990: 56–57) describes this dilemma in the following fashion:

> And (for blacks) to dispute the outcome of a conflict (with whites) would be to invite reprisals which would be likely to leave the person worse off than before. Under such conditions, the members of disadvantaged groups learn to put up with indignities (from whites) to contain their anger. Recurrent indignities that a person dares not protest promote a state of affairs in which aggressive impulses are likely to be frequent and strong, and vented against substitute targets, who are accessible and relatively powerless to strike back. The person who feels victimized in countless ways, large and small, is likely to have a short fuse in dealing with others, including his or her own family and friends.

For Balkwell, the inability to lash out at whites who routinely discriminate against them only exacerbates the situation by creating even more powerful aggressive impulses in blacks. And, because they dare not vent their rage on whites, blacks are forced to go in search of substitute targets, who are accessible and powerless including friends and family members. Even worse, the fact that blacks, angry over racial inequities, so frequently launch attacks on those near and dear bodes ill for black communities as it means that these neighborhoods are little more than an assemblage of residents primed to lash out at their neighbors.

Indeed Bernard (1990) describes urban ghettos as communities in which individuals live in close proximity to others who are in a nearly constant state of physiological arousal that he calls angry aggression. He argues that, in part, this heightened physiological arousal among urban poor blacks stems from the crowding, noise and limited recreational space that characterize urban living. As he sees it, these stresses of urban living are further compounded by the stresses associated with a lack of power and money that come from being in a low social position.

Although these conditions hardly distinguish urban poor blacks from urban poor whites, Bernard suggests that physiological arousal is more highly elevated among urban blacks because they also experience the stressors associated with living in a society that intentionally seeks to harm them through acts of racial discrimination. Therefore, he claims that individual blacks living in this highly elevated state of arousal are more prone to aggress and to develop rules that justify their anger and aggression towards their victims.

Much like the racial inequality theorists, Bernard also suggests that blacks are typically angry at whites but inclined to displace their anger onto other blacks because blacks are more accessible and more vulnerable. Hence in the course of justifying their anger and their aggression towards their victims, Bernard claims that blacks develop cultural rules that make it legitimate to transfer their anger at whites to proximate black victims. This bodes ill for black communities as it means that they are made up of a concentration of angrily aggressive individuals who are inclined to lash out at their neighbors. In such an environment, the rules for violence endlessly expand as more persons and situations are seen as sufficiently threatening to justify violent retaliation.

According to Bernard, the levels of injury required to satisfy those black males, who feel threatened, also spiral higher and higher in these communities making for ever more severe forms of violence. Hence, for him, the presence of a critical mass of angrily aggressive black individuals in an urban ghetto allows a subculture of angry aggression to form as the expanded rules for violence take on a life of their own. That they take on a life of their own is supposedly demonstrated by the fact that the expanded rules for violence get transmitted from one aroused ghetto resident to another and from one generation of black males to another through constant reinforcement.

PROBLEMS WITH RESEARCH ON THE PSYCHICALLY DAMAGED BLACK MALE

In order to determine if these theories work in the real world, criminologists try to figure out if there is a link between macrostructural measures of racial inequality and violence (Blau and Blau 1982; Balkwell 1990; Messner and Golden 1992). Racial inequality is typically measured as the average aggregate difference between blacks and whites in terms of their incomes or some combination of race differences in average income, education and occupation. Most studies rely on census measures to compute racial inequalities in aggregate income, education and occupation and then use arrest data to compute rates of violence (assaults and murders) in black and white communities. While the results from this research are inconsistent, some studies do show that those neighborhoods, cities or metropolitan areas with greater racial inequalities between blacks and whites also have higher black violent crime rates (Covington 1997; Krivio and Peterson 2000). And, each study that shows that greater racial inequalities are linked to higher black violent crime rates seems to provide additional social scientific proof that blacks are displacing their rage at whites into acts of violence aimed at other blacks.

Unfortunately, with this type of large-scale data (census data, arrest data) it is impossible to determine if exposure to these conditions of racial inequality actually penetrate the hearts and minds of individual blacks. Because these studies do not measure the actual attitudes of individual blacks towards racial inequality, it is unclear whether the blacks who are most resentful of racial inequalities are also the ones who are lashing out at other black people around them, as these theories suggest.

Hence, this research cannot confirm whether or not the murders, barroom brawls, gang fights and other acts of violence that plague the nation's ghettos are actually governed by internal emotions such as displaced rage at racial inequalities. For that reason, criminologists who do this type of macrolevel research have had to infer what goes on in the innermost recesses of black minds in the face of racial inequalities.

Not too surprisingly, the black self they have inferred is one which 1) is highly conscious of racial inequalities, 2) uniformly sees them as unjust, 3) experiences diffuse unfocused feelings of anger, resentment and frustration in the face of these inequalities and 4) routinely acts upon these heightened feelings of unfocused rage with aggressive behaviors aimed at relatively powerless black neighbors, friends and significant others. In other words, racial inequality theorists have constructed a black self that best fits their theory. And, because the black self they construct is based on mere inference, racial inequality theorists have enormous leeway to merely intuit a conception of black emotionality that enables them to make the necessary connections between their macrostructural indicators of racial inequality and violent crime rates.

Furthermore, because the black self imagined in these theories only copes in one way with racial inequalities—i.e., by turning to violence—this theory has the effect of treating blacks as a psychically damaged monolith. Unfortunately, this unresearched conception of the angrily aggressive black self is the weakest link in the theoretical chain because it is merely inferred. It is also the site at which racialization occurs as psychological traits, emotional makeup and moral character peculiar to African Americans are defined.

Yet, no matter how weakly supported their conceptions of the black self are, racial inequality theorists conclude that the black-on-black cycle of violence can be understood as a type of indirect and dysfunctional black resistance to white oppression. And, because they depict black violence as a kind of unrealistic racial conflict which is unconsciously and indirectly aimed at whites, blacks can be said to be "doing race" when they assault and kill their black friends, relatives and neighbors.

Hence, black violence is raced in racial inequality theories. By contrast, when whites assault and kill their white friends, relatives and neighbors, they are not seen as reacting to similar deprivations based on their race. In other words, because white racial status makes whites members of the "superior" race, it cannot possibly generate the kind of anger and frustration that would lead whites to lash out at other whites because of racial self-hatred. Therefore, white-on-white violence remains unraced with racial inequality theories.

Based on this perspective, most black murders could easily be attributed to displaced rage at whites as murder is an intraracial crime. In other words, 94 percent of black murder victims are killed by other blacks, while 86 percent of white murder victims are killed by other whites (Bureau of Justice Statistics 2009). However, a more likely explanation for this preponderance of black-on-black and white-on-white assaults and murders is the fact that violent black and white males have more access to victims of the same race in bars, on street corners and in rival gangs because the United States is a racially segregated society.

However, because the impulse violence of black males is explained by racial inequality theorists in terms of unique psychological functions not found in other race and ethnic groups, black males seem different from the rest of us. Simply put, the willingness of black males to injure and kill others because of their peculiarly dysfunctional makeup makes them seem more unpredictable and lacking in humanity than other Americans.

Moreover, by constructing a displaced aggression that is found only among blacks, these theorists not only explain race differences in violence, they also end up providing their readers with a theory of race-differentness. In other words, because they identify traits which define blacks as psychologically different from whites, they also end up telling their readers what it means to "be black." Of course, one byproduct of such thinking is that racial inequality theorists explain violence in different terms if the perpetrators are black as opposed to white. In other words, assaults and homicides by black men are described as acts of displaced racial aggression, while similar assaults and homicides by white males are typically seen as an effort to defend American notions of masculine honor.

COMMONALITIES BETWEEN BLACK SUBCULTURE OF VIOLENCE THEORIES AND RACIAL INEQUALITY THEORIES

In many respects, the blacks conceived of by racial inequality theorists are similar to those constructed by the black-subculture-of-violence theorists in that both argue that blacks have been damaged by their experience with white oppression. According to the racial inequality theorists, blacks have been broken emotionally and psychologically by racism, while the black-subculture-of-violence theorists argue that racism has so thwarted black men in their capacity to occupy mainstream masculine roles, that they have created self-destructive subcultures in which only violent masculinities get expressed.

Hence, in both theoretical traditions, blacks are constructed as morally, culturally and psychologically inferior to whites who have not been similarly impaired by racial oppression. Because these theorists describe blacks as damaged relative to "normal" whites, they reinforce the widespread belief in a racial hierarchy which defines whites as the moral, cultural and emotional superiors of damaged African Americans.

Theorizing about traits such as racially displaced aggression, racial self-hatred, angry aggression or the disputatiousness of the black subculture of violence and their role in producing black-on-black violence, then, becomes a way of drawing racial boundaries. After all, the seeming existence of these traits confirms that the residents of violent black ghettos exist in a world that is morally separate and apart from the white cultural mainstream. Indeed, because the blacks described in these theories are willing to countenance violence against their fellow blacks, they come across as denizens of an alien society (i.e., the ghetto), where a war of all against all is constantly being waged.

Because the theorists reviewed in this chapter expend so much effort in explaining how whole communities of black men have been rendered self-destructive by their rage at racism and their stunted masculinities, condemning the self-destructive violence in these communities—and the black rage and the stunted masculinities that presumably cause it—becomes the whole point of these analyses. These theories, then, have the effect of diverting attention away from the white oppression that has presumably led to black violence in these communities by focusing on the demonization of these communities instead.

For all of these theorists, then, living with racial oppression is disabling because it divides and atomizes the black community. Yet Cross and Strauss (1998) question whether black communities have been atomized because the bonds between African Americans have been destroyed by racism. While they acknowledge that the assumption that blacks merely accept and internalize the racially stigmatized images assigned to them is one that has been part of the social scientific discourse since the 1930s, they are fairly critical of this notion.

By way of rebuttal, they quote the well-known African American writer and anthropologist Zora Neale Hurston. In a collection of her works titled, *I Love Myself When I Am Laughing* (A. Walker 1979:153), Hurston wrote:

But I am not tragically colored. There is no great sorrow damned up in my soul, nor lurking behind my eyes. I do not mind at all. I do not belong to the sobbing

school of Negrohood who hold that nature somehow has given them a lowdown
dirty deal and whose feelings are all hurt about it. Even in the helter-skelter
skirmish that is my life, I have seen that the world is to the strong regardless of
a little pigmentation more or less.

Cross and Strauss go on to question the assumption that blacks are somehow "tragically colored" in more social scientific terms by arguing that blacks
may not simply accept and internalize negative images of themselves coming
from the larger society. Instead of atomizing black communities by causing
blacks to hate themselves and each other, they claim that negative images
of blackness may actually strengthen ties between blacks by causing them
to bond more closely with each other. In other words, by joining with other
African Americans for solidarity and social support, blacks may find that they
are better able to counter stigmatizing assaults from the white mainstream.

Indeed, for Cross and Strauss, blacks living in close proximity to other blacks,
who are similarly exposed to racial inequalities, might actually find that being
surrounded by other blacks relieves tensions. For example, having black neighbors, family members and friends may help African Americans bear up under
the strains of living in a racially hostile society by providing them with an outlet
to discuss, commiserate and solve problems associated with racial oppression.

Unfortunately, racial inequality and racial self-hatred theorists rule out
these possibilities by assuming that blacks automatically accept and internalize negative images of themselves. In so doing, they depict blacks as though
they are not in the least bit self-reflective. For these theorists, the experience
of living in a racially oppressive society is so overwhelming that it reduces
individual blacks to little more than a bundle of resentments, suppressed
hatreds, anger and suffering. For this reason, the blacks they describe are incapable of standing back from white racism, judging it, exploring it and then
proceeding to condemn it.

Because the blacks in racial inequality and racial self-hatred theories are
represented as little more than bundles of seething rage, they are unable to stop
themselves from committing self-destructive acts that do nothing to solve their
problems with white oppression. For that reason, racial inequality and racial
self-hatred theorists can claim that blacks are engaged in a kind of "unrealistic
conflict" that causes them to lash out at other blacks as an indirect way of attacking whites. However, it is important to remember that their constructions of
the black psyche have been inferred rather than actually observed.

Realistic Conflict and Black Voting Behaviors

Instead of inferring a black psyche that has been damaged by racial oppression, it might be better to get a handle on how blacks actually cope

with racial inequality by observing how they react to real-word incidents of discrimination. When such real-world situations are examined, there is considerable evidence of blacks' capacity for "realistic conflict." For one thing, the historical record indicates that blacks were fully capable of realistic conflict in their efforts to rid themselves of racial inequalities during the civil rights movement and the black power era of the 1950s, 1960s and 1970s.

Even today, blacks continue to demonstrate a capacity for realistic conflict as there are numerous recent examples of them bonding together with other blacks to voice their opposition to police brutality, racial intimidation, job discrimination, residential segregation and a whole host of other problems. (For examples, see chapters 2 and 3.) Indeed, given their record of protesting racial injustice, it is possible that blacks are more capable of realistic conflict than working-class and low-income whites. There is some evidence of this in black voting behaviors.

At least since the 1960s, large majorities of the black population have routinely voted for the Democratic Party, in part, because Democrats have historically been more inclined to support their economic and political interests than Republicans. For example, blacks achieved many of the rights that they sought during nonviolent demonstrations in the 1950s and 1960s because members of the Democratic Party passed legislation to guarantee black voting rights and then made a short-lived attempt to expand social programs that would help the black poor.

In the post-civil rights era, then, blacks have been more likely to support Democratic candidates than any other sociodemographic group because they see Democrats as more inclined to address their political and economic interests. This is clearly indicated by their recent voting behaviors as 88 percent of blacks voted for John Kerry in the 2004 presidential election and 90 percent supported Al Gore in the 2000 presidential election (Langer 2008; *New York Times* 2008).

Blacks have remained loyal to Democratic candidates not just because of longstanding Democratic support for their civil rights, but because they have tended to appeal to their economic interests as well. This was especially apparent in the 2008 presidential election when the Democratic nominee, Barack Obama, made voters' economic concerns the centerpiece of his campaign. In a time of growing economic crisis, as housing foreclosures and unemployment rates spiraled upward for Americans of all races, he promised to set up programs to help struggling homeowners and the unemployed (Calmes and Zeleny 2008).[2] Blacks responded enthusiastically to Obama's appeals to their economic concerns as fully 95 percent of blacks voted for him in the election (*New York Times* 2008).

The fact that millions of black males voted their economic concerns poses a problem for black-subculture-of-violence theorists because they fail to consider the work values and political beliefs of black males. Yet, because so many black males responded to Obama—and to Democratic candidates before him—who appealed to them by promising job creation, there is every reason to believe that many black males still define manhood in terms of living-wage work.

To be sure, Obama's appeal to black males also had a lot to do with the fact that he is black. However, the very fact that millions of black men turned out to support him also makes it difficult to give much credence to racial self-hatred theories that suggest that blacks hate themselves and other blacks. To the extent that their 2008 vote reflects an act of racial solidarity, there is reason to question the notion that blacks have necessarily internalized negative stereotypes of blackness from the larger society *en masse* and come to hate themselves and other blacks as a result.

Certainly, it could be argued that much of this black support for Obama came from older blacks, who are the least violent segment of the black population. However, even record numbers of blacks in the most violence-prone age-groups turned out to support Obama. Specifically, 2008 election turnout results indicate that fully 58.2 percent of blacks aged 18–29 who were eligible to vote showed up at the polls (Lopez and Taylor 2009). This is a very high turnout rate for young people in that age group and represents an 8.7 percentage point increase in turnout among young black voters over the 2004 election. Indeed, because so many young black voters showed up at the polls in 2008, their turnout rates surpassed those of 18–29 year old whites, Hispanics and Asian Americans. At the very least, figures like these suggest that claims of widespread black self-hatred and racial hatred should be greeted with skepticism.

Finally, the fact that blacks routinely vote in terms of their economic interests—both historically and in the 2008 election—also raises doubts about racial inequality theories. Racial inequality theories suggest that blacks are incapable of the kind of realistic conflict that would help them to collectively grapple with the obstacles to jobs, decent housing and quality schools that racial discrimination puts in their path (Blau and Blau 1982; Balkwell 1990). Yet, their willingness to vote as a bloc for candidates who support the lifting of these barriers suggests that they are still quite capable of realistic conflict.

White Voters and Realistic Conflict

Ironically, if voting behaviors are any indication, it is white voters who are incapable of realistic conflict. By the time of the 2008 election, white working-class and middle-class voters—much like black voters—were in the midst of an economic crisis as they saw their home foreclosure and unemployment rates soar. Yet, despite candidate Obama's appeals to their economic interests, he won only 43 percent of the white vote—a percent akin to the 41 percent of the white vote garnered by Democrat John Kerry in 2004 and the 42 percent of the white vote won by Democrat Al Gore in 2000 when there was no severe economic downturn (*New York Times* 2008).

That the majority of white voters supported the Republican candidate, John McCain, in the midst of a severe economic recession suggests that they were not inclined towards the kind of realistic conflict that would have involved them collectively behaving in ways that helped them to address obstacles to their economic recovery. After all, candidate McCain proved to be fairly ineffective at addressing their economic concerns.

For example, when it looked as if the financial industry was about to collapse in September of 2008, McCain temporarily suspended his campaign and postponed his first debate with Obama. He defended this seemingly impulsive move by claiming that the interruption was necessary in order for him to broker a solution to the financial crisis. However, a few days later, he rather awkwardly restarted his campaign and showed up at the debate even though he had failed to come up with a solution to the crisis (Nagourney and Bumiller 2008; Bumiller and Cooper 2008).

Yet, despite the fact that McCain failed to address the anxieties of white working- and middle-class voters reeling from rising unemployment and home foreclosure rates, he managed to win 55 percent of the white vote. He won over the majority of white voters by appealing to their cultural concerns rather than their economic interests. And, in fact, Republicans have long been able to win elections by making an appeal to white voters' cultural values rather than pocketbook issues. So, for example, George W. Bush managed to beat John Kerry 58 percent to 41 percent among white voters and Al Gore by 54 percent to 42 percent among white voters by garnering the support of socially conservative whites concerned about values (Martin 2008a; *New York Times* 2008).

Recognizing the importance of courting social conservatives, Republican candidate John McCain selected Alaska Governor Sarah Palin as his running mate during the 2008 campaign in order to signal to these voters that he embraced their values. Governor Palin had special appeal to conservative white voters, in part, because her decision to have a baby that she knew would be born with Down syndrome indicated a profound desire to live in accordance with conservative anti-abortion values (Vandehei and Kuhn 2008). Her history of moose hunting also endeared her to the many values voters who favored gun rights. Moreover, her support for the teaching of creationism in the public schools and for assigning religion a more prominent place in public life also enabled her to generate enthusiasm among conservatives for the GOP ticket. Basically, then, the Republican election strategy in 2008 involved waging a culture war against groups disliked by their socially conservative base (e.g., pro-choice groups, gun control organizations, etc.). They even managed to mount attacks against anti-Vietnam war radicals from the 1960s (Sinker 2008).

All in all, then, the majority of the white electorate in 2008 seemed to vote based on emotions like diffuse aggression that racial inequality theorists have traditionally attributed to blacks. In other words, many seem to have been driven by their hostile impulses towards those who did not share their values rather than by rational pursuit of their interests.

Of course, much white support for the GOP—and much black opposition to it—has long been based on the fact that the Republican Party has a history of appealing to white racial animus towards blacks in order to mobilize support. By running campaigns that focus on white fear of black crime, the Republican Party has been able to sow the seeds of racial hatred and division. So, for example, George H. W. Bush won the white vote by an impressive 19–point margin in 1988 by appealing to white fears that his Democratic opponent, Michael Dukakis, would be soft on black criminals like Willie Horton. And Ronald Reagan appealed to white fears that blacks benefited unduly from government programs offering "special privileges" with his talk of black welfare queens. Such appeals, made on racial grounds, helped him to win 56 percent and 64 percent of the white vote in 1980 and 1984 respectively.

While none of these policies served white economic interests, they did allow conservative white voters to symbolically lash out at blacks by voting for cuts in programs that were framed as primarily benefiting blacks—particularly at a time when blacks were thought to be the beneficiaries of too many "special privileges" left over from the 1960s.

Race may also have played a significant, if somewhat closeted, role in the 2008 campaign—particularly among the 29 percent of white voters who were deemed to be less racially sensitive. These less racially sensitive white voters were those who described themselves as harboring feelings of racial prejudice, having no interracial friendships and as not believing that blacks experienced any real discrimination (Langer 2008). Fully 43 percent of these less racially sensitive white voters admitted that a candidate's race affected their vote choice and it was these same white voters who were least likely to view Obama favorably and most likely to feel that he would do too much as president to appeal to the interests of blacks. While Republicans did not make direct use of Obama's race to mobilize the support of these white voters, they did try to raise racial suspicions indirectly by falsely claiming that he was a Muslim as a way of linking him to Islamic terrorists and by promoting the misconception that he was not really an American citizen (Weigel 2009; *Miami Herald* 2008; Martin 2008b).

All of this suggests that it is white voters who seem to be engaged in a kind of "unrealistic conflict" as they have long voted based on Republican appeals to their hostile impulses towards blacks (and other groups) rather than in terms of the rational pursuit of their economic interests. Blacks, by contrast, seem to be more inclined towards "realistic conflict" as they have long voted in support of Democratic candidates—black and white alike—with the hope of advancing their political and economic interests.

It may be, then, that centuries of living with racial inequality have not disabled the black community by sending ghetto residents into a war of all against all, as these theories suggest. Instead racial inequalities may actually have turned out to be *enabling*, precisely because they made blacks acutely aware that they live in a racially hostile society.

For example, racial inequalities can be said to be enabling when they induce black men to create protest masculinities in which they corroborate their blackness and their masculinity to each other, not through violence, but through displays of their resistance to racism. Indeed, it is those black men who subscribe to a masculinity formed in protest that are most inclined to condemn black-on-black violence because they define manhood in terms of unity and solidarity with other blacks.

Hence, because black men corroborate their blackness and masculinity to other black males in terms of their involvement in realistic conflict, expression of these race man identities becomes the way that black men "do race." Regrettably, these black male constructions of what it means to be black are never mentioned by the black-subculture-of-violence theorists and the racial inequality theorists discussed in this chapter. Yet, by overlooking these alternative definitions of black manhood, these theorists manage to convey the questionable notion that violence is the primary way that black males accomplish race.

NOTES

1. That academic criminologists and media elites make use of the same cultural explanations to make sense of black crime is hardly surprising as those in other media often turn to academic criminologists for expert opinion on crime and its causes. This is particularly true of news media as newspapers and broadcast news programs frequently interview or cite criminologists in their reports. Yet, even though criminologists theorize about links between blackness and crime in a manner akin to those in the media, what separates them from the media is their use of scientific tools and methods to back up their claims. Indeed, the reason that they are typically cited as

experts on crime in news reports is because they make use of scientific observation, scientific study designs and scientific research methods to validate their claims. By bringing these scientific tools to their theories on the links between blackness and violence, they have the capacity to scientize what "being black" really means. As a consequence, critiques of their "scientific" explanations of race turn on flaws in their observations, their study designs and their research methods. (See also note 1 in chapter 7 for additional definitions of the term "scientize.")

2. During the 2008 campaign, candidate Obama specifically promised to help economically stressed working- and middle-class homeowners by proposing a 90-day moratorium on home foreclosures. To address rising unemployment, he called for shoring up the social safety net by extending unemployment benefits and by promoting programs that would create jobs. In a further appeal to working- and middle-class families, he promised to cut taxes for the masses of Americans in middle- and low-income tax brackets, even as he called for a repeal of tax cuts for wealthy Americans making in excess of $250,000 (Calmes and Zeleny 2008).

Upon taking office, he immediately set about trying to address the economic woes of most Americans by signing a record $787 billion economic stimulus package into law. In keeping with his campaign promises, the stimulus package provided tax cuts to low-income and middle-class Americans. It also provided money to the states to shore up their social safety nets (unemployment benefits, food stamps, etc.) and finance infrastructure projects that would create jobs. Yet, despite widespread voter support for the stimulus package, only 3 Republican senators and 0 Republican congressmen supported the stimulus. In addition, several Republican governors signaled their opposition to the stimulus package by temporarily refusing to take portions of the stimulus money allotted to their states (Montgomery and Batheja 2009; *CNN Political Ticker* 2009; Stolberg and Nagourney 2009).

For example, the Republican governors of Texas and Louisiana said that they would turn down federal dollars for extended unemployment benefits in their states. Their fear was that their states would have to pay more for unemployment benefits when federal dollars ran out. Interestingly enough, the governor of Texas voiced his opposition to extending unemployment benefits in a time when 250,000 Texans had recently lost their jobs. It remains to be seen if large majorities of white voters—especially low-income and middle-class white voters—will continue to support GOP candidates, who refuse to address their economic concerns.

Chapter Five

Americanizing Black Violence

Making Criminology Race-Free

In the racial analyses of black violence discussed in chapter 4, white violence tends to disappear. White violence disappears because the criminologists who conduct these analyses begin by observing that black murder rates are seven times higher than white murder rates and then devote the rest of their effort to trying to explain why black murder rates are so high. In these analyses, then, white murder rates are treated like the norm and all of the focus is placed on explaining why black murder rates have reached such extreme levels. As a result, racial analyses of crime construct black violence as something that is foreign and different because of the sheer magnitude of the difference between black murder rates and white murder rates.[1]

With these theories, constructing black violence as something that is foreign and different has meant racializing black violence or assigning some black-specific trait (e.g., heightened disputatiousness, racial self-hatred, displaced aggression) to explain assaults and homicides in black samples. Criminologists also treat black violence as something foreign and different when they locate the origins of the black subculture of violence in conditions unique to the black past (slavery, Jim Crow). Because black violence is assigned separate motives, separate cultures and a separate history in these analyses, violent black subcultures appear to be un-American.

On the other hand, because white violence is taken to be normal, there is no corresponding tendency to understand it in terms of a "white experience." In other words, criminologists do not go in search of white-specific traits (except for hate crimes) to explain white violence. They also refrain from searching through historical records to find conditions unique to the white past that might explain the origins of the white subculture of violence. That no effort is made to identify the provenance of the white subculture of violence in some distinct and unique white past stems from the fact that white history is generally seen as American history. Hence, if the origins of violent white subcultures are found in America's past, it is not seen as a product of some kind of white racial history but rather as a product of American history. For these reasons, then, white subcultures of violence do not look like strange or un-American creations. Indeed because white history is American history, violent white subcultures appear to be as American as apple pie.

Because violence between whites was historically highest on the southern and western frontiers, criminologists attempt to identify the origins of white subcultures of violence by figuring out what conditions in these regions might have raised the level of white violence. And because white violence is typically higher among low-income and working class white males than middle- and upper-income white males, criminologists who study white violence also focus on the effects of gender (being male) and social class (Nisbett 1993; Gastil 1971; Black 1983, 1984; Courtwright 1996; Messerschmidt 1993).

Consequently, violent crimes committed by whites are analyzed in terms of a within-group analysis that divides up the white population by gender, region or social class. This means that there is a tendency to try to understand why white males, white southerners or working-class whites are more inclined towards violent behavior than white females, white non-southerners or middle- and upper-class whites respectively. Yet even as gender, region, and social class are privileged in analyses of white crime, these analyses remain race-free; in other words, race (being white) is not made to matter at all.

Americanizing black violence in ways so that it, too, no longer seemed alien, foreign and different, then, would mean abandoning the racial analyses of black crime described in the previous chapter and assessing assaults and homicides committed by blacks in much the same race-free way that the same violent crimes are examined among whites. In other words, instead of racializing black violence by going in search of black-specific traits to explain violence committed by black males, the focus would shift to nonracial characteristics like gender and social class to explain black crime.

Such an approach is easily defended for several reasons. For one thing, gender and social class seem to affect black violence in much the same way as they affect white violence in that males and the less affluent are more prone to violence in both populations. Moreover, violent behaviors look about the same in both populations in that the kind of macho violence that occurs in many ghetto-based bars also plagues bars in working-class and low-income white communities.

Not only does black violence look a lot like white violence today, it may also have the same history. After all, African Americans have been in the United States since 1619 and over the course of that long sojourn, they have been exposed to the same violent conditions on the southern and western frontiers as white Americans. For that reason as well, black violence—much like white violence—might be as American as apple pie.

In this chapter, then, I consider whether the racialization of black violence is really necessary or if black violence—like white violence—should also remain unraced. To explain what it means for violence to be unraced, I begin by reviewing research that analyzes the causes of white violence, largely because white violence is explained by nonracial variables like gender, age, region and socioeconomic status. In the course of reviewing these race-free analyses of the white subculture of violence, I not only examine theories that explain modern day white violence, but also theories that explain the origins of white violence in America's past.

By reviewing research on white violence, I mean to assess whether or not the longs-tanding tradition of leaving white violence unraced is reasonable. It is also my intent to explore the possibility that the same race-free analyses that are currently applied to white-on-white assaults and homicides ought to be applied to black-on-black violence. By examining whether a race-free analysis of black assaults and homicides is appropriate, I consider whether black violence, much like white violence, should be treated like just another reflection of the larger American love affair with violence.

THE UBIQUITY OF AMERICAN VIOLENCE

The notion that violence is as American as apple pie is easily defended as values favoring violence as a desirable form of masculinity are widely held throughout society. For example, there is evidence of the nearly universal respect accorded to the violent-male role in a number of sports as violent masculinities are routinely championed by professional athletes. Specifically, the goal in boxing is the explicitly violent one of knocking the other fighter out, while football games are won based on the strength and physical aggression of the players. In sports like hockey, the physical aggression of the game can even carry over into actual fights between rival teams.

Furthermore, it is not simply the players who act out these violent rituals in boxing arenas, hockey rinks and on football fields. By cheering them on, their millions of fans indicate that they, too, see these authorized forms of violence as a desirable expression of masculinity. Indeed sports fans have been known to become involved in acts of physical aggression, themselves, as they assault the players on rival teams by cursing at them and throwing drinks. Violent rioting by sports fans after championship games also occurs regularly whether the fans' favored teams win or lose (McKinley 2000; Drape 2002; Lipstyle 1999; Araton 2005; *New York Times* 2002). As the players and the millions of fans of these sports are drawn from all social classes and can be black or white as well as law abiding or criminal, there is every reason to conclude that values equating violence with masculinity are part of the American cultural mainstream.

Because violent masculinities receive such widespread acceptance, it is entirely appropriate to leave white violence unraced. In other words, violent acts committed by white males can be explained without reference to their whiteness because as the actions of professional athletes and sports fans suggest, respect for the violent-male role seems to be deeply ingrained in the cultural DNA. Because violent masculinities are rightly seen as an integral part of American culture, figuring out where these violent beliefs come from simply requires taking a look at American history.

The White Subculture of Violence in American History

Many criminologists, who look at the history of violence in this country, claim that the violent-male role was actually more commonplace and accepted in the past than it is today. For example, in his survey of American history, Donald Black (1983, 1984) argues that violence was a common way of resolving disputes in preindustrial times. In fact, he claims that in traditional America, much like other traditional societies where no formal legal code existed, violence and other crimes were forms of self-help.

By that, he means that, in preindustrial America, it was commonplace for violent crimes, such as assaults and homicides to be used as a form of self-help when husbands punished their wives for adultery or parents beat their kids for disobedience. Other crimes, such as arson and property destruction, were likewise used to settle disputes between neighbors, such as when one aggrieved party burned down the house of his neighbor or destroyed his animals or his crops. Theft was also used when warring parties pursued justice and punished their neighbors by stealing their livestock.

Sometimes these crimes of self-help would go on for years and some even escalated into blood feuds where reprisals were carried out against the offending neighbor, his blood kin and all of his descendants. Murders and assaults also figured in blood feuds between the races as lynchings and mutilations were used by white citizens against blacks as a way of punishing black men for their alleged rapes and harassment of white women (Beck and Tolnay 1990; Inverarity 1976).

In short, throughout much of America's past, homicides, assaults and other crimes were often committed to pursue justice, express disapproval, punish offenders and express the grievances of individuals or groups. Much like a number of other traditional societies, these crimes in traditional America were used as an alternative form of social control because the rule of law did not exist. In other words, because there was no formal legal system in place to resolve disputes over land, livestock, crops, or racial conflicts, private citizens routinely turned to self-help or the practice of taking the law into their own hands.

By describing violence and other crimes in these terms, Black is suggesting that most Americans back then might have seen some acts of violence as legitimate, just or even righteous when they were employed for self-help. And, because such violent acts were so widely accepted back then, there would have been no need to explain violence by identifying violent actors as members of a separate and deviant subculture of violence. There would also have been no need to argue that violent behavior was the manifestation of some underlying dysfunctional personality trait (such as displaced anger or racial self-hatred). Indeed because this largely white-on-white violence was such an integral part of the American cultural mainstream, there would have been no need to explain it in terms of the race of violent white males at all. Given its nearly universal nature, violence back then would have been regarded as normal and hence it could easily have remained unraced.

Regional Differences in White Male Violence

Nisbett (1993) also talks about the widespread use of violence among white males in preindustrial America without explaining it in terms of their race. Instead of race, he focuses on regional differences as he argues that white southerners have traditionally had higher rates of violence than white non-southerners. As he sees it, this is due to the fact that many of the European immigrants, who emigrated to the American south in the seventeenth and eighteenth centuries, hailed from herding backgrounds. While in Europe, herders had traditionally been disputatious because their entire livelihood could be so easily threatened by the theft of their herds. As a consequence, they found it necessary to develop reputations as the kind of men that would respond to even the most trifling insult with violence. For example, some shepherds were known to resort to violence if another shepherd merely threw a rock at one of their sheep. In fact, it was in their economic interest to use violent retaliation for even the smallest of slights, because it discouraged their rivals from escalating to more serious infractions such as theft.

In theory, the need for herdsmen emigrating from Europe to employ such violent tactics was only exacerbated when they arrived in America and settled on the southern and western frontiers. After all, there was no rule of law in place on the American frontier and their practice of taking the law into their own hands would have been even more necessary in preindustrial America than it had been in Europe. The violent herding cultures they formed were then passed on from one generation to the next in an American subculture of violence that presumably still lingers in the south and in other states settled by white southerners.

The fact that even today the south is usually the region with the highest homicide rates gives some credence to this argument (Bureau of Justice Statistics 2009). And, as further proof that this violent subculture survives, Nisbett cites survey data that indicate that even today white southerners are more inclined than white nonsoutherners to express the belief that most fathers expect their sons to fight if they are bullied at school. White southerners are also more likely than white nonsoutherners to argue that spanking is an appropriate way of disciplining their children, which suggests a greater willingness to resolve parent/child conflicts with violence. Yet, Nisbett manages to explain these regional white subcultures of violence without once mentioning whiteness. Instead, for him, the southern (white) subculture of violence is best regarded as a traditional adaptation to economic determinants like the demands associated with herding.

Courtwright (1996) also talks about the prevalence of white-on-white violence in preindustrial America without mentioning whiteness. He notes that such violence was especially common in places where young, unmarried males congregated. For example, many young unmarried white males, who went west to make their living, were congregated on the nineteenth-century western frontier because few white women initially went westward with them. Levels of white-on-white violence were quite high among these pools of young unmarried migratory workers who often moved about looking for work in construction, lumber camps and canneries. Many of them spent much of their lives alternating between these all-male workplaces and leisure time sprees that occurred in brothels and saloons, and any arguments they had in these places were typically settled with violence. The cowboys are probably best known for this practice of settling trivial disputes with violence on the western frontier as their early gunfights are still much celebrated in westerns on television and in film.

Industrialization and the Decline of Violence

Both Courtwright and Black suggest that levels of violence are not nearly so high today, and in different ways, offer explanations for why the customary violent masculinities practiced back then have been overtaken by less violent masculine roles today.

Courtwright (1996) claims that violence declined as more white men on the western frontier married after more white women followed them into the west. He also suggests that as jobs increasingly became available in cities in the industrializing America of the early twentieth century, many males found that they could live in one place and commute to work at the factory or some other industrial worksite. For the first time, then, it became possible for these men to give up their migratory occupations and settle down to married life.

As they settled into married life, they left behind the macho disputes of their nineteenth-century male-dominated social environments and thereby no longer felt a need to defend their masculine honor with violence on a daily basis. Indeed, as a consequence of their rising marriage rates, many of these men found themselves increasingly defining masculinity in terms of the non-violent male roles of family man and breadwinner.

Black (1984) offers a more far-reaching explanation for the decline in violence as he claims that the rampant violence of early America declined as a system of law enforcement developed and spread throughout the frontier. As the legal system expanded, there was less need for individual males to take the law into their own hands because the police force and the court system increasingly took over the role of resolving disputes between neighbors that had previously been settled with violent self-help.

The Survival of Violent Self-Help in Modern Day America

Still as Black notes, the legal system did not penetrate everywhere and hence a number of lawless spaces continue to exist in America today. After all, even in the America of today, people do still take the law into their own hands, particularly with private matters. It is in these modern day lawless spaces, then, where the practice of using violence to resolve disputes survives.

For example, even today disputes between neighbors may be resolved when one neighbor retaliates by vandalizing the property of the other or even by burning it down. Some of today's blood feuds can also arise from group conflicts where collective liability is assigned to a whole group of people. So, for example, modern conflicts between racial groups can mean that white residents in a community will burn crosses in the yard of any black person that happens to move into the neighborhood. Collective liability is also assigned by rival juvenile groups in a neighborhood, such as when a gang of teenagers like today's Bloods decides to engage in gang fighting with anyone they identify as a rival Crip.

However, unlike traditional America, where the individual defined when it was legitimate to use violence as a form of self-help, today it is the state which defines when violence is warranted. So, for example, when a husband assaults or kills his wife over adultery or poor housekeeping—much as he might have in traditional America—the state now prosecutes it as a crime with the husband defined as the offender and the wife as a victim. Or, when a teenager in conflict with her family runs away from home, the state can define the teenager as the offender for running away, return her to her home and treat the parents like victims. And while those using self-help (i.e., angry husband, teenage runaway) may still see themselves as the aggrieved party and resent the intrusion of the state, the modern state does have the power to define these acts of self-help as illegitimate and immoral and punish them as crimes. Nonetheless, modern Americans still persist in these crimes of self-help despite the fact that the state may intrude, label them as criminals and punish them.

Perhaps the fact that the state's legal codes do not typically penetrate into private disputes between family members explains why self-help is still used in conflicts between husbands and wives or between teenagers and their parents. After all, in many cases, family members in conflict may see their use of violence to resolve private disputes as legitimate. Indeed, spouses involved in domestic disturbances often attach so much legitimacy to their use of violence to resolve their disagreements that they do not think of calling the police even when one party is injured.

Private disputes between family members are not the only place where the state's legal code has no sway. The rule of law also does not reach into illicit markets such as illegal drug markets, prostitution rings or illegal gambling rings (Black 1984). This explains why buyers and sellers in these markets continue to settle disputes with crimes of self-help. For example, when drug dealers have disputes with their competitors over how to divvy up drug-selling turf, they cannot call the police, consult lawyers or go to court because drug selling is illegal. Instead, they have to fall back on the age-old custom of self-help, which may require them to assault or kill their rivals to settle their claims.

Hence, the fact that the state's legal codes, by definition, did not reach into the expanding illegal crack markets of the late 1980s and early 1990s helps to explain why drug-related murders surged in that period. Moreover, the decline in drug-related violence that followed in the mid-1990s only occurred as crack use became less popular and the stateless space of the drug marketplace contracted (Goldstein et al. 1997; Golub and Johnson 1997).

Black's concept of stateless spaces is also quite useful for understanding the modern-day subculture of violence. When males in modern America assault and kill each other in retaliation for trivial insults in bars and on street corners, they too are resorting to the long-standing custom of using violent self-help to resolve disputes (Felson et al. 1986; Katz 1988; Luckenbill and Doyle 1989; Wolfgang and Ferracuti 1967; Curtis 1975; Anderson 1990, 1994; W. Oliver 1994). This is because the modern legal code which condemns and punishes such violence also does not extend to the street corners and bars where the age-old rituals of "naming and claiming" persist. That disputants in bars and on street corners also reject formal resolution of their violent disagreements by the state is evidenced by the fact that even the victims of these assaults may refuse to call the police despite being injured. Instead, many prefer to resort to violent self-help by gathering up their friends and returning to the bar or the street corner where the assault occurred to seek revenge against the perpetrator.

All in all, then, Black's concept of self-help says a great deal about the nature of violence in America today. Because he suggests that the practice of using violence and other crimes to resolve disputes was widespread in traditional America, he can explain why it is still widely seen as legitimate and still respected even today. So, for example, he can explain why violence is still so widely respected across all social classes and among law-abiding and non-law-abiding citizens like the sports fans who champion the socially sanctioned violence of professional sports. He can also explain why violence is used to resolve disputes in low-income inner-city black high schools as well as in more affluent suburban white high schools like Columbine. And, he can explain why surveys show that blacks and whites are equally likely to hold violent values in surveys and why these same surveys indicate that the nonviolent are as likely to hold violent values as those who have been violent (Cao et al. 1997).

Still the fact that violence cuts across all social classes does not explain why low income and working-class Americans in general—and low-income and working-class blacks in particular—seem much more likely to actually act on these widely held beliefs and resolve their disagreements with assaults and homicides.

Social Class and the Survival of Violent Self-Help

One possibility is that the elevated levels of violence found among the poor and working class relative to the affluent can be explained by the fact that self-help may be more necessary in less affluent neighborhoods where the law is more likely to be absent or weak. After all, the law is less likely to be available in low-income white neighborhoods because poor whites cannot afford lawyers. As blacks are much more likely to be poor than whites, the inability to afford legal representation might be one reason that they have higher violent crime rates than whites. The law may also be especially weak or absent in black neighborhoods because residents may be less likely to call the police due to fears of police brutality.

If less affluent communities in general, and less affluent black communities in particular, are more likely to be stateless spaces where the law is absent or weak, then residents of these neighborhoods will be more likely to turn to self-help to resolve disputes with neighbors, strangers, intimates, and acquaintances.

Not only does the concept of self-help provide a distinctive way of looking at elevated levels of violence in black neighborhoods, it also raises a whole series of questions about the utility of racializing black violence by arguing that experiences unique to blacks explain their high violent crime rates.

For example, criminologists have long tried to make a case for the notion that black violence is somehow not a product of America's history with violence even though that is how white violence is explained. Instead they separate the black subculture of violence from the white subculture of violence by arguing that the former is the product of a separate history peculiar to blacks—namely the black experience with a history of slavery and Jim Crow. They also argue that the unique black experience of living in a socially isolated underclass neighborhood has damaged the black psyche in ways that make blacks uniquely prone to a heightened sensitivity to slights, racial self-hatred or displaced anger that lead to high levels of violence.

However, this brief review of the literature on the use of self-help in preindustrial America suggests that it might be more useful to consider the possibility that black violence might have the same origins as white violence in America's violent past. After all, black Americans were exposed to the lawless spaces of violent southern and western frontiers much like white Americans.

If black violence has the same origins as white violence in America's lawless past, then today's high rates of black violence might best be understood in terms of the survival of lawless spaces in modern day ghettos. If so, then there is no need to racialize black violence by setting it apart from white violence and suggesting that it has its own separate origins in a uniquely black history. Instead the focus should shift to an identification of those factors which help the practice of violent self-help to survive in black communities.

JAMES MESSERSCHMIDT AND THE CAUSES OF CONTEMPORARY WHITE MALE VIOLENCE

One explanation for why the use of self-help might have been better able to survive in both black and white low-income and working-class neighborhoods alike comes from Messerschmidt (1993). He argues that social class background may be important in explaining the decision to resort to violent self-help in today's America because low-income and working-class males are more likely to define masculinity in terms of violence. By contrast, he claims that this violent working-class definition of masculinity fares less well in middle- and upper-class communities because it is more likely to have been overtaken by a nonviolent definition of manhood.

In his efforts to explain how social class background shapes definitions of masculinity, he focuses on school-based adolescent peer groups. Adolescent peer groups are important social settings for defining masculinity because male roles are still being established during the teen years. Furthermore, in adolescence, masculine hierarchies are not tied to occupational rankings as adolescents cannot achieve masculinity like adult males do by working in a well-paid, high-status profession and assuming the role of head of the household. Because adolescents cannot achieve these hegemonic adult masculinities based on economic criteria, they focus on other definitions of maleness which are more accessible to them.

In addition, because adolescents have not established themselves in a lifelong career, the school-based youth subcultures they form tend to be centered on leisure time values that define maleness in noneconomic terms. This means that in adolescence the dominance, control and independence needed to define masculinity simply requires the expression of such traits as daring, the pursuit of excitement and violent aggression in leisure-dominated youth cultures (Matza 1964). Because teenagers lack access to the respected adult male roles of breadwinner and family man where these attributes can be expressed nonviolently, violent masculinities gain in importance for them because they allow them to express dominance and control in ways that are achievable.

Furthermore, for most of their teen years, adolescent males may feel that their masculinity is actually threatened. After all, school is required throughout their teens and many adolescent males may find themselves taking an oppositional stance to school because they see it as emasculating. School is perceived as emasculating because being a student is at odds with the dominance, control and independence that define manhood. Instead of these masculine traits, success in school requires such "unmanly" behaviors as following school rules and submitting to the authority of teachers and school administrators. In fact, any efforts to assert masculine dominance, control and independence in school are seen as acts of rebellion and can result in suspension or expulsion. School is also likely to be seen as emasculating because many of the teachers are women, which forces adolescent males to take orders from adult females. Moreover, the predominance of female teachers can also make the academic work that they promote seem feminizing.

As a result, delinquent behaviors including violence become a way of engaging in oppositional masculinities to counter the accommodations that males must make in school. In this context, then, violence becomes a resource to enable an adolescent male to achieve prestige in male gender hierarchies much like income is a resource for achieving prestige in adult male hierarchies. However, the willingness to use violence as a resource to express an oppositional masculinity is dependent on the adolescent's class background.

Masculine Roles and Affluent White Adolescents

Messerschmidt (1993) argues that middle- and upper-class boys are likely to express an accommodating masculinity at school by doing their homework, getting good grades and following school rules. In part, they obey adult orders and school rules and allow themselves to be emasculated, because they have to cooperate with adult teachers and the school administration as they typically head many of the student organizations in school. This gives them some limited power over other students as well as providing them with an incentive to accommodate themselves to the dictates of adult teachers and administrators.

Furthermore many of these males may be accommodating at school because school does provide them with some opportunities to achieve more acceptable forms of manliness through participation in supervised school sports. As athletes or sports fans, they can express the more traditional types of masculinity that promote violence, toughness, endurance and competitiveness.

They are also willing to be accommodating at school because their middle- and upper-class parents—often by their own example—socialize them to anticipate the hegemonic masculinity of adulthood that is defined by work in a middle-class or upper-class profession. Because their parents' (especially their fathers') own lives may help them to see that the pathway to a secure income from a middle- or upper-class occupation in adulthood begins in high school, they are able to understand the value of good grades in high school as a prerequisite for a college education and the necessary certification for a high-powered job. Indeed some middle- and upper-class parents even go so far as to plan their children's careers. For these reasons, then, boys from affluent households may be willing to resign themselves to the emasculating self-discipline and emotional restraint required in the school environment because their parents have succeeded in getting them to regard these accommodations as necessary for their future success.

However, their very emasculation in school makes affluent adolescents prone to assert oppositional masculinities outside of school in order to publicly re-establish a traditional masculine identity. Oppositional masculinities are typically expressed outside of school by drinking under age, gambling and committing a variety of pranks that include vandalism, minor theft and other forms of mischief. By raising hell in these ways, these affluent youngsters express the independence, dominance, daring and control that demonstrate their essential maleness to other boys. Delinquency outside of school, then, becomes a resource that enables them to counter the accommodations required in school and enhance their prestige in male gender hierarchies.

While all affluent adolescent males are capable of turning to these oppositional masculinities outside of school to cope with the accommodations required in school, the most susceptible to these forms of maleness are those middle- and upper-class males who are not academically successful and not interested in school sports. Hence, in one study of upper-middle-class white males, a clique of these boys dubbed themselves the "losers" and turned to drinking, vandalism and firebombing the cars of adult authority figures in the community as a way of constructing an oppositional masculinity because they were unable to achieve the limited masculine roles available in the school environment. For the most part, however, middle- and upper-class white males were not especially violent.

Oppositional Masculinities among White Working Class Males

However, the white working-class adolescents studied were inclined to express violent oppositional masculinities and as such had much higher rates of violence than those who hailed from the middle and upper class. The greater willingness of white working-class adolescents to express violent oppositional masculinities had a lot to do with the fact that many of them saw school as irrelevant. Their tendency to see school as less relevant than affluent white males is understandable.

Traditionally, academic success in school has had little value for white working-class adolescents because, up until recently, many of them have been able to follow their fathers into blue-collar jobs that did not require good grades in high school as a prerequisite for a college education. For many years, these same blue-collar jobs have also enabled their fathers to be the principal wage earner and head of the household and as a consequence, many working-class adolescents have been raised to believe that these blue-collar jobs are the basis for defining adult masculinity. Indeed, because they have been raised in working-class households, many white working-class teens have come to believe that "real men" would prefer the manual labor associated with blue-collar jobs to the mental labor associated with bookwork.

In school, then, working-class boys are inclined to bully the academically successful boys as they see them as headed for effeminate mental pursuits. And, because education has not been as relevant for them, working-class white teens have been less willing to assume the accommodating masculinities required in school. For that reason, they do not compete for offices in school organizations and the limited control over other students that these positions bring. Instead many choose to assert their masculine dominance and control in the emasculating environment of school by being disruptive in the classroom and by intimidating the smart students who obey school rules. In these ways, they demonstrate their rejection of the accommodating masculinities required in school.

To further distinguish themselves from the geeks and nerds who accommodate themselves to school rules, they also engage in fighting. Because fighting allows them to express their superiority to the academically successful males who conform to the feminizing dictates of school, these boys not only fight, but they also actively seek to start fights and talk about the best fighting strategies (Willis 1977, 1990). Because fighting is so central to their masculine standing in gender hierarchies, refusing to fight or being an inadequate fighter can destroy their reputations.

Furthermore, given the limited relevance of school to their futures, many feel free to express violent oppositional masculinities both inside and outside of school. For Messerschmidt, then, levels of violence are higher among working-class white males than among more affluent white males, because the former see violence as a way of doing working-class masculinities.

Unfortunately, their disdain for school means that many working-class white males will find themselves making considerably less money in their adult years than the geeks and nerds that they bully as the latter are likely to go on to college and get the higher-paying jobs that come with more years of schooling. Nonetheless, working-class white males unwittingly sacrifice their long-term financial interests in an effort to achieve masculine status in the short term.

They may also lose out financially in the long term because they are drawn into lower-paying working-class jobs at a young age. For example, Sullivan (1989) describes some working-class white males who started working at blue-collar jobs part-time during the school year and full-time during the summer as early as age 14. For many of these adolescents, these summer jobs become a stepping-stone to a lifelong occupation.

Yet, in taking on these jobs at an early age, many of these working-class white males eventually find themselves working for the geeks they used to bully when they become adults. Consequently, as workers on the shop floor, confined to manual labor that is often repetitive, demeaning and dangerous, they find themselves unable to meet the standards of a hegemonic adult masculinity that require a man to be independent, dominant and in control.

Still, they manage to construct their work as masculine by claiming that the manual tasks that they perform are an expression of a kind of rough and tough manliness that requires them to be physically strong, steely, tenacious and active in order to complete their work. By contrast, they label the men in middle management from whom they take orders as sycophants and paper pushers and dismiss the kinds of mental work they do as effeminate. As fathers, it is likely that they are able to convey their disdain for this kind of effeminate, mental work to their children, thereby reproducing contempt for the passive, mental life in their sons and reinforcing their sons' scorn for the academic work required in school.

OPPOSITIONAL MASCULINITIES AMONG BLACK MALES

Clearly, violence thrives among teenaged white males because it becomes a way of "doing working-class masculinity." Because black males are disproportionately raised in working-class and low-income households, they may likewise be seen as "doing working-class masculinity" when they turn to violence. In other words, much like their white male counterparts, many young working-class and low-income black males will be completely incapable of seeing school as relevant because schooling has not traditionally prepared them for prestigious, well-paying occupations. Instead, their parents and many of the adults around them are unemployed, underemployed or working at low-status service industry jobs.

Because school has not historically been linked to high-powered middle-class jobs in their communities, black youngsters may likewise be expected to conclude that school has little relevance for them. If so, much like working-class white males, they too will feel free to express oppositional masculinities both inside and outside school. Violent crime, then, is likely to be high among working-class and low-income black males.

In fact, violent crime rates should be even higher among working-class and low-income black males than they are among working-class white males because the latter at least have traditionally had access to blue-collar jobs starting in their teen years. By contrast, black teenagers have traditionally lacked access to these jobs and have therefore been more likely to turn to moneymaking crimes to buy clothes, music and other goods that adolescents find desirable (Sullivan 1989).

Black Adolescents and Blue-Collar Work

Royster (2003) argues that even today black adolescents are less able than white adolescents to secure the more desirable blue-collar jobs left over after deindustrialization (e.g., jobs in construction, auto mechanics, plumbing, computer repair, and carpentry). She comes to this conclusion after interviewing 25 black adolescents and 25 white adolescents.

At the time of her interviews, all of the young male interviewees in her study were 2-3 years beyond high school and trying to establish themselves in a blue-collar trade. The black males and white males she interviewed had a lot else in common as well as they had both attended the same high schools, had the same instructors and in many cases had trained in the same blue-collar trades. Further, both instructors and other students agreed that the black males and the white males in her sample were among the strongest students. Moreover, the black and white males in her sample shared formal access to the same job-listing services and work-study programs.

Yet, despite the fact that they seemed to start out on equal footing, the black males she interviewed were already less likely to be employed in the skilled trades than the white males less than 3 years after high school. They also made less money per hour, had lower-status positions, received fewer promotions and experienced more and longer bouts of unemployment.

Royster argues that these disappointing outcomes for the black males in her sample were largely due to racially exclusionary practices in the blue-collar trades which occurred at various points along their career paths. To begin with, the white male teachers of these young men were far more helpful to the white males in their classes than to the black males. For example, even as the white male teachers verbally encouraged their black male students, they were more inclined to provide their white students with information about actual job vacancies or referrals and to assist them in securing their first job. Indeed, in some instances, white teachers directly recruited white males for specific jobs and were more inclined to vouch for them with employers.

The advantages that these young working-class white males enjoyed extended beyond school, as their white fathers, uncles, brothers, and friends often provided them with information about job openings as well. Even the women in their lives including mothers, aunts, and girlfriends (and their families) helped them to secure blue-collar work despite the fact that these males were young, inexperienced and in many instances immature and un-disciplined as well. Some white males even found work in the trades through casual contacts with other white male blue-collar workers in local neighborhood taverns, bars and restaurants.

In short, job opportunities were plentiful for these young white males because they came from white working-class family backgrounds and lived in white working-class neighborhoods. For example, Royster describes a case in which a young white busboy managed to get into a union apprentice program because of these neighborhood contacts, while in another case, a white pizza delivery boy managed to get a job as a refrigeration specialist. Clearly, then, inexperience was no barrier to securing employment in a skilled trade for the white males in her sample.

Moreover, many of them managed to secure work even if they had not made good grades in high school or even if they lied about their work experience. Some even got second chances after negative experiences at previous jobs by returning to their white male high school teachers to secure additional job references. Hence, one young white male managed to get another job after verbally abusing his employer. And another young white male managed to hide his prison record for a burglary conviction and secure a job at a burglar alarm company.

This is in stark contrast to the experiences of the young black males she interviewed, who were forced to fall back on a far less effective job search network of black family members and friends to secure work. Furthermore, Royster claims that the black males in her sample would never have been able to find another job in the skilled trades if they had the negative work histories or criminal records of some of their white counterparts.[2] Moreover, even those black males who managed to secure work without these blemishes on their record often found themselves subjected to discrimination and racial insults by white employers on the job and the frustrations of being passed over for promotions. However, unlike their white counterparts, if they left these jobs due to job dissatisfaction or because they were fired, they were typically unable to find other employment in the skilled trades. Instead of a lateral move to a comparable skilled labor job, many found themselves on a downward spiral into low-skill, low-pay service sector jobs for which they were overqualified. And, those who rejected these service sector jobs in food service or retail and insisted on remaining in the blue-collar trades often found themselves subjected to longer and longer bouts of unemployment while they looked for skilled work.

Clearly, then, Royster's findings indicate that black male entry into blue-collar work is still limited by the discriminatory practices of white males who continue to recruit, hire and fire workers along racial lines. Unfortunately this racial apartheid in the blue-collar trades has dire consequences for black males as it makes them less able to support a family and less capable of developing the kinds of job search networks that might assist future cohorts of black adolescents in securing work.

All in all, then, the oppositional masculinities that lead to violence both inside and outside school may be especially likely to develop in black high schools where there is less exposure to employment traditions that prepare them for work in middle- and upper-class professions. Hence, much like white working-class adolescents, black working-class adolescents are also likely to find the mental work required in school to be irrelevant and effeminate and thereby threatening to their fledgling masculine identities.

However, unlike white working-class adolescents, working-class black adolescents are less able to fall back on work in the blue-collar trades even if they are alienated from school. Furthermore, unlike white working-class adolescents, they are far less likely to come from households where there is a tradition of males achieving masculinity as the sole breadwinner and head of the household based on the capacity to support a family with the income from blue-collar work. Because discriminatory practices mean that they are still frequently excluded from even the blue-collar trades, their tenuous status in the labor force may make it that much harder for them to age out of the violent and criminal lifestyles that typically begin in adolescence (Steffensmeier and Allan 2000; Hawkins et al. 2000).

This means that in black low-income and working-class neighborhoods, violent masculinities can thrive because there is so little exposure to alternative working traditions in either white-collar jobs that require more education or in blue-collar jobs that require access to a white-male-dominated job recruitment network.

By arguing that violent masculinities thrive among adolescents from blue-collar or low-income backgrounds, then, these theorists manage to explain violence in terms that privilege age, gender and class over race. And, because adolescent black males are far more likely to come from working-class or low-income backgrounds than white males, these theorists allow for the possibility that high violent crime rates among blacks may simply mean that more of them are likely to live in communities where oppositional masculinities still thrive.

Unattached Males and Black-on-Black Violence

However, it is not simply class-based definitions of masculinity that explain high rates of black violence. Because of the exit of blue-collar jobs, marriage rates are low and therefore there are now large pools of unattached black men living in black working-class and low-income neighborhoods (U.S. Census Bureau 2006). In many ways, these pools of unattached black males resemble the pools of unattached white males on the nineteenth-century western frontier.

Back then, levels of bachelorhood were high among nineteenth-century white males because they went west without white females to find work in migratory jobs in construction, lumber camps, and canneries. In their male-dominated social environments, a highly disputatious subculture of violence formed as arguments were often resolved with fistfights and gun battles. Because these men had to defend their masculine honor in macho disputes on a daily basis, it is understandable why levels of violence were so high. The fact that violent arguments only thrived back then because these men lived and worked in such male-dominated environments is made clear by data indicating that their violent crime rates declined rapidly when they deserted these macho all-male environments for marriage after the westward migration of white females (Courtwright 1996).

Today's black ghettos with their low marriage rates can also be seen as places where men, unattached to a family, are likely to congregate and interact frequently with other males in a male-dominated environment. Hence, in ghetto bars and on street corners, black men once again resolve their macho disputes with violence in a manner akin to white males on the nineteenth-century western frontier. It comes as no surprise, then, that levels of violence are especially high in the modern deindustrialized black ghetto—much as they were on the preindustrial western frontier.

Hence, by looking at American history and the conditions that led to elevated levels of violence back then, it is possible to argue that the black subcultures of violence on view in today's urban ghettos are not a break from the American cultural mainstream. Instead, they appear to be one of the surviving lawless spaces where private disputes are settled with violence. For that reason, black disputatiousness and sensitivity to slights need not be raced as a unique black cultural reaction to slavery, Jim Crow or to living in a ghetto. Nor does black disputatiousness need to be understood as an outgrowth of racial self-hatred, racial group hatred or as a coping mechanism in the face of racial inequality. Instead a review of American history suggests that black violence is as American as apple pie because today's black ghettos simply resemble nineteenth-century America with their low marriage rates, male-dominated environments and surviving lawless spaces.

PRIVILEGING CLASS OVER RACE IN ANALYSES OF BLACK VIOLENCE

If nothing else, the previous sections indicate that social class background can induce black males and white males alike to express masculinity in very different ways. For that reason, then, it might be wise to consider whether what many criminologists describe as race differences in violence might not really be social class differences in violence. After all, black males are more likely to be poor than white males as they have considerably lower incomes on average and are more likely to be unemployed. They are also far less likely to complete four years of college than white males, which limits their access to jobs in middle- and upper-class professions (U.S. Census Bureau 2006; S. Walker 1990; Hawkins et al. 2000; Harris and Shaw 2000).[3] And, while a high school education without any college puts all males at a disadvantage in the job market, even white males with only a high school education enjoy certain advantages over black males because they have been better able to move out of the central cities and gain access to blue-collar jobs (W. Wilson 1996; Royster 2003).

The devastating impact that the exodus of blue-collar jobs has had on black urban communities is most visible in those black inner-city neighborhoods where homicide rates are at their highest. For example, in a study comparing black and white homicide rates in the 124 largest cities, Krivio and Peterson (2000) found enormous differences in the socioeconomic status of blacks and whites living in these cities. Specifically, they found that urban blacks in their sample were far more likely than urban whites to live in neighborhoods where they were surrounded by large concentrations of poor people and by males aged 16 and over that were either unemployed or out of the labor force entirely. The converse was also true as residents of these socially isolated black census tracts were also less likely to encounter persons employed in professional or managerial positions. Cut off from employment and opportunities for employment, it should come as no surprise that these disadvantaged black neighborhoods had the highest murder rates.

Over and above these measures of neighborhood disadvantage, urban poor black communities were also disadvantaged by having a much greater concentration of female-headed households than white communities. A high concentration of female-headed households in a neighborhood is generally believed to be a measure of disadvantage because it is assumed that children raised in these households are subject to less supervision, more instability and inadequate childhood socialization (Rainwater and Yancey 1967). Presumably, because of the limited supervision, instability and inadequate socialization, children raised in these homes are more prone to crime and violence during adolescence.

However, this interpretation of the relationship between female-headed households and high black murder rates is very controversial (Rebellon 2002; Harris and Meidlinger 1995). For one thing, research on young black males raised in urban poor two-parent households where the father is present actually had *higher* rates of violent delinquency than young black males raised in female-headed households where the father is absent. Moreover, young black males from two-parent households were *more* likely to become delinquent at a much younger age than those from female-headed households (Harris and Meidlinger 1995). In fact, several studies suggest that the presence of a father seems to only lower the risk of delinquency for whites, while actually raising it for blacks in some cases.

Moreover, research that examines delinquency rates for children of all races shows that children raised in single-parent households do not have the highest crime rates. Rather this research shows that it is children raised in two-parent families with a stepparent—a common household structure in white middle-class neighborhoods—that are actually more inclined to turn to crime than children raised in female-headed households (Rebellon 2002). All of this suggests that high black murder rates do not stem from poor socialization in female-headed households.

Still, even if a concentration of female-headed households in an inner-city black neighborhood is not linked to high homicide rates due to family instability and faulty socialization, it does signal that there are large pools of unattached males in a neighborhood. Put differently, neighborhoods with a large concentration of unattached single, separated or divorced females running a household are, by definition, also neighborhoods with a large pool of unattached single, separated or divorced males living there. If so, then, the fact that urban blacks are more likely to live in neighborhoods where they are surrounded by a high concentration of female-headed households also means that they are surrounded by large pools of unattached males.

As studies of nineteenth-century white males on the western frontier indicate, violence is likely to be high in communities where there are such large pools of unattached males because of the incessant need to defend masculine honor in macho environments (Courtwright 1996). Perhaps, then, a concentration of female-headed households in today's black ghettos should not be taken to be a measure of instability and poor supervision in these households, but rather should be seen as a proxy measure of a concentration of unattached males in a neighborhood.

When neighborhood disadvantage is measured in terms of a concentration of poverty, jobless males, single-parent households (as a proxy for unattached males), and limited access to neighbors working in professional and managerial occupations, it has a significant positive effect on homicide rates for both blacks and whites (Krivio and Peterson 2000). In other words, the higher the concentrated level of neighborhood disadvantage measured in these terms, the higher the homicide rates.

Indeed, living in such structurally disadvantaged communities had more of a direct effect on white homicide rates than black homicide rates—although the effect was significant for both races. Because living in an urban neighborhood with low socioeconomic status has a significant impact on homicide rates regardless of race, then isolating the true effect of race differences on homicide—independent of the effects of social class—would mean controlling for these neighborhood class differences.

In order to isolate the true effect of race differences, independent of social class, it is necessary to compare black juveniles living in socioeconomically disadvantaged urban poor neighborhoods to white juveniles living in urban poor neighborhoods with equivalent levels of socioeconomic disadvantage. However, efforts to make these comparisons have not generally been successful because the most socioeconomically disadvantaged inner-city white communities typically do not have poverty rates or unemployment rates as high as those found in urban poor black neighborhoods.

For example, Krivio and Peterson (2000) found that 95 percent of blacks in the 124 cities that they studied lived in communities that were saddled with considerably more socioeconomic disadvantage than white inner-city neighborhoods. In other words, the urban blacks in their study were far more likely than urban whites to live in communities where they were surrounded by concentrations of jobless males, female-headed households (i.e., pools of unattached males) and little contact with persons in managerial or professional occupations.

This suggests that many urban poor blacks live in neighborhoods where local working traditions and job networks may do little to help them prepare for white-collar jobs or gain access to blue-collar work. Under these conditions, a tradition of defining masculinity in terms of violence can flourish. It comes as no surprise, then, that these structurally disadvantaged black neighborhoods had higher murder rates than the white urban neighborhoods.

Because urban poor black neighborhoods are more disadvantaged than urban poor white neighborhoods, statistics that suggest that black males are seven times as likely to commit murders as white males are misleading. Such statistics are misleading because they are basically comparing *all* black males to *all* white males without controlling for the enormous socioeconomic differences between the types of communities in which blacks and whites live. Because the significant socioeconomic differences between black and white neighborhoods have not been taken into account, the 7:1 race gap in crime is basically comparing apples to oranges. In other words, it is comparing two socioeconomically dissimilar populations. If socioeconomic differences do actually account for this large race gap in homicides—and not race differences—then the 7:1 race gap in homicides should be greatly reduced if class differences are controlled.

However, because blacks and whites do not live under similar socioeconomic conditions in real life, no comparison of equally disadvantaged populations is possible. For that reason, Phillips (2002) tries to make an apples-to-apples comparison between socioeconomically comparable black and white populations by creating a black population with the same socioeconomic status as the white population by statistical means.[4] When she does so by treating blacks as if they had the same structural advantages as whites, she finds that the black/white gap in homicides is greatly reduced. In other words, she finds that if blacks had the same income levels as whites and were as likely to be employed as whites and were as likely to achieve a college education as whites, then the race gap in homicides would be reduced by 69.1

percent. In other words, much of the seeming race difference in homicides really turns out to be a class difference in homicides. She cautions that even this substantial reduction may be on the low side as she can only consider the kinds of large-scale, quantifiable, structural variables that can be gleaned from census data.

SUMMARY AND CONCLUSIONS: AMERICANIZING BLACK VIOLENCE

Any analysis which starts out by trying to figure out what is different about blackness and how black-specific traits might lead to violence both defines blacks in terms of their crime problems and deprives blacks of a certain complexity. Whites are never subjected to this kind of racial reductionism in criminological research. Instead, whether they are poor or affluent, criminologists treat individual whites as if they can all be good and bad, honest and dishonest, noble and self-centered. Apparently none of them are ever hounded by the kinds of demons that plague entire communities. However, criminologists do construct whole communities of black people as if they are all consumed by uniquely black emotions like racial self-hatred or displaced rage at whites or an oversized sensitivity to slights that drives them to violence. One of the main justifications for constructing these uniquely black traits has been the very large race gap in homicides.

This chapter examines research that raises questions about this kind of racial reductionism, in part, by looking at studies which suggest that the oft cited 7:1 race gap in homicides is inflated. According to the criminologists that do this research, this seemingly very large race gap in homicides is inflated because it comes from national statistics which compare all blacks in the United States to all whites without taking into account how differently the two populations are distributed. For these researchers, the only way to calculate a true race difference in homicides is to compare black and white populations which are comparable in all other ways except race.

Because the poor and unemployed are more likely to commit murders regardless of race and because blacks are more likely to be poor and unemployed than whites a 7:1 black/white homicide ratio that does not control for poverty and unemployment differences between blacks and whites grossly exaggerates the race difference. Therefore, in order to gauge the true effect of race on violence, it is necessary to at least control poverty and unemployment before trying to calculate a race difference.

The fact that the race gap is greatly reduced after criminogenic factors like poverty and unemployment are controlled raises some serious questions about traditional racial analyses of crime. After all, if race differences in violence are small in socioeconomically comparable black and white populations, then there is no justification for racializing black violence by lumping blacks together and distinguishing them from whites through the construction of separate motives, separate subcultural values and separate histories in order to explain their violence.

In other words, high murder rates may not signal that blacks have coped with racial self-hatred, hatred of other blacks and displaced aggression by turning to violence. Rather elevated levels of black violence may indicate that violent masculinities are just as attractive to today's working-class and low-income black youth as they are to today's working-class and low-income white youth. The fact that there is a race gap in murder may simply mean that a larger proportion of blacks are working class and poor.

Moreover, this research suggests that high black murder rates may not be the product of a separate black history with slavery and Jim Crow conditions that has caused them to become disputatious. Rather it may signal that as Americans they have been exposed to the same lawless spaces that led to white-on-white violence on the frontier and that these lawless spaces have just been better able to survive in the structurally disadvantaged conditions characteristic of the modern day black ghetto. Perhaps, then, black violence should be viewed as just another reflection of the long-standing American love affair with violence.

Hence, if black violence were to be Americanized by being analyzed in the same terms as white violence, then, racial analyses which suggest that "being black" somehow makes a person more prone to violence would be replaced with race-free analyses that privilege age, gender, and socioeconomic status over race.

NOTES

1. The most frequently cited homicide rates are computed based on arrest statistics that come from the Uniform Crime Reports (UCR) and the Supplementary Homicide Reports (SHR). Unfortunately, the UCR and the SHR only measure what they call black/white differences in homicides. This is something of a misnomer because Latinos are included with whites in arrest statistics. Thus, it is more accurate to say that racial comparisons based on UCR or SHR data are really comparisons between blacks and nonblacks rather than comparisons between blacks and whites.

2. In a study with interesting implications for the stigma attached to black males by employers, Pager (2003) had pairs of fictitious job applicants fill out job applications. There were no differences between the males in each of the pairs; except that one male in each pair claimed that he had served time in prison for possession of cocaine.

As might be expected, those males with a supposed criminal record were a lot less likely to get a call back from an employer. However, even a white male applicant who claimed that he had spent time in prison had a *better* chance of getting a call back from an employer than a black male without a prison record.

3. 2003 census data indicate that black males are about three times as likely to live below the poverty line as white males. Specifically, 7.2 percent of white males live in poverty compared to fully 22 percent of black males. White males are also twice as likely to complete at least four years of college as 32.9 percent of white males over 25 years of age have a bachelor's degree or more compared to only 16.6 percent of black males (U.S. Census Bureau 2006). White males also have considerably lower unemployment rates than black males. Indeed, white male unemployment has generally been about half that of black males since the 1950s (S. Walker 1990). In August 2009, when a severe economic downturn elevated unemployment rates for everyone, white unemployment rates stood at a very high 8.9 percent, while black unemployment rates stood at an astronomical 15.9 percent (Bureau of Labor Statistics 2009).

Unfortunately, homicide data, which show that black males have murder rates that are 7 times as high as those of white males, do not take these race differences in poverty, education and unemployment into account. Yet, poverty, education and unemployment have an enormous impact on homicide rates in their own right. Hence, in order to isolate the true effect of race on homicide, it is absolutely essential to control for race differences in poverty, education and unemployment.

4. Instead of using Uniform Crime Report (UCR) or Supplementary Homicide Report (SHR) statistics to obtain counts of homicide *offenders*, Phillips (2002) uses National Center for Health Statistics (NCHS) data to obtain counts of homicide *victims*. This is a legitimate approach because murder is an intraracial crime. In other words, 86 percent of white victims are killed by whites and 94 percent of black victims are killed by blacks (Bureau of Justice Statistics 2009). Hence, the race of the victim is a very good proxy measure of the race of the offender. Still, Phillips cautions that she might not get the same results if she used the more traditional measures of homicides based on UCR and SHR arrest statistics (see note 1). On the other hand, by using NCHS data on homicides, she is able to separate Latino homicide victims from white homicide victims and compute distinct homicide rates for each of the 3 largest sociodemographic groups—namely blacks, whites and Latinos. Hence, the homicide data she uses do a better job of capturing race and ethnic differences than those derived from UCR and SHR arrest data.

Section II

CINEMATIC AND ACADEMIC IMAGES OF BLACK FEMALE CRIMINALS AND VICTIMS

Chapter Six

Black Women on the Silver Screen

In previous chapters, I have examined how males "do masculinity" in their relationships with other men with an eye to explaining how doing masculinity can lead to violence. However, males do not simply establish manhood in the context of their relations with other men; they also establish their masculinity in their relationships with women. And just as the masculinities most frequently fostered in popular culture are defined in terms that require males to demonstrate their dominance and control over other men, achieving masculinity in popular culture likewise requires that males be able to provide evidence of their dominance and control over women.

Even in a chapter on cinematic constructions of women, then, it is important to consider how males demonstrate their masculinity in popular culture because images of women in popular culture are typically constructed in ways that enable men to establish their masculinity. That women are defined in terms that help men to affirm and promote their masculinity is not especially surprising. After all, the institutions of popular culture are controlled by men—particularly white men.

For example, white males are overrepresented among writers, producers and directors in the film industry, and they likewise dominate The Academy of Motion Picture Arts and Sciences that determines which pictures and performances will be awarded an Oscar (Chideya 1995; Mapp 2003). Their dominance in the film industry is important because it enables them to decide on what characters will be created and what stories will be told, and their overrepresentation in the Academy of Motion Picture Arts and Sciences gives them the power to determine exactly what constitutes excellence in moviemaking.[1]

The female characters they create have come in for a good deal of criticism from a number of feminist film critics. For example, these critics have accused Hollywood of devaluing both their black female and white female characters in a gender hierarchy which assigns lesser worth to women than men (Manatu 2003; Dines et al. 1998; Humm 1997; hooks 1981, 1992, 1993). By this they mean that Hollywood writers demean their female characters by focusing on them not as whole persons in their own right, but rather on how they rank in terms of their interactions with men.

In order to conform to the standards of appropriate male/female behavior required in Hollywood, feminist critics claim that female characters are typically ranked in terms of their degree of femininity. As a consequence, they claim that the film industry is best able to stigmatize its female characters by describing them in terms which suggest that they have somehow deviated from the standards of femininity as they are defined by the industry.

Unfortunately, African American women face the dual dilemma of being both female and black in a popular culture which values neither. This means that, unlike white females, black females are devalued even further on screen because of their race. Hence, unfavorable comparisons have long been made between black women and white women in a female hierarchy which makes distinctions between women of different races based on their femininity. White female characters have generally been placed at the top of this female hierarchy because they are represented as behaving in a feminine fashion in male/female relationships. Black female characters, by contrast, generally fall at the very bottom of this race-based female hierarchy as their conduct in male/female relationships is depicted as deviating from the standards of culturally approved notions of femininity (Manatu 2003; hooks 1981, 1992, 1993; Jewel 1993; Humm 1997).

Any discussion, then, of black female images in popular culture must take both the gender hierarchy and the race-based female hierarchy into account. Hence I will begin by looking at how gender hierarchies have long defined all women—black and white alike—as inferior to men and then follow that with a consideration of how race-based female hierarchies have traditionally defined black women as inferior to white women by representing them as less feminine.

THE GENDER HIERARCHY AND
THE GENDERED DIVISION OF LABOR

In many ways, standards for defining women as inferior to men grow out of a gendered division of labor which has traditionally relegated women to subordinate roles in both the paid labor force and the private household. This gender hierarchy was in evidence as long ago as preindustrial times when America was still largely an agricultural society. Back then, women performed a number of tasks on the farm that allowed these households to be self-sufficient. Yet, despite their contributions, the head of the household was always the father or husband who divvied up the work load and made all decisions. In these patriarchal households, women simply obeyed the dictates of their fathers or husbands and in that context, passivity and dependence came to be associated with femininity (Messerschmidt 1993).

As the nation industrialized, work was removed from the home. And, as the workplace moved from the farm to the factory, work came to be rewarded with wages. Yet even with the rise of wage labor, males continued to dominate and control female labor at work and at home. Hence, even when women worked, their jobs were lower paid than those of males and came with considerably less authority and control. Women also continued to be subordinated at home as the division of labor in the household required them to be responsible for most of the housework and child care.

Gradually, women were discouraged from working at even the low-paid jobs to which they had been relegated in the industrial labor force as their work came to be seen as a threat to the wages and job security of men working in the trades. Hence, working-class and upper-class men alike urged women to leave the factories and confine themselves to the household by accusing married women who tried to work of deserting their children and trying to steal men's jobs. Single women who tried to work were likewise stigmatized for working as they were said to lack the proper feminine socialization that would have trained them to be competent wives and mothers (Messerschmidt 1993; Higginbotham 2005).

Clearly, then, industrialization-shaped definitions of white masculinity and white femininity as being a good husband increasingly came to be equated with being the sole wage earner in the family who earned enough so that his wife would not have to work. In complementary fashion, white femininity came to be equated with being a full-time mother and housewife (Messerschmidt 1993).

As they were increasingly confined to the home, white women found their position as workers devalued because as housewives they worked for free. As housewives, they were also extremely dependent on their husbands, who were often the sole wage earners in the family. These conditions held sway until the latter half of the twentieth century when a number of jobs held by white males were outsourced and many white females were forced to return to work, at least on a part-time basis. These women quickly found out that the gendered division of labor was still in place as they were often segregated into jobs that had a mostly female workforce (clerical work, nursing, teaching, etc.). And, as they soon discovered, jobs with a mostly female workforce continued to be characterized by low pay and limited authority (Shapiro 2005; Reskin and Padavic 2005; Zinn and Eitzen 2005).

Clearly, then, white females have a history of being devalued as workers. Yet, not all white females regard this as problematic. After all, femininity has never been measured in terms of a woman's standing in the occupational hierarchy like masculinity. Instead, since preindustrial times, femininity has been equated with weakness, dependence and passivity, and hence by passively obeying the dictates of their husbands and fathers, many women have been socialized to believe that they are "doing femininity" (Manatu 2003; Collins 1991; hooks 1981; Giddings 1992; Messerschmidt 1993).

Doing femininity has also traditionally meant that women should confine themselves to the private sphere as wives and mothers rather than striking out in the public sphere to try to achieve status in high-powered jobs. For that reason as well, many women have been more willing to consent to gender inequalities in the paid labor force because of the ways in which a male-dominated society has traditionally defined femininity.

To be sure, this definition of femininity brings with it certain costs; but, it also assures white females of certain rewards. By confining themselves to the feminine roles of wife and mother, they achieve social respectability and by expressing feminine traits like weakness, dependence and passivity, they are assured of male protection. And, even though their willingness to labor for free as wives and mothers makes them totally dependent on their husbands, it simultaneously encourages their husbands to achieve masculinity by providing them with economic security (Jewel 1993; hooks 1981).

However, since the 1970s, these constructions of womanhood have increasingly been contested. Feminists, in particular, have been critical of the fact that the feminine ideal has defined the highest calling for women as being a wife and mother. As such, they argue that these traditional standards of femininity have led to the stifling of female ambition and achievement by discouraging women from pursuing higher education and a full-time career.

Partially, in reaction to these feminist critiques, more and more white females have sought a college education since the 1970s and they now make up a larger share of many high-powered professions. Yet even in these jobs, women often encounter an old-boy network that prevents them from rising to the top of their profession. Moreover, there is still sex segregation in the labor force as many high-paying, high-powered jobs still have predominantly male workforces (e.g., engineering, computer sciences, politics) even as women continue to be hired to work in jobs staffed by largely female workforces (e.g., teachers, clerical workers, nurses). That these female-dominated jobs continue to pay less and command less authority means that even today white women (as well as black women) make considerably less money than white males. Hence even today, feminists find themselves calling for equal pay for equal work (Reskin and Padavic 2005; Zinn and Eitzen 2005).

Feminists have likewise been critical of a definition of femininity that has traditionally labeled housework as women's work. After all, even today when so many women work, they often find themselves coming home to work a second shift as they continue to be more responsible for cooking, cleaning, child care and care of aging parents than their husbands. Feminists, then, still find themselves demanding better family-leave policies and increased funding for child care to enable women to balance their responsibilities in the paid labor force with the unpaid work they perform in the private sphere of the family (Reskin and Padavic 2005; Risman 2005).

Many in the women's movement have also been critical of the traditional feminine ideal that continues to encourage women to see passivity and dependence as ways of doing femininity. Even today, many working women find themselves passively following the dictates of their husbands because their lower pay in the paid work force can mean that the husband's higher wages give him the authority to make more decisions in the household (Reskin and Padavic 2005). This dilemma is even more pronounced for those housewives and mothers who do not work as they are totally dependent on the wages of their husbands. This kind of dependence has also been a source of concern because it can thrust women into poverty in the event of a divorce and make women less willing to leave physically abusive husbands.

Female Sexuality in a Male-Dominated Popular Culture

The fact that women continue to be so dependent on men has other repercussions as well. Because so many women continue to be partially or fully dependent on men for their economic survival, they often find themselves selling their sexuality in order to attract a male. As a consequence, female sexuality has traditionally been defined by males as they alone rank women in terms of what they find desirable. This means that many of the images of female sexuality in a male-dominated popular culture have been developed for male enjoyment rather than for female enjoyment (Manatu 2003; Dines et al. 1998; Humm 1997).

Hence, despite the sexual revolution and improvements in contraception that should have given females more control over their own sexual expression, images of females in popular culture still afford males enormous influence over female sexuality. And because it is males who so frequently rate female sexuality in popular culture, images of female sexuality often say more about what it takes to affirm masculinity rather than providing audiences with any insight into how women perceive their own sexuality (Humm 1997; Messerschmidt 1993).

Among other things, affirming heterosexual masculinity in popular culture has meant that men should be able to demonstrate an insatiable appetite for women that requires them to be able to perform sexually at all times. As a consequence, a number of images in male-dominated popular culture measure maleness in terms of a man's capacity to make numerous sexual and romantic conquests (e.g., James Bond movies). When this metric is used, women are reduced to mere objects whose only purpose is to affirm masculinity by playing the role of sexual or romantic conquest. And, when taken to the extreme, this kind of female objectification can mean that in many films, women are reduced to mere body parts meant to draw only the audience's voyeuristic gaze. Males, by contrast are more frequently presented as complete social subjects with whom the audience can identify (Humm 1997; Davies and Smith 1997; Dines et al. 1998).

If gender inequalities were the only consideration, then this chapter on constructions of womanhood would focus on the numerous criticisms of these images of femininity as they are defined in popular culture. However, any effort to consider how both race and gender shape constructions of black womanhood dictates that these images of femininity be taken as the standard—no matter how problematic they might be. After all, they are the basis for making distinctions between black women and white women in a white-male-dominated popular culture, where black women are often constructed as inferior to white women because they are depicted as less feminine.

Hence, I will simply stipulate that the notion that a woman's worth should be measured in terms of her femininity has been contested and then proceed to consider how this problematic notion of femininity is used to make distinctions between black women and white women.

BLACK WOMEN AND THE FEMALE RACIAL HIERARCHY IN POPULAR CULTURE

From the outset, it should be noted that blacks (and other minorities) have been considerably less capable of conforming to these definitions of masculinity and femininity than whites. After all, racial discrimination has meant that black men have traditionally had much higher rates of unemployment than white men. As a consequence, black women have been less able to live up to these mainstream definitions of femininity, as they have had to work—traditionally as maids in white households (Collins 1991; Higginbotham 2005).

While black males and black females have been forced to come up with their own definitions of masculinity and femininity in light of these constraints, they have not been able to disseminate them because they do not control the institutions of popular culture. As these institutions are still controlled by white males, definitions of masculinity and femininity in popular culture are still very much defined by white males.

In a white-male-dominated popular culture, then, the racial inferiority of black women characters is often expressed in terms of their low ranking in a race-based female hierarchy which continues to rank women in terms of their femininity. And, despite its problematic nature, a woman's femininity in this female racial hierarchy is often based on her possession of such superficial "feminine" traits as beauty and virtue. Females who lack either beauty or virtue, then, are subject to be punished in film narratives, while those who possess these feminine traits are all too often revered and rewarded. (This contrasts sharply with a male hierarchy which can rank males—even physically unattractive males—based on more substantial character traits such as courage, intelligence, strength, honesty or a sense of justice.)

Consequently, many negative images of black females in popular culture show them as lacking in beauty or virtue or both. For example, many long-standing negative images of black women represent them as unattractive, de-sexed mammies who lack the kind of beauty required to meet the standards for feminine beauty that are set by white women (Manatu 2003; Jewel 1993; hooks 1981, 1992, 1993; Bogle 1994; Guerrero 1993; J. Jones 1992; Lubiano 1992).

Unfavorable comparisons are also made between black women and white women in terms of virtue or their willingness to subscribe to society's moral codes. Hence, white females have traditionally been depicted as the standard bearers for femininity by displaying a willingness to conform to a moral code that demands virtue in women. Black females, by contrast, have long been represented as women who demonstrate a willingness to deviate from society's moral codes because of their lack of virtue. By depicting black women as "bad girls" or oversexed Jezebels, lacking in virtue, it has always been possible to hold them up to public shame even as white women were placed on a pedestal because of their innocence and purity (Manatu 2003; Jewel 1993; hooks 1981, 1992, 1993; Bogle 1994; Guerrero 1993; J. Jones 1992; Lubiano 1992).

A Brief History of the Female Racial Hierarchy

White women's superior status in a female hierarchy that defines them as true women, by dint of their femininity, began to emerge as far back as slavery. Back then, beliefs about black women's inferior status were starting to take shape based on the notion that they were the defeminized opposites of feminine white women (Giddings 1992).

Historically, black women were defeminized because of differences in the way in which whites constructed heterosexuality amongst themselves as opposed to the ways in which they constructed heterosexuality among blacks. Amongst themselves, whites defined heterosexuality in terms of clearly demarcated masculine and feminine roles and traits. Hence, white women were traditionally depicted as true women based on their incumbency in the ultimate feminine roles of wife and mother. As wives and mothers, they typically expressed feminine traits such as innocence, weakness, nurturance, passivity and a lack of sexual passion (Manatu 2003; Collins 1991; hooks 1981; Giddings 1992; Messerschmidt 1993; Jewel 1993).

These feminine roles nicely complemented the masculine roles that white males assigned themselves in that the male role required that men accord these innocent, weak and passive women respect and provide them with economic security and protection. In fact, one measure of status for a white male was the respect accorded his white wife, mother or sister. Indeed, it was considered an insult to his masculine honor if his wife, mother or sister was dishonored, and he was duty bound to retaliate for any such insults or have his masculinity questioned (Gastil 1971). Hence, whites defined themselves in terms of a sexual binary in which white women were what white men were not.

Yet even as whites laid out clearly demarcated and complementary sex roles for themselves, they made little effort to differentiate between their female and male slaves. Instead of a sexual binary, whites treated their black slaves as if a sexual symmetry prevailed between black men and black women. After all, there was little need to make sexual distinctions between male and female slaves as both were regarded as subhuman (Jewel 1993).

Indeed because they were slaves, it would have been difficult to apply a feminine ideal developed for white women to black women. After all, as slaves, the world of black women was the public sphere of work rather than the private sphere of hearth, home and family. As bondswomen, they could not be protected from extreme poverty, violence or the hostile world outside their families like many white women. And, as inferior, subhuman slaves, they could not be placed on a pedestal like white women, nor could they be perceived as passive, dependent or in need of protection.

Instead of treating black female slaves like true women (i.e., white women), then, slaveowners treated them more like black males. For example, black women were forced to labor in the fields right alongside black males. They were also expected to work as hard as the males, which meant no attention was paid to the fact that black women had less strength and endurance than black males.

In truth, taking physical differences between male and female slaves into account would have meant less profit for white male slaveholders as it would have meant much less labor was expected of black women. By constructing black male and black female slaves as if they were governed by a sexual symmetry, then, white slaveholders made slavery that much more efficient and more profitable for themselves (Jewel 1993).

Over and above similarities in their treatment as slave labor, black females and black males were punished in much the same way as both could be stripped naked and publicly beaten by whites (hooks 1981; Jewel 1993). For example, hooks (1981) cites the case of a black female slave who was stripped naked and brutally beaten in public for failing to bake a pie to her white owners' specifications. Such public beatings were likewise meted out to free black women as in the case of Eliza Gallie.

In 1853, Ms. Gallie was arrested, tried and convicted for stealing cabbages from a white man's property. As a free black woman, she had sufficient assets to hire four attorneys to appeal her conviction. Yet, despite her lawyers' best efforts in her defense, her conviction was upheld. Convinced a second appeal would be futile, Ms. Gallie resigned herself to her punishment, which consisted of being beaten on her bare back at the public whipping post.

Commenting on the Gallie case, Jewel argues that it was actually quite common for black women to be whipped naked in public for minor infractions. By her estimation, such public spectacles, where African American women were beaten right out in the open, only served to remind black women—both slave and free alike—that they did not have the same rights as whites.

Such public humiliations also served to defeminize black females by indicating to them that they were not deserving of the protections and respectability accorded true women (i.e., white women). Indeed, the fact that black women could be subjected to public beatings and the violation of their rights as a matter of course is a testament to the power of antebellum stereotypes that depicted them as pseudomales, little different from black males, and as such, undeserving of the protections accorded true women.

The public whippings of black women also sent a message to black men that they could do nothing to stop this public debasement of the black women in their lives whether they were their wives, mothers, sisters or daughters. As such, these public punishments of black women also functioned to emasculate black males who were forced to stand by helplessly and watch these beatings unable to take on the masculine role of protector.

There were other similarities in the treatment of black females and black males as well. Because both female and male slaves were looked upon as animals, black female slaves were routinely pranced about naked on auction blocks and fondled by white male auctioneers like livestock—just like male slaves. Indeed, because black women were slaves, antebellum society could hardly have been expected to exempt them from these incessant little molestations due to concerns about their feminine modesty.

And just as there was no need for the dominant white society to concern itself with any feminine sensibilities that black females might have had about being exhibited on an auction block and fondled like cattle, it also did not have to concern itself with how black women might have felt about being sold into lifelong slavery where sexual assaults and public whippings were routine (hooks 1981; Lerner 1972; Manatu 2003; Jewel 1993). Instead of concerning itself with how slave women might have been traumatized by the incessant rapes and molestations, antebellum society proceeded to stereotype black women as oversexed Jezebels who not only consented to these sexual liaisons, but actually brazenly initiated sexual relations with white male slaveowners and overseers.

As loose, animalistic women, who enjoyed sex, the black Jezebels of antebellum myth were depicted as the unvirtuous opposites of white women. Back then, the thinking was that virtuous white women would have preferred jumping off a cliff to succumbing to sex with black males, and therefore trauma in the face of sexual victimization was an emotional state reserved for true women—i.e., white women. By contrast, early American myths regarding the sexually aggressive black Jezebels initiating sex with white males fostered the notion that black females could not be raped and indeed could not even be expected to be traumatized by rape (hooks 1981; Jewel 1993; Manatu 2003; Lerner 1972).

Hence, a female hierarchy emerged in slavery in which true womanhood was equated with the virtuous, sexually passive, delicate, and dependent white female. And, because they were the standard bearers for femininity, white women were eligible for the rewards of the feminine including chivalry, protection, and respectability. By contrast, black women came to be seen as strong, shameless, wanton and sexually forward—just like black men (Collins 1991). Hence they emerged from slavery being stereotyped in terms which suggested that they were grotesquely unfeminine in a time when femininity was equated with delicacy, virtuousness, modesty and a want of sexual passion.

Certainly, the treatment of black women during slavery provides ample evidence that they were perceived by whites as more like black men than white women and as such, no more in need of protection than black males. And, because they were stereotyped as wanton, pseudomasculine deviants from the female sex role, they hardly seemed to require the protections accorded to truly feminine women—i.e., white women.

Hollywood and the Minimization of Black Female Oppression

In many ways, then, slavery was every bit as oppressive for black women as it was for black men. Yet, in some ways, the oppressiveness of racial domination during slavery and its aftermath has been more visible and better documented for black men. After all, there are any number of accounts of how white domination of black males was expressed in the form of whippings and mutilations, which gave way to lynchings and castrations in slavery's aftermath.

This is not to say that Hollywood did not try to minimize the racial oppression of black males by depicting them as lazy coons, toms or harmless sidekicks to whites (e.g., Bill "Bojangles" Robinson, Rochester, Stepin Fetchit), who were content to be dominated by their white masters first in slavery and then in the aftermath of slavery as servants in white households (Bogle 1994). By portraying black male characters that seemed to consent to their domination, these films suggested that racial domination was not especially onerous for black men. If news accounts of the lynchings and castrations from the real world had not intruded on these big-screen images of happy-go-lucky black men, the film industry might have succeeded (Bogle 1994; D. Jones 2005; Guerrero 1993).

With black females, however, the minimization of racial oppression was more successful. For one thing, Hollywood was able to erase a history of racial violence directed at black women by simply not showing the public beatings. There were also few cinematic scenes depicting antebellum cultural practices that allowed white males' easy sexual access to black female slaves whether they were on slave ships, on the auction block, working in the fields or working in slaveowners' households (hooks 1981; Jewel 1993; Lerner 1972). Most films likewise ignored the black female slaves who labored as field hands. Instead Hollywood largely depicted black women cooking and cleaning for their white owners during slavery much as they would have cooked and cleaned in their own households. With such images of black female servitude, then, it was possible to depict slavery in terms that suggested that it was not especially burdensome for black women.

And, because slavery was depicted in terms that suggested it was not particularly oppressive for black women, it was possible for the film industry to persuade audiences that the black women shown on screen raising the children of their masters were truly willing to consent to their own domination. Hence in film after film, black women, cast as mammies, could be seen happily suffering and sacrificing for their white employers and their children (e.g., *Imitation of Life, Gone with the Wind*).

Indeed the loyal, contented and long-suffering mammy was a crucial character in a number of films because it allowed Hollywood to openly depict a racial hierarchy between women in its early days. Hence, in film after film, white females were cast as slaveholders and mistresses of the house, while black women were cast as the loyal, unfeminine, de-sexed mammies who willingly waited on them first in slavery and then later in freedom (Manatu 2003; Bogle, 1994; Collins 1991; hooks 1981, 1992; Jewel 1993).

In fact, the first black person to win an Oscar of any kind was black actress Hattie McDaniel, who won for her portrayal of Mammy in the 1939 pro-Confederacy classic, *Gone with the Wind*. Working as Scarlett O'Hara's loyal house slave, Mammy, Ms. McDaniel embodied the image of a black woman content to suffer and sacrifice for her white owners. As evidence that she consented to her own domination, Mammy was shown rejecting freedom so that she could remain Scarlett's loyal servant even after emancipation. And because Mammy's role was apparently so vital in justifying the slave-owning south in the film, Hattie McDaniel managed to best white actress Olivia de Havilland (who played Melanie in the film) to win the award for best supporting actress—even in the racially intolerant time of 1939 (Mapp 2003).

The Female Racial Hierarchy and Romance

As slaveholders and later mistresses of their households, white women achieved much of their social status on the big screen by acquiring a husband who could provide them with economic security and access to the high-status feminine roles of wife and mother. Hence, Hollywood routinely cast white females in the role of romantic leads who expended much energy throughout the film in establishing their feminine desirability by seeking expressions of tenderness from the leading man so that the imaginative act of falling in love could take place (Manatu 2003). Women who pursued romance in these films were then rewarded with society's highest honors for doing femininity which included social respect, defense of feminine honor and a husband who provided social status, economic security and access to the roles of wife and mother.

Yet, as women ranked at the bottom of the female hierarchy, black women were typically excluded from these romantic roles and thus, their feminine wiles were not on display. Rather, in their relationships with black men, they were often cast as masculinized pseudomales who competed with men for the male role rather than establishing their femininity through romance. For example, black women were routinely cast as Sapphires who demeaned and emasculated their husbands and suitors with verbal put-downs. They were also cast as matriarchs who went even further and emasculated black men by completely taking over the masculine role of breadwinner (Manatu 2003; Collins 1991; hooks 1981, 1992; Bogle, 1994).

The tendency of Hollywood to defeminize black females is also evident in its construction of them as "bad girls" like traditional oversexed Jezebels or modern-day whores. Roles which depict black females as bad girls are de-feminizing as they force their incumbents to express a masculine sexuality rather than a feminine sexuality. In other words, like men, black women in these roles pursue sex rather than romance. Much like men, bad black girls also pride themselves on their sexual prowess. And, like men, they are often eager to initiate sexual intercourse rather than waiting around to be wooed like a feminine romantic lead (Manatu 2003).

Because they do not express a feminine sexuality, bad black girls are de-nied the rewards accorded true women including respectability, protection and defense of honor. In fact, they hardly seem to require such protections as their ill-famed promiscuity induces them to shamelessly make themselves sexually accessible and allow themselves to be sexually exploited by the men in their lives.

The First Bad Black Girl: The Oversexed Jezebel

Cultural beliefs suggesting the existence of a bad black girl or oversexed black Jezebel began in slavery when black female slaves were said to initiate sex with white male slaveholders and overseers. As a consequence, many black females came to be seen as sexual outlaws much like black males as both were depicted as constantly lusting after whites (hooks 1981; Jewel 1993; Manatu 2003; Lerner 1972; Collins 1991). Moreover, these myths suggested that across-race desire was asymmetrical for much like white females did not find black males desirable, white males were not presumed to find black females desirable.

Of course, by suggesting that these masculinized black female slaves shamelessly initiated sex with white males, the oversexed Jezebel myth ab-solved white males of any responsibility for sexual assaults on black females. And when coupled with representations of them as unattractive, de-sexed mammies, these early stereotypes suggested that white males could not pos-sibly find them desirable, thereby indicating that black women had to be the aggressors in any black female/white male liaisons.

Of course, such myths were also the basis for a long-running tradition in which the pain and suffering of black female rape victims could be studiously ignored. In fact rather than talking about the sexual victimization of black females, these myths inscribed white male innocence by suggesting that black females were so oversexed and lacking in virtue that they could not be raped (hooks 1981; Manatu 2003).

Racial myths about a masculinized, oversexed black female slave ever-ready to initiate sex also helped to shore up the female hierarchy in which white women were depicted as superior because of their virtue, desirability and sexual passivity. As oversexed Jezebels, black female slaves could be judged to be inferior because of their undesirability, sexual forwardness and lack of virtue.

Black Rape, White Rape: The Difference It Makes

This same race-based female hierarchy that distinguished virtuous, sexually passive white women from unvirtuous, sexually aggressive black women also explains the very different ways in which the rapes of black females and white females were treated during slavery and Jim Crow. Even the suspicion that a white female had been raped by a black male was sufficient to mobilize the white community to avenge itself on the black community with extralegal acts that included lynchings, pogroms, murders and other forms of vigilantism (Inverarity 1976; Beck and Tolnay 1990). Even the legal system specified more severe penalties (including death) for black men who raped white women than for white men who raped white women (Walker et al. 2004).

Yet in this system where the rape of a white female by a black male was punished severely—both legally and extralegally—the rape of a black female by a white male was rarely punished (Walker et al. 2004). While some states did specify minor penalties for the rape of a black female slave, it is doubtful that many black females made it to court to see their attackers punished with even these greatly reduced penalties as black female slaves could be flogged, imprisoned or put to death if they attempted to fight off or kill their white male attackers (hooks 1981; Collins 1991; Jewel 1993). Instead of justice, black females were burdened with myths that converted their rapes into consensual sex by depicting them as the initiators in any sexual encounter that occurred with more powerful white males (Jewel 1993; Manatu 2003; hooks 1981, 1992; Collins 1991).

In a case of art imitating life, Hollywood early endorsed this cultural practice of treating white rapes more seriously. In fact, the 1915 Hollywood classic *Birth of a Nation* was little more than a vindication of the custom of unleashing white vigilantes when a white woman's virtue was at stake. Yet even as *Birth* urged the avenging of a white female's honor, real-world accounts from that period suggest that whites continued to resist treating black women as if they were respectable ladies deserving of equal protection from sexual assaults.

This is demonstrated in a 1912 account written by a black woman who tells of the dominant society's resistance to taking her assault by a white employer seriously:

> I remember very well the first and last work place from which I was dismissed. I lost my place because I refused to let the madam's husband kiss me. He must have been accustomed to undue familiarity with his servants, or else he took it

as a matter of course, because . . . soon after I was installed as cook, he walked up to me, threw his arms around me, and was in the act of kissing me, when I demanded to know what he meant, and shoved him away. I was young then, and newly married, and didn't know then what has been a burden to my mind and heart ever since; that a colored woman's virtue in this part of the country has no protection. I at once went home, and told my husband about it. When my husband went to the man who had insulted me, the man cursed him and slapped him, and—had him arrested! The police judge fined my husband $25. I was present at the hearing, and testified on oath to the insult offered me. The white man, of course, denied the charge. The old judge looked up and said: "This court will never take the word of a nigger against the word of a white man" . . . I believe nearly all white men take and expect to take undue liberties with their colored female servants—not only the fathers, but in many cases the sons also. Those servants who rebel against such familiarity must either leave or expect a mighty hard time if they stay. (cited in Lerner 1972)

That the legal system in early twenthieth-century America could refuse to punish this white male for his harassment and in fact, could decide on punishing the woman's husband instead indicates at least two things. First, it demonstrates that the legal system endorsed Jim-Crow-era custom that allowed white males' easy sexual access to their black female employees. Secondly, it is further evidence that the early-twentieth-century American legal system gave its stamp of approval to the emasculation of black men as such penalties would have served as a reminder to them that they could not take on the masculine role of protecting their wives, mothers, sisters or daughters from these abuses.

And yet, the same white males who felt entitled to easy sexual access to black women during slavery and Jim Crow would never have thought of allowing anyone to molest or assault their white wives, daughters or sisters in similar fashion. Regrettably, this double standard made sense in light of cultural beliefs at the time. Back then, distinctions made between black women and white women defined white women as the kind of virtuous and delicate feminine creatures that required protection from such crude sexual advances. By contrast, black women were stereotyped as mammies and oversexed Jezebels and as such they were deemed either too masculinized and sexually unattractive or as too oversexed and lacking in virtue to require similar protections (Jewel 1993; Manatu 2003; hooks 1981).

REINVENTING THE BAD BLACK GIRL MYTH: FROM OVERSEXED JEZEBELS TO SEX WORKERS

Clearly, the film industry in the early twentieth century was more than happy to show off the existing racial hierarchy rather than challenging it. Consequently, when it came to black females, the film industry simply borrowed many of the negative stereotypes of black females from antebellum literature, law and custom that had long defined them as women of little social worth.

For example, in the early days, prior to the civil rights movement, Hollywood routinely made use of cinematic images of the desexed mammy to attach inferiority to black womanhood and show off the racial order to movie audiences. By parading one loyal black mammy after another before the movie-going public, the film industry was able to graphically depict a racial order that was defined by black women showing deference to white female slaveholders in films set in the slave era or to white female mistresses of the house in films set after slavery (e.g., *Gone with the Wind*, *Imitation of Life*).

However, these roles always had the potential to generate negative audience reactions in a democracy where all persons are presumably created equal. It comes as no surprise, then, that these roles gradually became problematic as the race privilege denoted by the role of the white female slaveholder or mistress of the household increasingly came to be seen as an illegitimate symbol of racial oppression—particularly in the aftermath of the civil rights movement (Collins 1991). As a consequence, fewer and fewer white female slaveowners and their compliant black mammies were shown on the silver screen. Yet, even as the role of the loyal and subservient black mammy declined, new negative images of black female characters came along to replace it.

Since the civil rights movement, depicting a female hierarchy in which white women can be seen as superior to black women has meant a revival of the old myths that depict black females as bad girls like oversexed Jezebels (Manatu 2003; hooks 1981, 1992). However, this time, the oversexed Jezebel from American slavery has been resurrected as a modern day prostitute or some other sex worker rather than as a slave. Beginning with the blaxploitation movies of the 1970s followed by ghetto action movies beginning in the 1990s, black females have increasingly been trotted out before the cameras as prostitutes, strippers, lap dancers and other sex workers. There is ample evidence of this in a wide variety of films including *Independence Day, Girl 6, Jungle Fever, South Central, Boyz n the Hood, Mona Lisa, Baby Boy* and a host of other movies.[2]

COMMONALITIES BETWEEN OLD-FASHIONED
BLACK JEZEBELS AND MODERN-DAY SEX WORKERS

By depicting black females as prostitutes (and other sex workers), these recent films can be said to be channeling old-fashioned images of the oversexed black Jezebel from antebellum literature, custom and law largely because modern-day prostitutes and old-fashioned Jezebels have so much in common. For one thing, much like the old-fashioned black Jezebels of the antebellum south, today's black prostitutes can be portrayed on screen as hypersexual and lacking in virtue. Hence both images—either the traditional oversexed Jezebel or contemporary sex worker—function to deny black female characters respectability. Furthermore by representing black women as either prostitutes or Jezebels, Hollywood can continue to uphold the racial order among women as both images automatically place black females at the bottom of a female hierarchy based on virtue.

Routinely depicting black women as prostitutes or sex workers is also a good way to demean them because sex workers are seen as the very antithesis of true womanhood. After all, true women often express their femininity in their relationships with men by using their virtue or sexual inaccessibility as a bargaining chip to extract favors from men in either courtship or marriage. By contrast, sex workers are paid-for women who are paid precisely because they have agreed not to use the denial of sex as a weapon. So, for example, prostitutes and other sex workers can be paid to allow themselves to be looked at, touched or titillated by their male clients. Alternatively, they can also be paid to be sexually aggressive and proposition their clients for sex if it furthers their clients' fantasies. Indeed some sex workers will even pretend to be sex starved in order to make their male clients feel more desirable (Allison 1994).

In the nineteenth century, clear-cut distinctions were being made between prostitutes of all races and respectable white women like wives and mothers. Evidence that such distinctions were made comes from a group of late-nineteenth-century regulationists, so named because of their failed attempt to head off the criminalization of prostitution by promoting its regulation (Messerschmidt 1993). To make their case, the regulationists argued that white men were driven by an excessive sex drive, while white women were governed by an equally strong asexuality.

To address the conflicting needs of the two sexes, then, they argued that prostitution should be legal and regulated rather than outlawed because regulation would provide men with an outlet for their sexual instincts while simultaneously protecting delicate and asexual white wives and sweethearts from men's crude sexual demands. In other words, prostitutes were to be treated as a separate caste of women who were not to be protected from the sexual excesses of men like respectable women. Instead their function was to protect more respectable women from the kinds of sexual debasement for which they were paid.

As noted, prostitutes were not alone in being exempted from protection from the excessive sexual instincts of men as nineteenth-century cultural beliefs and custom also held that *all* black women (even black wives and sweethearts, who did not work in the sex trade) were wanton and sexually available (Lerner 1972). Hence, cultural beliefs that assume an overlap between black women and prostitutes are quite old. And, because prostitutes of all races and black women were both seen as lacking the virtuousness of respectable white wives and mothers, prostitutes back then, much like old-fashioned black Jezebels, did not warrant any of the rewards accorded true women such as respectability and protection (Messerschmidt 1993; Collins 1991).

Modern-Day Treatment of Prostitutes

This traditional unwillingness to grant prostitutes and other sex workers the protections accorded true women persists even today. For example, even though both the prostitute and the male client who buys her sexual services are guilty of crimes, prostitutes are still far more likely to go to jail than their male clients (Raphael 2006). Further, in the event that they are raped, today's prostitutes have no credibility to press rape charges as the police are not likely to believe them. And because serial rapists are aware that prostitutes are not likely to be protected by the legal system, they often target them for serial rapes.

Not only are prostitutes unable to receive protection from rape, but they are also not likely to be protected from physical abuse as some johns pay for the right to assault them as a way of realizing their sexual fantasies. In fact, because they are so vulnerable to beatings, serial killers often target them for their killing sprees precisely because they know that no one will believe their complaints or protect them (Raphael 2006). That they are not seen as virtuous and respectable, then, is cause for exempting them from the protections accorded respectable women much as oversexed black Jezebels were exempted from protections from sexual assaults during slavery.

A number of feminists have long decried prostitution as one of the most sexist of professions because its very job description gives male clients the license to buy and sell prostitutes as if they were objects without any human dignity (McCaghy and Capron 1994; Raphael 2006).[3] And, in fact, the johns who buy their services are paying them purely to provide sexual gratification. Hence, depending on the john's definition of sexual gratification, prostitutes can be paid to provide services that range from extraordinary stimulation for the impotent to acting out elaborate rituals for men who can only be fulfilled by sadomasochistic fantasies that require that the prostitute allow herself to be physically abused or otherwise degraded.

Prostitutes are also objects of convenience for male buyers who do not wish to waste time with dating, entertaining, phony professions of emotional commitment or any other courtship rituals in order to have sex. They are also handy to have around for male travelers like salesmen, conventioneers, military personnel or long-distance truck drivers seeking quick and easy sexual outlets (James 1977).

Moreover, in a society where masculinity is defined in terms of numerous and varied sexual experiences, buying the services of a prostitute can also enable a man to improve his self-image. For example, for those men who define their self-worth and potency in terms of the quantity of sexual experiences they have had, buying sexual services from a prostitute becomes a quick way to add to the number of their experiences and enhance their self-esteem. And for males who define masculinity in terms of the variety of sexual experiences they have had, being able to quickly buy women who represent the exotic, the forbidden or the sexually ideal as symbolized by body parts (long legs, large breasts, etc.), race/ethnicity (black women, white women, Latinas, Asians, etc.) or persona (little girl-like women) is certainly expedient. Having such a diverse group of women (representing a variety of exotic sexual experiences) at their beck and call is especially appealing for those males who might otherwise have trouble approaching such a wide variety of women due to their own shyness or cultural taboos.

Moreover, males seeking to bond with their male friends can also hire sex workers like prostitutes or strippers to provide the entertainment at fraternities or stag parties (James 1977). In these all-male environments, such entertainment reinforces masculinity norms that place high value on maleness by devaluing women through the use of rituals that reduce them to sex objects and commodities (Boeringer et al. 1991; Allison 1994; Dines et al. 1998).

Justifying the Debasement of Prostitutes

That the males who hire sex workers often debase and abuse them in the course of realizing their fantasies is easily justified by the fact that these women are paid to perform these services. Indeed, the sex trade represents one of the last bastions of human transactions that leaves males totally free to pursue their fantasies—no matter how racist, sexist, brutal, or degrading.

The fact that prostitutes are so frequently debased and abused also seems warranted because women who become sex workers are thought to do so voluntarily. The thinking here is that modern-day prostitutes are motivated to enter the sex trade because they are so promiscuous (Raphael 2006; McCaghy and Capron 1994). Such assumptions seem to be borne out by interviews with prostitutes in which some report that they begin multiple sexual experiences at ages as young as 10 to 13 after only the briefest periods of acquaintance-ship with their sexual partners. Indeed, because so many adult sex workers report such early promiscuous behavior, some researchers have even claimed that sex workers have physiological and genetic predispositions that make them prone to enter and persist in a life of prostitution (McCaghy and Capron 1994). In short, they are described as if they are born promiscuous.

This notion that sex workers are distinct from "normal" females because of personality traits or genetic predispositions that make them naturally oversexed assumes that girls who grow up to work as sex workers enter these trades voluntarily because of an innate hypersexuality. However, a fair amount of research on prostitutes indicates that many enter the sex trade only after falling victim to rape or incest as young girls (Chesney-Lind and Shelden 1992; Raphael 2006).

Because so many prostitutes report that their careers in sex work begin only after they are subjected to childhood incest or rape, it seems highly probable that many may not enter the trade voluntarily. In other words, many may not be oversexed or genetically predisposed to promiscuity so much as they are the involuntary victims of abusive early childhood experiences. And, if many do not enter the trade voluntarily, but because of childhood abuse, then their eventual involvement in sex work cannot be blamed on defects in their personalities or on their genetic predispositions.

That early childhood experiences with rape or incest can socialize a young girl to believe that she is little more than a sexual object to be used for the enjoyment of others is understandable. Many children exposed to these early traumatic experiences might come to see their sexuality as an efficient means of gaining affection and attention. Moreover, the loss of self-esteem that comes with such childhood trauma and feelings of worthlessness–especially when it goes unpunished or unreported—could prepare them to accept the abuse, violence and debasement that often come with sex work (Raphael 2006; McCaghy and Capron 1994).

Young girls, who are sexually or physically abused by family members, are also prone to run away from home especially when they fear reporting their assaults or when nothing is done even when they do report their abuse. Unfortunately, when they run away, many are forced to live on the streets where they are often encouraged to support themselves by selling their bodies (Chesney-Lind and Shelden 1992; Raphael 2006). Hence, any tendency for female runaways to see themselves as worthless objects that exist for other people's gratification due to sexual abuse at home would only receive further reinforcement on the streets.

All in all, then, the notion that sex workers voluntarily enter the sex trade because they are hypersexed can safely be described as implausible. Still, promoting such a notion serves to divert attention away from the sexually oppressive childhood experiences that might drive many females into the trade. In that sense, then, modern-day myths about promiscuous young girls choosing sex work have much in common with age-old myths of oversexed Jezebels, which suggest that black women eagerly entered into relationships with slaveholders and overseers of their own free will. And much as is the case with myths about today's sex workers, antebellum myths also deemed the hypersexuality of the old-fashioned black Jezebel to be an essential part of her nature rather than a reflection of her powerlessness in a brutal slave system.

Black Females as Whores in the Era of Crack Cocaine

Because prostitutes deviate farthest from a feminine ideal based on virtue, depicting black women as prostitutes has been one way to evoke old images that stereotype them as inferior to white women in the female racial hierarchy. Hence, the trend towards portraying black women as prostitutes and other sex workers that began with the rise of blaxploitation films in the early 1970s and persisted into the 2000s has meant that their low ranking in the female racial hierarchy has often been based on their lack of virtue.

The recent popularity of this image of the black female as whore was only reinforced by the rise of crack-cocaine use in the late 1980s. As crack became more popular, more and more black women were represented as crack whores involved in trading sex for crack or some other drug in a number of 1990s films including many ghetto action movies (e.g., *Jungle Fever*, *Boyz n the Hood*, *South Central*).

Of course, white actresses have also played prostitutes in a number of popular or critically acclaimed movies including *Klute*, *L.A. Confidential*, *Pretty Woman*, *Hardcore* and *Traffic*. Still, it is worth noting that the white prostitutes in each of these films were also rescued and rehabilitated by the leading men. Hence they were able to exit the role of the whore by the end of the movie.[4]

More important than narratives which ultimately end in their rehabilitation, many of the white females cast in these roles also literally exit the role of the whore by the end of the movie by going on to reinvent themselves in other parts as wives, mothers, ingénues, political heroines, adventuresses, romantic heroines and a host of other nonsexual roles. Because black actresses are less likely to be reinvented in these nonsexual roles and more likely to be typecast as prostitutes, long-standing notions of black female hypersexuality are more easily reinforced when they are depicted as sex workers on the big screen (Manatu 2003).

In some ways, this recent tendency to represent black females as drug whores in the wake of the recent crack epidemic is surprising because it has little to do with reality. After all, recent national surveys consistently show that black females are equally likely or somewhat *less* likely to experiment with illegal drugs than white females.[5]

Moreover, the relationship between illegal drug use and prostitution, now being advertised with today's black crack whores, is hardly unique to the recent crack epidemic. In fact, one of the earliest historical references to females willing to sell their bodies for drugs was to white prostitutes addicted to opium in the 1870s. However, back then, the public was less concerned about the hypersexuality of these white prostitutes and more concerned about protecting white girls from respectable families from being lured into prostitution by Chinese American males, who were selling opium in opium dens. Indeed this desire to protect white females from being lured into prostitution was, in part, used to justify the outlawing of opium dens in San Francisco in 1875 (Brecher et al. 1972).[6]

Protecting black women from drug addiction and prostitution, however, does not seem to be the theme of many recent films that depict their involvement in the crack-sex trade. Instead, these films only seem to be interested in documenting how degraded black crack whores are. So, for example, black director John Singleton includes a cameo of a black crack whore publicly offering sex in exchange for crack in the ghetto action classic, *Boyz n the Hood* (1991). A few years earlier, black director Spike Lee cast Halle Berry as a crack whore who could be seen shamelessly peddling her body to passersby on the street in exchange for crack in *Jungle Fever*. A few years later, Ms. Berry would go on to reprise this role, by once again playing a crack whore named Khaila in white director Jake Gyllenhall's film, *Losing Isaiah* (1995).

However, *Losing Isaiah* goes beyond *Jungle Fever* and *Boyz n the Hood* by making the black crack whore, Khaila, the lead character in the picture. Furthermore, most of the other black female characters in the film are depicted as women who have become prostitutes and whores because of their addiction to crack-cocaine. Having constructed most of its black female characters as crack whores, the movie then proceeds to focus on how the crack addiction of these black women has caused them to violate the standards of the ultimate feminine role—namely that of a mother.

The Female Racial Hierarchy in *Losing Isaiah*

In the opening scenes of the movie, Khaila (Berry) is thrown out of a crack house because her infant son, Isaiah, is crying. She proceeds to hide him in a box in a garbage dumpster and then goes off to smoke crack. Waking the next morning from her crack-induced stupor, she returns to the dumpster to find that Isaiah is gone and gradually comes to believe that he is dead.

Later, when she is arrested for possession of marihuana, the audience follows her as she boards the prison bus with the other female prisoners on her way to a drug treatment program. While in treatment, Khaila attends a group therapy session where she is surrounded by other female crack addicts like herself, who are talking about what bad mothers and whores they are. In an act of self-condemnation, one black mother even confesses to the group that many of their children probably know that they are "hos."

This theme of the black woman as crack addict and bad mother is also dramatized in a later scene when one of Khaila's pregnant girlfriends is taken to the hospital where she miscarries, presumably after smoking crack. In earlier scenes, this same crack-addicted, bad black mother can be seen alternately screaming at her kids and neglecting them.

In part, then, *Losing Isaiah* represents black females in terms of a number of negative images—including whore, drug addict, and bad mother. In so doing, it places most of its black female characters on the lowest rung of a female racial hierarchy which ranks women in terms of their virtue and their roles as wives and mothers. It likewise depicts the female hierarchy by intercutting scenes of Khaila's drug addiction, prostitution and abandonment of her son, Isaiah, with scenes from the life of a white female social worker named Margaret (Jessica Lange), who is depicted as a good wife and mother.

Margaret first appears on screen when she encounters Isaiah after Khaila leaves him in a dumpster and an ambulance rushes him to the hospital where Margaret works as a social worker. Margaret eventually decides to adopt Isaiah, despite some objections from her husband and her daughter. Some time later, after Isaiah has lived with Margaret and her family for several years, Khaila discovers that he is still alive. At that point, she hires a Legal Aid lawyer and prepares to go to court to regain custody of Isaiah because as her lawyer argues black babies belong with black mothers.

In the courtroom scenes that follow, black single motherhood is put on trial as Khaila—now an ex-addict and an ex-prostitute—is forced to confess to the court that she was once a whore who traded sex for crack. As further evidence of her lack of virtue, she also admits that because Isaiah was conceived when she was working as a crack whore, she does not know the identity of Isaiah's father. Moreover, despite her exit from crack addiction and sex work, her status as a mother is still questionable as she confesses that she will have to raise Isaiah alone without a father on her inadequate income with no support system to help her.

In light of her past, the audience is not likely to have much sympathy for Khaila, who is after all a black female ex-addict and ex-prostitute, who left her tiny baby in a garbage dumpster. By contrast, Margaret, Isaiah's white adoptive mother, comes across as a sympathetic character, who loves Isaiah very much and very much wants to raise him, despite any problems that Isaiah might encounter by living as a black child in an all-white world.

In light of Khaila's past, Isaiah's white adoptive mother, Margaret, clearly has a higher ranking in the female racial hierarchy than his black birth mother, Khaila. After all, Margaret can offer Isaiah a loving, stable two-parent family in a middle-class home. Even the toddler, Isaiah, seems to be aware of the superiority of the white world—despite his tender age. This is evidenced by the fact that he keeps demanding to see his adoptive mother Margaret when the state forces him to go live with his birth mother Khaila in her shabby ghetto apartment. Eventually, even Khaila is forced to recognize Margaret's superiority as a mother as she calls on Margaret to help Isaiah make the adjustment to his "descent" into ghetto life.

As it cuts back and forth between Khaila and Margaret, then, the film foregrounds a female racial hierarchy based on virtue and motherhood in which black women are ranked at the bottom as unvirtuous whores and negligent mothers, while white women are ranked at the top as virtuous, nurturing wives and mothers.

And, while the race-based female hierarchy depicted in *Losing Isaiah* takes every opportunity to point up the inferiority of its black female characters, its depiction of the female hierarchy can hardly be described as racist. In that sense, then, the racial pecking order that it visualizes is preferable to earlier versions of the female hierarchy that were depicted in the pre-civil rights era. Back then, the racial inferiority of black women was often dramatized by depicting them as black slaves and maids, who were intensely loyal and submissive with the white women—whether slaveholders or mistresses of the house—for whom they worked. However, since the civil rights movement as the relationship between white female mistresses of the house and their black female slaves or servants came to be seen as a form of racial oppression, far fewer loyal black mammies have appeared on screen.

In *Losing Isaiah*'s more modern iteration of the female racial hierarchy, Khaila's low status in that hierarchy stems from the fact that she has chosen the life of a drug addict, bad mother and whore. Hence, the racial inferiority of the black female character in this film is explained by her assimilation of black underclass cultural values. In other words, it is Khaila's commitment to a decadent underclass lifestyle that explains her involvement in bizarre cultural practices like the crack-sex trade or her abandonment of her son—and not racial oppression. As a result, the female racial hierarchy depicted in *Losing Isaiah* represents an improvement over the old pre-civil rights version because it is clearly not the product of a system of racial oppression.

Indeed, because white racial oppression is not implicated in Khaila's low status in the female hierarchy, a white female like Margaret is provided with the space to comment on Khaila's inferiority as a mother. So, for example, Margaret can call Khaila a junkie and say that she belongs in prison without any fear of being seen as racially insensitive or politically incorrect because Khaila is so clearly responsible for her own inferiority.

From Whores to Symbolic Whores

Certainly the easiest way to depict a female racial hierarchy based on virtue is to contrast black oversexed Jezebels or modern-day whores to virtuous white wives and mothers—such as occurs in *Losing Isaiah*. However, in some ways, it has become more difficult to construct the kind of female racial hierarchy that ranks women based on their sexual purity, particularly since the sexual revolution. After all, since the 1970s, beliefs about sex and white women's virtue have changed in the larger society, and Hollywood has accommodated itself to these cultural shifts. As a result, white females have routinely come to be depicted as having a sexual history on screen. In fact, because sex sells, a sex scene is now almost required in many movies.

Since the sexual revolution, then, male filmmakers have had to erect a hierarchy of female virtue that does not simply pit prostitutes and sex workers against women who are not involved in the trade, like innocent girlfriends, wives or mothers. In the post-sexual revolution era, then, they have increasingly come to rely on a hierarchy of female virtue that makes more subtle distinctions between "bad girls" and "good girls" within the non-sex worker population of girlfriends, wives and mothers. Generally they have accomplished this by allowing a sexually active white female to establish her femininity through romance and the courtship process.

Hence, to preserve a racial order that defines black women as "bad girls" and white women as "good girls" (despite a sexual history), it has been necessary for Hollywood to rely on ever more negative depictions of black female sexuality (Manatu 2003). Filmmakers have often accomplished this by excluding black females from romantic roles. This means that while white girlfriends with a sexual history are still routinely cast in romantic leads where they pursue the roles of wife and mother, black girlfriends with a sexual history are more often cast as bad girls or symbolic whores, who pursue relationships with men based on sex rather than romance. Hence, for many of the black women characters that appear on screen, there typically is no courtship process.

Manatu (2003) examines how black male and white male filmmakers alike depict black females as bad girls or symbolic whores in a number of films released between 1986 and 2001. In part, she claims many directors have been able to portray their black female characters as symbolic whores, who are wholeheartedly sexual beings, by omitting any mention of their careers, family roles or political beliefs. Instead of showing any interest in any of these areas, their black female characters are depicted as exclusively interested in men. Moreover their single-minded focus on men is portrayed as sexual rather than romantic.

Roles which depict black females as symbolic whores are defeminizing as they force their incumbents to express a masculine sexuality rather than a feminine sexuality. In other words, like men, black women in these roles pursue sex rather than romance and pride themselves on their sexual prowess like men (e.g., *Boomerang* 1992). Much like men, symbolic whores also initiate sex with men rather than waiting around to be wooed like a feminine romantic lead (Manatu 2003). In other words, symbolic whores take on the traditional male role by propositioning men for sex and by initiating sexual relations with them.

Much like men, they are also depicted as eager for sex and conveniently enough see men only as potential sex partners or as sources of financial support. And, when symbolic whores solicit men for sex, their approach tends to be sexual rather than romantic as they use crude and degraded language to make their desires known. Finally, to make their reduction to mere sexual beings complete, many male filmmakers also show these black symbolic whores in the midst of coitus performing crude sex acts.

Because romance is downplayed in their relationships with men, there is typically little dating or courtship in these films. And because the black women in these films are uninterested in romance, they are typically portrayed pursuing multiple sexual partners rather than committing themselves to a romantic courtship with a single partner.

Indeed, because they are so single-mindedly focused on sex, many of these women seem to have little interest in men as people. Hence, there are few friendships shown in which these symbolic whores treat the men in their lives as whole people with nonsexual characteristics. In a similar vein, because these women are not shown in friendships with men, the men in their lives do not treat them as whole people with nonsexual characteristics.

In many ways, then, the black symbolic whore is just an unpaid variant of the prostitute or other sex worker (call girl, stripper, lap dancer, etc.) that, like them, is always available for sexual gratification. And, because both sex workers and symbolic whores treat men like sex objects, it gives the men in these films license to treat them like sex objects in return. Hence, black girlfriends depicted as unpaid symbolic whores can legitimately be abandoned after sexual gratification in a manner akin to paid sex workers.

Also, because they do not express a feminine sexuality, neither sex workers nor black symbolic whores are accorded the rewards of the feminine that include respectability and defense of honor. In many ways, then, both the sex worker and the symbolic whore call up the image of the oversexed black Jezebel from slavery as they are just as sexually accessible and inclined to consent to temporary, degraded sexual relationships with the men in their lives as the old-fashioned black Jezebel. That symbolic whores and sex workers are just as promiscuous as the oversexed Jezebels who precede them means that no effort need be made to defend the virtue of any of these black female characters.

This tendency to represent black females as prostitutes, whores, symbolic whores or other hypersexuals characterizes other media as well—most notably, music videos. Yet, what typically goes missing from each of these media is the characterization of black females as conforming to the feminine ideal either as ingénues or romantic heroines. In the absence of such role diversity, black female characters are not depicted as innocent or romantic. And, because they are not represented in more universal terms, it is almost impossible for an audience—either black or white—to identify with the black women they see on screen as many will have trouble seeing themselves in terms of the sex workers, whores or symbolic whores they play.

Moreover, because the sole function of these black female characters seems to be to provide sexual gratification or sexual affirmation for the males in these films, they are reduced to little more than props. Hence their characters are typically underdeveloped, which means that viewers are not provided with any access into the interior lives of these women. Instead of empathy or understanding, their characters are likely to induce audiences to empathize with the male characters in the film, who inevitably dismiss these women for their violations of the feminine role.

As noted previously, white females also play sex workers. However, they more frequently play romantic heroines, bored housewives, political heroines, psychopaths, adventure seekers and a host of other nonsexual roles. Because of the diversity of the roles they play, audiences are variously able to see white females as wanton or innocent or dramatic or funny or committed to some noble political cause. And, because their roles are so diverse, audiences are better able to see themselves in white female characters as they find themselves rooting for them, condemning them, laughing at them or laughing with them. The fact that their private emotions are on display also makes it possible for an audience to gain some insight into the interior lives of the white female characters they see. As a consequence, viewers more readily find themselves identifying with the white women they see on screen and relating to their cultural perspective.

With their diverse characterizations, then, white females set the standard for womanhood. Nowhere is this more apparent than in romantic movies.

Doing White Femininity in *Four Weddings and a Funeral*

White females routinely play the romantic lead in movies and through these roles "do femininity" by establishing themselves as desirable. It is possible, then, to gain some understanding of how romantic roles enable white women to express femininity by examining the popular British romantic comedy *Four Weddings and a Funeral*. This Oscar-nominated film, with its all-white cast, follows the courtship of a male and female named Charles and Carrie over the course of the *Four Weddings and a Funeral* named in the title.

Charles first spies Carrie at the first of these four weddings and immediately begins to pursue her. Even if not all viewers would immediately define these characters as attractive, it is clear from the story line that they are both regarded as highly desirable because both are surrounded by suitors. Hence, as Charles makes his way towards Carrie, he finds himself outpaced by other men who get to her first. This clearly communicates to the audience that Carrie is a catch. Charles is likewise depicted as a prize and something of a playboy as he is constantly being pursued by abandoned ex-girlfriends seeking to re-establish a relationship with him.

However, unlike many of the other women in the film, Carrie, the romantic lead, does not pursue Charles, but rather is pursued by him. Hence, she is able to establish her desirability and her femininity by passively waiting for him to approach. Because Charles pursues her from the film's opening scenes, he is forced to put her on a pedestal throughout much of the movie as she is always dangling just out of reach—particularly when she goes off to marry another man. In the course of the courtship, then, Charles attempts to show off his more attractive nonsexual qualities with her. For example, he attempts to show her his charming and witty side in one scene where he can be seen toasting the bride and groom as the best man at the first wedding. Charles' wit and charm are also on display for the audience to see in his interactions with his circle of close female and male friends.

Carrie is likewise depicted as a charming and sensitive person with Charles as she encourages his sometimes awkward advances. Even their sex scenes are characterized by amusing banter and sexual double entendres rather than crude sex acts. Moreover, it is clear that Carrie sees Charles as a whole person as she can be seen treating him like a friend rather than a sexual partner when she invites him to help her pick out a wedding dress for her marriage to an older and much wealthier man. She likewise treats him like a friend when she offers him emotional support by missing her honeymoon to attend the funeral of one of his best friends.

Audiences can be expected to identify with both these characters, in part, because their more attractive nonsexual characteristics are consistently on display. Furthermore, they are provided with some access into the interior life of the previously caddish Charles who awkwardly tries to tell Carrie that he loves her just before her wedding to another man. In a later scene, an equally vulnerable Carrie appears at Charles' wedding to another woman to reveal that she still cares for him. Because the audience can see themselves in both these characters, they are inclined to sympathize with them in their more vulnerable moments and root for them to rid themselves of any competing romantic entanglements and make a commitment to each other.

Yet, despite the fact that Carrie has an extensive sexual history and, in fact has had more sexual partners than Charles, she is never reduced to a symbolic whore. In part, she is still able to establish her femininity as a romantic lead character because she is consistently courted by men throughout the picture. Indeed, because she is consistently pursued by a number of suitors, she is able to express a very traditional feminine passivity by waiting for men to come to her. Moreover, neither she nor her suitors use crude, degraded language when negotiating for sex. Even her sex scenes with Charles are characterized by warmth and tenderness rather than crude sex acts. As a consequence, even in these scenes, the focus is on Carrie's feminine attempts to establish intimacy rather than on her raw sexuality.

Even in a scene in which she recounts a number of risqué sexual experiences from her past to Charles, Carrie does not appear to be hypersexed because she has already established her femininity by treating Charles like a whole person rather than a sex object. He, in turn, returns the favor by treating her like a complete human being rather than a symbolic whore. And, because their more appealing nonsexual characteristics are consistently on display as they interact with each other and with Charles' friends, the sexuality of both these characters seems to be a mere afterthought.

Black Female Hypersexuality in *Monster's Ball*

However, when black women are depicted in male/female relationships, they are often not depicted as romantic figures. In a number of their on-screen male/female relationships, their characters do not fall in love; instead they have sex. And because black women are so frequently excluded from romantic roles, they are often unable to "do femininity" by making themselves appear desirable and feminine. There is evidence of this in the film *Monster's Ball*.

Written and directed by white males, Marc Forster, Will Rokos, and Milo Addica, *Monster's Ball* was not an especially popular film. Nonetheless, it is an important one for talking about representations of black females in the cinema as Halle Berry became the first black woman to win the Oscar for Best Actress for her depiction of the film's black female lead character, Leticia Musgrove.

The Leticia Musgrove role was originally offered to black actress Angela Bassett, who turned it down because she felt it was too demeaning (Mapp 2003). And, in fact, the Leticia Musgrove character does evoke the age-old image of the oversexed Jezebel as during the course of the film, this black female character is forced to make sexual overtures to the bigoted white male lead character.

In the opening scenes of the movie, Leticia is widowed as her black husband is executed for murder. Yet, despite the death of her husband, Leticia is not represented as a grieving widow, but rather as a sexual being. Working as a waitress in the wake of her husband's death, she has no interest in her career nor does she seem to have much interest in her friends or her community. Even the potentially positive feminine role of a mother concerned about comforting a son, who has just lost his father to an execution, is denied to her. Instead she is depicted as an abusive mother, who slaps her son and calls him a "fat little piggy," even as the son anxiously awaits a last phone call from his father on death row.

In fact, her role as a sexual being receives so much emphasis in this Oscar-winning movie that after her husband's execution, her son's death, her loss of her job, and her imminent eviction from her home, she only seems to be interested in sexual gratification. As a consequence, when she comes upon a bigoted white male named Hank after this series of disasters, she is not depressed or withdrawn; instead she is depicted as in wanton pursuit of sexual pleasure. Her pseudomasculine traits are fully on display as she assumes the role of symbolic whore by brazenly propositioning Hank for sex. Her sexual propositioning of Hank is also crudely delivered as she uses explicitly sexual language, devoid of any romantic overtones, as she assures him that she is only interested in sexual gratification. This is followed by an overlong sex scene where she can be seen engaging in degraded sexual acts.

Because Leticia is such a single-mindedly sexual being, the film's narrative is able to dispense with any of the niceties associated with a romantic courtship. Hence, Hank is never forced to pursue her or court her by treating her as if she is desirable. Instead, in the time-honored fashion of a slave era Jezebel, it is Leticia who propositions Hank for sexual gratification. And, because Hank never pursues her, Leticia is never presented as a trophy and hence her status at the very bottom of a race-based female hierarchy, defined by beauty and desirability, is preserved.

Further, because Leticia pursues Hank, he is never forced to compromise his racially superior status as a white male by courting her or by trying to charm her or persuade her to date him. This is just as well as any attempts on the part of Hank to pass himself off as a charming and attractive suitor would have been difficult because before meeting Leticia he has clearly hated black people and only recently executed Leticia's black husband. Indeed, given his history, it is difficult to see how Leticia would have been attracted to him even if he had attempted a courtship. Hence, to avoid straining the audience's incredulity too much, the narrative is conveniently structured in such a way so that Leticia does not find out about Hank's involvement in her husband's execution until the end of the film after their sexual relationship has begun.

And, just as there is no need for Hank to show off his positive attributes to court Leticia, there is also no need for her to display any attractive qualities that might explain his interest in her. Certainly Halle Berry is a physically beautiful woman, but the film's narrative denies her the desirability that such beauty usually brings by turning her into a masculinized sexual aggressor who can be seen crudely propositioning Hank for sex in a manner that calls up her crude sexual propositioning in earlier roles as a crack whore in films like *Jungle Fever* and *Losing Isaiah*.

Because there is no courtship, there is also no need for Leticia to showcase nonsexual characteristics like wit, charm, or tenderness that generally induce men to court women. Indeed her dialogue as she initiates the sex act is reduced to animalistic grunts and expressions of sexual satisfaction rather than more human expressions of warmth or tenderness that might elicit emotional intimacy.

Indeed, because of the film's single-minded focus on this black woman's hypersexuality, the Leticia character is severely underdeveloped. The only thing the audience learns about the interior life of Leticia Musgrove is that she becomes eager for sexual gratification after a whole series of tragedies. Other than her agency in propositioning Hank for sex, she shows no agency in other aspects of her life such as trying to grapple with her many problems. As a consequence, the Leticia character has virtually no personality at all, which makes it hard for her to evoke much emotional response from the audience.

Indeed, because her character is so underdeveloped, she is reduced to a mere prop who serves only to provide Hank with sexual gratification and affirmation of his dubious sexuality while speeding him along in his road to racial redemption. The fact that Leticia's role is so poorly fleshed out also makes it difficult to see how it was worthy of the Oscar for best actress. Still, the fact that Hollywood's premier award was bestowed on a black woman for the role of an oversexed Jezebel and symbolic whore shows the continuing importance of stereotypes that represent black females as hypersexual.

THREATENING MALE DOMINANCE: THE BLACK MATRIARCH

While black sex workers and symbolic whores are denigrated because they have the same sexuality as males, at least they conform to the standards of a gender hierarchy which requires male dominance over women. Hence, even though these characters negate the femininity of black women, they are not a threat to the masculinity of their male lead characters. Indeed, oversexed Jezebels, sex workers and symbolic whores all do much to uphold the gender hierarchy by providing sexual affirmation for the male characters in starring roles. However, there are some additional stereotypes of black females that negate their femininity by representing them as a threat to black male dominance in the gender hierarchy.

This is particularly true of the black female matriarch, who generally appears on screen as the black single mother in charge of a female-headed household. The black single mother or matriarch figure threatens the male dominance required in a gender hierarchy because black women in this role appear to usurp the male roles of breadwinner and head of the household. By taking command of the traditional male role as head of the household, the black single mother/matriarch emasculates the black male as her status as the breadwinner in the family is proof that her counterpart, the black father/patriarch, is unable to support his family.

Obviously, black women depicted as matriarchs are also masculinized figures because they must express many masculine traits like dominance and control as they wield authority in their families. In addition, black women portrayed as matriarchs are also defeminized because they are unable to express feminine traits like dependency and passivity since they head their own households. As a consequence, they are easily devalued in a female racial hierarchy because they have been stripped of their feminine traits.

Moreover, because the black matriarch's takeover of the male role of household head has the effect of emasculating the black father, the black matriarch and her mate, the absent black father, constitute two parts of a dysfunctional couple, namely the strong masculinized black woman/weak emasculated black male dyad (hooks 1992, 1993; Jewel 1993).

The strong black woman/weak black man dyad serves the dual function of negating both the black woman and the black man in the pair as both are deviating from the standards of hegemonic masculinity and femininity in a kind of role reversal. In a number of ghetto action movies, then, the characters go to some trouble to demonstrate that they recognize that the black matriarchal household is a "perversion" of the natural order of things and attempt to restore the gender hierarchy. For example, a central theme in the ghetto action classic *Boyz n the Hood* seems to be to demonstrate that female-headed households are a distortion of the gender order by depicting boys raised in female-headed households as if they are more likely to become mired in a life of crime, violence and poverty than boys raised with a man in the household. (See chapter 3 for review of *Boyz*).

Boyz accomplishes this by following the escapades of Doughboy, a black male raised in a female-headed household who grows up to be violent and is eventually killed in the ghetto cycle of black-on-black violence. The perils of Doughboy's upbringing in a matriarchal household are made clear when Doughboy's life is compared to his neighbor Trey, who was raised by his father and grows up to be a law-abiding young man who goes on to college. Early on, when Trey is quite young and having disciplinary problems at school, his mother, Reba, realizes the dangers of raising Trey alone as a black single mother and sends him to live with his father, Furious Styles, in a patriarchal household. Reba later congratulates Furious after Trey turns out so well. Other single mothers in *Boyz* also seem to associate female-headed households with the downfall of their sons as they can be seen trying to persuade Trey's father, Furious, to give them advice on how to raise their sons.

This notion of the female-headed household as the cause of black male violence is likewise dramatized in the ghetto action film *South Central*. (See chapter 3 for review of *South Central*.) In this film, the black single mother, Carole, is both a drug addict and a whore, who works as a prostitute to support her drug habit. As a consequence, she neglects her 10-year-old son Jimmie by refusing to fix his meals or make sure he goes to school. Because of Carol's neglect, Jimmie is raised by the local street gangs and is stealing car stereos for them by the tender age of 10.

The film's premise is that the only thing that can save Jimmie from a permanent life of crime is the chance to be raised by his father, Bobby. Hence, in scene after scene, Bobby, Jimmie's father, is presented as a superior and more nurturing parent than Carole, Jimmie's mother, despite the fact that Bobby is also a violent gang leader, drug dealer, and murderer who ultimately goes to prison for his many crimes. Despite all that, it is only after Bobby is released from prison and goes on a quest to find and raise his son that little Jimmie can be saved from his inevitable descent into a life of crime.

Like so many other ghetto action movies, then, *South Central* defeminizes and devalues its black female character, Carole, by portraying her as both a negligent mother and a whore. Indeed because ghetto action films so frequently depict black female characters that deviate from the traditional feminine roles of wife and mother, Jacquie Jones (1992) argues that these movies have the effect of placing black women in the accusatory space. In other words, by routinely casting black females as "hos" and incompetent single mothers, she claims that black male filmmakers are accusing black women of having destroyed the black community with their teen pregnancies and female-headed households.

Jones, then, goes on to argue that these age-old stereotypes of black females as "hos" and bad mothers have acquired new uses in that their characters are now being manipulated in ways so that they transform audience distaste for the transgressions of the black male characters in the film into sympathy by vilifying the black female characters.

So, for example, in *Boyz n the Hood*, Jones claims that blame for young black males killing each other is ultimately not assigned to the young black males themselves; rather the image of the black female matriarch is called up to explain black male violence. And, because the narrative in *Boyz* suggests that the poor parenting skills of black women who head single-parent families ultimately turn their sons into gangbangers, audiences may find themselves experiencing some sympathy for these poorly socialized young black males even as some of their antipathy shifts to black matriarchs for their role in raising their violent sons.[7] Representing black women as incompetent matriarchs, then, becomes another way to discourage audiences from caring about the black women they see on screen.

THE BLACK FEMALE SAPPHIRE AS A THREAT TO THE PATRIARCHY

In many ways, black matriarchs have much in common with another stereotypical image of black womanhood, namely the Sapphire. After all, black women who portray either matriarchs or Sapphires on screen are both represented as threats to black male dominance. However, unlike the black matriarch who is often forced to raise her family alone without a male present, the Sapphire role requires the presence of an African American male. Indeed, it is through black Sapphires and their mates that audiences typically see a black couple interact (Jewel 1993).

In the context of their relationships with black males, the classic black female Sapphire is generally presented as a headstrong, talkative and sassy know-it-all. By contrast, the Sapphire's black male partner is usually stereotyped as dishonest and inclined towards cunning and trickery. In fact, it is his dishonesty which provides her with an opportunity to emasculate him at every turn with her verbal put-downs. Hence, the interaction between the Sapphire and her black male partner typically consists of her demonstrating her virtues and morals even as she calls attention to his lack of virtues and morals. In some ways, then, the Sapphire stereotype is a "two-fer" as it ascribes negative traits to both the bossy, overbearing black female character and her dishonest black male partner.[8]

Because the Sapphire is one of the few black female characters actually shown interacting with her black mate, Sapphire and her black male mate can be used to depict the conflict-ridden black couple. In fact, once the stereotypical character of a black female Sapphire is introduced into a film, her presence forecloses any possibility of a black couple being shown in a loving, romantic relationship. Representing black couples in terms of this particular strong black woman/weak black man dyad, then, serves a number of functions.

Black feminist writer, bell hooks (1993) describes some of these functions and the ambivalent reaction of black female audiences to being represented as Sapphires in the following terms:

> She (Sapphire) was even then backdrop, foil. She was bitch — nag. *She was there to soften images of black men, to make them seem vulnerable, easygoing, funny, not threatening to a white audience. She was there as man in drag, as castrating bitch, as someone to be lied to, someone to be tricked, someone the white and black audience could hate.* Scapegoated on all sides. She was not us (black women). We (black women) laughed with the black men, with the white people. We laughed at this black woman who was not us. And we (black women) did not even long to be there on the screen. How could we long to be there when our image, visually constructed, was so ugly? We did not long to be there. We did not long for her. We did not want our construction to be this hated black female thing—foil, backdrop. Her black female image was not the body of desire. There was nothing to see. She was not us. (emphasis mine)

From Sapphires to Hyper-Sapphires (Bitches)

Despite the fact that Sapphires could regularly be seen bossing around their inadequate black male mates, they were generally treated like comic figures. Not only was the audience meant to laugh at their bossiness and not take them seriously, their black male partners were usually shown laughing them off as well. More recently, however, a black female hyper-Sapphire has emerged in popular culture, and this souped-up version of the old stereotype is depicted as a lot more threatening to men. Indeed some black women film critics have dubbed this new, more hostile hyper-Sapphire role as the Bitch role (J. Jones 1992; Manatu 2003; hooks 1993).

Because they are more hostile and threatening than the comic Sapphires of the past, these new hyper-Sapphires are much better at softening the images of black men and making them appear even more vulnerable and less threatening to a white audience. This strategy of constructing a black woman as a hyper-Sapphire in order to soften the image of a black male and make him appear more vulnerable to a white audience was very much in evidence during the real-world incident of the Anita Hill/Clarence Thomas hearings.

In 1991, Clarence Thomas was nominated by President George Herbert Walker Bush to become a Supreme Court Justice, and law professor Anita Hill appeared at his Senate confirmation hearing to raise questions about his suitability for the high court by revealing how he had sexually harassed her when she worked for him at the Equal Employment Opportunity Commission. On its face, it would seem that many Americans might have been inclined to sympathize with Professor Hill as she reported being the victim of his harassment. Therefore, in order to garner at least some support, Thomas' white handlers had to find a way to spin the story so that Thomas became the victim and Anita Hill became the victimizer.

Lubiano (1992) explains how Thomas' handlers succeeded in transferring the sins of the black male (Thomas) to the black woman (Hill), thereby placing her in the accusatory space. She argues that Thomas' white male supporters dusted off the old Sapphire myth and beefed it up to show how Hill's charges of sexual harassment actually threatened and victimized Thomas. She terms the new hyper-Sapphire image constructed by Thomas' white male handlers as the Black Lady or the Black Female Overachiever and defines her as a woman who has achieved success through her educational attainments and her high-status career.

Because of her accomplishments, the Black Female Overachiever is marked by her Sapphire-like tendency to hold her own in a debate with a male rather than passively agreeing in truly feminine fashion. Yet, unlike the prattling comical Sapphires of the past, the Black Female Overachiever's economic independence, ambitiousness and ladylike tendency to reject male sexual advances actually turns her into a threat to black male dominance.

Given these characteristics, Black Female Overachievers can easily be depicted as victimizers as their male-like achievements are seen as a betrayal of the patriarchy—especially the black patriarchy. Indeed, their overachievement is thought to ensure the underachievement of the black male. With their construction of this hyper-Sapphire, then, Thomas' handlers transformed him into the victim of emasculation by the Black Female Overachiever, Anita Hill.

Paul Haggis, the white male writer and director of *Crash*, likewise makes use of the emasculating hyper-Sapphire to transform his black female character from a victim into a victimizer. Awarded the Oscar for the best picture of 2005, *Crash* is an important movie because it was hailed by many white and black film critics alike as providing an accurate picture of race relations in America (Hsu 2006).

Haggis wrote and directed this film after being robbed during a carjacking, which may explain why the film opens with two black males robbing the white district attorney and his wife of their Lincoln Navigator in a carjacking. In a later scene, two white male police officers can be seen illegally stopping innocent black motorists while looking for the two black carjackers who have stolen the white District Attorney's Lincoln Navigator.

In the course of their round-up of black suspects, the police pull over an innocent black couple and force the husband to get out of the car and submit to a sobriety test. The black wife, Christine, then, begins to argue with one of the white male officers named Ryan. Officer Ryan responds to Christine's outrage over the illegal search by treating her like a common criminal, and forcing her to get out of her Navigator and submit to a search just like her husband. Then, in an act all too reminiscent of slavery and Jim Crow, Ryan, the white cop, pats Christine down and sexually assaults her as though she is little more than chattel to be fondled on the auction block. Moreover, this white male cop molests this black woman right in front of her black husband who is powerless to stop it.

In many ways, then, this scene from *Crash* conjures up images from slavery and Jim Crow when white males acted as if they should have easy sexual access to any black female they saw. Moreover, much as was the case during slavery and Jim Crow, the black husband in *Crash* is emasculated as he is powerless to stop the white male's sexual advances. Finally, in an additional throwback to America's racist past, the white male police officer in *Crash* is never punished for the racial profiling, the pat down of both the wife and the husband or the sexual assault.

Instead, the white male filmmakers in *Crash* strive to make the unpunished sexual violation of Christine seem normal by turning her into a hyper-Sapphire. Hence, in the moments after Christine has been illegally profiled, searched, and molested by Ryan, the white cop, and after the armed white cops have driven off, she does not use these precious moments (when the audience is primed to sympathize with her) to make an appeal to the audience by expressing anger, fear, shame, or any of the other feelings that one typically associates with the victims of sexual assaults. In this, she is nothing like the white female victims of yore who would rather jump off a cliff than succumb to the sexual advances of a black male. Rather *Crash* depicts her as devoid of any emotions suggesting anger at her molester and in so doing sidesteps a golden opportunity to persuade audiences to care about Christine and her plight or to insist on punishment for the white cop who has molested her.

Rather than expressing her outrage at the white cop who has just molested her, Christine turns on her black husband instead and calls up the negative role of the hyper-Sapphire as she goes about castigating him for not protecting her. Hence, the audience's sympathies shift in these crucial emotional moments after the assault, from this black woman who has just been victimized by a sexual assault to her husband, Cameron, as he is verbally castrated by his wife for failing to protect her from armed white cops.

Not only is Christine transformed from victim to victimizer with her verbal assault of Cameron, her outburst also allows her to serve the time-honored

Sapphire function of softening her black male mate by making him appear more vulnerable and less threatening to a white audience. Cameron's image is softened for white audiences in other scenes as well as he is emasculated by the armed white cops when they initially order him to get out of the car and then search him in front of his wife. He is humiliated yet again as he has to stand by and watch helplessly as one armed white cop molests his wife right in front of him. And then after the white cops finish humiliating him and making him appear less threatening to a white audience, the audience gets to watch Christine join in his emasculation as she berates him for failing to protect her.

Indeed because Christine ultimately is transformed into such an unsympathetic character, the audience may be willing to let Cameron off the hook as he decides against pursuing justice for his wife because he is fearful that the publicity of filing sexual assault and racial profiling charges against the police department will undermine him at his white-male-dominated workplace (where he is further emasculated). And yet several scenes later, Christine finds herself apologizing to Cameron for her outburst even as her sexual violation remains unpunished.

Not only does Christine let her husband off the hook for failing to help her pursue justice, but the very next day, events conspire so that she is forced to let Ryan, her white male attacker, off the hook as well. Rather than seeing him punished for his sexual assault, the story line forces Christine to embrace her white male molester instead and express her gratitude to him as he pulls her from her burning car to save her life. Hence the white cop is never punished for his illegal search or sexual assault of this black woman. Instead he is transformed into a hero as he rescues the black woman he has recently victimized from certain death. Indeed, the image of a frightened and grateful Christine embracing the white cop who has saved her life after molesting her the day before is apparently so symbolic of modern-day race relations that it is used to advertise the film; a picture of the rescue appears on the cover of the DVD version of the film.

During slavery and Jim Crow, the fact that nothing was done about sexual assaults on black females was evidence of their powerlessness as it indicated that society felt that their virtue was unworthy of protection. And, yet even though this long-standing image of black female virtue as undeserving of protection is evoked in *Crash*, a number of white film critics described it as "one of the best Hollywood movies about race," and prominent black film critics gave it ringing endorsements as well (Hsu 2006).

These endorsements seem strange in light of the fact that it is generally unsettling to see a female subjected to the humiliation of being sexually molested. Indeed in a number of films where white women are sexually assaulted, the film focuses on pursuit of justice for the white female victims involved (e.g., *The Accused, Anatomy of a Murder, Chinatown, Dolores Claiborne*). The fact that a black woman's molestation can go unpunished in an Oscar-winning film about race relations indicates that a female racial hierarchy in which white women are on top and black women are at the bottom is still alive and well.

That black female characters can be violated with impunity also attests to the power of racial myths to normalize sexual assaults on black women. In other words, by presenting Christine as an emasculating, defeminized hyper-Sapphire, *Crash*'s filmmakers succeed in justifying her exemption from protections that are generally extended to white female characters on screen. This is not hard to understand as the film industry's insistence on locking black women into unsympathetic, stereotypical roles—such as that of an emasculating hyper-Sapphire—enables audiences to watch the suffering of black female characters with cold-blooded disregard. Thus numbed to the suffering of the black women characters they see, audiences are likely to find it easier to see the sexual violations of black female characters proceed without penalty. Depicting black women as Sapphires, then, can camouflage modern-day black female powerlessness by making the failure to protect them or punish racial assaults against them seem less objectionable.

The Female Racial Hierarchy and Domestic Violence

Audiences, unable to sympathize with a browbeating Sapphire like Christine, are likely to be even less sympathetic when black female hyper-Sapphires are portrayed as going beyond mere verbal abuse and character assassination of black men to outright physical abuse of black male characters. Such physical abuse is most likely to occur within the confines of an intimate partner relationship (e.g., married, cohabiting or dating couples).

Feminist thinking on domestic conflicts that occur in real life has long been that violence between intimate partners is a by-product of living in a patriarchal society in which males are socialized to believe that they should dominate and control women. Presumably, when men in a patriarchal society come to believe that their male dominance has been threatened, they feel they have a right to resort to various forms of psychological, economic and physical abuse against their female partners. In theory, males are also likely to use various forms of abuse in the event that their female partners actually leave or threaten to leave a relationship. For many feminists, then, the classic case of intimate partner violence involves a clearly defined victim—the woman—being abused by a clearly defined victimizer—a larger and physically more powerful male—whose patriarchal authority has been threatened

(Belknap and Potter 2005, 2006; Wallace 1996; Ptacek 1997; Dobash et al. 1992; Dobash et al. 1998).

This classic scenario of intimate partner violence involving a male abuser and an abused female victim is dramatized in a film with an all-white cast called *Dolores Claiborne*. The title character, Dolores, is a white woman married to a chronically unemployed white male named Joe. Dolores (played by Kathy Bates) supports both Joe and their daughter, Selena, by working as a maid, and because Dolores is forced to support the family, Joe's male dominance is threatened leading him to abuse her. Joe begins his abuse of Dolores with psychological tactics including taunts about her being fat, undesirable and a lousy cook. He then rapidly escalates to physical abuse by hitting her with a wooden plank. Dolores' pain and suffering in the face of that blow is clear as she is temporarily unable to stand and fix dinner after Joe hits her.

When she is finally able to stand, she attempts to defend herself by threatening Joe with an axe. However, her self-defense ends with mere threats as she throws the axe in Joe's lap and tells him to use it on her if he can stand having their daughter walk in and witness her mother being killed. Joe quickly retreats and miraculously never physically abuses Dolores again. Instead of physical abuse, he next resorts to trying to gain control over her money by stealing her savings. This attempt at economic abuse likewise fails as Dolores is able to have the stolen savings returned to her. It is only when Dolores comes to suspect that Joe is sexually abusing their daughter, Selena, that she lures him to his death.

Yet despite Dolores' need to protect herself and her daughter from Joe's physical and sexual abuse, she never once engages in violence by striking a blow against him. As a consequence, Dolores' clear-cut status as a victim is preserved because she never once resorts to violent masculine behaviors. Because Dolores is so clearly the victim, she is able to draw enormous audience sympathy. Indeed because viewers are likely to be so sensitive to her plight, it is likely that many will find themselves rooting for her by the movie's end as she survives Joe's abuse and triumphs by escaping prosecution for his murder, winning the respect of their daughter Selena and inheriting millions of dollars.

And yet, while *Dolores Claiborne* dramatizes the classic one-sided version of domestic violence in which a man whose patriarchal authority has been threatened abuses his female partner, there is some research done on real-world couples, which suggests that the roles of male abuser and abused female victim are not always so clear-cut. For example, some studies suggest that couples' conflicts may be more symmetrical as they show that women are equally or even more likely to hit and kick their male partners than vice versa (Wallace 1996; Moffit et al. 2001; Giordano et al. 1999; Strauss and

Gelles 1990). By suggesting that both parties are involved in abuse, such studies make it more difficult to distinguish the victim from the victimizer.

Even more controversial are studies that suggest that the roles of female victim and male victimizer may actually be reversed in what is called the battered man syndrome (Steinmetz 1978). The battered man syndrome refers to those couples' conflicts in which males are subjected to emotional and physical abuse at the hands of their abusive female partners. By depicting the female as the batterer and the male as the victim, the battered man syndrome constitutes yet another example of the strong masculinized woman/weak emasculated man dyad. In this case, the female batterer is masculinized because of her willingness to initiate and sustain violence, while the male is emasculated because of his unwillingness to defend himself from his female batterer.

Clearly, those who claim that there is such a thing as a battered man syndrome question classic feminist conceptions of domestic abuse that suggest that violence typically involves the male partner striking the female. As support for their contention that it is females who batter males, they point to research which shows that women are more likely to hit and kick men than vice versa (Strauss and Gelles 1990; Giordano et al. 1999; Moffitt et al. 2001). They then use these findings to argue that many of these women who hit and kick men are not simply using violence to defend themselves or their children from violence provoked by men. Rather, for them, these findings indicate that it is women who actually initiate the violence in many couples. Moreover, these researchers make a case for taking the battered man syndrome seriously by pointing to research that shows that some males suffer serious injury or even death at the hands of their female intimate partners (Moffitt et al. 2001; Giordano et al. 1999; Bureau of Justice Statistics 2009; Rennison and Welchans 2000).

Studies suggesting a battered man syndrome obviously raise questions about feminist assertions that describe couples' conflicts solely in asymmetrical terms that involve a violent male battering his passive, nonviolent female partner. For those who accept the battered man syndrome, then, violence between couples is more symmetrical, with women every bit as violent as men.

Not surprisingly, feminists regard the battered man syndrome as a myth. In part, they question whether such a syndrome exists because they note that the violence perpetrated by males is much more serious than that perpetrated by females. To support their assertions, they point to research that shows that females are more likely to be severely injured or even killed by males than vice versa. Even worse, they argue that this myth of a violent woman who batters her male partner is actually dangerous as it denies victimhood to women who try to defend themselves when they fight back (Belknap and Potter 2005,

2006; Miller and White 2003; Chesney-Lind 2002; Strauss and Gelles 1990; Rennison and Welchans 2000; Bureau of Justice Statistics 2009). Their thinking is that by fighting back, women might risk being defined as batterers and prosecuted for domestic violence themselves. (See Chapter 7 for a review of social scientific research on these arguments.) In other words, women might be punished for deviating too far from culturally approved standards of femininity when they defend themselves in an abusive relationship.

The Battered Man Syndrome in *Baby Boy*

Whatever the merits of these arguments, the violence depicted in the feuding couple in the black coming-of-age picture *Baby Boy* hews more closely to the battered man syndrome than to the classic scenario of domestic violence in which the female is the victim. In scene after scene the young, unemployed black male in the couple, Jody, is subjected to psychological and physical abuse at the hands of his black girlfriend, Yvette. Yvette is abusive because she feels threatened by Jody's sexual liaisons with other women and exasperated by his tendency to borrow her car for days at a time stranding her and their son and forcing them to walk or take the bus. Hence, when Yvette first confronts Jody about other women, she begins by verbally abusing him. Jody responds to her taunts by simply walking away, which only seems to encourage her to follow him out the door and escalate to violence by hitting him and punching him. Yet, despite the fact that Jody is the classic threatened patriarch suffering from long-term unemployment, living with his mother and forced to depend on Yvette for a car, he goes through much of the movie without once returning a blow. The only incident in which he returns Yvette's violence comes after she has repeatedly cursed at him and hit him and then finally socked him very hard.

Only after she has landed this last hard punch does he quickly and unthinkingly punch her back. She falls down crying about being punched although she apparently is not injured. Jody is immediately apologetic, carrying her to the bedroom and trying to make up and he is never seen hitting her again.

Yet, even though there is scene after scene of Yvette striking Jody, the classic domestic violence scenario in which a male whose patriarchal authority is threatened resorts to physical abuse to control his female partner is merely mentioned rather than actually dramatized in *Baby Boy*. So, for example, Jody alludes to his mother's prior physical abuse by a boyfriend, but there are no scenes in which this classic male-on-female violence is actually shown on screen.

By verbally and physically abusing Jody, Yvette repeatedly violates the norms of true womanhood and therefore turns herself into a less sympathetic character. Her repeated abuse of Jody, in turn, makes him a more sympathetic character as he manfully resists returning her violence. And Jody is the kind of character that is very much in need of audience sympathy as he is himself violating the norms of true masculinity with his chronic unemployment and his dependence on his mother and Yvette for money and a car. Hence, the relationship between the abusive Yvette and the dependent Jody constitutes just another example of the strong emasculating black woman/weak emasculated black male relationship.

Because Yvette's constant psychological and physical abuse of Jody is a violation of traditional norms of femininity, her character manages to reinforce long-standing stereotypes of black women that depict them as masculinized, in this case because of their violent aggressiveness. Moreover, when compared to white females grappling with physical abuse by their white male partners in films such as *Dolores Claiborne*, Yvette's character represents black females as more violently aggressive with their male intimates than white females.

The masculinized black female hyper-Sapphire is also a fixture in other films with all-black casts. For example, Taraji P. Henson, who plays Yvette in *Baby Boy* is once again cast as the violently aggressive black woman in the 2007 film *Talk to Me*. In *Talk to Me*, she plays Vernell, the girlfriend of 1970s Washington, D.C. black activist, shock jock and ex-convict Petey Greene. When Vernell catches Petey in bed with another woman, she holds a broken bottle to Petey's throat and forces the other woman to leave. Still brandishing the broken bottle, she then kicks Petey out of his own apartment without his clothes, thereby forcing him to walk through the streets naked to a friend's apartment. Yet, despite Vernell's outrageous behavior, *Talk to Me* repeatedly depicts both her and Petey's buffoonery as characteristic of black male/female relationships in a period of 1970s black activism.

NOTES

1. White males likewise have enormous control over news media as they account for the vast majority of newspaper editors and television news directors (Chideya 1995). As such, they can determine the tone and content of news. Because they control so many popular culture and media platforms, they are able both to perpetuate myths about African Americans as entertainment and then depict these same myths as reality in news outlets. Much of the racial lore that they disseminate in these media defines whites as the standard bearers for appropriate male and female behavior and then stigmatizes black males and black females as sex role deviants for their failure to conform to these "white" standards.

2. See Manatu (2003) for reviews of a number of additional films in which black women play sex workers and symbolic whores.

3. Actually, there is considerable disagreement among feminists about how to frame prostitution. While some regard prostitution as the ultimate indicator of a patriarchal society because it defines women as body parts for the use and enjoyment of men, other feminists see it as an expression of sexual freedom. For the latter group of feminists, prostitutes and other sex workers have liberated themselves from a feminine ideal based on virtue and have freely chosen to use their bodies and their sexuality in ways that openly violate male-defined standards of femininity (Raphael 2006). Sadly, this view is challenged by the fact that so many sex workers suggest that their entry into sex work is not motivated by free choice, but rather by a history of childhood sexual abuse.

4. Narratives in which the prostitute is rescued and rehabilitated by the leading man have also been faulted because the male hero remains the arbiter of the female's virtue (Manatu 2003; Humm 1997).

5. During the 1990s when black female crack users were receiving so much attention on the silver screen, national survey data show that black females were equally or less likely to report illegal drug use than white females. For example, in 1991, when the crack cocaine epidemic was in its heyday, roughly one-third of black females and one-third of white females reported some kind of illegal drug use (mainly marijuana use) in the National Household Survey on Drug Abuse (National Institute on Drug Abuse 1991). By 1995, roughly one-third (31 percent) of white females were still reporting illegal drug use in the same survey, but only 24.7 percent of black females reported illegal drug use (Substance Abuse and Mental Health Services Administration 1996). And, by 1998, 33.1 percent of white females continued to report illegal drug use compared to only 26.4 percent of black females (Substance Abuse and Mental Health Services Administration 1999).

These race differences also show up when black and white female respondents are asked to report on their cocaine use alone. In the 1990s, when all forms of cocaine are considered, including powder cocaine, freebase and crack cocaine, a larger percentage of white females report cocaine use than black females—largely because of their preference for powder cocaine. So, for example, in 1991, 9.7 percent of white females report using some form of cocaine compared to 7.6 percent of black women. By 1995, some 9.2 percent of white females report some form of cocaine use compared to a mere 4.2 percent of black women. And, by 1998, 9.2 percent of white females once again report some form of cocaine use compared to 5.6 percent of black females. It is only when women are asked about crack cocaine specifically that a larger percentage of black women report crack cocaine use. Crack cocaine also turns out to be one of the least popular of drugs in this survey. Hence, in 1991, a mere 2.6 percent of black females reported crack cocaine use compared to 1.1 percent of white females. In 1995, 1.9 percent of black women reported crack cocaine use compared to 1.1 percent of white females. And, by 1998, 2.7 percent of black females reported crack use compared to 1.2 percent of white females.

6. In part, the outlawing of opiates in San Francisco must be understood in terms of a nineteenth century effort to criminalize prostitution. Back then, some feminists promoted the criminalization of prostitution by equating it with slavery. They claimed that white women did not enter prostitution voluntarily, but were often forced into it

or lured into it by men. Hence, they equated the trafficking in white women with a white slave trade. As many of these feminists had earlier participated in the abolitionist movement, describing prostitution in these terms was meant to be a rallying cry (Messerschmidt 1993).

7. It is also important to note that films like *South Central, Losing Isaiah* and *Boyz n the Hood* were released when Republicans were trying to dismantle big government programs by denouncing black women on welfare as incompetent mothers. By depicting black welfare mothers as sexually depraved drug addicts and by linking them to the delinquency and violence of their sons, these films offered visual support for Republican condemnations of welfare.

8. While the original Sapphire on the radio program *Amos and Andy* was part of a married couple, some of the later Sapphires have put down black males to whom they were not married. So, for example, Florence, the maid, on the television comedy *The Jeffersons* was a Sapphire, who regularly leveled insults at her black male employer, George Jefferson. Aunt Esther, the sister-in-law of Fred Sanford, likewise played the Sapphire to Fred Sanford in the television sitcom *Sanford and Son*.

Chapter Seven

Black Women, Violence and Masculinization

The female racial hierarchy, described in chapter 6, ranks women of different race and ethnic groups in terms of their conformity to the standards of true womanhood and rewards them for their conformity. Chief among the rewards for true womanhood is chivalry. Among other things, chivalry rests on the principle that women should be protected from male violence like rapes and assaults, but only if they conform to patriarchal standards of what it means to be a woman. Because true women are first and foremost white, white females who conform to male-defined standards of true womanhood by being passive and weak can expect to be rewarded with protection from male violence.

Unlike white women, however, African American women have never been perceived as meeting the standards of true womanhood. Beginning with slavery, traditional media outlets like newspapers and literature routinely portrayed them in ways that negated their femininity. After that, Hollywood and other more modern forms of media kept up the practice of denying them feminine status by casting them in roles that conveyed the impression that they had violated the standards of true womanhood. Because they were stereotyped as women who lacked femininity, it was possible to justify exempting them from the protections accorded true women.

One of the most common ways to depict them as violating the standards of true womanhood has been to masculinize them by representing them as women whose behaviors mimic those that are generally expected of men. Hence, since slavery, they have been portrayed as oversexed Jezebels who were as sexually aggressive as any man. Because they were characterized as sexual aggressors, they did not seem to need the protections from rape that true women required and hence they were not to be protected from sexual violence—particularly sexual violence perpetrated by white male slaveholders.

The film industry has also masculinized them by depicting them as a threat to male dominance. So, for example, they have routinely been portrayed as matriarchs who set out to emasculate black males by taking over the household and assuming the traditional male role of breadwinner. As masculinized matriarchs who usurped the male role and presumably passed on a penchant for crime and violence to their sons, they and their children were not deemed worthy of protection from poverty, destitution and homelessness. In fact, this image had become so powerful by the 1990s that conservative politicians managed to depict households headed by black single moms as unworthy of welfare payments and use it to successfully defend the evisceration of the entire program.

Hollywood has also masculinized black females by depicting them as women who imitate "male" behaviors by turning to violence. Indeed in films like *Baby Boy* and *Talk to Me*, they can even be seen turning the tables on black males by using violence to bully and intimidate the men in their lives. Showing black women on screen involved in violent assaults is a good way to masculinize them because violent crimes like murder and assault are considered to be quintessentially "masculine" behaviors. It is not hard to see why as males are about nine times as likely to be arrested for violent acts like murder as females and four times as likely to be arrested for aggravated (serious) assaults (Federal Bureau of Investigation 2008). Because these male/female differences in violence have long been recognized, the practice of masculinizing women by depicting them as violent is a very old one and one that is not just confined to Hollywood.

In fact, for more than a century, a number of academics have brought the tools of science to bear on establishing the reality of such notions. And, after satisfying themselves that these notions are real, they have used their research to justify policies for reducing the violence of masculinized women.

In this chapter, then, I trace the history of these notions from the early twentieth century to the present. By taking a critical look at the academic research that has grown out of these ideas, I mean to home in on the kinds of policies that this research has encouraged. And, because black women, in particular, have been described as masculinized in this discourse—particularly in academic discourse on domestic violence—I also consider how academic researchers have used images of violent, male-like black women to justify policies that deny them protection from domestic violence.

RACIAL CONSTRUCTION, FEMALE VIOLENCE AND MASCULINIZATION IN THE EARLY TWENTIETH CENTURY

More than a century ago, the Italian doctor Cesare Lombroso was among the first criminologists to describe the rare woman who became involved in crime and violence as more masculinized than the masses of normal, noncriminal women. As he saw it, criminal women and criminal men alike were both genetic throwbacks to an earlier stage of evolution. As primitive throwbacks living in communities where they were surrounded by normal, more evolved, law-abiding people, the criminals he described were clearly out of sync with the rest of society (Lombroso-Ferrero 1911; Klein 1995; Akers and Sellers 2009; Vold, Bernard and Snipes 2002).

Claiming that it was possible to recognize these crime-prone primitives by their atavistic physical features, Lombroso used autopsies and physical observations of criminal and normal males, to identify the physical features that distinguished the two populations. Based on these observations, he concluded that criminal males tended to have larger jaws and teeth than normal, noncriminal males; they were also distinguished by their extraordinarily long arms, double rows of teeth, flat noses and by ears that stood out from their heads (Akers and Sellers 2009; Vold, Bernard and Snipes 2002).

Lombroso did similar comparisons with females to identify traits that distinguished criminal women and prostitutes from normal, noncriminal women. He found that the atavistic traits that distinguished criminal women and prostitutes from normal, noncriminal women included physical features like moles, dark hair and excessive body hair. Moreover, because Sicilian women made up a large share of the imprisoned Italian female criminals that he studied, he also included darkness and shortness as atavistic markers of criminality in women.

The fact that females had much lower crime rates than males presented Lombroso with something of a problem, however. After all, like most thinkers of his day, he assumed that males were further along on the evolutionary scale than women and therefore morally and psychically superior to them. Hence, to explain lower female crime rates, he argued that women simply had fewer of the biological defects that predisposed to crime than males. Indeed, to make clear that he was not conceding the existence of any equality between the sexes, he described women as child-like, because they were inclined to be revengeful, jealous and morally deficient like children. He, then, went on to argue that these innate child-like defects were neutralized by inherently feminine traits like passivity, piety, maternity, sexual coldness, lack of passion and an undeveloped intelligence, which kept female crime rates low (Klein 1995).

On one hand, then, true women lacked many of the superior traits found in men; on the other hand, many of their innately inferior feminine qualities also made them considerably less inclined to commit crimes. Clearly, then, a woman who lacked the feminine qualities that made normal women less criminal could be very criminal indeed. Hence, in Lombroso's way of thinking, criminal women were more "masculine" than normal women because they lacked many of the feminine traits that discouraged criminality in normal women.

As he saw it, criminal women had psychic and emotional characteristics that were more like those of males including a male-like tendency towards passion rather than the lack of passion that characterized true women. Moreover, after conducting autopsies and observations of criminal women, he concluded that criminal women were also more physically similar to men than they were to normal women in terms of their skulls and cranial capacities.

Clearly, for Lombroso, masculinity in a man was a good thing because it signaled a more advanced stage of development. However, he considered masculinity in a woman to be a defect as it presumably made women more prone to criminal behavior. Lombroso was not alone as a number of European and American thinkers of his day thought of the sexes in these terms. Indeed, American sociologist W. I. Thomas argued that the population groups in which women were most like men tended to be the inferior races (Klein 1995). Hence, in describing the American racial hierarchy, Thomas claimed that in the more highly evolved white race, and in civilized white nations in general, there were huge physical and psychic differences between males and females. Conversely, he claimed that in inferior racial groups like American blacks and Native Americans, there were fewer differences between the sexes as the women in these inferior races were more masculinized. For him, then, sexual symmetry was one marker of the genetic inferiority of the nonwhite races, while a sexual binary in which white women were what white men were not was one indicator of superiority in the white race.

By characterizing the white race in terms of a sexual binary and the black race in terms of sexual symmetry and by using these distinctions to denote white racial superiority and black racial inferiority, Thomas sounded a lot like American slaveholders during the slave era. Long before Thomas, they too had argued that there were huge biological, psychological and emotional dissimilarities between white males and white females even as they assumed that black females and black males were quite similar. In fact, because black female slaves were thought of as surrogate black males, they were often treated in much the same way as black male slaves (Jewel 1993).

The Policy Implications of Lombroso's Research

Lombroso's research sparked a number of studies that were intended to replicate his findings among biological and psychological theorists in Europe and America in the late nineteenth and early twentieth centuries (e.g., Hooton 1939; Dugdale 1877; Goddard 1914). In an effort to test his claims, these researchers set about trying to identify the biological and psychological defects that best distinguished criminals from noncriminals and predisposed the criminal population to commit crimes.

Because criminals were thought to be born with the biological and psychic defects that predisposed them to crime, many of these theorists argued that these born criminals could not be socialized to see their criminal behavior as wrong like normal, more evolved individuals. This created a dilemma for society as it meant that these genetic throwbacks had to somehow be prevented from preying on the more evolved law-abiding members of society. However, for many of these early-twentieth-century theorists, who thought that the biological and psychic defects of the criminal were permanent and inherited, there was no hope of adjusting the criminal to society. For them, then, reducing crime meant identifying and containing these born criminals before they could do too much damage. Moreover, in order to prevent crime in subsequent generations, some argued that the population of born criminals should also be sterilized so that their criminal predispositions could not be passed on to their children and their children's children (Hooton 1939).

Racial Construction, Policy and the Decline of Lombrosian Criminology

While Lombroso's theory was popular in the early years of the twentieth century, it had been almost completely discredited by the middle of the century (Akers and Sellers 2009). Several factors account for its gradual demise. For one thing, Lombroso's theory was initially debunked by other biological and psychological theorists who attempted to replicate his findings and failed to find that the genetic defects he identified—or any other genetic defects—distinguished criminals from noncriminals (Akers and Sellers 2009; Vold, Bernard and Snipes 2002).

Moreover, by the 1930s and 1940s, American sociologists increasingly began to fault these early biological and psychological theorists for their essentialism (Klein 1995). In their way of thinking, the overreliance on individual differences in innate biological and psychological defects or essences to explain crime caused Lombroso and his disciples to totally ignore the economic and social forces outside of the individual that might result in criminal behavior. As these sociologists saw it, social and economic forces like poverty and living in an urban community might cause even normal persons without biological and psychological defects to commit crime (see, e.g., Shaw and McKay 1942; Merton 1938; Sutherland 1939).

Thus, while Lombroso and his disciples might have explained a woman's involvement in prostitution in terms of her defective biological or psychological makeup, these sociologists eschewed such talk of an abnormal biological or psychological essence at the core of the individual criminal (Klein 1995). Instead they were more inclined to argue that an extra-individual factor like poverty might make a low-income woman more likely to turn to prostitution than a more affluent woman as an alternative way of making money. Moreover, unlike Lombroso and his disciples, these sociologists were actually able to show that social and economic conditions outside the individual like poverty and urban living were actually linked to crime.

The eventual demise of Lombroso's theory also had a lot to do with some of its more controversial policy implications. Because he argued that whole races of people could be crime prone due to biological and psychological defects, his theory encouraged policies that would have kept the more crime-prone races from reproducing as a way of reducing crime. His thinking also had implications for immigration policies because it advanced the notion that a nation's crime rates could increase if it was "invaded" by crime-prone immigrants. Consequently, it gave a boost to national policies that would exclude crime-prone or defective "races" of people from a nation as a way of keeping crime rates low (Lombroso-Ferrero 1911).

As an Italian doctor conducting research in Italy, Lombroso claimed that a biological predisposition to crime was associated with the low-income Sicilians who were overrepresented in the Italian prisons he studied. Hence, based on his theory, Sicilians should have come in for more state oversight and containment as a crime prevention measure. In the United States, it was the new immigrant populations of Italians, Irish, Poles and Jews that migrated to the United States in the nineteenth and early twentieth centuries who were thought to be crime prone. Because they were not regarded as "white" back then, but as members of separate, inferior races, the notion that they were biologically defective and crime prone was one argument that could be used to defend policies to limit their immigration (Brodkin 1999; Patterson 1997).

The fact that the theories of Lombroso and his contemporaries urged these kinds of controversial policies has caused a number of modern-day criminologists to look back on these early-twentieth-century biological and psychological theories of crime as dangerous They were considered dangerous because they defined high crime rates in a racial or ethnic group as evidence of biological and psychological inferiority and then used these assumptions about the inferiority of a whole "race" of people to justify exclusionary social policies (Akers and Sellers 2009).

The policies that grew out of Lombrosian thinking were considered dangerous in other ways as well. Because he assumed that criminals were genetic throwbacks with permanent, inherited biological and psychological abnormalities that predisposed them to crime, his thinking encouraged policies like the sterilization of those identified as born criminals as a way of preventing future crime. In fact, in the early years of the twentieth century, thousands of Americans were sterilized as part of the eugenics movement on the premise that they were biologically defective. While American whites were certainly sterilized, it should come as no surprise that a number of African Americans were sterilized as well. Moreover, these American eugenicist assumptions regarding the biological inferiority of whole races of people were later used to justify even more dangerous social practices like genocide as this kind of thinking presumably helped to shape Nazi justifications for the extermination of the entire Jewish "race" (Kuhl 1994).

For all of these reasons, then, Lombroso's theory had been fully discredited by the 1950s. By then, many criminologists dismissed him as a crackpot and reasoned that his theories had ultimately turned out to be wrong because he failed to practice science in a value-free manner. By that, they meant that he and his contemporaries had allowed their own personal biases about the inferiorities of women and nonwhite races to shape their science rather than engaging in the kind of scientific inquiry that was free of such gender and racial biases. Even worse, they claimed that because this biased science gave credence to pre-existing racial and gender prejudices, it had resulted in the institution of some very dangerous social policies. Still, because he was one of the first scholars to scientize the study of crime, Lombroso has been called the father of criminology. Hence, today most criminologists follow his approach by applying the scientific method to the study of crime even as they completely reject his theory.[1]

Replacing Biological Abnormalities with Cultural Abnormalities

Still, even though criminologists rejected his belief that racial and gender differences in female crime rates could be explained by biological or psychic abnormalities, they increasingly began to account for these differences in terms of cultural abnormalities. Hence, the early-twentieth-century notion advanced by Lombroso and his contemporaries that nonwhite women were more masculinized and thereby more prone to crime was revived in terms that suggested that the criminality of nonwhite women was due to cultural abnormalities rather than biological abnormalities. And, because the black race, in particular, was thought to include a larger proportion of male-like women than the white race, the resulting symmetry between the sexes among blacks once again became a mark of inferiority that was to be explained in cultural terms.

Taken at face value, these claims of sexual symmetry in the violent behaviors of blacks are difficult to defend because there are huge gender differences in violence among blacks and whites alike. For example, in 2002, white males in the murder prone age group of 18- to 24-year-olds had murder rates that were nearly 10 times as high as those of white females in the same age group. The gap between black males and black females was even larger as 18- to 24-year-old black males had murder rates that were more than 17 times as high as those of 18- to 24-year-old black females. Hence, at least, when it comes to murder, there is nothing to support the notion of sexual symmetry in violence among blacks. However, it has been possible to depict black women as masculinized relative to white women as the murder rates of 18- to 24-year-old black females were a little over 4 times as high as those of 18- to 24-year-old white females (Renzetti 2006).[2]

This gap between the murder rates of black females and white females has existed for some time and has in large part been explained by black women's greater propensity for killing their husbands, boyfriends, ex-husbands and ex-boyfriends than white women (Bureau of Justice Statistics 2009; Gauthier and Bankston 1997; Renzetti 2006). It is this observed black female propensity for the use of lethal violence against their intimate partners, then, that has often been interpreted as evidence of their masculinization. In other words, their high rate of intimate-partner homicides has been taken as an indicator that they are more likely to act like males and use violent intimidation in conflicts with their male intimates. And, because their high intimate homicide offending rates indicate a greater tendency to use lethal violence against a male partner, black women are seen as more inclined to violate the standards of true womanhood that require real women to be more passive and retiring in their disputes with the men in their lives.

CULTURAL EXPLANATIONS OF BLACK FEMALE VIOLENCE

One early cultural explanation for high rates of black female involvement in killing their male partners comes from Wolfgang and Ferracuti (1967). As they saw it, a kind of sexual symmetry prevailed in black couples with black females exhibiting behaviors that were every bit as violent as those of black males because they were both members of the black subculture of violence.

Wolfgang and Ferracuti originally developed the concept of a black subculture of violence to explain why black males killed other black males at such high rates. Their thinking was that black men who belonged to a subculture of violence were more likely to consider even trivial matters (improper stare, jostle, playing the dozens, etc.) as serious affronts and attack those who had insulted them in these ways if they did not apologize (see chapter 4). Because apologizing was equated with cowardice, neither male in one of these trivial disputes was willing to back down and thus a fight could ensue ending in severe injury or death. Indeed among males who belonged to a subculture of violence, assaulting someone or even killing them over such trifles was a badge of honor because it was seen as an expression of masculinity.

While Wolfgang and Ferracuti also assumed that homicides among white males could be explained by a white subculture of violence that defined violence as an expression of masculinity, they felt that the black subculture of violence had more of an impact on its members than the white subculture of violence. For that reason, they claimed that black males had higher homicide rates than white males because their violent black subcultures heightened their penchant for violence. They were also able to make their case that the black subculture of violence sharpened the predisposition to violence in its members by pointing to the extremely high murder rates of black females.

In a study of homicides in Philadelphia in the 1950s, Wolfgang found that black females actually had homicide rates that were considerably higher than those of white males in Philadelphia (Wolfgang and Ferracuti 1967). This finding was especially surprising because violence is generally seen as a way of doing masculinity.

Wolfgang and Ferracuti proceeded to explain these high black-female murder rates by arguing that not only were black males members of the black subculture of violence, but that black females were members as well. As such, they claimed that black females were just as inclined to turn to violence in response to minor disputes as the males. Hence in lovers' quarrels between black male and black female intimates, they claimed that both parties were often itching for a fight and both parties were equally reluctant to back down. Hence, they described violence in black couples in the following terms:

> Physical aggression is often seen as a demonstration of masculinity and tough-ness. . . . If homicide is any index at all of physical aggression, we must re-member that in the Philadelphia data, *non-white females* (i.e., black females) *have rates often two to four times higher than the rates of white males.* Violent behavior appears more dependent on cultural differences than on sex differ-ences, traditionally considered of paramount importance in the expression of aggression. It could be argued, of course, that *in a more matriarchal role than that of her white counterpart*, the Negro female both enjoys and suffers more of the male role as head of the household, as parental authority and supervisor; that *this imposed role makes her more aggressive, more male-like, more likely to respond violently.* Because most of the victims of Negro female homicide offenders are Negro males, the Negro female may be striking out aggressively against the inadequate male protector whom she desperately wants but often cannot find or hold. (Wolfgang and Ferracuti 1967, emphasis mine)

Hence Wolfgang and Ferracuti are suggesting that the high rate of black-female intimate homicide offending is evidence that they are seeking to demonstrate their masculinity, dominance and toughness just like males. For them, black female membership in the black subculture of violence coupled with their status as matriarchal heads of households are such powerful conditions that they have masculinized black women and caused them to deviate from the standards of true womanhood.

Certainly, Wolfgang and Ferracuti could have interpreted the high rates of black female violence in intimate partner relationships as evidence of their need to defend themselves from the inordinately high levels of black male violence directed at them. However, they succeeded in converting this seeming tendency on the part of black women to defend themselves into abnormal behavior by claiming that it was a reflection of their membership in the dysfunctional black subculture of violence and their incumbency in the matriarchal role.

Of course, by defining black female self-defense as abnormal, they were assuming that the corresponding white female failure to defend themselves from their white male batterers was normal feminine behavior. Hence, even though more white females may have died at the hands of their male intimates because of their failure to defend themselves, their low rate of intimate homicide offending was treated as normal. With this interpretation of race differences in female homicides, then, the white female ranking at the top of the female hierarchy could be preserved because white women conformed to the standards of true womanhood.[3]

Feminist Explanations of Black Female Violence

Of course, Wolfgang and Ferracuti were writing in the days before the white middle-class feminist movement really took off. It took white middle-class females to make the case that women who killed their male intimates were only defending themselves from battering by their male partners. After all, the black females that Wolfgang and Ferracuti constructed as male-like lacked the kind of clout in academic circles that was needed to make the case that their violence in the face of male abuse was neither "masculine" nor "feminine" behavior, but rather a normal human effort at self-preservation.

Feminists also explained the race differences in the rate at which females killed their male intimates in very different terms than Wolfgang and Ferracuti. For them, the fact that black females were more likely to kill their male partners than white females was only an indicator that black females might be defending themselves from extremely abusive black males. And, in fact, national homicide data indicate that black females are more likely to be murdered by their black male intimates than any other race or ethnic group (Bureau of Justice Statistics 2009, 2009a). According to feminist arguments, then, this high rate of male violence might in turn precipitate high rates of black female violence in self-defense.

Clearly, then, for many feminists, it is males who are typically at fault for relationship violence because as they see it, men in patriarchal societies are socialized to believe that they should dominate and control women. Because the male need to dominate women is presumably so strong, they claim that some men are inclined to resort to various forms of psychological, economic and physical abuse if they feel their patriarchal authority is threatened in any way (Belknap and Potter 2006).[4]

Female Relationship Violence: Self-Defense or Sexual Symmetry?

As feminists describe it, then, intimate partner violence is the kind of crime that involves a female victim and a male perpetrator, who subscribes to a patriarchal ideology that requires him to dominate and control his wife or girlfriend. Hence, for them, intimate-partner violence typically begins with a male batterer heaping physical abuse upon his wife, girlfriend, ex-wife or ex-girlfriend because he feels his male authority has been threatened. In such situations, they claim, females may resort to violence only as a way to defend themselves.

However, even today, there are some critics of this kind of feminist think-ing who continue to explain female involvement in intimate-partner violence in terms that masculinize and pathologize it. That is because these critics question the notion that females are always the victims in domestic violence, who only engage in violence to defend themselves or their children from an abusive male. Instead, as the critics see it, women are quite capable of initiat-ing violence on their own that can lead to male injury and death.

Hence, unlike the feminists who see intimate-partner violence in asymmet-rical terms—with a male perpetrator and a female victim—these critics argue that violent behaviors in an intimate-partner relationship are characterized by sexual symmetry or conflicts in which men and women are equally abusive in their relationships (Moffitt et al. 2000; Moffitt et al. 2001; Giordano et al. 1999). For those who explain intimate-partner violence in terms of sexual symmetry, women who attack men and women who return violence after be-ing battered by a male are often just as violent as their male partners.

Indeed in some cases, these critics claim that a woman may actually batter a man without him returning the violence—a phenomenon that some refer to as a battered man or battered husband syndrome (Steinmetz 1978). Hence, because they see relationship violence in terms of sexual symmetry, their research tends to be geared towards identifying those factors that might cause women to be just as violent as men. As such, this research has particular relevance for black females in light of their tendency to kill their intimate partners at higher rates than white females.

African Americans, Sexual Symmetry and the Code of the Streets

Writing after the feminist movement, Anderson (1994) offered a new cultural explanation as to why there was sexual symmetry in violence among blacks. Moreover, he suggested that such similarities in violence between the sexes might be expected to increase as he claimed that a new more masculinized black female had appeared on the horizon. However, he was not especially concerned with explaining black female involvement in intimate partner violence. Rather, the new more violent black female that he described was more likely to be involved in fights at school and gang fighting. Still, because he provides an explanation of why black girls might be motivated to mimic male violence, his explanation has some relevance for explanations of all forms of black female violence.

As he describes it, black females and black males alike are both trying to achieve manhood and thus both are inclined to use violence when they feel slighted by others. In his description of how young black girls resort to violence in order to achieve manhood like the boys, Anderson sounds a lot like Wolfgang and Ferracuti, who suggest that both sexes are inclined to respond with violence in the face of trivial insults because they are both members of a black subculture of violence. However, for Anderson, instead of the subculture of violence, black girls are conforming to what he calls the code of the streets. Hence, he describes their violence in the following terms:

> Increasingly, (black) *teenage girls are mimicking the boys and trying to have their own version of "manhood."* Their goal is the same [as black boys] to get respect, to be recognized as capable of setting or maintaining a certain standard. They try to achieve this end in the ways that have been established by the boys, including posturing, abusive language, and the use of violence to resolve disputes, but the issues for the girls are different. Although conflicts over turf and status exist among the girls, the majority of disputes seem rooted in assessments of beauty (which girl in a group is "the cutest"), competition over boyfriends, and attempts to regulate other people's knowledge of and opinions about a girl's behavior or that of someone close to her, especially her mother. . . . A major cause of conflict among girls is "he say, she say." . . . As with much gossip, the things said may or may not be true, but the point is that such imputations can cast aspersions on a person's good name. The accused is required to defend herself against the slander, which can result in arguments and fights often over little of real substance. . . . Here, again is the problem of low self-esteem, which encourages youngsters to be highly sensitive to slights and to be vulnerable to feeling easily "dissed." (Anderson 1994:92, emphasis mine)

Certainly white girls and black girls alike are likely to form cliques and argue over which girl is the cutest or dresses the best and girls of all races compete over boyfriends. That these kinds of conflicts are ubiquitous among girls is indicated by the popularity of the gossip magazines positioned at the supermarket checkout counter, which are meant to appeal to teenaged females of all races with their never-ending discussion of these topics. However, Anderson suggests that a type of sexual symmetry exists between black girls and black boys that causes black girls to be more likely to resolve such arguments with violence than girls in other racial and ethnic groups. And, much like Wolfgang and Ferracuti, Anderson claims that this sexual symmetry in violent behaviors stems from the fact that both black males and black females are seeking manhood in an oppositional subculture that requires conformity to a code of the streets in which the use of violence is required to maintain reputations.

For him, this oppositional subculture is black-specific as it is a response to the alienation and frustration that only economically marginalized black males and black females experience as a result of the persistent joblessness and racism that confines them to the underclass. In fact, Anderson warns that unless the cycle of joblessness and racism that fuels this quest for manhood is broken, violence for black male and black female teens alike is only likely to escalate.

Because he suggests that black girls are seeking to achieve manhood with their use of violence just like the boys, his theory could certainly explain black female involvement in fights at school or in violent adolescent gangs. It could also be expanded to explain relationship violence in young black couples as both parties in these disputes would, in theory, be inclined to use violence in response to any disagreements in their efforts to achieve manhood. Indeed, because Anderson claims that teenaged black girls are seeking manhood, it might even explain a battered man syndrome in which these girls might batter their black male partners even if their partners never return the abuse.

Critique of Cultural Explanations of Sexual Symmetry

Clearly, then, both the theories of Wolfgang and Ferracuti and Anderson manage to revive age-old ideas about sexual symmetry in the violent behaviors of black females and black males. However, instead of using biological or psychic defects to explain this seeming sexual symmetry among blacks, they rely on cultural explanations.

Wolfgang and Ferracuti, in particular, developed their theory about sexual symmetry in violent behaviors among blacks using homicide data—specifically data on homicides in Philadelphia in the 1950s. Because these data showed that black females killed their partners at rates that were higher even than those of white males, this seemed to confirm their hypothesis that the black subculture of violence had a more powerful impact on black female behavior than even sex role norms that discouraged such violence in women.

Moreover, they claimed that some of the male-like aggressiveness that they observed in black women was due to their status as matriarchs. In other words, they argued that black women had become more male-like in the process of taking over the masculine roles of breadwinner and head of the household and thus may have become more violent as a result.

However, national homicide statistics do not actually support this notion that large numbers of black females have been masculinized by their membership in the black subculture of violence. Even if one looks at all types of homicides involving all categories of victims (including intimate partners, strangers, acquaintances and family members), females of all races committed a total of 1,330 homicides in 2007 (Puzzanchera and Kang 2008). Although black females were responsible for a disproportionate 44.7 percent of the homicides committed by women, that translates into a mere 595 homicides committed by black women. In a population of a little over 19 million black women, these 595 violent acts can hardly be taken as evidence of widespread male-like or matriarchal tendencies in black women (U.S. Census Bureau 2006).

Moreover, even if the black subculture of violence did make substantial numbers of black females more likely to kill their intimate partners, its influence seems to be subsiding. For example, when nationwide trends are examined for intimate-partner homicides only, they indicate that the number of black males killed by a spouse, ex-spouse, girlfriend or ex-girlfriend fell by a whopping 83 percent between 1976 and 2005. This suggests that black females may be considerably less violent towards their black male intimates than they were when Wolfgang and Ferracuti conducted their classic study (Bureau of Justice Statistics 2009, 2009a; Rennison and Welchans 2000). Black males likewise seem to be considerably less violent with their female intimates as well as in the same time period, the number of black females killed by a male intimate partner declined by a full 52 percent.[5]

Considerably less dramatic were the drops in intimate homicides that occurred in the white population during this period. While the number of white males killed by a spouse, ex-spouse, girlfriend or ex-girlfriend fell by an impressive 61 percent, the number of white females killed by an intimate partner declined by a mere 6 percent. In part, the decline in white female victims was so small because the *number* of white males killing their white female intimates in 2005 was about the same as it had been in 1976 (Bureau of Justice Statistics 2009, 2009a). And, for white girlfriends killed by a boyfriend or ex-boyfriend, the homicide victimization *rates* were actually higher in 2005 than they were in 1976.

Because overall declines for black couples were far more substantial than those for white couples, black and white rates for intimate-partner homicides have converged over the years. Hence, even if the notion of a black subculture that masculinized black women and made them violent was persuasive in the past, it seems a lot less persuasive today.

These trends also raise questions about Anderson's notion that black girls in the underclass have recently become more inclined to use violence to resolve disputes in their attempts to achieve manhood. If this is so, it is certainly not showing up in the intimate homicide trends, which indicate a precipitous drop in the number of black females killing off their male intimates. Moreover, the fact that there has been a decline in overall black female homicide offending rates that involve all kinds of victims raises additional doubts about Anderson's argument that a new, more violent black female has emerged on the horizon to become involved in girl fights at school and gang fighting. In particular, the fact that there seems to have been a drop-off in killings by 14- to 17-year-old black girls between 1990 and 2003 suggests that there is no trend afoot for black girls to use lethal violence to seek manhood just like the boys (Renzetti 2006).

PSYCHOLOGICAL ABNORMALITIES AND FEMALE VIOLENCE REVISITED

As noted previously, the kinds of cultural explanations promoted by Anderson and by Wolfgang and Ferracuti only became popular once the notion that violence in women could be explained by biological and psychological defects lost favor. However, of late, these kinds of biopsychological explanations for female violence have been enjoying something of a comeback in more modernized form.

For the most part, the modern biopsychological theorists have concentrated on trying to explain the high crime rates of males—particularly black males—in terms of their supposed biological and psychological abnormalities in a manner akin to early-twentieth-century criminologists (e.g., Wilson and Herrnstein 1985; Moffitt 1999).[6] Hence, when these theorists turn to explanations of female violence, they have a tendency to resurrect some of Lombroso's early-twentieth-century ideas about biological and psychological defects in violent women. This has been especially true of the research on female violence in intimate partnerships.

More than one hundred years ago, Lombroso claimed that women who suffered from biological and psychological abnormalities would be more likely to resort to violence just like men. Hence, when applied to today's research on violence in intimate relationships, his theories have prompted a similar search for underlying psychological abnormalities—and to a lesser degree, biological and physiological abnormalities as well—to explain female violence in their intimate relationships.

Given the fact that black females have traditionally had such high rates of involvement in intimate-partner homicides, these updated versions of biopsychological theories would seem to have particular relevance to them. In the next few sections, then, I will examine some of these more recent biopsychological theories and consider how they might account for high rates of black female involvement in intimate-partner violence.

One of the newer biopsychological theories of female violence comes from Moffitt and her colleagues (2001). They revive some of the early-twentieth-century ideas by identifying the kinds of emotional and psychological abnormalities that might cause a woman to resort to violence in her relationships. Their research is based on a study of sexual symmetry in violent behaviors in an all-white sample of dating, cohabiting and married couples in Dunedin, New Zealand.

Unlike Wolfgang and Ferracuti, they do not use homicide statistics to measure levels of intimate-partner violence. After all, murder is only the tip of the iceberg when it comes to relationship violence as most conflicts in couples do not escalate beyond nonlethal assaults. Therefore, instead of using homicide data, they asked the men and women that they interviewed if they had actually assaulted their partners by slapping, strangling, hitting, or kicking them or by beating them up or using a weapon against them.

When such scales of nonlethal assaults were used to measure intimate-partner violence in earlier research, they generally showed that females were actually more inclined to assault their male partners than males were to assault their female partners (Strauss and Gelles 1990). Moffitt and her colleagues obtained similar results as the women in their sample were more likely to physically abuse the males than vice versa. Hence, while 40 percent of the males in their sample of 360 couples reported slapping, strangling, kicking, hitting, beating up, or using a weapon against their partners, fully 50 percent of the women in these couples reported that they too had committed many of these violent acts as well.

For Moffitt and her associates, then, these findings demonstrate that females are just as violent as males in conflicts between couples. As such, they raise doubts about feminist assertions that couples conflicts are caused by a male seeking to dominate his female partner with violence. Because the females in their sample seem to batter their male intimates at equal or even higher rates than vice versa, they suggest that female motivations for relationship violence may be the same as males.

For them, the trait that motivates females to be as violent as males is one they call negative emotionality. Hence, in order to study the effects of negative emotionality on couples' violence, they interviewed their Dunedin, New Zealand, sample of couples at two points in time. In time 1, when the study subjects were 18 years old, both females and males from this birth cohort were asked to participate in the study by responding to items measuring negative emotionality.

Negative emotionality was measured by 49 true-false items which asked respondents if they "often got irritated at little annoyances," or "sometimes experienced anger or anxiety without knowing why." Efforts were also made to gauge the extent to which respondents were prone to using aggressive strategies by asking them if it was true that "when someone hurts me, I try to get even." Hence, those who scored high on negative emotionality tended to describe themselves in their responses as nervous, vulnerable, prone to worry, emotionally volatile, and unable to cope with stress. They were also inclined to circle items in which they described themselves as having a low threshold for feeling tense, fearful, hostile, angry, callous, and suspicious. And, based on their own self-descriptions, respondents with negative emotionality had a tendency to expect mistreatment from others and to see the world as peopled with potential enemies. Finally, those scoring high on the negative emotionality scale reported that they were more likely to seek revenge for slights, enjoyed frightening others and were more likely to remorselessly take advantage of others.

At time 2, when the study subjects were 21 years old, the original study participants were asked to bring their intimate partners to a second interview, and as a result the researchers were able to interview 360 couples (339 heterosexual couples) about their relationships. At age 21, only 7 percent of the couples were married, while some 52 percent were dating and 41 percent were cohabiting; on average, the relationships for these couples had lasted 26 months.

It was during this second interview that they asked the original study subjects and their partners about their relationship violence. Because the original study participants had been questioned about their negative emotionality at age 18, it was possible to determine if those reporting negative emotionality at age 18 were more violent in their intimate partnerships at age 21. For their partners, who were not part of the original study, questions were asked about both negative emotionality and involvement in violent behaviors within the couple at age 21 only.

Among other things, they found that a good deal of violence by women in their sample occurred in conjunction with abuse by the male partner, which is consistent with the feminist assertion that women are only violent in conflicts between couples when they are trying to defend themselves. However, they also found that some 18 percent of the women in their sample had perpetrated abuse on a male when the male had not reciprocated. To them, this indicated that nearly a fifth of women could be violent even when they were not defending themselves, which is a finding more consistent with the battered man syndrome than feminist arguments suggesting female self-defense. Furthermore, all of the women involved in violence in their study scored high on negative emotionality, whether they were simply reciprocating male violence or involved in one-sided abuse of males.

Moffitt and her associates claim that the fact that all of the violent females in their study shared the same personality traits raises questions about the feminist notion that women only become involved in violence to defend themselves. By their reasoning, if females were only violent when they were defending themselves, it does not seem likely that such women would share personality traits with women involved in one-sided abuse of males. Indeed one would expect these women to have little in common. However, because they found that females who were involved in violent acts (both one-sided and reciprocal) at age 21 were more likely to have reported negative emotionality at age 18, they claimed that it was this violence-prone psychological trait that predisposed females to violence as opposed to a simple need for self-defense against male battering.

They also found that the males in their sample who were involved in violence against their female partners were more likely to report negative emotionality at age 18 than males not involved in violence. Hence, the fact that both females and males who were inclined to batter their partners shared the same psychological profile (negative emotionality) only provided further support for their claim that there was sexual symmetry in violent behaviors.

Because negative emotionality makes both sexes more irritable, vengeful, prone to anger and desirous of retaliation for past arguments, they hypothesized that couples in which both female and male partners shared these traits would have particularly high levels of mutual abuse. In such couples, they reasoned a woman might batter her partner both as an expression of her negative emotionality as well as in reaction to his negative emotionality and vice versa. Hence, violence in these couples was expected to be especially high because of mutual additive effects in which one partner's abuse was a reaction to the other partner's irritability, vengefulness, inclinations to anger and desire for retaliation for past arguments. This was borne out in their study, as they found that abuse was more likely when both partners reported negative emotionality than when only one partner reported negative emotionality.

They hypothesized that there might be additional reasons for doubting feminist self-defense arguments about female relationship violence, particularly if they could demonstrate that women who battered their partners also had a history of assaulting nonpartners. And, in fact, the women in their study who abused their intimate partners were four times more likely to have been involved in violence against a nonintimate in the same year as compared to women who were not abusive. This finding casts doubt on feminist assertions because it indicates that women are not just violent in situations in which they are defending themselves or their children against a violent male partner, but that they are also violent in situations in which no such self-defense is required.

That women who are violent with their intimates seem to be violent with everyone across a variety of circumstances is also consistent with the notion that a personality trait like negative emotionality—that can be expected to operate across situations—may be driving women to be violent across situations rather than a situation-specific need for self-defense. Furthermore, in keeping with the sexual symmetry argument, the same finding applied to males as well. In other words, males who abused their partners were also more likely to be violent across situations as well (see also Moffitt et al. 2000).

In explaining the origins of the violent predisposition that they called negative emotionality, Moffitt and her colleagues claim that it is inherited and likely to be a permanent part of the personality. Hence, they are suggesting that women who are violent in domestic disputes are psychologically different from women who do not resort to violence in their intimate relationships. The fact that they describe these traits as inherited also suggests that they see women with negative emotionality as biologically or physiologically distinct as well.

Because they assume that negative emotionality is permanent and heritable, they argue that it can first manifest itself in early childhood and then persist throughout the teen years and on into early adulthood. Hence, the fact that they find that eighteen-year-old girls who score high on negative emotionality are more likely to resort to violence in their relationships at age 21 at least provides evidence that this trait persists from the late teens to young adulthood.

However, while Moffitt and her colleagues were only able to find evidence of the link between psychological predispositions and violence over a three-year period, from age 18 to age 21, they cite a study by Giordano and her associates (1999) which finds evidence of such violent predispositions over a somewhat longer time period. Moreover, Giordano and her colleagues find evidence of violent psychological predispositions in a sample of black and white American females. Consequently, their study suggests that the research of Moffitt and her colleagues on New Zealand women might be generalizable to explanations of violence among black and white women in the United States.

Female Violence across the Life Course

In a two-stage study, Giordano and her colleagues asked black and white urban teenagers in Toledo, Ohio, to report on their delinquency when they were between the ages of 12 and 19. Using a scale to measure intimate-partner violence that resembled the one used in the New Zealand study, they then re-interviewed these same respondents about their involvement in intimate-partner violence some 10 years later when they were in their twenties.

They found that self-reported delinquency in the first wave of interviews conducted in the teen years was one of the best predictors that females would later report committing violent acts in conflicts with their intimate partners in their second interview in their twenties, some 10 years later. Because this indicated that violent females were likely to be violent across situations—both in fights at school as teenagers and then later in disputes with their boyfriends as young adults—it seemed to confirm the New Zealand study results that likewise suggested that female violence was not situation-specific. There are other similarities in the Toledo and New Zealand studies as well as both suggest that female violence can be understood in terms of a life course or developmental perspective. In other words, both studies provide evidence that a female propensity for violence in the teen years (negative emotionality, delinquency) simply continues into young adulthood in the form of violence in intimate partnerships.

Much like the New Zealand study, Giordano and her colleagues also included some measures of personality traits that might have predisposed their teen respondents to intimate partner violence as young adults. For example, they asked the young adults (age 22-29) in the second wave of their study to think back to their teen years and determine if they were viewed as trouble-makers. In the same second wave interview, they also asked their young adult respondents to report on whether or not they currently saw themselves as angry.

Their scale measuring angry self-concepts in young adulthood included items such as "when people say or do something that hurts me, I usually try to hurt them back," "I can be a pretty mean person," "I have a lot of trouble controlling my temper," and "when I drink, I sometimes become pretty mean." Clearly, then, the Giordano study's measures of angry self-concepts in adulthood were similar to some of the items measuring negative emotionality in the Moffitt study.

Furthermore, much like the New Zealand research, Giordano and her colleagues found that these two personality characteristics—the troublemaker self-concept as a teenager and the angry self-concept as a young adult—were modest predictors of female involvement in intimate-partner violence in their young adult years.

In addition, they found that a history of juvenile delinquency, a trouble-maker self-concept as a juvenile and an angry self-concept as an adult were all associated with male involvement in partnership violence as well. This result offered further support for the sexual symmetry argument as it suggested that males and females were motivated to resort to violence for the same reasons.

Still, at best, Giordano's study merely demonstrates a correlation between these psychological traits (troublemaker self-concept as a juvenile, angry self-concept as an adult) and intimate-partner violence as she first asked her female and male respondents about these personality characteristics during the second wave interview at the same time that she was asking them about their involvement in domestic violence. Hence, unlike the New Zealand study, her study does not prospectively assess the impact of the personality measures over the life course of her respondents as they progress from delinquency in their teen years to violence in conflicts with their intimate partners in their twenties.

Race, Sexual Symmetry and Intimate Partner Violence

Still, despite these limitations, both of these studies seem to provide support for the notion that there is sexual symmetry in violent behaviors as both suggest that the same psychological profile may be motivating males and females to become involved in intimate-partner violence. Moreover both studies provide some support for developmental and life course perspectives that assume that males and females with violence-prone psychological characteristics in common (negative emotionality, troublemaker self-concepts, angry self-concepts) are simply expressing them first with involvement in juvenile delinquency during their teen years and then expressing them later in their twenties in the form of violent battering of their male and female partners.

Such findings would seem to have particular relevance for the African American couples in the Giordano study, as the black females and the black males in her sample were much more likely to be involved in intimate-partner violence than the white females and white males in the study. Hence, it is at least possible that these black females and black males may be more likely to have personality characteristics like angry self-concepts, troublemaker self-concepts or negative emotionality that make them prone towards violence first as teenagers and then as young adults.

If so, this bodes ill for these black couples as it could translate into mutual additive effects. In other words, personality traits like the negative emotionality or angry self-concepts of black females might only reinforce the negative emotionality or angry self-concepts of their black male partners making it all the more likely that violence will escalate as each partner initiates and returns violence.

Over and above the seeming psychological predispositions to violence, Giordano and her colleagues also considered the possibility that influences in the larger cultural environment might make the urban girls that they studied more prone to relationship violence. In particular, they note that the fact that some of the girls in their study live in "marginal, economically depressed areas where fights between girls are common," coupled with exposure to violence in their families while they are growing up, could be having an effect.

They argued that this early exposure to violent resolution of conflicts might have socialized the urban poor females in their study to view violence as an acceptable way of coping with conflict in their teen years long before they used violence to respond to conflicts in their intimate-partner relationships as young adults. In other words, once these violent, antisocial behavior patterns were established as a way of resolving conflicts as teenagers, these inner-city girls might have been more likely to persist in using violence to settle disputes with boyfriends or husbands in young adulthood. This would seem to account for why the female respondents in the Giordano study who reported delinquency as girls were more likely to be involved in relationship violence as young adults.

Anderson's research on the code of the streets (1994) would seem to be of some relevance here as he notes that in urban poor black neighborhoods, teenaged girls are socialized to seek manhood just like the boys by using violence to resolve disputes. Because Giordano finds race differences and sex differences in violence in separate equations in her study that indicate that blacks and females report more relationship violence in their twenties than their urban white or male counterparts, it could be interpreted as evidence that early exposure to a black urban cultural influence like the code of the streets might make it more likely that the violent repertoires that blacks and female adolescents learn as teenagers only persist into adulthood.

CRITIQUE OF PSYCHOLOGICAL
EXPLANATIONS OF FEMALE VIOLENCE

Because blacks have higher rates of intimate-partner violence than whites, the Moffitt and Giordano studies might lead to the conclusion that this means that they may be more likely to have the underlying emotional predispositions (troublemaker self-concept, angry self-concept, negative emotionality) that induce men and women in couples to abuse each other. Hence, much as was the case in the early twentieth century, this research could further the notion that there are racial differences in the psychological abnormalities that make females prone to violence. However, both studies promote this controversial notion by using research that is plagued with fundamental problems with measurement—much as was the case with biopsychological theories in the early twentieth century.

Problems with the Measurement of Intimate-Partner Violence

What is particularly troubling is the way in which they operationalize their dependent variable, namely intimate-partner violence. In both the Moffitt and Giordano studies, partner violence is measured in terms of vague and often trivial forms of assault like pushing, slapping, kicking, biting and hitting. Measures of nonlethal violence like a slap or a hit are problematic because they can cover everything from a playful tap to being slapped or hit so hard that a jaw is broken or teeth are loosened. The inclusion of these vague, trivial items, then, makes it appear that men and women are equally violent when men are far more likely to injure or kill women with their slaps and hits. Hence these scales have the effect of minimizing the dangers of male-to-female violence while maximizing the dangerousness of female-to-male violence (Belknap and Potter 2006; Miller and White 2003).

Moreover, by simply measuring partner abuse with vague, trivial nonlethal violent acts, their measurement scales make it appear that the sexes hit each other for the same reasons and thereby obscure any patriarchal intent that might lie behind male abuse of women. According to feminist theories, such patriarchal intentions cause men to perpetrate violence on women in efforts to dominate and control them on the assumption that, as males, they are entitled to wield power over women in keeping with patriarchal ideology. That these attempts at dominance often work is evidenced by the fact that many women respond to repeated battering by their male partners by becoming docile, fearful and obedient (Belknap and Potter 2006; Miller and White 2003).

However, when women slap and hit their male partners, their intent is not to dominate and control the men in their lives in the belief that they are entitled to be in charge as matriarchs. Nor do the men in their lives neces-sarily respond by becoming docile, fearful and obedient. Yet, because sexual symmetry researchers assert gender parity in violence based on a measure that includes a simple count of hits and slaps, they ignore the possibility that males and females might initiate violence for radically different reasons and that their violence might have radically different results.

Research by Miller and White (2003) shows the importance of looking at the motives behind female violence rather than relying on a simple count of hits and slaps. They surveyed some 70 delinquent or at-risk black female and black male teenagers in St. Louis, Missouri, using a scale of intimate-partner violence that was similar to that used by Moffitt and Giordano. In keeping with the Moffitt and Giordano findings, the black females in their study were more likely to push, shove, slap, kick, bite and hit their black male boyfriends than vice versa. Although this could have been interpreted as evidence that these girls were seeking to dominate and control their boyfriends, Miller and White found that these black girls primarily slapped and hit their black boy-friends because they suspected them of seeing other girls.

It is important to note that many of the at-risk black males "battered" by these black females likely subscribed to a code of the streets that dictated that violence should be used against any male that might hit, slap or even stare at them too long. Yet, they clearly saw the violence of their girlfriends in quite different terms. Many of them went out of their way to avoid reciprocating when their girlfriends hit or slapped them; in fact, many of them just walked away. Some of them laughed when their girlfriends "abused" them in these ways and they laughed when they told their black male friends about their girlfriends hitting them. Some were flattered when their girlfriends hit them as many were, in fact, seeing other girls, and their girlfriends' anger and "abuse" did much to reinforce their player image. Clearly, then, their girl-friends' "abuse" did not make these males fearful, docile and compliant.

Instead of reacting to black female "abuse" with fear, many of these males dismissed their girlfriends' violence as trivial and ineffective and merely saw it as evidence that they were emotionally out of control. Indeed because their assumption was that their girlfriends couldn't really hurt them, they did not feel in the least bit threatened. And because their girlfriends' "abuse" was not perceived as threatening, many of them felt that a male should just walk away.

The belief that males should just walk away from girlfriends who hit or slapped them was widely espoused by many of the black males and black females in the study whether they had been involved in hitting their intimate partners or not. Males and females alike felt that it was unmanly for boys to hit girls precisely because girls represented no physical threat. In addition, some of the males opposed reciprocating female violence for reasons having to do with chivalry as they feared they might hurt their girlfriends if they hit back. Indeed one black male respondent said he had been taught by his mother not to hit women and added that he would not want a male hitting his mother or his sister.

Hence, when hit, some males might push their girlfriends away or grab them to avoid further violence. While technically these pushes and grabs might qualify as male "abuse" of females on a partner violence scale such as those used in the Moffitt and Giordano studies, it is clear that the intent of these males was to restrain their girlfriends, settle them down and protect themselves from further hits or slaps rather than abuse.

This study, then, makes it clear that a simple count of hits, slaps and kicks made by males and females in the course of their conflicts may be a poor measure of abuse—at least in terms of the way that feminists define abuse. When feminists initially referred to male abuse of women, they were talking about male battering. By battering, they meant the male's systematic use of violence or threats to exert power, induce fear and control their female partners (Osthoff 2002). Because separate, isolated hits and slaps can occur without being motivated by an ongoing desire to coerce or control the partner, a simple count of these violent acts cannot be taken as an indicator of the systematic violence that is implied by terms like abuse or battering. As such, then, the scales of intimate-partner violence used in these studies are a poor way to test the battering described in feminist theory.

To identify real battering requires putting these separate hits, slaps and kicks in context by identifying the batterer as the person who initiated the violence. Distinguishing the batterer from the battered victim also means determining who is using violence as part of a campaign to dominate and control and who is merely defending themselves from an ongoing campaign of abuse. Because the measures of relationship violence used in the Moffitt and Giordano studies merely record one-time hits, they cannot distinguish the partner who is the primary aggressor or instigator from the partner whose slaps and kicks are self-defensive efforts to respond to a history of victimization. Hence, by decontextualizing the violent event, these scales manage to make female relationship violence look every bit as serious as male relationship violence (Osthoff 2002; S. Miller and Meloy 2006; Dasgupta 2002).

Sexual Symmetry Research and the Bootstrapping of Female Violence

Still, despite these fundamental problems with measurement, the notion of gender parity in partnership violence promoted by the Moffitt and Giordano studies has been described and even sensationalized in popular culture—most notably in newspaper reports and on television news broadcasts and talk shows (Dasgupta 2002; S. Miller and Meloy 2006). And, as noted, in the previous chapter, it has likewise been dramatized on the silver screen, particularly in films with all-black casts (e.g., *Talk to Me, Baby Boy, What's Love Got to Do With It?*). Moreover, Moffitt's and Giordano's findings that suggest that intimate-partner violence is nothing more than men and women involved in mutual abuse of each other is likewise reflected in criminal justice policy.

One bit of evidence that this research has affected policy comes from the fact that criminal justice practitioners have become increasingly proactive about intervening with girls involved in minor forms of acting out (Steffensmeier et al. 2005). Such early interventions are encouraged by both these studies because their findings suggest that every minor female scrape, fight or delinquent act from childhood through the teen years might be predictive of more serious violence to come in the form of female violence in intimate relationships during the young adult years. Indeed, even without overt delinquent acts, the mere evidence of disturbing emotional states in young girls like a propensity for anger or seeking revenge or a low threshold for feeling tense, hostile or suspicious (i.e., negative emotionality) might presage a predilection for violence in adult relationships..

That is because both the Moffitt and Giordano studies take a developmental approach which assumes that the attitudes, emotions and antisocial behaviors that they identify signal some underlying trait like an angry self-concept, a troublemaker self-concept or negative emotionality that can distinguish a violence-prone female from a normal nonviolent female. And because both studies foster the belief that these emotional and psychological problems can appear early in life—perhaps in childhood or the early teens—and persist into adulthood in the form of serious relationship violence, state regulation of girls who manifest these attitudes and behaviors appears to be warranted.

Presumably, this tendency on the part of police and prosecutors to take even trivial forms of female violence more seriously has come as part of a larger trend toward early identification and enhanced legal control over those deemed to be problem individuals or problem groups. Because youth are typically included among these problem individuals or groups, the police have become more inclined to intervene earlier and more often for even the most insignificant of youthful transgressions. In other words, rather than waiting around to arrest teenagers when they commit some serious act, the police have become more proactive about arresting young people for trivial indiscretions on the premise that crackdowns on minor antisocial behaviors by juveniles will prevent major crimes in the future.

For example, with zero tolerance policing, the police have arrested juveniles—especially juveniles in minority neighborhoods—for loitering or disorderly conduct on the unproven assertion that these sweeping dragnets of minor miscreants somehow manages to draw in serious criminals (see chapters 2 and 3 for discussion of zero tolerance policing). Prosecutors have then proceeded to back up this trend towards enhanced policing of trivial forms of delinquency by punishing even the most minor youthful indiscretions with severe penalties (McArdle and Erzen 2001). They do so by lumping verbal intimidation, antisocial behaviors and minor acts of violence in together with serious forms of physical aggression that result in injury. By lumping minor and serious acts together, they are able to "charge up" or bootstrap simple assaults into aggravated assaults (Steffensmeier et al. 2005).

Most of this criminal justice system emphasis on early recognition and proactive intervention with even minor youthful indiscretions is targeted at males. And, in fact, there is a much larger, much criticized developmental literature that suggests that underlying biological, physiological and psychological abnormalities in male children and teenagers may indicate that they are at-risk for future involvement in a career in serious crime and violence (i.e., becoming career robbers, burglars, drug dealers, etc.) that can last for much of their adult life (Wilson and Herrnstein 1985; Moffitt 1999). Hence, this kind of research makes proactive interventions with populations of boys who are deemed to be "at-risk" for lengthy adult careers in crime seem warranted.

However, such research on the factors that lead to careers in serious crime and violence in males has traditionally not focused on identifying at-risk females because there are so few female career criminals. For example, a study on the 1958 birth cohort in Philadelphia found that only about 1 percent of females were chronic juvenile offenders, who were likely to persist in serious criminal behavior for much of their adult life (Siegel 2008). Nonetheless, the Moffitt and Giordano studies reviewed in this chapter suggest that similar weight should be given to early recognition and proactive intervention for minor antisocial behaviors in both girls and boys on the premise that even trivial outbursts early on might lead to severe forms of violence in their intimate-partner relationships in young adulthood.

Unfortunately, when this kind of research is translated into policies that encourage police and prosecutors to charge up minor juvenile outbursts into serious aggravated assaults, it can have more of an impact on assault arrests for teenaged girls than teenaged boys. This is because so much girl violence is minor while a larger share of violence among boys tends to actually be more serious and aggravated—with no need for bootstrapping. Recent trends in assault arrests seem to confirm this hypothesis that female violence is being bootstrapped as the rate of increase in assault arrests for females has outpaced that for males.

For example, when assault trends are examined for males and females in all age groups, male assault arrests declined by 17.3 percent between 1994 and 2003 even as female assault arrests increased by 14 percent in that same period (Steffensmeier et al. 2005; Renzetti 2006). If only juvenile trends are considered, the data offer even more support for the notion that the police may be charging up minor female scrapes into serious offenses as the number of boys arrested for aggravated assaults increased by a mere 13 percent between 1980 and 2003 even as the number of aggravated assault arrests for girls increased by a whopping 96 percent (Renzetti 2006). Clearly males are still far more likely to be involved in serious assaults than females as they had aggravated assault arrest rates that were nearly four times as high as those of females as recently as 2007 (Federal Bureau of Investigation 2008). Still, the fact that female arrests for aggravated assaults are increasing at a much faster pace than those of males suggests that the sexes may eventually converge in terms of their arrests for assault.

While Steffensmeier and his colleagues interpret these trends as evidence that the police and prosecutors are increasingly including girls in the at-risk population and bootstrapping their minor antisocial acts into more serious offenses, another interpretation is possible. An uncritical interpretation of these assault arrest trends might suggest that they are real. If that is the case, then the rise in female assault arrests would simply indicate that females have actually become more violent in recent years. Such an interpretation would certainly be consistent with Anderson's claim that black girls, at least, are becoming more like blacks boys in terms of using violence as a way of seeking manhood.

However, it is difficult to argue that an increase in the number of females arrested for assaults necessarily reflects an actual increase in assaults by females because assaults are such vague and poorly defined crimes. One reason for this murkiness is that there is no agreement across police departments around the country about what constitutes an assault or what distinguishes an aggravated assault from a simple assault. Hence, while the most clear-cut aggravated assaults involve severe bodily injury or the use of a weapon, distinctions can blur between aggravated assaults and simple assaults because both categories also include mere attempts to inflict severe bodily harm. Because there is such fuzziness about the difference between a simple and an aggravated assault, police and prosecutors around the country have enormous leeway to bootstrap simple outbursts or minor assaults into more serious aggravated assaults.

For that reason, Steffensmeier and his colleagues claim that the recent increases in female assault rates do not reflect an actual increase in girl violence, but rather an increased tendency for the criminal justice system to arrest and charge girls with serious assaults for acts that formerly would have been charged as simple assaults or received no charges at all. Hence, they conclude that it is not girls' violent behaviors that have changed; it is the tougher enforcement and charging practices of police and prosecutors that have changed.

So, for example, family-centered fights at home which involve a girl hitting her mother or throwing something at her in the course of an argument about her boyfriend or her loss of virginity or her poor grades can now end in an assault arrest for the girl if the parents decide to press charges. Previously, they claim, such family conflicts might have been handled as status offenses (offenses for juveniles only) and the girl might have been charged with lesser violations like incorrigibility, running away from home, disorderly conduct or with being a minor in need of supervision.

Because the charges for these acts were considerably less serious in the past, the corresponding punishments were also less severe as many of these family conflicts were resolved without arrest or detention. Nowadays, though, such private family conflicts between girls and their parents are increasingly being converted into public criminal matters with more arrests and possible detention for the girls involved. Presumably, this bootstrapping of family conflicts has had more impact on increases in assault arrests for girls than boys because parents have historically made more of an effort to control their daughters' behavior than their sons (especially daughters' sexual behaviors) and so daughters may have many more conflicts with parents than sons because of the parents' attempts to assert more control.

Moreover, Steffensmeier and his colleagues claim that the charging up of girl violence has not just been confined to family conflicts as youth violence at school is now being taken more seriously, including girl fights in and around school. Indeed, growing concerns about school safety have resulted in more police or security guards being posted on school premises and therefore it is easier for the police to make an arrest when a fight occurs (Herbert 2007; New York Civil Liberties Union 2007, 2007a, 2009).

To be sure, many of these zero tolerance policies—especially zero tolerance at school—have translated into crackdowns on boys as well as girls. However, because a larger proportion of girl fights at school and at home have traditionally been minor scrapes that have been less likely to result in death or injury than the violence perpetrated by boys, the widening of the criminal justice net to include ever more minor school-based offenses as grounds for an arrest has meant that violence by girls has been subjected to more bootstrapping than violence by boys.

To make their case that recent increases in juvenile assault arrests for females reflect bootstrapping and not real increases in girl violence, Steffensmeier and his colleagues hypothesize that if these increases were real, they would show up both in the arrest data generated by the police as well as in data not generated by the police. For that reason, they attempt to determine if these same increases in female assaults also appear in trend data drawn from self-report surveys and national victim surveys, because the data from these surveys are not generated by the police. In fact, victim surveys were initially conducted to be an independent check on arrest data because they ask assault victims to report on whether the person who assaulted them was male or female instead of asking the police. Similarly, self-report studies were also meant to be an outside check on police-generated arrest data as they ask male and female high school students to report whether they have assaulted someone rather than relying on police reports.

When they compare the arrest trends reported by the police to the trends generated by victim surveys and self-report surveys, they find that neither victim surveys nor self-report surveys of youth show any increase in female violence from 1980 to 2003. Hence, they conclude that there have been no real changes in female violence since 1980. Moreover, they argue that the fact that only arrest data show an increasing percentage of females being arrested for aggravated assaults merely indicates that bootstrapping or tougher enforcement by police and prosecutors—who control the number of girls arrested—has simply made girls more arrest-prone.

Chesney-Lind (2002) argues that this kind of bootstrapping has especially affected black girls leading to an increase in their arrests for girl fights in particular. There are some studies which bear out this out as they show that police officers stationed in high schools have grown increasingly more likely to arrest students for minor disruptive acts that would formerly have been handled as school disciplinary measures and that a disproportionate number of these police officers are stationed in black and Latino high schools. As a consequence, minority students in these high schools are more subject to see their minor antisocial behaviors bootstrapped into serious criminal acts, worthy of an arrest (Herbert 2007; New York Civil Liberties Union 2007, 2007a, 2009). And, while this trend towards overpolicing has mainly affected minority males, minority females have been affected as well.[7]

Moreover, bootstrapping is not simply confined to girls involved in minor scrapes at school or to girls in conflict with their parents. Bootstrapping has also resulted in more adult females being arrested for intimate-partner violence as the police are now more inclined to arrest both the male and female when they are called to a house in response to a domestic violence call. Presumably, these dual arrests also contribute to the rising number of female assault arrests (Chesney-Lind 2002; Belknap and Potter 2005, 2006).

African American Females, Bootstrapping and Dual Arrests

To many feminists, this practice of dual arrests may seem especially repugnant as it was during the course of the 1970's women's movement that more women started to come forward to talk about their abuse by male partners and to complain about police and prosecutors who did not take their complaints of intimate-partner violence seriously. Back then, the tendency of the criminal justice system was to treat male battering of women as little more than a disturbance of the peace. And, some have claimed that they were particularly dismissive of pleas from abused black women that they do something about the violence.

However, since the 1980s, the police have increasingly been required to make an arrest when a domestic violence incident is reported to them although it is not certain that they always do. Moreover, prosecutors have increasingly been pushed towards prosecuting these cases as assault because of no-drop policies that do not allow them to drop the charges even if a woman changes her mind about pressing charges (Belknap and Potter 2006).

As police and prosecutors find themselves pressured to take more of these assaults seriously and arrest and prosecute, there has been something of a backlash. Increasingly, when the police are called to a home because of a domestic disturbance, they are likely to make dual arrests in which they arrest both the man and the woman. Hence women who may call the police because they see themselves as victims may increasingly find themselves being treated like offenders as they are arrested right alongside the man who has battered them. The police are more likely to make dual arrests when a woman fights back, particularly if when they get to the house after answering a call, they find the woman is still fighting as she tries to defend herself.

There is some evidence that black females are more likely than white females to be arrested when the police make dual arrests (Chesney-Lind 2002; Belknap and Potter 2005, 2006; S. Miller and Meloy 2006; Dasgupta 2002; Osthoff 2002). And, to some degree, the greater application of this perverse policy to black females in which victims are arrested and punished like offenders seems to be based on police perceptions of black females as deviating from gender norms of what constitutes a "good" domestic violence victim.

Both the media and feminist literature have constructed the ideal type battered woman victim as nice, delicate, submissive, helpless and passive because she has been paralyzed by her male partner's systematic abuse. Hence, when the police respond to a domestic violence call and find a mouthy, angry, aggressive, and often drunk woman who may still be violently defending herself from her male partner, they may be inclined to arrest both parties. The chances for a dual arrest are further enhanced if such a woman diverts some of her angry aggression from her partner to the police. Because the police may be inclined to dislike these women, they may find it easier to see them as perpetrators rather than victims and arrest them.

Moreover, with all the cultural baggage attached to black women that has long defined them as domineering, overbearing and emasculating, they may be perceived as deviating furthest from the standards of the passive, submissive ideal type domestic violence victim by the arresting officer and thus be more subject to arrest than white females (Osthoff 2002; S. Miller and Meloy 2006; Dasgupta 2002).

The Policy Consequences of Dual Arrests

Clearly, then, the police have the power to transform a battered woman victim into an offender simply by deciding to arrest her. This has numerous consequences for the women who are taken into custody. For one thing, once these women are arrested, they may be pressured into pleading guilty to assault charges because they may be threatened with jail time or the loss of custody of their children (S. Miller and Meloy 2006). Moreover, a battered woman who is arrested for a single episode of hitting her male partner may find her whole history of being the victim of male battering erased by one isolated incident of self-defense.

Once these women plead guilty and are legally designated as offenders, it can set in motion a whole series of other negative events. As offenders, they are denied the protections accorded those legally designated as victims, and hence they may find it difficult to issue a restraining order against their male partners. They are even likely to be denied access to shelters for battered women and to other victim assistance services because they are not seen as victims.

Shelters are likely to turn women arrested as batterers away because they also subscribe to the notion that the real female victims of male battering are not violent because they are too paralyzed by all the abuse to defend themselves from their batterers. As a result, many shelters simply accept the police designation of these women as batterers because of their arrests for violence and refuse to provide services or advocate for them because they are vehemently opposed to working with those that they perceive to be "perpetrators" of domestic violence of either sex (Dasgupta 2002; Osthoff 2002; S. Miller and Meloy 2006).

Women arrested as perpetrators may also find themselves treated like surrogate males as they may be required to enroll in batterer treatment programs just like the boyfriends or husbands arrested with them (S. Miller and Meloy 2006). These batterer treatment programs were originally designed for males, who had been arrested for battering their female intimates and then mandated to attend these programs by the courts as an alternative to incarceration.

The hope was that these treatment programs could persuade these males to stop battering the women in their lives by helping them to recognize what triggered their anger and teaching them how to redirect their anger into constructive channels so that they were no longer beating up their wives or girlfriends. For those males who did not make sufficient progress towards nurturing, egalitarian relationships or for those who violated program rules regarding attendance, treatment could be extended. And, for some males, the failure to be rehabilitated could even result in termination from the program and possible incarceration or re-incarceration.

Understandably, a number of anti-domestic-violence advocates have expressed vehement opposition to mandating battered women to these batterer intervention programs simply because they have been arrested for violence. Their thinking is that many of the women arrested and mandated to these programs may have only used violence to defend themselves from years of intimidation and bullying by the men in their lives. If this is the case, these women may not need to be taught to reject violence in favor of a nurturing, egalitarian relationship. Moreover, teaching them how to redirect their own anger into constructive channels may do little to stop the men in their lives from abusing them.

Yet, despite the fact that batterer intervention programs may be totally inappropriate for the battered woman who has been arrested for violence, Moffitt and her colleagues (2001) have suggested that violent women should be treated in the same couples therapy sessions as their violent male partners. They contend that such conjoint therapy is to be recommended because their research suggests that men and women who use violence in a relationship do so because of the same underlying psychological conditions—namely negative emotionality.

As they see it, couples therapy for both partners is important because it makes it possible for the female's negative emotionality to be treated. They claim that a woman diagnosed with negative emotional it should also receive treatment because their research shows that a woman's negative emotionality actually fuels a man's violence. From their perspective, then, treating the man's negative emotionality while the woman's negative emotionality goes untreated can mean that her untreated negative emotions will lead to new violence even after the man is treated.

By contrast, anti-domestic-violence advocates have argued that women coerced to accept treatment in batterer intervention programs may come to regard the whole criminal justice system as alienating and unfair. Indeed a number of women arrested and mandated to one of these programs (separate from the male program) have expressed outrage at the police for the initial arrest and made it clear in the course of their treatment that they had only used violence to defend themselves or their children from male abuse (S. Miller and Meloy 2006).

This has led some antiviolence advocates to conclude that these women would be better served if police and prosecutors made more of an effort to contextualize female relationship violence and identify those women, who were only using force in self defense. Once women who use violence in self-defense are identified, the thinking is that they should be referred to community-based domestic violence shelters where they can be treated like victims. Of course, this would mean that more domestic violence shelters would have to expand their definition of victimhood to acknowledge that battered women who use violence in self-defense are still victims (Osthoff 20002; Dasgupta 2002; S. Miller and Meloy 2006).

SUMMARY: CONTINUITIES IN RESEARCH ON RACE, FEMALE VIOLENCE AND SEXUAL SYMMETRY

It should be clear by now that there are numerous similarities between the biological and psychological theories espoused by Lombroso and his early-twentieth-century contemporaries and those used to explain female violence today. More than a hundred years ago, Lombroso and his contemporaries relied on their biases about the nature of appropriate female behavior to define normal women as feminine and distinguish them from criminal women whom they regarded as male-like. Back then, criminal women were seen as masculinized because they lacked the kinds of feminine qualities that discouraged crime and violence in normal women and because, in theory, they more closely resembled men than normal women in their biological, physiological and psychological makeup.

Today's biopsychological theories continue to essentialize violence in women although they rely more on psychological defects to distinguish normal nonviolent women from abnormal violent women than was the case in the past. Hence, current research on female violence suggests that the differences between normal women who are nonviolent in their intimate relationships and abnormal women who are violent in their relationships lie in differences in their personalities. Specifically, abnormal personality traits like negative emotionality, angry self-concepts and troublemaker self-concepts are said to predispose women to intimate-partner violence. And, for Moffitt and her associates (2001), at least, these violent predispositions are likely to be permanent and inherited, which suggest some underlying biological or physiological abnormalities as well.

Yet, because these theorists attach such significance to the supposed psychological abnormalities of women who are violent in their intimate partnerships, they manage to totally ignore the possibility that violent women may simply be defending themselves from violence initiated by their male partners. The fact that they are unable to determine if a woman is merely defending herself from male violence has a lot to do with the fact that they measure relationship violence in terms of isolated hits and slaps and thus fail to contextualize it. With these flawed metrics, they are unable to determine which violent partner is the primary aggressor or instigator and which partner may merely be engaged in self-defense. Hence, because of shortcomings with their measures, they are able to downplay the role that patriarchal ideologies might play in causing a male to systematically batter his female partner as part of a campaign to dominate and control her.

Not only do both the early-twentieth-century theorists and today's theorists share a tendency to see violence as an indicator of biological, physiological and psychic abnormalities in the individual woman, they both also share a tendency to use female violence to make racial distinctions. In the early twentieth century, Lombroso and his contemporaries claimed that the inferior nonwhite races, with their masculinized women, were characterized by similarities in violent behaviors between the sexes or sexual symmetry. By contrast, they argued that the superior white races were characterized by a sexual binary in which males and females diverged significantly in terms of their biological and psychic characteristics and therefore in terms of their use of violence.

Back then, there were a number of inferior nonwhite "races" including immigrant populations of Poles, Irish, Italians and Jews, who had recently migrated to the United States. Of course, African Americans had long been regarded as the most inferior racial group in the United States—and elsewhere—and black females had been constructed as more violent and male-like throughout the slave era. Early-twentieth-century American scholars, then, simply repeated many of the claims left over from slavery to argue that black inferiority, in part, rested on a pronounced similarity between the sexes among blacks rather than the more normal sexual binary found among whites.

Today, only blacks are considered a distinct and inferior racial group in the United States as the rest of the formerly nonwhite "races" have now become "white" (Brodkin 1999; Patterson 1997). Hence, distinctions are now drawn between black females and white females, based on this expanded definition of the white race. The fact that black females are more likely to kill their intimate partners than white females has meant that age-old stereotypes of a male-like, physically aggressive black female are still part and parcel of the research on female violence.

So, for example, Wolfgang and Ferracuti as well as Anderson argue that black females and black males are both prone to violence because they are both members of the black subculture of violence. And for Anderson, the sexual symmetry that characterizes black male and black female behaviors means that black girls turn to violence to achieve manhood just like the boys. While the theories of Moffitt and Giordano do not single out blacks directly, their research would clearly interpret the seemingly high rate of intimate-partner violence in black couples as evidence that they are plagued by more of the underlying psychological defects that are thought to predispose to violence in black women and black men alike. Hence, all of this research encourages the belief that seemingly high rates of black female violence in intimate partnerships should be taken as a modern-day marker of racial inferiority among blacks.

Moreover, because this research suggests that this propensity for relationship violence may appear as early as the teen years, it encourages a search of the history of black females for even minor scrapes with peers or family members from their teens onward because these otherwise insignificant outbursts could be interpreted as evidence of a propensity for future episodes of serious violence in their intimate partnerships.

Much as was the case in the early twentieth century, these modern-day studies come to these conclusions about female violence, sexual symmetry and race using measures that have been highly contested. However, once again, these researchers have managed to use their flawed metrics to scientize the notion that female violence in a relationship reflects underlying psychological defects and thereby affect policy.

Back when Lombroso and his contemporaries wrote, they used questionable research methodologies to claim that policies like sterilization of criminals were necessary to prevent crime in future generations because of permanent and inherited biological and psychological defects in criminal women and criminal men alike. Today, the notion that women and men are motivated to be violent because of the same underlying psychic defects (e.g., negative emotionality) justifies disturbing policies like dual arrests in which women who are violent in relationships are arrested right alongside their male batterers rather than being protected like victims.

The ability of these modern sexual symmetry theorists to affect policy largely stems from their success in pathologizing females who use violence—even those who use violence to defend themselves from abusive males. By claiming that these women suffer from psychological abnormalities, they have been able to steer clear of acknowledging the possible legitimacy of female anger in the face of male bullying and battering and back away from arguments that define female relationship violence as a normal, human reaction to male efforts to dominate them. As such, these researchers manage to blame the female victim of male battering for her own victimization.

By claiming that women's violence in relationships is the product of abnormal violent predispositions, the sexual symmetry researchers also promote the idea that relationship violence can only be reduced if these women can somehow be treated and rehabilitated. Hence the policy prescriptions that flow from these theories focus on controlling and changing the individual woman who defends herself from male violence rather than changing the patriarchal ideologies which urge males to believe that they should be able to batter and dominate the women in their lives in the first place. Much like their early-twentieth-century forebears, then, the current sexual symmetry researchers have succeeded in scientizing their own biases about the nature of appropriate female behavior. This time around, their notions about true womanhood have enabled them to justify forcing the female victims of abuse to adjust to their abuse rather than changing the patriarchal ideologies that cause it.

All of this has particular relevance for black women as mainstream American culture has always framed them as deviating from the standards of appropriate female behavior. Long before the term sexual symmetry was coined, there was a belief that black women could be every bit as violent and overbearing as any male. Indeed as far back as slavery, black women were seen as so male-like that they were even treated much like black men by being forced to work right alongside them plowing, planting and harvesting (hooks 1981). Back then, black women were constructed as masculinized or male-like because they were seen as strong enough to do the work of any man. And, because their femininity was negated, their exemption from the protections accorded true women (i.e., white women) seemed warranted.

There is some anecdotal evidence that battered black women may currently be more likely to be exempted from protections from male battering today because of these long-standing racial biases and prejudices. After all, some recent studies suggest that black females have been disproportionately subjected to dual arrests, in part, because they are perceived as more male-like and more violent than white women by the police. Apparently, then, these age-old constructions of African American females as masculinized and undeserving of the chivalry accorded true women continue to be real in their consequences.

NOTES

1. Lombroso wrote his original treatise on *L'uomo Delinquente* (The Criminal Man) in 1876 only a few years after Charles Darwin's 1859 publication, *Origin of Species*. Hence, his tendency to see criminals as throwbacks to an earlier stage of evolution is understandable. While his notion that criminals were biologically defective primitives was subsequently dismissed, he did manage to scientize the study of

crime in several ways. First, he stated his theory by hypothesizing that there was a relationship between classes of observable phenomena. Specifically, he hypothesized that persons with biological defects were more prone to commit crimes. Because both biological defects and criminal behaviors are observable phenomena, he was able to use the scientific method to determine if his hypothesis that biologically defective persons were prone to crime was true. He did so by comparing criminal and noncriminal populations to see if criminals were more likely than noncriminals to possess the biological defects that he claimed signaled a proclivity for criminal behavior. Furthermore, he made it explicit that a particular set of biological anomalies (e.g., large jaws, extra long arms, double rows of teeth, etc.) indicated a propensity for crime thereby making it possible for other scientists to replicate his study and confirm or disconfirm his results. The fact that his results were not found to be valid after numerous replications, in part, explains why his theory was ultimately rejected as wrong.

Still, despite the fact that his theory was eventually discredited, other criminologists have followed his approach to bringing the tools of science to bear on the study of crime. Hence, they too begin by hypothesizing that there is a relationship between some set of observable variables and crime. They, then, proceed to once again test whether the proposed variables lead to crime with direct observations. And, as was the case in Lombroso's day, the original study is generally followed by other studies that replicate the original in an effort to confirm or disconfirm the original findings. However, unlike Lombroso, most criminologists today do not use biological variables to explain crime. Instead, they are more likely to rely on sociological variables (e.g., socioeconomic structure) or psychological variables (e.g., personality traits) to explain crime (Vold, Bernard, and Snipes 2002; Hoover and Donovan 2004).

2. That females become involved in "masculine" crimes like homicides and assaults so infrequently is generally explained by the fact that they do not see violence as a way of achieving status and prestige with their peers like males do. In fact, involvement in violent behaviors like assaults and homicides may actually cause females to lose status with their peers because these behaviors are seen as violations of the feminine role (Messerschmidt 1993; Heimer and De Coster 1999).

3. Even in the cinema, racial hierarchies are constructed not by depicting whites as superior, but rather by portraying them as normal. Once whiteness is defined as the norm, blackness can be defined as abnormal and inferior by dint of being what whiteness is not (Davies and Smith 1997). And, if blackness is used to signify the subnormal or the abnormal, numerous white ethnicities (e.g., Italian, Irish, Polish, Jewish, etc.) can be united under the same umbrella as normal because they are not black. Blackness then functions to secure the ethnic inclusiveness of whiteness. And, because blackness signals the abnormal, dysfunctional and negative, whiteness (i.e., not blackness) can signal the positive, the normal and the functional.

4. The data show that the male tendency to resort to physical abuse seems to be especially pronounced among low-income men, perhaps because they are not able to dominate the women in their lives by economic means (Rennison and Welchans 2000; Bureau of Justice Statistics 2009a). This has enormous implications for levels of black male abuse as their high unemployment rates and low incomes signify that they disproportionately lack access to the kinds of jobs and incomes that would en-

able them to dominate and control their female partners by economic means. As a consequence, they might be more likely to turn to violence as a way of wielding authority over their female partners than more affluent white males. After all, affluent white males would be better able to dominate and control their female intimates by maintaining control over the purse strings.

5. Data on the victims of intimate-partner homicides identify them in terms of their relationship to their killers. Hence, victims can be listed as the killer's spouse, ex-spouse, boyfriend, girlfriend, ex-boyfriend or ex-girlfriend. Because a few of these homicides may involve homosexual couples, a girlfriend might be killed by a girlfriend in a lesbian couple and a boyfriend might be killed by a boyfriend in a gay couple. Still the assumption is that the overwhelming majority of victims of intimate-partner homicides are part of a heterosexual couple. For that reason, declines in the number of males killed by an intimate partner are generally taken to mean that fewer females are killing their male partners. In the same vein, declines in the number of females killed by intimate partners suggest that fewer males are killing their female intimates.

Hence, because most blacks are married to blacks, a decline in the number of black males killed indicates that fewer black females are killing their black male partners. Similarly, a decline in the number of black females killed by intimate partners suggests that black males are less likely to kill their partners. To some degree, this applies to whites as well because whites are likely to marry other whites. However, with homicide data, the category "white" includes all non-black race/ethnic groups—including Hispanics and non-Hispanic whites.

6. These modern biopsychological theories have come in for severe criticisms, often for some of the same reasons as earlier versions of these theories espoused back in Lombroso's day. For example, Lombroso and his contemporaries were faulted for ignoring social, economic and environmental factors outside the individual that might explain crime. Furthermore, these early-twentieth-century theories often failed to stand up to empirical testing as many of their hypotheses turned out to be untestable, illogical or just plain wrong. In addition, many of the studies designed to test these theories were plagued by methodological weaknesses.

Many of the more modern biopsychological theories suffer from the same tendency to downplay or ignore social, economic and environmental factors outside the individual that might explain crime. They are also plagued by some of the same methodological deficiencies as the earlier research. For example, critics have accused some of the more recent biopsychological studies of using poor measurements of criminality, small sample sizes, and poor study designs, and they have questioned the generalizability of their findings as well. Some critics have also complained about their tendency to use unrepresentative samples of prisoners and their failure to examine whether affluent white-collar and corporate criminals suffer from the same biological and psychological defects that they seem to find in many of the low-income criminal populations that they study (Katz and Chambliss 1995; Akers and Sellers 2009).

7. Since taking over control of school safety in 1988, the New York Police Department (NYPD) has assigned more police officers to the New York City public schools. These school safety agents report to the police department and not to school authorities. Although their mission is to prevent crimes from occurring on school premises,

teachers, students, parents and school principals have accused them of abusing their authority by acting belligerently and overpolicing the schools. By overpolicing, they mean that these school safety agents have turned what were previously minor school disciplinary matters into crimes.

Hence, students have been sprayed with mace or even arrested for disruptive acts like being late to class, writing on desks, dress code violations, smoking cigarettes, cutting classes or bringing cell phones into class. Such policies have the effect of creating a new category of crime or status offense for those schools in which these police officers are stationed. This is a problem for black and Latino students because these officers are disproportionately posted in their high schools. Hence they are more likely to suffer the consequences of being overpoliced, which can include a greater likelihood of acquiring a juvenile record in the event that they are arrested. Such a record can make it harder for them to get into college, obtain a scholarship or get a job. It can also make it more likely that they will drop out of high school or be pushed into a GED program. Indeed, some have argued that this might be the intent of some of these high schools; because if students with low test scores are pushed out in these ways, it improves the school's average test scores.

For the most part, this practice of overpolicing the schools has been targeted at male students. However, female students are hardly immune. For example, in one particularly telling case, a 16-year-old girl was arrested by a high school safety agent for using a curse word in the hallway (Herbert 2007). When the school's principal attempted to intervene to stop the arrest because he saw it as excessive, he too was arrested along with a school aide that came to his defense. The police then proceeded to parade the principal before the media in a humiliating "perp walk," and school authorities briefly suspended him after his arrest before later reinstating him. Both the police commissioner and the district attorney supported the police officer in this dispute, although the charges against the girl were later dropped because no crime had been committed.

Chapter Eight

Comforting Fictions

Black Women, Hollywood and Color-Blind Racism

After reading much of the media and academic discourse on black females from the previous chapters, a reader might conclude that the biggest threat to black women comes from their relationships with black men. In part, their relationship problems seem to be a product of their own overbearing and domineering dispositions as demonstrated by stereotypical figures like black matriarchs and Sapphires. Indeed, to read some of the academic literature on black women, one might even conclude that the angry hostility that these black female caricatures exhibit towards black males might even have biological roots.

In fairness, Hollywood has also placed some of the blame for the stark divisions between black females and black males on black men, who have been depicted as overbearing and abusive with the women in their lives in such well-known films as *The Color Purple* and *What's Love Got to Do with It?* Indeed, with all this focus on the battle between the sexes, the predicament of black females seems remarkably similar to that of white females as women in both races seem to be coping with the problems brought on by living in a patriarchal society.

Yet, with all of this focus on the divisions between men and women, racism is not depicted as a problem for black women at all. However, it is racism that segregates black women into the same resource poor black ghettos as black males. And because black women are consigned to the same urban poor neighborhoods, they attend the same underfunded schools that do little to funnel them into living-wage blue-collar work or to prepare them to obtain a college education as a stepping-stone to a professional career.

Racism, then, more than patriarchal black males, might seem to account for at least some of the difficulties that black women face. Indeed, the fact that black women have to grapple with racially discriminatory conditions

271

that white females do not have to face is made clear by data on educational attainment. Black females have less education than white females as 80.8 percent of black women have graduated from high school compared to 90.1 percent of white females (U.S. Census 2006). Moreover, only 18.5 percent of black females over 25 years of age have completed college compared to fully 28.4 percent of white females. This last statistic, in particular, suggests that segregation into underfunded schools may be taking its toll on black women. And, given the fact that a college degree is increasingly required for living-wage work, this low level of college completion by black women bodes ill for their financial futures.

Because less education usually presages low-wage work and high unemployment, it should come as no surprise that black females are far more likely to be poor than white females. For example, in 2003, 26.6 percent of black females lived below the poverty line compared to only 9.1 percent of white females (U.S. Census Bureau 2006). And, while less educated white females have the option of escaping poverty by marrying an employed white male, black females are considerably less able to exercise this option. That is because the black males who surround them are much more likely to be less educated, poor and unemployed like they are and thereby less able to support them or a family. For example, only 16.6 percent of black males over 25 had completed college compared to fully 32.7 percent of white males; as a consequence these black men had less access to higher-paying jobs (U.S. Census 2006). Black males were also less likely to complete high school than white males (80.4 percent vs. 89.9 percent).

Even when black men do complete high school, they have traditionally had less access to the living-wage blue-collar jobs that could be obtained with a high school degree than white males due to racial discrimination in the skilled trades (W. Wilson 1996; Royster 2003). Given these circumstances, then, black males are more likely to be poor than white males as 22 percent of black males live below the poverty line compared to 7.2 percent of white males. Hence, in a world where over 90 percent of blacks who marry marry other blacks (Manatu 2003), the fact that so many black males are poor and unemployed means that less educated black females typically do not have the option of depending on the earnings of an employed black male for support. And when many of these women turn to welfare to support themselves and their families, they find themselves facing demonization by white conservatives and restrictions on their welfare payments (Albelda et al. 1996).

Because the source of so many of their problems seems to be white racism, it would seem that black women might be willing to look past their differences with black males and join with them in the struggle against racial oppression. Yet, because so many media and academic images foreground the battle between black women and black men, they fail to show them coming together to struggle against racism. For that reason, black women and black men alike come across as lacking in any kind of racial consciousness. This is a striking misrepresentation of black women as they have a long history of joining with black males to fight the forces of racial oppression. One early example of this comes from the life story of Harriet Tubman, who as far back as slavery, became known for rescuing more than 300 slaves from servitude as a conductor on the Underground Railroad. Ms. Tubman began her legendary rescues after her own successful escape from slavery in which she started out with her two brothers on the road to freedom. When her brothers lost heart on the difficult trip northward and turned back, it was Ms. Tubman who made her way to freedom and then returned south at least 19 more times to rescue other black slaves. Later during the Civil War, Ms. Tubman would go on to serve as a spy, scout and guerilla leader for the Union Army (Lerner 1972).

By the 1890s, another black woman named Ida B. Wells became famous for her struggle against racial injustice. Working as a teacher and writing part-time for black newspapers, she exposed the inadequate school facilities available to black children and was fired from her teaching job as a result. She then took up journalism full time and became one of the owners of a paper called the *Memphis Free Speech*. In her columns, she appealed to race pride and called on her black readers to take up the struggle against racial discrimination.

After three black men that she knew were lynched, Ms. Wells began her own one-woman crusade against lynching. Claiming that lynchings were simply another expression of the barbaric nature of southern racism, she argued that most of the black men lynched were wrongly accused of raping white women to justify this particular form of racial intimidation. Her campaign against lynching brought a swift reaction as her newspaper's office was destroyed and her life was threatened. Forced to leave the south, Ms. Wells settled in Chicago where she continued to lecture, organize and write in opposition to lynching (Wells-Barnett 1895; Lerner 1972).

Ms. Tubman and Ms. Wells are just two of countless black women who might properly be called race women. Yet, in the years before the civil rights movement, Hollywood routinely ignored politically conscious black women like Ms. Tubman and Ms. Wells and instead represented black women as apolitical mammies who were so loyal to their white masters and mistresses that they consented to their own domination rather than protesting the system of racial stratification.

Despite the film industry's insistence on depicting black women as apolitical mammies, black women in the real world continued to participate in the struggle for racial justice. This was especially apparent during the civil rights movement of the 1950s and 1960s and the black power movement of the 1960s and 1970s as both social movements sparked a rise in political consciousness in the black community.

The black power movement, in particular, precipitated a political reawakening in black communities across the country by urging black people to reject traditional stereotypes that defined them as lazy, irresponsible and inferior. Instead, movement leaders urged blacks to embrace images of themselves as powerful, assertive, intelligent, courageous and resolute in their struggle against racism. As leaders of the black power movement saw it, victory in the struggle against racial injustice required that America go beyond the dismantling of Jim Crow laws that came in response to the civil rights movement. For them, the solution to the race problem required nothing less than ridding American society of the racist policies and practices that had been built into all of its major institutions from the nation's founding.

The political reawakening that the civil rights and black power movements sparked in the black community did not simply affect black men; it affected black women as well. And, for many of these newly conscious black women, becoming a race woman in the 1960s and 1970s meant uniting with their black sisters and brothers in racial solidarity. It also meant rejecting the old sense of racial inferiority and taking pride in being black. Hence, black women around the country began raising their own racial consciousness and that of others around them by acquiring a sense of African Americans' proud past and a new love for other black people (Healey 1997; Connor 1995).

However, with its call for restructuring major American institutions in order to rid them of their racist policies and practices, the black power movement generated a sense of threat in the dominant white society (Healey 1997). Perhaps that is why Hollywood completely ignored the major political reawakening that was then going on in the black community. In fact, instead of dramatizing the lives of the many race women then emerging in black neighborhoods across the nation, the film industry actually chose to step up its production of apolitical black female characters.

This trend began in earnest with the rise of blaxploitation films in the early 1970s and continued with the ghetto action films that emerged in the early 1990s. Taking no notice of the many newly politicized black women in the real world, filmmakers after the 1970s chose instead to parade a steady stream of politically unconscious black prostitutes, symbolic whores, drug addicts, negligent mothers, robbers, burglars and con women before movie audiences.[1] Hence, in the place of black women protesting against racial injustice in the real world, they substituted black women characters on the big screen that only seemed to be concerned about making money, finding their next drug fix, neglecting their children or pursuing sexual pleasure.

Instead of expressing race pride and pride in themselves as black women, the black women characters depicted on screen were portrayed as women who hated themselves. And when these black women characters were not mired in their own self-hatred, they seemed to be involved in exhibiting their hatred for black men. Hence, the many black female Sapphires and matriarchs in Hollywood's strong black woman/weak black man dyads were routinely represented as either so disappointed in black men or as so hostile to them that it would have been hard to imagine these female characters joining with black men in the struggle for racial justice.

Clearly, then, the film industry's insistence on depicting black women in terms of these apolitical stereotypes has meant that other more realistic representations of politically conscious black women get short shrift. Recent Oscar-winning films—like *Crash* (2005) and *Monster's Ball* (2001)—only continue in this tradition.

In fairness, however, the negation of black female political consciousness is not the primary focus of either of these films. Rather, the black female characters in both these films are stereotyped as politically unconscious Sapphires and symbolic whores because such apolitical figures are least likely to offend white viewing audiences. By contrast, white viewers might be expected to find scenes of racially conscious black women struggling against racial discrimination a bit off-putting because so many whites have convinced themselves that discrimination based on race has ceased to exist.

As many whites see it, the United States is now a color-blind society in which they and everyone else can get ahead based on their own talent, hard work and perseverance and not because being white still assures them of certain privileges. Hence, they have convinced themselves that if blacks are still mired in poverty, it is because they have created cultures in which education and hard work are not encouraged. To support their assertions, they then point to inner-city neighborhoods in which the residents seem intent on destroying each other. They are reinforced in these beliefs by Hollywood, news media and academia, which all routinely circulate images of a ghetto-based war of all against all in which black criminals can be seen preying on their law-abiding black neighbors or black youth can be seen preying on black adults or black men and black women can be seen preying on each other.

In the next few sections, then, I will review some of the research that talks about how many white Americans have managed to convince themselves that the racially discriminatory practices of the past have disappeared from American institutions and been replaced by a system that is based on a meritocracy that no longer privileges some individuals based on their white skin color alone. This will be followed by a lengthy examination of how Hollywood, in particular, strives to avoid offending its white viewership by producing films that ignore the powerful racist institutions that allow their white characters to continue to discriminate against blacks. In the course of this discussion, particular emphasis will be placed on the kinds of black women characters that have to be created in order to avoid offending white audiences.

TALKING PAST EACH OTHER:
BLACKS AND WHITES CONSTRUCT RACISM

That many white Americans feel more comfortable with a definition of racism that avoids talking about racist institutions is evidenced by research, which shows that whites make use of a variety of strategies to sidestep this issue (Blauner 2006; Gallagher 2003). One strategy that white Americans use to avoid talking about institutionalized racism is to construct racism in individual terms.

When whites define racism in individual terms, they typically mean that racism is best understood in terms of concepts like prejudice and discrimination or the racially biased beliefs and actions of individuals. When the race problem is reduced to a problem of individuals, it means that individual whites can only be described as racist if they hold hostile attitudes and beliefs about blacks and are inclined to defend or justify these beliefs in terms of racial stereotypes. Furthermore, because individual whites who are prejudiced against blacks might act on their beliefs and discriminate against blacks, individual racism can also refer to individual acts of discrimination.

Conversely, according to this definition, individual whites cannot be described as racist if they think and act in ways that suggest they are blind to skin color. In other words, whites cannot be said to be guilty of racism if they do not express prejudiced beliefs and do not personally discriminate against blacks. For that reason, many white Americans do not see themselves as racist because they do not personally subscribe to racial prejudices nor do they personally discriminate against blacks (Blauner 2006; Gallagher 2003).

By contrast, the same research shows that blacks are more likely to see racism not as the expression of prejudiced individuals but rather as a reflection of substantial power differences between blacks and whites. For them, these power differences are best indicated by the unequal treatment that blacks receive due to numerous racist policies and practices that are built into the institutions and daily operations of American society as a whole (Healey 1997; Blauner 2006; Gallagher 2006).

It was fairly easy to see this kind of institutionalized racism in the daily operations of the Jim Crow south before the civil rights movement. Back then, when individual whites expressed their prejudices and hostilities towards blacks by refusing to sit at the same lunch counters or stay in the same hotels, their anti-black prejudices were backed up by powerful southern legal institutions which enforced separate and unequal public accommodations for whites and blacks. Similarly, when individual whites openly opposed hiring blacks for certain jobs or admitting them to public colleges and universities, these individual prejudices were backed up by legal institutions in southern states, which excluded blacks from desirable jobs and state-supported universities.

By limiting black access to high-status jobs and a college education, institutionalized racism placed blacks at a disadvantage in terms of achieving the American dream. And to guarantee that these racial inequalities would be maintained, southern political institutions at that time made use of poll taxes, literacy tests, violent intimidation and other roadblocks to prevent blacks from voting for elected officials who might challenge institutionalized racism in the south.

To sum it all up, then, blacks are inclined to define racism in ways that make white power central by focusing on institutional racism (Frankenberg 1999; Blauner 2006; Gallagher 2003). However, by relegating racism to expressions of individual prejudice and discrimination, whites have managed to define racism without talking about power at all. In light of their penchant for defining race and racism in such distinct ways, Blauner (2006) argues that blacks and whites are talking two separate languages when it comes to race. And because their separate world views about racism are so far apart, they often end up talking past each other in a manner no different from the way that men and women talk past each other (Tannen 1990).

For example, in a study where Blauner (2006) asked blacks and whites to describe their views about race and racism, he found that his black and white respondents were especially likely to talk past each other on the issue of whether or not blacks could be racist. A number of the blacks in his study argued that there was no such thing as black racism because, in their view, racism required power and blacks as a social group did not have the kind of power needed to oppress whites.

By contrast, the whites in his study argued that black racism was fully possible based on their assumption that racism referred to the biases and prejudices of individuals rather than to the policies and practices of major American institutions that limited resources based on skin color. Because the white respondents defined racism solely in terms of the personal biases and acts of individuals, they assumed that it was just as possible for individual blacks to be racist as individual whites. In other words, they reasoned that black racism was possible because individual blacks could hold racially biased beliefs about whites and could express that bias in acts of reverse racism or discrimination against whites.

Black Racism, White Racism: The Difference It Makes

Critics of definitions of racism that equate it with individual prejudice have faulted this personalizing of racism precisely because it treats blacks and whites as if they are on equal footing. In other words, by suggesting that black racism is somehow equivalent to white racism, such constructions of racism ignore the fact that no matter how virulent black antiwhite prejudice may be, it has no impact on white life chances. In other words, blacks who are biased against whites are in no position to exclude them from jobs or educational opportunities and thereby limit their access to the good life.

Prejudiced blacks also cannot call on a powerful criminal justice system to deny whites their civil liberties or single them out for arrest and imprisonment simply because they are white. In short, individual blacks—no matter how biased—do not have the power to oppress whites. By contrast, these critics argue, whites do have the power to oppress blacks through a variety of social institutions. And, once the white power reflected in racist institutions is acknowledged, it is quite clear that white racism and black racism are not equal.

The inadequacies of a definition of racism that relegate it to the personal prejudices and discriminatory acts of individuals are immediately apparent when applied to the system of racial stratification that existed in the south of the 1950s and 1960s. Back then, there were innumerable instances of racial violence that indicated that white racism was all too often characterized by a one-two punch in which the racist attitudes and acts of individual whites received the backing of powerful racist institutions (Knowles and Prewitt 1969).

Hence, to use the particularly brutal case of Emmett Till as an example, when highly prejudiced white individuals killed and mutilated this black teenager over his alleged flirtation with a white woman, this could rightly have been classified as the racist act of white individuals. However, what really demonstrates the difference in power between the races was not this particular hate crime itself, but the fact that the sovereign state of Mississippi refused to seriously investigate Till's murder and punish the white men that killed him. Clearly, then, terms like individual prejudice and discrimination would have been inadequate to define racism back then, because such terms ignore the role that powerful southern institutions played in providing support for individual acts of white bigotry.

Certainly, it can be argued that in today's world, the kind of institutional racism that existed in the pre-civil rights era is now a thing of the past. Yet, even as the more blatant Jim Crow practices of the pre-1960s south have faded, blacks find themselves forced to do battle with a more subtle form of modern racism. And, despite being less blatant than the racism of the Jim

Crow south, modern-day racism is still sufficiently powerful to enable whites to limit black access to economic opportunities and the good life (Healey 1997).

So, for example, when today's blacks find themselves segregated in resource-poor neighborhoods with schools that do not prepare their children for high-status jobs, they experience the kind of modern racism that limits their opportunities to achieve the American dream. Or, when blacks find themselves excluded from even blue-collar jobs because of the color of their skin, they once again encounter the kinds of economic constraints that result in racial inequality (Royster 2003). Modern racism is also expressed in the contemporary policies and practices of a white-dominated police force which can single blacks out for surveillance and searches due to racial profiling or disproportionately imprison them for offenses for which whites typically are allowed to remain free (e.g., nonviolent drug offenses).

Once again, terms like individual prejudice and individual discrimination seem insufficient to account for these forms of modern-day racism because the kinds of contemporary structural practices that result in the exclusion of blacks from white neighborhoods or desirable blue-collar jobs do not even require individual biases and prejudices.

Nonetheless, by ignoring the impersonal system of racial stratification that continues to exclude blacks from economic opportunities, whites can claim that America is now a color-blind society in which skin color no longer matters. Believing that America has now become a color-blind utopia in which equal opportunity exists for all also enables many whites to argue that any privileges that they used to enjoy for being white have disappeared with the blatantly racist institutions of the Jim Crow south.

White Investment in a Color-Blind America

Despite its many problems, the color-blind stance favored by whites dominates media discourse on race and racism. This is hardly surprising as whites—particularly white males—dominate the institutions of popular culture including film, television, news media, and newsmagazines. Hence, these elites might be expected to allow their own belief in a color-blind America to influence the images they circulate. And, as noted, many of these media elites might also be inclined to take a color-blind stance on race in order to appeal to a largely white audience that may actively resist seeing racism as an ongoing structure of white power and position.

In part, white audiences might be expected to resist regarding racism as an impersonal, oppressive, structural force because they confuse the white racism of a social structure with accusations that they as white individuals are personally racist. Some might also be sensitive about their own possible investment in a modern-day system of racial stratification that allows them to enjoy a certain number of privileges just for being white. Moreover, some whites may vehemently reject such definitions of racism because it allows them to argue that their own higher status in the socioeconomic hierarchy is a direct result of their determination, hard work and willingness to invest in education rather than some now defunct white privilege. However, to sustain this vision of a color-blind America in which skin color is no longer a basis for allocating resources or meting out justice, whites have to find a way to ignore ongoing social, political and economic arrangements that continue to privilege them (Gallagher 2003).[2]

Because white audiences might be sensitive to constructions of racism that equate it with an impersonal social structure in which they enjoy white privilege, they may not be entertained by films which portray racism in these terms. On the other hand, they may feel more comfortable if a kind of individual racism is visualized on screen because individual racism means that blacks and whites alike can be guilty of racism.

Perhaps, then, this explains why the racism depicted on film is typically constructed in terms of individual prejudice, bias and acts of discrimination rather than in terms of an impersonal structure of racial domination. In such films, where racism is reduced to interpersonal conflict between individual black bigots and individual white bigots, ugly portrayals of white racism can be balanced by equally ugly portrayals of black racism or reverse racism. Black racism and white racism have likewise been placed on equal footing in classic television sitcoms like *All in the Family* or *The Jeffersons.*

It is only in films set in the pre-civil rights era that Hollywood constructs racism as a structure based on white power and privilege that excludes and exploits blacks. Only in films set in the bad old days before the 1960s can images of blacks being subjected to separate and unequal public accommodations or being denied entrance to all-white schools and universities be shown. Only in films set in the Jim Crow past can blacks be shown being subjected to racial injustice at the hands of white mobs or a white-dominated criminal justice system in the form of lynchings, pogroms and other racial violence.

And yet this willingness to release films set in the bad old days of Jim Crow segregation that construct racism as an underlying structure based on white power and white privilege does nothing to tamper with the color-blind stance that suggests that America is now a land of equal opportunity. Indeed, the fact that the Jim Crow segregation, the pogroms and the lynchings of that era have all disappeared actually serves as a testament to how much racial progress the United States has made since the 1960s. As such, these films set in the bygone days of Jim Crow segregation seem to offer support to the view that institutional racism is no longer a central force in American society. Presumably, then, it can be argued that any racism that remains today is now confined to the personal biases and prejudices of racist individuals—both racist white individuals and racist black individuals alike.

In a world where the discourse in media and popular culture routinely reduces modern-day racism to individual prejudice and discrimination, the absence of politically conscious black female characters on the silver screen makes perfect sense. Historically, black women have had their political consciousness raised by being forced to cope with an environment in which they have to struggle against powerful racist institutions. To depict such women on screen, then, would mean talking about the powerful racist institutions against which they struggle. However, all such images of racist institutions can be completely erased in a world where racism is reduced to interpersonal conflict between biased blacks and biased whites on a level playing field. Therefore, Hollywood's penchant for constructing racism in terms which equate black racism with white racism goes a long way towards explaining why politicized black women are typically banished from most films set in modern-day America.

In the next few sections, then, I will examine how black characters are depicted in films that focus on institutional racism in the Jim Crow past. This will be followed by some discussion of how filmmakers treat black characters—especially black female characters—in films set in modern America that reduce racism to individual prejudice.

INSTITUTIONAL RACISM IN THE PRE-CIVIL RIGHTS ERA: *ROSEWOOD*

One movie that hearkens back to the pre-civil rights era when blacks were routinely oppressed by racist institutions is black director, John Singleton's film *Rosewood* (1997). *Rosewood* is based on a true story in which the black town of Rosewood, Florida, was burned to the ground by a white lynch mob in 1922, and the blacks who survived the rampage were forced to flee their homes.

The movie opens as the white sheriff hears rumors that a black man named Jesse Hunter has just escaped from the chain gang and may be headed towards Rosewood. A few scenes later, a white woman walks out in the street and screams that she has been beaten and raped by a nigger. The audience is aware that, in actuality, the woman has been beaten by a white boyfriend and is only claiming a black man has assaulted her to keep her white husband from finding out about her adulterous affair. Nonetheless, on the assumption that the black man who has raped her is Jesse Hunter, the white sheriff gathers together a mob of angry white men in town and they set off with their hound dogs in search of Jesse Hunter to avenge her spoiled honor.

In the course of their search for Jesse Hunter, the white mob beats, lynches, mutilates and kills any black male in their path. They also shoot one black woman dead on the front porch of her home when she dares to say that a white man was responsible for the rape of the white woman and not a black man named Jesse Hunter. After silencing this black woman with a bullet, the white mob continues its reign of terror by lynching and killing other black women along with black men. Eventually, all the surviving black women, men and children are forced to flee their homes and make their way to the city of Gainesville to escape these vigilantes.

Rosewood, then, graphically depicts the kind of Jim Crow era racism which involved the entire white community attacking the entire black community. Moreover, it makes clear that the anti-black hostilities and biases of individual whites had been institutionalized into Rosewood's legal structure as the local all-white police force and local judges not only refuse to punish the rampaging white mob, but actually help to form the posse of white male avengers.

So, for example, as the white mob goes about lynching, killing and mutilating blacks at will, the white sheriff accompanies them and witnesses much of their mob violence, but does nothing to stop it. Similarly, when a white judge is called into town to look into the death of one of the black men that has been lynched, he simply notes that the black man has been castrated and that ears, fingers and other body parts are also missing from the blood soaked corpse. Yet this judge does nothing to stop the murders and mutilations as he does not pursue an investigation and simply declares the death as due to "mischief at hands unknown." The sheriff will later call on this same judge to get him to send white male reinforcements from other towns to help the local whites continue their massacre of the local blacks.

Clearly, then, the kind of racism depicted in *Rosewood* is not based on mere individual prejudice in which the hostilities of whites and blacks towards each other can somehow be equated because they are on equal footing. Concepts like "black racism" and "reverse racism" would have no meaning in the America depicted in *Rosewood* because the blacks in this film so clearly lack the power to enforce any antiwhite biases they might have. Instead, *Rosewood* depicts a racial hierarchy in which only one group has power—namely whites. After all, the whites as a social group clearly had the power to attack blacks as a social group. And, the masses of blacks under attack in *Rosewood* clearly had no power to stop these attacks.

Rosewood likewise shows how white skin privilege functions as even a white female who makes the most dubious claims of rape by a black male can expect the full white community to turn out to exact the most horrid forms of revenge on the black community. Black skin, by contrast, denotes a lack of privilege as the criminal justice system refuses to intervene to protect the black community from the rampaging white mob.

Because *Rosewood* takes an unsparing look at an America in which white racism has teeth, it also shows how black identities are forged as the African Americans in the film are clearly forced to band together to escape the vengeance of a white mob. Hence, the black women in *Rosewood* are not depicted as Sapphires in hostile relationships with the black men in the film. Rather the black women and black men in the film are depicted as caring deeply about each other as they bravely go about trying to save themselves and their children from this episode of racial terrorism.

Institutionalized Racism in *A Lesson Before Dying*

The whites-only justice depicted in *Rosewood* is largely enforced by a rampaging white mob acting outside the law even as agents of the legal system look on. However, in *A Lesson Before Dying* (1999), viewers get a clearer picture of how thoroughly white racism had infiltrated legal institutions in the Jim Crow south as it is the legal system alone which enforces a more subtle race-based justice with no help from white vigilantes.

In *Lesson*, a black man named Jefferson accompanies two black friends to a liquor store where the white shopkeeper kills one of Jefferson's friends because he thinks the friend is trying to rob him. Jefferson's other friend and the white shopkeeper, then, get involved in a shootout and end up killing each other. All of this happens in the space of a few seconds with Jefferson merely witnessing these events in shock. It is clear to the audience, then, that Jefferson is a mere bystander, who is innocent of any crime himself.

However, because a white man has been killed by blacks, the all white male jury that hears Jefferson's case seems intent on convicting him of murder and sentencing him to death. About the best defense that Jefferson's attorney can mount to try to avoid a death sentence is to try to persuade the white male jurors of Jefferson's biological inferiority. Hence he claims that Jefferson has no more brains than a hog and, as such, would have been incapable of planning to rob and kill the white shopkeeper. Yet, despite the attorney's efforts to persuade the white jurors by appealing to their deep-seated racist beliefs that a black man is not fully human, the jury convicts Jefferson of murder and sentences him to death.

Many of the blacks living in this town are not surprised by the jury's verdict which condemns Jefferson to death for being in the wrong place at the wrong time as they know that when a black man kills a white man, someone black has to die. Resigned to the injustice of the sentence, the black townspeople take it upon themselves to try to restore some sense of dignity to Jefferson in his last days so that he can face his execution like a man.

Hence, the teacher at the local black school is dispatched to the jail to teach Jefferson that blacks at least see him as a man and not a hog. And while all of the whites in the town continue to argue that the sentence is fair and that he should die like an animal, the black teacher takes up the task of teaching Jefferson a lesson about dying with dignity in the face of gross racial injustice. Even the black children in town visit Jefferson in his cell in his final days to say goodbye and give him gifts treating him like a martyr to racial injustice rather than a monster deserving of execution.

Because *Lesson* occurs against a backdrop where a legally sanctioned system of racial stratification is clearly in view, the audience is once again able to see how blacks came to be politicized in their efforts to cope with legal injustice. And because white power and privilege are clearly visible in this miscarriage of justice, atonement for these wrongs on the part of individual whites is not put forward as a solution for reconciling the condemned black man to this gross injustice. Rather it is the black community which bands together to make Jefferson's last days comfortable. Hence in *Lesson*, the audience sees black men, women and children uniting in racial solidarity to take a stance against racial injustice as they offer their support to Jefferson.

Racism in the Legal System Today

Of course, both *Lesson* and *Rosewood* were set in small southern towns in the bad old days before the civil rights movement. Hence, for those who claim that America has now progressed past racial injustice, it might be tempting to argue that the institutionalized racism that is the subject of these two films is a thing of the past. To be sure, it is difficult to imagine that the kind of white pogrom depicted in *Rosewood* could go unpunished today. Indeed in 1993, some 70 years after the Rosewood rampage, the Florida House of Representatives paid reparations to the black survivors of the massacre, largely due to appeals made by one black survivor of the pogrom.

Yet, even though the kind of massacre by white vigilantes seen in *Rosewood* might be a thing of the past, the kind of racial injustice in the administration of the death penalty seen in *Lesson* continues to exist even today. Indeed, ongoing racial bias in administration of the death penalty, in part, led the Supreme Court to declare it unconstitutional in 1972 as disproportionate numbers of the poor, blacks and other unpopular groups were being executed (Swarns 2006). It was only reinstated some four years later after the court had been reassured that newly revised death penalty statutes would prevent any further race and class bias in executions.

Yet, despite these revisions, there is considerable evidence that racial bias in the administration of capital punishment survives even today. For example, research suggests that despite the fact that few murders involve blacks killing whites, those blacks who kill whites are the most likely to end up on death row. By contrast, those whites who murder a black victim have the least chance of ending up on death row (Sorenson and Wallace 1999; Baldus, Woodworth and Pulaski 1990; Paternoster 1984; M. Smith 2000). Racial bias, then, still affects policy and practice in legal institutions as modern-day American courts continue in their age-old tradition of punishing the taking of white life more severely than the taking of black life.

Yet, despite continuing injustice in its administration, capital punishment continues to be legal, in large part, because it is widely supported by the public—particularly whites. For example, a 2006 Gallup poll showed that fully 71 percent of whites supported capital punishment, while a meager 38 percent of blacks were in favor of executions (Maguire and Pastore 2007). In addition, some studies show that at least some of that white support for the death penalty is fueled by white racial hatred of blacks as whites who express more antiblack prejudice are more likely to support the death penalty (Cohn and Barkan 2004). Hence, today, much as in the Jim Crow era, the racial biases of individual whites continue to be backed up by legal institutions which administer the death penalty in a racially discriminatory fashion.

In its haste to execute black males who kill whites, the legal system has been found to tolerate an inordinate number of errors. In fact on January 31, 2000, Governor George Ryan of Illinois halted all executions in his state because of what he described as the criminal justice system's "shameful record of convicting innocent people and putting them on death row . . ." (Johnson 2000). A year after the moratorium, *Monster's Ball* was released. And yet, despite ongoing concerns about racial bias in the death penalty, *Monster's Ball* managed to tell a story about the aftermath of the execution of a black man without once mentioning the controversy.

RACISM IN THE POST-CIVIL RIGHTS ERA: *MONSTER'S BALL*

Much like *Lesson, Monster's Ball* examines the execution of a black man by white executioners. However, unlike *Lesson* and *Rosewood, Monster's Ball* is set in the period after the civil rights movement. As such, it does nothing to threaten the belief in racial progress favored by white audiences. In part, this is accomplished by constructing a kind of racism in which individual whites are simply bigoted or prejudiced. In that context where racism is reduced to individual prejudice, the race problem can be solved by individual whites ridding themselves of their prejudices. However, for individual whites to successfully redeem themselves for past acts of racism, several things have to happen.

For one thing, the institutionalized racism that continues to mar administration of the death penalty must be made to disappear in the film so that the audience can focus on the atonement of a lone white male. Secondly, racism has to be perceived as an individual, personal behavior that can be rectified by individuals rather than as part and parcel of criminal justice institutions. *Monster's Ball* accomplishes this in several ways.

First, unlike *A Lesson Before Dying*, where the white male-dominated criminal justice system is executing an innocent black man, in *Monster's Ball*, there is no possibility of an unjust execution. Instead, the black man who is electrocuted is consistently treated as guilty. Indeed, he comes close to confessing his own guilt as he describes himself as a "bad man" to his son. Because the fairness of the death penalty is not in question in *Monster's Ball*, there is no need to consider the errors that continue to plague administration of the death penalty in the real world off-screen.

Secondly, while *Lesson* foregrounds racial injustice in the administration of the death penalty by focusing on the condemned black man and the attempts made by the black community to make the wrongfully executed man's final days dignified, in *Monster's Ball*, institutional racism in the legal system disappears altogether as the story focuses not on the condemned black man, but on the white males who will execute him. In fact, it is altogether necessary that no mention be made of institutional racism in the death penalty in *Monster's Ball*, because it is all about the racial redemption of one of the white male executioners named Hank. Hence, while it is the black community that marshals its resources to try to make the condemned man's final days dignified in *Lesson*, these functions are largely taken over by two white male executioners—Hank and his son, Sonny—in *Monster's Ball*.

In the movie's opening scenes, Hank can be seen working very hard to help the condemned black man, Lawrence Musgrove (played by hip-hop musician, Sean Combs), remain calm in his final hours. Indeed the white male writers, Will Rokos and Milo Addica, who wrote the Oscar-nominated screenplay for *Monster's Ball*, compare executioners like Hank to priests or social workers because of their dedication to helping the condemned man spend his last hours in a state of inner peace (*Monster's Ball* 2001). The writers also humanize the death team that pulls the switch by focusing on what an emotional experience it is for them to kill a man and how much emotional control they have to maintain to make sure that the condemned man remains calm and peaceful. To that end, they show Hank and the death team praying before the execution to prepare themselves to escort a fellow human being to his death.

Because Hank has risen to the position of lead executioner by successfully conducting executions devoid of any affect, he becomes incensed when his son, Sonny, violates the death team's standards of emotional control by actually bonding with the condemned man. Hence, in the condemned man's final hours, Sonny can be seen giving the soon-to-be executed black man, Lawrence Musgrove, some paper and pencils to draw with and lighting his cigarettes. Because Sonny makes an emotional connection with the condemned black man, he loses his self-control and throws up as he leads Lawrence to be strapped into the electric chair. After the execution, an angry Hank attacks Sonny for losing emotional control, and other members of the death team are forced to pull father and son apart.

Yet, even though these opening scenes of the execution show Hank and Sonny comforting the condemned black man on his way to the chair, these two white male executioners never even remotely question the injustice of a system that has a history of disproportionately avenging itself on black males (especially black males who kill whites) in its quest for retribution. Hence, while these white male executioners are depicted as human enough to be revolted by electrocuting another human, their revulsion largely stems from their personal involvement in flipping the switch; they express no opposition to the death penalty itself.

By concentrating on the humanization of the white male foot soldiers that carry out state executions, then, *Monster's Ball* manages to smooth over the practice of racial discrimination in the administration of the death penalty and thereby avoid any reference to the need for change in the legal system. Indeed by humanizing the death penalty system's white male operatives, the film goes a long way towards humanizing the death penalty system itself.

As such, the film supports the racial status quo. After all, audiences viewing *Monster's Ball* would be correct in assuming that an error-ridden death penalty process would continue to put a disproportionate number of black men on death row even as they are assured that the state's executioners consider it a professional obligation to make the condemned man's final hours calm and peaceful.

Individual Racism and the Denial of Responsibility

Having made the institutional racism that continues to plague the death penalty process disappear, the writers of *Monster's Ball* are then free to reduce racism to individual racism and focus on the racial redemption of one lone white male, namely Hank (played by Billy Bob Thornton). They accomplish this by showing how Hank has been hurt by his own racist acts and, as a consequence, has become motivated to break with his racist past and transform himself into a nonracist human being. And even though the film's creators hold Hank responsible for his own racist behavior, they go to some trouble to minimize his responsibility for his own bigotry.

So, for example, in their commentary on the film's DVD, the filmmakers note that it is the state that is ordering Hank to kill other men and hence he cannot be seen as fully responsible for killing black men, but rather should be seen as someone who is just doing his job. Indeed, the writers claim that executioners like Hank are as much a prisoner of the system as the condemned men who are about to die (*Monster's Ball* 2001). Hank's actions, then, are depicted not as a reflection of internal psychological factors like white bigotry—which has been found to be related to support for the death penalty—but rather as a product of external factors like the demands of the criminal justice system. By minimizing Hank's responsibility for his own actions, then, the film's creators turn him into a more sympathetic character.

They minimize Hank's responsibility for his racism in other ways as well by suggesting that working as an executioner may actually foster Hank's racial prejudice because his bias against blacks may make it easier for him to do his job. In other words, because Hank sees blacks as subhuman, it is easier for him to kill them. Once again, then, they suggest that Hank is not fully responsible for his antiblack attitudes but rather has learned to dehumanize blacks in the course of his on-the-job training as an executioner.

Moreover, as the filmmakers make clear, the job of executioner is frequently passed on from father to son in real life, and therefore the antiblack prejudice that may be encouraged on the job can also be passed down in families (*Monster's Ball* 2001). Hence, they make Hank part of a family in which the job of executioner is passed on from one generation to the next. In the film's opening scenes, Hank can be seen trying to teach his son Sonny (played by Heath Ledger) the fine art of killing a man much as his father, Buck, a retired executioner, has taught him. It is almost immediately apparent that Hank may have acquired his own hatred of blacks from his father Buck, as Buck (played by Peter Boyle) is clearly an unrepentant bigot. *Monster's Ball*, then, succeeds once again in minimizing individual white males' responsibility for their own racist beliefs by focusing on how they might be socialized to their biases in their own families.

The Journey to Racial Redemption

Because *Monster's Ball* is all about Hank's racial redemption, much of the film is taken up with following Hank's spiritual progression from racial bigotry to racial tolerance. Hence, at the beginning of the movie before Hank begins his journey towards racial redemption, he is depicted as a bigot who has seemingly found it easier to execute black men because of his apparent hatred for all black people. This is evident in an early scene when Hank can be seen shooting at some black kids to scare them off his property when they come to visit his son Sonny. It is only after Hank and Sonny have executed Lawrence Musgrove that events conspire to induce Hank to begin the process of racial atonement.

Returning home after the execution, Hank is still angry at Sonny for being so unprofessional and losing emotional control as they go to strap the condemned black man in the chair. Hence, when they return home, father and son continue their dispute. Eventually, Hank grows so angry at Sonny that he tries to throw him out of the house physically even as Sonny manages to fend him off by pulling out a gun. At first, Sonny turns the gun on Hank to defend himself and then he turns the gun on himself and shoots. After Sonny's suicide, Hank hurriedly buries him and then closes off his son's room and locks it.

In DVD commentary on the film, the claim is made that Hank's outsized anger at his son for establishing an emotional connection to the condemned black man is driven by the fact that Sonny has not become a racist like him. In other words, while Hank's father, Buck, has successfully passed on his hatred of black people to Hank, Hank has not succeeded in passing on his own bigotry to Sonny. The thinking seems to be that Hank tragically overreacts to his son's failure to inherit his bigotry because in his heart, Hank really wishes to be as free of bigotry as his son (*Monster's Ball* 2001). It is his son's tragic suicide, then, which pushes Hank to begin his journey towards racial redemption.

After Sonny's suicide, then, Hank quits his job as lead executioner, burns his prison guard uniform and opens a gas station. Then, later, as the film's narrative would have it, he comes upon Leticia Musgrove (the black wife of the black man he has just executed). Leticia is trying to flag down a car to rush her injured son to the hospital after a car accident and Hank reluctantly rushes them both to the hospital. After Leticia's son dies in the emergency room, Hank comforts her as she weeps at the death of her son.

Leticia and Hank now have both lost their sons and it is that shared grief which begins to bind them together. From that point on, then, the filmmakers no longer concern themselves with the things that might keep Hank and Leticia apart such as a racist legal system that has allowed Hank to legally kill her husband. Instead, much of the rest of the movie is given over to depicting their budding relationship and documenting the sacrifices that Hank makes to maintain his relationship with Leticia.

So, for example, the audience sees Hank putting his bigoted father in a nursing home after he calls Leticia a nigger, naming his gas station after Leticia and allowing her to move in with him after she is evicted from her own home. With each of these sacrifices, this white man breaks with his racist past even as he also makes amends with the black woman he has recently widowed.

And, because the film is focused on individual racism and the redemption of a single white male, Hank's sexual liaison with Leticia becomes one major marker of his racial redemption. Of course, the film's single-minded focus on Hank's redemption is only possible because the institutional racism that continues to mar the death penalty process is nowhere to be found in *Monster's Ball*.

Certifying Racial Redemption: The Role of Black Characters

It is not enough that an individual white male undertake a journey from racial bigotry to racial redemption on his own. In order for a racial redemption ceremony to be successful, there also need to be black characters who can forgive bigoted whites for their racist pasts. The two main black characters in *Monster's Ball*, Lawrence Musgrove and Leticia Musgrove, both serve this function admirably in the film.

Lawrence Musgrove first serves this function by bonding with the two white male executioners, Hank and Sonny, who are slated to electrocute him. In Lawrence's final hours, Hank and Sonny sit outside his cell and watch him, and then prepare him to be electrocuted by shaving his head and helping him into a diaper for the moment when he soils himself as the electricity courses through his body. Lawrence responds to these little courtesies by drawing portraits of both Hank and Sonny—the two white men who will soon kill him—and then hugging both of them in his final hours.

Indeed, as the filmmakers note, the white executioners, Hank and Sonny, are the last humans that Lawrence bonds with before his death. Thus, by the little courtesies that Lawrence extends to the white men who will soon kill him, he demonstrates that he does not hold them responsible for their actions. All of this is made to seem reasonable because as the filmmakers note, Hank and Sonny are just doing their job.

The character of Leticia Musgrove serves a similar purpose in that she too must help the white male character, Hank, atone for his racist past. Hence, because it is the white male's absolution which is the central focus of the film, *Monster's Ball* must also ready the Leticia Musgrove character to be willing to grant Hank absolution. This is no mean feat as Leticia must eventually forgive the white male who has executed her husband. Hence to prepare Leticia to forgive Hank for his racist past, the writers first have to make Leticia give up any identification with blacks or black causes. It does this in several ways.

First, Leticia Musgrove is depicted as a black woman with no black friends or confidants. Unlike *Lesson*, then, there is no evidence of a black community that might empathize with her as her husband faces execution. And, because Leticia is depicted as a black woman alone, who is not surrounded by other blacks, there is no need to show black friends, relatives or coworkers who might express any anger or hostility about racial injustice in the white-dominated legal system that has executed her husband. Moreover, as a black woman alone, Leticia does not act as if she is concerned about racism in the death penalty herself. And yet, in the real world off screen, polls show that blacks are far more opposed to the death penalty than whites, precisely because they fear racial discrimination in the way executions are meted out (Walker et al. 2004; Cohn and Barkan 2004; Maguire and Pastore 2007). Yet, at no point in the film does Leticia even once raise questions about the fairness of the death penalty as blacks do in real life.

On a more emotional level, the audience might have expected Leticia to at least display feelings such as grief, sorrow or despair as her husband is about to be executed. After all, these are the types of emotions that one expects of the families of condemned men in real life even if they do not voice concerns about racial injustice in the legal system. Instead, *Monster's Ball* dredges up the age-old black female stereotypes of Sapphires, abusive mothers and over-sexed Jezebels to characterize Leticia's emotional reactions to her husband's execution.

First, Leticia plays the Sapphire when she and her son, Tyrell, go to visit Lawrence for the last time before his execution. Thus, while an audience might have expected a married couple like Lawrence and Leticia to cry or pray or talk about the unfairness of the death sentence in their final moments together, Leticia plays the Sapphire instead when she coldly tells Lawrence that she has only come to visit him for the last time so that he can say good-bye to his son. Then, for good measure, she adds that she is tired of coming to the prison to visit him after 11 years and leaves without hugging him or kissing him for the last time or showing him any affection. Only their son, Tyrell, is predictably upset at his father's impending death as he cries and then hugs his father refusing to let go. In the face of Leticia's obvious hostility, all Lawrence can do is turn to Tyrell and promise to call him before he is executed.

Afterwards, when Leticia and Tyrell go home to await a final phone call from Lawrence (that never comes), Leticia finds out that the overweight Tyrell has been eating candy bars behind her back. At that point, she begins to verbally and physically abuse him by calling him a "fat little piggy" and "a fat ass" and slapping him until she finally knocks him down on the floor. Hence, Leticia also does not complain about the unfairness of the death penalty to her grieving son or cry or pray with him as his father is about to die. Instead, she reacts to her son's grief over his father's death by playing the stereotypically abusive black mother.

Indeed, the only time the audience sees Leticia happy, affectionate and (sexually) fulfilled is when she plays the oversexed Jezebel with Hank, the white executioner, a few scenes later. And like every other oversexed Jezebel, in her sex scenes with Hank, Leticia projects the sexuality of a man as she initiates sex with Hank rather than waiting to be pursued like a feminine romantic lead. Moreover, just like a man, she makes it clear that she is pursuing sex in her relationship with Hank rather than romance. She, then, makes her final break with her now executed black husband by pawning the wedding ring that he has given her to buy Hank a hat.

Racial Redemption and Racial Dominance

In many ways, the character Hank manages to have it both ways in *Monster's Ball*. On one hand, he becomes more sensitive to the plight of blacks as the movie progresses. On the other hand, he is able to demonstrate his newfound racial sensitivity without giving up any of his power. Davies and Smith (1997) argue that this two-pronged approach to representing white male dominance on-screen has become more common in films released since the civil rights movement and the women's movement.

In theory, as oppressed groups like blacks and women have increasingly contested their subordination in a racist, patriarchal system, more "liberal" white male characters have been paraded before movie audiences to express their sensitivity to the plight of the very blacks and women that they oppress. By showing that they are sensitive to the struggles of those they oppress, these characters have been able to redeem themselves for their oppression *without giving up any of their power.*[3]

In the case of blacks, liberal white males presumably redeem themselves for racial oppression—while simultaneously legitimizing their dominance— by solving the problems of individual blacks. And, in fact, Hank spends much of his time in the movie solving Leticia's many problems. Yet, his racial dominance over the two lead black characters, Leticia and Lawrence, is never in any doubt. That his racial dominance remains intact is indicated by the fact that he is able to execute a black man in one scene and then a few scenes later get involved in a sexual liaison with the all too willing black wife of the man he has just executed. Indeed, the crude sex scenes between Hank and Leticia have the added advantage of sexing up his racial dominance over her in a way that his dominion over Lawrence in the execution scenes cannot be eroticized.

Hence Hollywood awarded the first best actress Oscar to a black woman for playing a Sapphire who is hostile, demeaning and abusive with the black men in her life (her husband and her son), even as she acts out the role of oversexed Jezebel with the very white male who has executed her black husband. Audiences looking for a black woman who acts like a race woman engaged in the struggle against racial injustice will not find her in *Monster's Ball* as the Leticia character displays few emotions other than those one typically associates with apolitical Sapphires and oversexed Jezebels—namely, cold-blooded hostility and anger towards black men combined with sexual aggressiveness and lust towards white males.

The Failure of Racial Redemption in *Rosewood*

Because racism is reduced to the individual biases and prejudices of whites in *Monster's Ball*, the sexual liaison between the black female character, Leticia, and the white male character, Hank, becomes central to Hank's redemption. Yet in a similar sexual liaison between a black female and a white male in *Rosewood*, their affair does not constitute a marker of white racial tolerance and redemption. In large part, this is so because racism in *Rosewood* is not constructed as simple individual prejudice but rather as institutionalized racism. In other words, the Jim Crow era America depicted in *Rosewood* is a society based on a blatant system of racial stratification, which is openly upheld by the police and judges.

Because institutionalized racism in the legal system is situated front and center in *Rosewood*, the film graphically demonstrates the futility of efforts on the part of individual white males to redeem themselves particularly when those efforts occur against the backdrop of a system of racial stratification.

Hence, in *Rosewood*, a middle-aged white shopkeeper named John Wright, who has formed a casual sexual liaison with a very young black girl named Jewel, who works in his store, rather quickly finds that he cannot save Jewel or his black customers and neighbors from being massacred by a rampaging white mob. Indeed, once the white lynch mob begins its rampage against the black townspeople in *Rosewood*, Jewel's cousin comes to the store and insists she leave the white shopkeeper and the store. After all, the cousin is well aware that Jewel's casual affair with the white shopkeeper will not protect her from the bloodthirsty white mob.

Hence, because *Rosewood* is focused on racial oppression and not on white racial redemption, the sexual liaison between Jewel and Mr. Wright is not depicted as evidence of Mr. Wright's racial tolerance. Moreover, because the ugly racial hostilities of the white mob that destroys Rosewood are the central theme of the film, it is impossible to sex up their affair. Instead, *Rosewood* is actually one of the few films to depict the shame and humiliation that a black father experiences as he is unable to protect his daughter from sexual exploitation by a white male.

Hence, in one scene where Jewel and her father are desperately trying to flee the white mob, the father initially refuses to let Mr. Wright hide him in his house to protect him because he accuses Mr. Wright of having sexually exploited his daughter. However, the father is eventually forced to relent and reluctantly let Mr. Wright hide him because he is wounded and cannot run from the white vigilantes.

Yet, Jewel, herself, does not relent. Instead she is so ashamed of her sexual exploitation at Mr. Wright's hands that she refuses to let Mr. Wright hide her and leaves her father with him. She, then, sets off on her own, deciding to take her chances with the white lynch mob rather than be protected by Mr. Wright. Later Mr. Wright will be forced to surrender her father to the lynch mob and then watch as they kill him. Then, on his way back home after he witnesses them killing Jewel's father, Mr. Wright unsuspectingly passes Jewel's lifeless body lying alongside the road as the white mob has killed her too.

Rosewood, then, does not trade in the usual stereotypes that depict black females as oversexed and eager to consent to sexual liaisons with white males; rather it shows the shame they experience in the black community because of their sexual misuse by more powerful white males. Unlike *Monster's Ball*, then, *Rosewood* makes no effort to eroticize white racial dominance.

In fact, with its graphic depiction of the kind of racist legal institutions that only mete out justice to whites, *Rosewood* does not provide the space for a racial reconciliation ritual in which one white male alone can atone for his racism. Instead *Rosewood* portrays the Jim Crow south as a place where black men, women and children are forced to band together to flee a white mob. Hence, despite being confined to minor roles, the black women depicted in *Rosewood* look like race women. And in a context where their very survival depends on all the black townsfolk cooperating to survive an episode of white racial terror, their solidarity with the black male characters in the movie makes sense.

MODERN-DAY RACISM IN *CRASH*

Clearly, then, the way in which racism is depicted in a film's narrative has an impact on the kinds of black and white characters constructed. Because *Monster's Ball* invokes the notion of racism as individual prejudice and totally sidesteps any mention of institutionalized racism in the administration of the death penalty, it is possible for the film to promote the notion that any racial bad feelings between blacks and whites can be rectified by changes in individual attitudes and behaviors.

The filmmakers of *Crash* likewise choose to construct racism in terms of individual biases and prejudices. In order to accomplish this, they too have to sidestep any reference to institutionalized racism in the legal system, much like the filmmakers in *Monster's Ball*.

In *Crash*, institutionalized racism in the legal system takes the form of racial profiling or the police practice of singling out blacks for stops and searches. Racial profiling is simply an illegal variant of the legal practice of criminal profiling. In the real world, state and local police as well as U.S. Customs agents have developed criminal profiles that are meant to identify the characteristics that single out those individuals who are most likely to be involved in crimes like carrying illegal drugs or participating in gangs. (See chapter 3 for more discussion of racial profiling.)

Racial profiling refers to the practice of using race (being black) as a basis for defining someone as suspicious in a criminal profile. Because criminal profiles reflect the accumulated hunches of the police, undue reliance on race as a criterion in a criminal profile may allow the antiblack biases of individual police officers to creep into profiles developed by a mostly white police force. And, once race is made an indicator in a criminal profile, these biases can become an institutionalized part of police searches.

Apart from the overreliance on race, critics of racial profiles have claimed that the criteria used to define blacks as suspicious in these profiles are often so broadly drawn that almost anyone black could be suspected of a crime and hence be subjected to an illegal search. So, for example, with some drug courier profiles, black motorists have been deemed suspicious and searched for drugs if they were driving new, expensive cars or alternatively if they were driving old, inexpensive cars. Blacks carrying too much luggage or too little luggage or those driving leased vehicles have likewise been considered suspect. Given these wide ranging criteria, blacks have disproportionately been searched for drugs as motorists on the highways or as travelers at airports around the country. This is hardly surprising as the expansive criteria in racial profiles give police the discretion to search any and all blacks that they want to search (Russell 1998; Cole 1999; Meeks 2000; Covington 2001).

Most of these drug courier profiles have targeted black males, but black women travelers have also been suspected of being drug couriers if they had hair weaves, long nails and carried Fendi bags. Because this was a popular fashion style among young black women at the time, such criteria had the effect of converting a wide swath of the black female population into criminal suspects (Covington 2001; Meeks 2000).

In another example of racial profiling, black women travelers landing at Chicago's O'Hare airport were deemed suspect and singled out for searches if they flew in from the Caribbean. The thinking behind this practice was that black women flying in from the Caribbean might have swallowed drugs or hidden them in their body cavities in order to smuggle them into the country. As a consequence, many were subjected to X-ray searches. Indeed black female travelers at O'Hare were subjected to nine times as many intrusive X-ray searches as white female travelers (Meeks 2000; Covington 2001). Yet, despite long-standing racial myths that depict white females as innocent, the white females searched were actually twice as likely to be carrying drugs as the black females searched. Eventually some of the black females searched at O'Hare sued and the practice was discontinued.

One black woman named Yvette Bradley described one of these searches in grueling detail. Flying into the United States from Jamaica, she went through the initial checkpoint like all the other passengers, and then a white male customs agent shunted her off into another line for a secondary luggage search. As the customs agent had no computer terminal, his decision to send some passengers to the line for the secondary luggage search was clearly based on his own hunches. When Ms. Bradley joined the line for the secondary luggage search, she noticed that the line mainly included other black women like herself. And while waiting in line to be searched, she noticed that a group of college-age white males flying back from a spring break spent in Jamaica were being allowed to pass through customs with no need for a secondary search. This is somewhat surprising as surveys show that white males are considerably more likely to use illegal drugs than black females (National Institute on Drug Abuse 1991; Substance Abuse and Mental Health Services Administration 1996, 1999).

Watching the college-age white males breeze through Customs, Ms. Bradley complained to one of the white male customs agents that she should have worn a blond wig and blue contacts so that she, too, could have been waved through. The customs agent responded by glaring at her as he pawed through her luggage throwing everything in her bag around haphazardly and asking her where she lived, where she worked and exactly what she had done on her Jamaican vacation. He then ordered her to go to the door of another room for yet another search. This proved to be the worst part of Ms. Bradley's ordeal as she was subjected to a body search by two female customs agents—one white and one black—upon entering the room.

Ms. Bradley describes the white customs agent's search as especially humiliating and intrusive as she claims that the agent dallied over her breasts and genitals and even pushed her undergarment inside her as she checked her body cavity for drugs. While Ms. Bradley felt sexually violated after the search, U.S. Customs, at that time, described it as a routine pat-down. Ms. Bradley, however, did not see it as routine as she proceeded to file a complaint with U.S. Customs.

The pat-down endured by Yvette Bradley in 1999 looks remarkably similar to the pat-down experienced on-screen by Christine in the 2005 movie, *Crash*, except in many ways the movie version of the pat-down was much worse. First, unlike Ms. Bradley who was searched by a woman, Christine in the movie was subjected to an invasive body search by a racist white male police officer named Officer Ryan. Moreover, unlike Ms. Bradley in real life, Christine and her husband, Cameron, in the movie, never sue the police department for the illegal search. Furthermore, instead of being punished or even reprimanded for the illegal search and sexual molestation, the film's plot is concocted in a way so that Officer Ryan is eventually turned into a hero.

That Officer Ryan is heroicized in the movie is surprising in light of the fact that the kind of racial profiling that led to Ms. Bradley being singled out in real life had been discredited and outlawed in the real world by the date of the film's release in 2005. In fact, in the film, Ryan's partner, Officer Hanson advises against a stop and search of Christine and Cameron because as he tells Ryan, racial profiling is illegal. Clearly, then, the filmmakers for *Crash* could easily have addressed institutional racism in the criminal justice system in this scene. Instead, they managed to deflect all attention from the kind of systemic racism in the legal system that allows for these kinds of round-ups of African Americans, in part, by distorting the ways in which blacks react to such searches in the real world.

Camouflaging Racial Oppression in *Crash*

For example, in the real world off screen, a black couple subjected to sexual assault and an illegal search by white cops might have been expected to sue the police department or at least complain to a civil rights organization. Perhaps, that is why *Crash* does not allude to lawsuits or civil rights organizations, for to do so would have meant acknowledging the illegitimacy of these abuses of black civil rights.

Indeed, instead of trying to point up the illegitimacy of Ryan's racist search, *Crash* seems to be geared towards making the racism depicted in this scene appear less objectionable. One way the film accomplishes this is by individualizing and psychologizing racism rather than depicting it as institutionalized practice in the legal system

In part, *Crash* individualizes and psychologizes racism by equating it with the personal biases and hatreds of individuals. Once racism is framed in terms of the personal prejudices of individuals, it is possible for the filmmakers to dramatize both white racism and black racism in *Crash*. After all, if racism is reduced to the personal biases and discriminatory acts of individuals, blacks can be just as racist as whites.

Hence, even as *Crash* depicts the kind of institutional racism that affords white cops like Officer Ryan the power to pull over innocent black motorists, hold them at gunpoint and humiliate them in any way they so choose, it also points to ways in which white police officers like Ryan are victimized by individual blacks. In so doing, *Crash* succeeds in putting blacks and whites on equal footing by equating racism with a round robin in which one black individual first discriminates against one white individual and that white in turn discriminates against another black and on and on and on.

For example, before molesting Christine, Ryan talks about a case of reverse racism in which his father lost his business because he was forced to compete with black-owned businesses due to affirmative action. Moreover, in another example of black racism or reverse racism, the movie zeroes in on scenes of a black female case manager at Ryan's father's insurer telling Ryan that she will not pay for health care that might ease his father's suffering. While the black female case manager is following her company's policies rather than expressing racial bigotry towards Ryan's father, Ryan seems to see it as an act of black racism. Presumably, it is these experiences with "black racism" and "reverse racism" that motivate Ryan to illegally stop Christine and Cameron and sexually molest Christine (Hsu 2006).

Not only does black racism allow blacks to discriminate against whites for the filmmakers of *Crash*, it also means that blacks can discriminate against other blacks. For example, in an early scene one black carjacker named Anthony complains of his victimization by black racism to his fellow black carjacker. According to Anthony, the black waitress who has just served them in a restaurant is guilty of "black racism" because she waited on the white customers before serving them. Presumably the waitress's act of black racism towards Anthony was motivated by her prejudices against other blacks in that she assumed that because they were black, they would be less likely to tip. In that sense, her act of black racism, as Anthony terms it, was no different from the kind of prejudice and discrimination that defines individual acts of white racism. In other words, much like white waitresses who might act in similar racist ways towards black customers, the black waitress, in Anthony's estimation, held hostile attitudes and beliefs about other blacks and proceeded to discriminate against them by offering them poor service.[4]

Individual Racism and Racial Redemption in *Crash*

Because *Crash* avoids any consideration of institutional racism and focuses instead on the personal prejudices and discriminatory acts of individuals—be they black or white—it is able to provide the space for a racial reconciliation ritual in which one lone white male can atone for his own individual racist acts.

Hence, the film's narrative conveniently allows Ryan to redeem himself for his molestation of Christine the very next day, when he fortuitously pulls her from her burning car to save her life. Under these circumstances, Christine is forced to forgive him as she gratefully holds on to him as he is saving her life. And with Christine's forgiveness, Ryan's racial redemption is complete, even as his institutionally backed racial profiling and sexual molestation go unpunished.

And while Ryan's white partner, Officer Hanson opposes the search of Christine and Cameron from the beginning, he too manages to redeem himself for his participation in the wrongful search of the innocent black couple. He does so first by demonstrating his principled opposition to racial profiling when he complains to his black supervisor about Ryan's behavior and asks to be assigned another partner. With his complaint, Hanson, does more to look out for the interests of Christine and Cameron than they do themselves because they never file a formal complaint about their illegal search. In fact, throughout much of the picture, the white officer Hanson seems to be the person most concerned about addressing institutional racism in the police force—certainly he is far more concerned about it than any blacks in the film. Predictably, then, it is Hanson's black supervisor who refuses to order an investigation of Ryan's racist behavior, despite Hanson's complaint, because he is fearful of losing his job if he pursues the complaint. In other words, Ryan's racist acts ultimately go unpunished because of the timidity of his black supervisor.

Failing to get justice for Christine and Cameron from his black supervisor, Hanson manages to redeem himself anew by saving Cameron's life the next day when Cameron is stopped again by white and Latino police officers in his Lincoln Navigator. In this scene, Cameron is still angry about the search and molestation of his wife from the previous day and is refusing to submit to yet another search by the police. As he curses at the police and refuses to kneel and put his hands on his head to be searched, the police draw their guns and are about to shoot him for resisting arrest. At that point, Officer Hanson conveniently drives up and tells his fellow officers to hold their fire. As a consequence, Hanson saves Cameron from almost certain death at the hands of the police by talking Cameron down, convincing his fellow officers of Cameron's innocence and allowing Cameron to drive off unsearched.

Because racism in *Crash* is reduced to personal prejudices and individual acts of discrimination, it is possible for lone white males like Ryan and Hanson to solve the race problem in *Crash*. Moreover, Ryan's and Hanson's redemptive acts mean that there is no need for the kinds of system-wide policy changes required to eliminate the practice of racial profiling. In other words, because Officers Ryan and Hanson redeem themselves, there is no need for Christine or Cameron to sue the police department for racial profiling or join with other blacks to protest institutional racism in the criminal justice system.

Trivializing Racism

Perhaps unwittingly, *Crash* demonstrates the perils of personalizing and psychologizing racism by equating it with individual prejudice and discrimination rather than institutional racism. For one thing, by depicting racism as personal, it is able to trivialize Ryan's white racism by equating it with black racism. In other words, because white racism and black racism are treated as equivalent, the kind of white racism demonstrated in Ryan's racially discriminatory search of Christine and Cameron can be equated to the reverse racism of the black case manager at Ryan's father's insurance company who refuses to provide coverage for treatment of Ryan's father's illness.

Similarly, Ryan's racial profiling can also be equated with the black-on-black racism that involves a black waitress providing the black carjackers with inferior service at a restaurant. These false equivalencies are only possible because the film fails to examine the institutionalized racism in the criminal justice system that provides individual white policemen like Ryan with the legal authority to single out blacks for searches.

BLACK WOMEN AND THE CRIMINAL
JUSTICE SYSTEM IN THE REAL WORLD

Once again, such a world where black racism and white racism are equal is only possible if no consideration is given to the kind of institutional racism that exists in the real world to back up individual white antiblack prejudices. So, for example, in the real world, the antiblack prejudices and suspicions of individual whites can be backed up by the kind of institutionalized racism that results in black females being subjected to nine times as many X-ray searches as white females based on drug courier profiles developed by customs officials. And, yet, it is this kind of real-world systemic racism in which there are power differences between black and whites that never makes it to the silver screen.

Moreover, in the real world, outside Hollywood, black women do not simply fall victim to the kind of institutional racism that allows them to be singled out for X-ray searches or searches of their body cavities in the course of the legal system's efforts to find drugs. They are also more likely to be imprisoned for their drug offenses than white females, despite the fact that white females are equally likely or even *more* likely to use drugs than black females.

One reason that black females are more likely to be subject to racial profiling, heightened police surveillance and disproportionate incarceration for crime has to do with the fact that when the police go into black communities to crack down on black males, they also crack down on black females. This is in stark contrast to police crackdowns in the white community, where the police often confine their arrests to white males even as they avoid arresting white females because of chivalry.

Presumably, the police extend chivalry to white females they suspect of crimes and avoid arresting them because they wish to protect white women, are reluctant to use physical force against them, wish to avoid seeing them punished and are concerned that an arrest will be harmful for them and their families—particularly for white mothers raising children (Klein 1995; Visher 1983).

That the police make distinctions between white male and white female suspects is borne out in one study which shows that the police are far less likely to arrest white females suspected of crimes than white males suspected of crimes (Visher 1983). However, even though the white female suspects in the study benefited from chivalry, black females suspected of crime in the same study did not. In other words, the police in the study were every bit as likely to arrest black female suspects as black male suspects. And because white female suspects benefited from chivalry, while black female suspects did not, black female suspects were more likely to be arrested than white females suspected of crimes (Visher 1983).

Further evidence that the police do not extend chivalry to black women comes from research on domestic violence. As noted in the last chapter, black women who call the police to complain of battering by their male partners can sometimes find themselves being arrested for domestic violence right alongside the men who abuse them. Unfortunately, then, there is still a fair amount of research that indicates that institutionalized racism is alive and well in the post-civil rights era, particularly when the police are making decisions about whether or not to arrest a woman.

That a white-male-dominated police force makes few distinctions between black male suspects and black female suspects has a lot to do with the fact that both sexes can be considered dangerous. Evidence that the police can construct black women as dangerous comes from a chilling anecdote involving a fatal encounter between a black homeless woman named Margaret Mitchell and two police officers in Los Angeles.

The two officers were investigating stolen shopping carts and confronted Ms. Mitchell about the shopping cart she was pushing (Purdum 1999). According to the officers, when they tried to stop Ms. Mitchell to ask if her shopping cart was stolen, she refused to stop and began shouting profanities, brandishing a foot-long screwdriver and threatening to kill them. The officers drew their weapons and claim that Ms. Mitchell then ran, stopped, threatened them again and lunged toward the male officer. The male officer reported that he then ducked, stumbled and shot her in the chest, killing her. Despite the fact that he was carrying a gun, this officer reported that *he feared for his safety against this tiny 5 foot, 1 inch tall, 100 pound, 55-year-old black woman holding a screwdriver.*

While some witnesses questioned the police account of events, the police commissioner defended the killing as legitimate police work. Furthermore, a consultant to then Mayor Richard Riordan's office echoed the police and defended the killing by saying, "It sounds . . . like two officers confronted with what they considered to be a very *dangerous* situation. . . ." Clearly, then, the legal authorities in Los Angeles sanctioned the police killing of a petite, middle-aged black woman over something as trivial as an allegedly stolen shopping cart, largely by constructing her as dangerous.

SUMMARY AND CONCLUSIONS:
BLACK WOMEN, WHITE AUDIENCES

Despite ample evidence that the modern-day biases, fears and antiblack prejudices of individual whites continue to be backed up by legal institutions in the real world, films set in the post-civil rights era like *Crash* fail to acknowledge that American society is still based on a 400-year-old system of racial stratification in which whites have more power than blacks and a history of using the criminal justice system to enforce these power differences. Instead, *Crash* portrays a racism that is not defined by white power and its enforcement at all, but rather by a kind of toothless individualized racism that merely reflects personal biases and hatreds.

By personalizing and psychologizing racism, the makers of *Crash* manage to depict a raceless society in which blacks and whites suffer equally from some variant of "white racism," "black racism" or "reverse racism." Yet, despite their refusal to acknowledge institutional racism, the filmmakers in this award-winning film claim to provide a faithful rendering of what race is really like in America.

Unfortunately, as the aforementioned real-world incidents of institutionalized racism in the criminal justice system indicate, black females have less access to the civil rights and protections afforded white females and it is the police that are often involved in making sure that the civil rights of black women are not respected. Because black women are far more likely to have their civil rights violated by the police, they are far more likely to suffer the humiliations, injuries and even death that come with these infringements on their rights.

In the real world, black women protest these violations of their rights. However, that kind of motivation to resist racism is glaringly absent in the black female characters depicted in Oscar-winning films like *Crash* and *Monster's Ball*. That the filmmakers in these movies have seen fit to banish race women from their films has a lot to do with the fact that such politicized characters only make sense when black women can be seen doing battle with a powerful system of racial stratification. Because racism is reduced to the personal biases and prejudices of individuals in both *Crash* and *Monster's Ball*, racial conflicts in these films are confined to those that occur between individuals and not those that pit black women against a dominant white power structure. Hence, because there are no images of racist institutions, there is no need for the black women in these films to be seen raising their voices against the racial injustice that surrounds them.

Instead, the black female characters in these films are portrayed as so lacking in political consciousness that they seem not to have been touched by any of the movements for racial justice or gender justice that took off in the 1960s or the 1970s. Unlike the black female protesters of that period, neither Christine (in *Crash*) nor Leticia (in *Monster's Ball*) expresses any pride in her race or any awareness of sexism. And, because they are so devoid of any political consciousness, both women also seem indifferent to joining with other blacks in collective solidarity in a struggle against racial injustice; they especially seem unmotivated to join with the black men in their lives to do battle against racist institutions.

Leticia is actually cut off from the black males in her life early in *Monster's Ball* as her black husband is executed and her young black son dies. The film's creators also do not permit her to have ties to any other blacks that might join her in protesting racial injustice in the administration of the death penalty. Similarly, in *Crash*, Christine and her husband Cameron do not complain to other blacks about their ordeal with the police nor do they seek to form ties with other blacks to protest their mistreatment by the police. Furthermore, despite her sexual molestation, Christine also seems to be completely unaware of sexism; hence she does not turn to a women's advocacy group for advice on how to cope with her sexual molestation. Instead, many of the problems faced by both Leticia and Christine are magically solved by the very white males who have created them.[5]

Certainly, it could be argued that the racial ferment of the 1950s, 1960s and 1970s is a thing of the past and hence the race woman identities fostered in that era may no longer be so popular. If that is the case, then, the kind of race pride that was so widespread among the masses of black women in that period might today be confined to a handful of black female activists and black leaders. Under these conditions, representing Christine and Leticia as politically unconscious women would not be a distortion of authentic black women in the real world off screen.

However, there is ample proof that many black women still get involved in protesting racist conditions. For example, when blacks protested police harassment, police brutality and police killings of unarmed black New Yorkers in the wake of the police shooting of Amadou Diallo in 2000, black women marched and demonstrated right alongside black men. Then, once again, in the fall of 2007, when more than 10,000 black college students took buses to Jena, Louisiana, to protest the criminal justice system's excessive punishment of the young black men known as the Jena 6, black women marched right alongside black men to demonstrate against this injustice. Nevertheless, Hollywood chose not to transfer these images of authentic black women protesting racial injustice to the silver screen.

In similar vein, the filmmakers for *Crash* likewise failed to represent Christine in terms similar to the black women travelers in the real world who experienced racial profiling at Chicago's O'Hare Airport. Hence, even though authentic black women in the real world outside the movie studios sued U.S. Customs agents after being subjected to racial profiling, the writers for *Crash* had the fictional Christine endure her ordeal with white police officers in silence. This is understandable; because if these real-world images of black females being forced to sue Customs over discriminatory searches had been brought to the silver screen, they would have provided proof positive that institutionalized racism exists even in modern America. As such, they might have been seen as off-putting to white audiences who still accept the more comfortable fiction of a color-blind America.

Other recent evidence of black women's ongoing resistance to racism comes from their voting behaviors. There is a long history of black females and black males alike encountering obstacles when they try to vote—particularly in the period before passage of the Voting Rights Act of 1965. Before 1965, African Americans who tried to exercise their right to vote were often disenfranchised by poll taxes, literacy tests, white primaries, grandfather clauses or outright violent white intimidation (Hines 2006).

Unfortunately, these discriminatory practices seem to have survived the civil rights era—albeit in more subtle form. For example, there were successful efforts to disenfranchise many black voters in Florida as recently as the presidential election of 2000—in a year in which the presidency was decided by fewer than 600 votes in Florida.

Nationwide, some 90 percent of black voters supported Al Gore that year and hence the successful suppression of their vote in Florida must have contributed mightily to his ultimate defeat.

While black Floridians had registered to vote in droves for the 2000 presidential election, in part, because they were unhappy with then Governor Jeb Bush's decision to get rid of the state's affirmative action laws, many of these registered black voters were eventually silenced at the polls because so many of their votes were ultimately rejected (Hines 2006). This is indicated by the fact that ballot rejection rates were much higher in Florida's predominantly black counties than in its predominantly white counties, largely because so many black voters cast their votes on outdated and faulty voting machines—particularly the error-prone punch card machines with their now infamous hanging chads.

However, in the years after the election debacle in 2000, Hollywood chose to ignore this glaring example of institutionalized racism and instead turned to reducing modern-day racism to "black racism" or "reverse racism" in films like *Crash*. This is unfortunate because there is evidence that black voter suppression continued on into the recent presidential election of 2008.

With black voter turnout high in 2008 because so many African Americans wanted to cast their vote for the first black president, many blacks were urged by the Obama campaign to vote early—particularly in highly contested states—to make sure their votes got counted (Saulny 2008). Yet, election officials in a number of the highly contested states seemingly did not do enough to prepare for the predictable surge in black voter turnout (Funk and St. Onge 2008). Hence, in the days immediately before the November 4 election, there were scenes of black women and black men alike waiting in long lines to cast their votes early. In some cases, the lines for early voting required an eight- to ten-hour wait (Weiner 2008).

While these 2008 scenes of thousands of black citizens waiting in long lines to cast a vote early were in many ways just as inspiring as scenes of blacks protesting for the right to vote in the 1960s civil rights movement, it was hard not to see comparisons between the long lines in 2008 and the poll taxes, literacy tests and black voter intimidation of the pre-civil rights era. After all, both the pre-civil rights era poll tax and the long lines outside voting booths in 2008 would have had the self-same effect of suppressing the black vote (Weiner 2008). Seen in these terms, then, scenes of blacks waiting in line to vote in 2008 simply provide a modern-day image of black women—and black men alike—resisting racism. And yet this image of racially conscious black women waiting to vote is at odds with the images of apolitical black women that continue to be trotted out on the silver screen.

Yet even though Hollywood continues to depict its black women characters as depoliticized, it represents its white female characters as politically engaged. So, for example, white females are occasionally cast as political heroines struggling for progressive causes like workers' rights or ending environmental pollution (e.g., *Norma Rae, Erin Brockovich*). This, despite the fact that the majority of white females in the real world have voted for Republican candidates in all of the presidential elections from 1972 to 2008, even though the GOP politicians they support have actually sought to quash workers' rights or allow corporations to pollute the environment. Moreover, many of the same Republican candidates that the majority of white females in the real world have supported have also come out in opposition to the liberal feminist causes (e.g., abortion rights, equal pay for women, etc.) that many politicized white female characters can be seen supporting on screen.

By contrast, black females in the real world have just as consistently supported Democratic presidential candidates at higher rates than any other sociodemographic group (including black men) from 1972 to 2008 (*New York Times* 2008). Much of their support is based on the Democratic Party's historic support of civil rights legislation in the 1960s as well as its ongoing efforts to fund big government programs that help the poor and working men and women. In fact, in the 2008 election, black female support for the Democratic Party reached new heights as a larger percentage of black women turned out to vote than any other group—including white men and white women.[6] Between the 2004 and 2008 presidential elections, white voter turnout actually dropped by 1.1 percent while the turnout for black women and black men rose by 4.9 percent—unquestionably because of Barack Obama's candidacy (Lopez and Taylor 2009; Roberts 2009).

Yet, despite the fact that millions of black women in the real world consistently vote in accordance with their political and economic interests, they are still boxed into screen roles where they play apolitical characters caught in a time warp before the movements for civil rights, black power and women's rights.

Still, the fact that Hollywood avoids representing black women as politically sophisticated is completely understandable. Exposing movie audiences to recent scenes of black women suing U.S. Customs over racial profiling, protesting racism in the criminal justice system in Jena, Louisiana, or New York City, facing roadblocks to voting in 2000 and 2008 or of them turning out in record numbers to support the first black president would have the effect of calling attention to the persistence of institutionalized racism. And, by calling attention to images of politicized black women struggling against institutionalized racism in its myriad modern-day forms, these real-world scenes might do much to challenge the notion of a color-blind America that is still so relentlessly promoted in popular culture.

NOTES

1. Many of the films reviewed in chapter 6 demonstrate how Hollywood has stereotyped black women as masculinized matriarchs or overbearing Sapphires intent on usurping the patriarchal authority of black men. In addition, a number of films released since the late 1980s have treated their black female characters like surrogate

males by showing them involved in "masculine" behaviors like crime. Hence, black females have been variously cast as con women, burglars, robbers and drug dealers in films like *Ghost, Burglar, Set It Off, Dead Presidents,* and *Jackie Brown.* By casting black women in these roles, it has been possible to represent them as conniving, underhanded, dishonest and, in some cases, as violent, intimidating and dangerous just like black males.

2. Interestingly enough, it is those whites who believe that institutional racism has ended who are most likely to express the greatest racial animus towards blacks. For example, in a poll taken in June 2008 in the midst of the presidential election campaign, those whites who claimed that racial discrimination had ended were those least likely to voice support for candidate Obama (Langer 2008). They were also more likely to report that they harbored feelings of racial prejudice and had no interracial friendships. That the notion that racial discrimination had ended was most commonly expressed by the least racially sensitive whites is understandable in light of the ways in which the GOP has repeatedly promoted this belief in the end of racial discrimination. As Republican politicians explain it, the so-called end of racial discrimination means that big government programs that provide blacks with "special privileges" are no longer needed. In other words, Republican politicians have long sought to persuade their constituents that racism has ended as a way of justifying the dismantling of social programs—apparently with some success. Perhaps, many whites also allow themselves to be persuaded that racial discrimination has ended because that makes it easier for them to convince themselves that their own achievements are based solely on their own talent and hard work rather than some now defunct and discredited white skin privilege.

3. In the case of women, the film industry has increasingly felt the need to shore up the patriarchy with its white female viewers—particularly since the feminist movement. Presumably, it has done so by creating white male characters that demonstrate their sensitivity to the plight of the white women around them without giving up any of their power (Davies and Smith 1997). One way to accomplish this is to have the male character experience some of the same oppression that women have traditionally experienced. So, for example, in *Disclosure,* a white male is subjected to sexual harassment at the hands of his female boss. Another example comes from the comedy *Mr. Mom,* in which a laid off auto exec takes on the role of house husband as his wife is forced to start a high-powered career in order to support the family. As a house husband, this "Mr. Mom" suddenly finds himself able to empathize with the other housewives around him as he finds himself facing the same stifling of his career ambitions that many women experience. Happily, patriarchal authority is restored at the end of both films as the harassing high-powered female boss is eventually punished in *Disclosure* and the househusband gets his job back, while his wife returns to her "natural" state as a mother and housewife in *Mr. Mom.*

4. In fact, when black customers received poor service from white waitpersons at restaurants like Denny's and Cracker Barrel, they saw it as evidence of institutional racism and successfully sued both companies (Gallagher 2003). In similar vein in *Crash,* the black carjackers seem to be suggesting that the poor service that they receive from their black waitress is an example of black racism. By creating this false

equivalency between black racism and white racism, the makers of *Crash* manage to once again trivialize institutional racism.

5. It is worth noting that this depoliticization of black women characters is not confined to films about racial redemption that are marketed to white audiences. Many of the ghetto action films reviewed in chapter 6 likewise turn their black women characters into apolitical symbolic whores, drug addicts and criminals.

6. In 2008, 68.8 percent of black women, who were eligible to vote, turned out to vote. This compares to a turnout rate of 66.1 percent for white females and white males combined. Overall turnout for black females and black males combined stood at 65.2 percent and, in fact, 2 million more blacks voted in 2008 than in 2004. For black women, in particular, their record turnout in 2008 represents a 5 percent increase over their turnout rate in 2004, which stood at 63.7 percent. Predictably, the overwhelming majority of these black women (96 percent) threw their support to the Democratic candidate, Barack Obama, in 2008. Black women have also been the strongest supporters of other Democratic candidates in elections going back to 1972. Hence, between 1972 and 2004, some 86 percent to 94 percent of black women voted for the Democratic candidate for president (*New York Times* 2008; Lopez and Taylor 2009; Roberts 2009).

Bibliography

Adler, Patricia. 1993. *Wheeling and Dealing*. New York: Columbia University Press.

Akers, Ronald, and Christine Sellers. 2009. *Criminological Theories: Introduction, Evaluation and Application,* 5th ed. New York: Oxford University Press.

Albelda, Randy, Nancy Folbre, and The Center for Popular Economics. 1996. *The War on the Poor: A Defense Manual.* New York: The New Press.

Allison, Anne. 1994. *Nightwork: Sexuality, Pleasure and Corporate Masculinity in a Tokyo Hostess Club.* Chicago: University of Chicago Press.

Anderson, Elijah. 1994. "The Code of the Streets." *The Atlantic Monthly* (May): 80–94.

——. 1990. *Streetwise: Race, Class and Change in an Urban Community.* Chicago: University of Chicago Press.

Araton, Harvey. 2005. "Pro Basketball: One Year After Pacer-Pistons Fight, Tough Questions of Race and Sports." *New York Times*, October 30.

Associated Press. 2007. "Teenager in Jena Six Pleads Guilty to Lesser Charge." December 4.

——. 1994. "US Reports $1 Billion in Welfare Overpayments in '91." *Boston Globe,* April 12, p. 14.

Bachman, Jerald, Lloyd Johnston, and Patrick O'Malley. 1990. "Explaining the Recent Decline in Cocaine Use among Young Adults." *Journal of Health and Social Behavior* 31:173–184.

Baldus, David, George Woodworth, and Charles Pulaski. 1990. *Equal Justice and the Death Penalty: A Legal and Empirical Analysis.* Boston: Northeastern University Press.

Balkwell, James. 1990. "Ethnic Inequality and the Rate of Homicide." *Social Forces* 69, no. 1 (September): 53–70.

Banfield, Edward C. 1970. *The Unheavenly City: The Nature and the Future of Our Urban Crisis.* Boston: Little, Brown.

Barkan, Steven. 2001. *Criminology: A Sociological Understanding,* 2d. Upper Saddle River, NJ: Prentice-Hall.

Barry, Dan. 2000. "One Legacy of a 41-Bullet Barrage Is a Hard Look at Aggressive Tactics on the Street." *New York Times*, February 27.

Barry, Dan, and Marjorie Connelly. 1999. "Poll in New York Finds Many Think Police Are Biased." *New York Times*, March 16.

Barstow, David. 2000. "Antidrug Tactics Exact Price on a Neighborhood, Many Say." *New York Times*, April 1.

Bass, Sandra. 2001. "Out of Place: Petit Apartheid and the Police." Pp. 43–53 in *Petit Apartheid in the U.S. Criminal Justice System: The Dark Figure of Racism,* edited by Dragan Milovanovic and Katheryn K. Russell. Durham, NC: Carolina Academic Press.

Beck, E. M., and Stewart Tolnay. 1990. "The Killing Fields of the Deep South: The Market for Cotton and the Lynching of Blacks, 1882–1930." *American Sociological Review* 55 (August): 526–539.

Belknap, Joanne, and Hilary Potter. 2006. "Intimate Partner Abuse." Pp. 168–184 in *Rethinking Gender, Crime and Justice: Feminist Readings,* edited by Claire Renzetti, Lynne Goodstein and Susan Miller. Los Angeles: Roxbury.

———. 2005. "The Trials of Measuring the Success of Domestic Violence Policies." *Criminology and Public Policy* 4, no. 3 (August): 559–566.

Bennett, William J., John J. Dilulio, Jr., and John P. Walters. 1996. *Body Count: Moral Poverty and How to Win America's War against Crime and Drugs.* New York: Simon and Schuster.

Bernard, Thomas. 1990. "Angry Aggression among the 'Truly Disadvantaged.'" *Criminology* 28: 173–194.

Black, Donald. 1984. *Toward a General Theory of Social Control.* New York: Academic Press.

———. 1983. "Crime as Social Control." *American Sociological Review* 48: 34–45.

Blau, Judith, and Peter Blau. 1982. "The Cost of Inequality: Metropolitan Structure and Violent Crime." *American Sociological Review* 47: 114–129.

Blauner, Robert. 2006. "Talking Past One Another: Black and White Languages of Race." Pp. 17–25 in *Race and Ethnicity in Society: The Changing Landscape,* edited by Elizabeth Higginbotham and Margaret L. Anderson. Belmont, CA: Wadsworth.

Boeringer, Scott, Constance Shehan, and Ronald Akers. 1991. "Social Contexts and Social Learning in Sexual Coercion and Aggression: Assessing the Contribution of Fraternity Membership." *Family Relations* 40: 58–64.

Bogle, Donald. 1994. *Toms, Coons, Mulattoes, Mammies & Bucks: An Interpretive History of Blacks in American Films.* 3d ed. New York: Continuum.

Boyd, Todd. 2000. "Commentary." *Superfly.* DVD. Warner Brothers.

Brecher, Edward M., and the Editors of *Consumer Reports.* 1972. *Licit and Illicit Drugs.* Boston: Little, Brown and Company.

Brodkin, Karen. 1999. *How Jews Became White Folks and What That Says about Race in America.* Piscataway, NJ: Rutgers University Press.

Brooks, Thomas. 1970. "U.S. 1970: The Radical Underground Surfaces with a Bang." *New York Times*, March.

Bumiller, Elizabeth, and Michael Cooper. 2008. "McCain to Suspend Campaign to Work on Economy." *New York Times,* September 24.

Bureau of Justice Statistics. 2009. "Homicide Trends in the US." Washington, DC: US Department of Justice, Office of Justice Programs, Bureau of Justice Statistics. http://www.ojp.usdoj.gov/bjs/homicide.htm (accessed July 20, 2009).

——. 2009a "Intimate Partner Violence in the U.S." Washington, DC: US Department of Justice, Office of Justice Programs, Bureau of Justice Statistics. http://www.ojp.usdoj.gov/bjs/intimate/victims.htm. (accessed July 20, 2009).

Bureau of Labor Statistics. 2009. Labor Force Statistics from the Current Population Survey. http://www.bls.gov/CPS (accessed September 20, 2009).

Butler, Judith. 1993. "Endangered/Endangering: Schematic Racism and White Paranoia." Pp. 15–22 in *Reading Rodney King, Reading Urban Uprising,* edited by Robert Gooding-Williams. New York: Routledge.

Butterfield, Fox. 2000. "Cities Reduce Crime and Conflict without New York Style Hardball." *New York Times*, March 4.

CNN Political Ticker. 2009. "Jindahl to Reject $98 million, Less Than Sanford, Perry. March 13.

Calmes, Jackie, and Jeff Zeleny. 2008. "Obama Details Plan to Aid Victims of Fiscal Crisis." *New York Times,* October 13.

Campbell, Anne. 1986. "Overview." Pp. 3–13 in *Violent Transactions: The Limits of Personality*, edited by Anne Campbell and John J. Gibbs. Oxford: Basil Blackwell.

Cao, Liquan, Anthony Adams, and Vickie Jensen. 1997. "A Test of the Black Subculture of Violence Thesis: A Research Note." *Criminology* 35: 367–379.

Chesney-Lind, Meda. 2002. "Criminalizing Victimization: The Unintended Consequences of Pro-Arrest Policies for Girls and Women." *Criminology and Public Policy* 2, no. 1 (November): 81–90.

Chesney-Lind, Meda, and Randall Shelden. 1992. *Girls Delinquency and Juvenile Justice.* Belmont, CA: Brooks/Cole.

Chideya, Farai. 1995. *Don't Believe the Hype: Fighting Cultural Misinformation about African-Americans.* New York: Penguin Books.

Cohn, Steven, and Steven Barkan. 2004. "Racial Prejudice and Public Attitudes about the Punishment of Criminals." Pp. 33–47 in *For the Common Good: A Critical Examination of Law and Social Control,* edited by Robin Miller and Sandra Lee Browning. Durham, NC: Carolina Academic Press.

Cole, David. 1999. *No Equal Justice: Race and Class in the American Criminal Justice System.* New York: The New Press.

Collins, Patricia Hill. 1991. *Black Feminist Thought: Knowledge, Consciousness and the Politics of Empowerment.* New York: Routledge.

Comer, James. 1985. "Black Violence and Public Policy." Pp. 63–86 in *American Violence and Public Policy,* edited by Lynn Curtis. New Haven: Yale University Press.

Conklin, John. 2003. *Why Crime Rates Fell.* Boston: Allyn and Bacon.

Connor, Marlene Kim. 1995. *What Is Cool?: Understanding Black Manhood in America.* New York: Crown.

Cooper, Michael. 1999. "Dinkins among 14 Arrested in Protest of Police Shooting." *New York Times,* March 16.

Coser, Lewis. 1968. "Conflict: Social Aspects." Pp. 232–236 in *International Encyclopedia of the Social Sciences,* volume 3, edited by David Sills. New York: MacMillan.

Courtwright, David. 1996. *Violent Land: Single Men and Social Disorder from the Frontier to the Inner City.* Cambridge: Harvard University Press.

Covington, Jeanette. 2004a. "Drugs and the Racial Divide: Selective Punishment of Black Drug Offenders." *Souls* 6 (1): 4–15.

———. 2004b. "Drug War Prisoners: Incapacitation and the Limits of Drug Policy." Pp. 246–265 in *For the Common Good: A Critical Examination of Law and Social Control,* edited by Robin Miller and Sandra Lee Browning. Durham, NC: Carolina Academic Press.

———. 2003. "The Violent Black Male: Conceptions of Race in Criminological Theories." Pp. 254–279 in *Violent Crime: Assessing Race & Ethnic Differences,* edited by Darnell Hawkins. New York: Cambridge University Press.

———. 2001. "Round Up the Usual Suspects: Racial Profiling and the War on Drugs." Pp. 27–42 in *Petit Apartheid in the US Criminal Justice System: The Dark Figure of Racism,* edited by Dragan Milovanovic and Katheryn K. Russell. Durham, NC: Carolina Academic Press.

———. 1999. "African American Communities and Violent Crime: The Construction of Race Differences." *Sociological Focus* 32, no. 1 (February): 7–24.

———. 1997. "The Social Construction of the Minority Drug Problem." *Social Justice* 24, no. 4 (Winter): 117–147.

———. 1995. "Racial Classification in Criminology: The Reproduction of Racialized Crime." *Sociological Forum* 10, no. 4 (December): 547–568.

Crisis—Digital Edition. 2007. "NAACP Leads Rally on Jena—September 20, 2007, Save the Date: Will You Be There for Justice?" August/September.

Cross, William E., and Linda Strauss. 1998. "The Everyday Functions of African American Identity." Pp. 267–279 in *Prejudice: The Target's Perspective,* edited by Janet Swim and Charles Stangor. San Diego: Academic Press.

Curtis, Lynn A. 1975. *Violence, Race and Culture.* Lexington, MA: Lexington Books.

Dasgupta, Shaunta Das. 2002. "A Framework for Understanding Women's Use of Nonlethal Violence in Intimate Heterosexual Relationships." *Violence Against Women* 8: 1364–1389.

Davies, Jude, and Carol A. Smith. 1997. *Gender, Ethnicity and Sexuality in Contemporary American Film.* Edinburgh: Keele University Press.

Dines, Gail, Robert Jensen, and Ann Russo. 1998. *Pornography: The Production and Consumption of Inequality.* New York: Routledge.

Dobash, Russell, R. Emerson Dobash, Kate Cavanagh, and Ruth Lewis. 1998. "Separate and Intersecting Realities: A Comparison of Men's and Women's Accounts of Violence against Women." *Violence Against Women* 4: 382–414.

Dobash, Russell, R. Emerson Dobash, Margo Wilson, and Martin Daly. 1992. "The Myth of Sexual Symmetry in Marital Violence." *Social Problems* 39: 71–91.

Donziger, Steven, ed. 1996. *The Real War on Crime: The Report of the National Criminal Justice Commission.* New York: Harper Collins.

Drake, St. Clair, and Horace Cayton. 1945. *Black Metropolis: A Study of Negro Life in a Northern City.* New York: Harcourt, Brace and Company.

Drape, Joe. 2002. "Colleges Pondering Prevention after the Latest Sports Riot." *New York Times,* November 26.

Dugdale, Richard. 1877. *The Jukes: A Study in Crime, Pauperism and Heredity.* New York: Putnam.

Dwyer, Jim. 2007. "An Infamous Explosion and the Smoldering Memory of Radicalism." *New York Times,* November 14.

Eder, Richard. 1976. "Film: 'Underground,' a Documentary." *New York Times,* May 10.

Federal Bureau of Investigation. 2008. *Crime in the United States, 2007.* Washington, DC: Federal Bureau of Investigation.

Felson, Richard, William Baccaglini, and George Gmelch. 1986. "Bar-Room Brawls: Aggression and Violence in Irish and American Bars." Pp. 153–166 in *Violent Transactions: The Limits of Personality,* edited by Anne Campbell and John J. Gibbs. Oxford: Basil Blackwell.

Fischer, Claude S., Michael Hout, Martin Sanchez Jankowski, Samuel Lucas, Ann Swidler, and Kim Voss. 2005. "Why Inequality?" Pp. 9–15 in *Great Divides.* 3d ed., edited by Thomas M. Shapiro. New York: McGraw-Hill.

Foster, Mary. 2007. "La. Protests Hark Back to '50s, '60s." Associated Press. September 20.

Frankenberg, Ruth. 1999. "Thinking through Race." Pp. 467–475 in *Race and Ethnic Relations in the United States: Readings for the 21ˢᵗ Century,* edited by Christopher Ellision and W. Allen Martin. Los Angeles: Roxbury.

Funk, Tim, and Peter St. Onge. 2008. "2.5 Million in North Carolina Have Voted Early." Charlotteobserver.com November 3.

Gallagher, Charles A. 2003. "Color-Blind Privilege: The Social and Political Functions of Erasing the Color Line in Post Race America." *Race, Gender & Class* 10: 22–37.

Gans, Herbert J. 2005. "The Uses of Undeservingness." Pp. 85–94 in *Great Divides: Readings in Social Inequality in the United States,* 3d ed., edited by Thomas M. Shapiro. New York: McGraw-Hill.

Gastil, Raymond. 1971. "Homicide and a Regional Culture of Violence." *American Sociological Review* 36: 412–427.

Gauthier, DeAnn, and William Bankston. 1997. "Gender Equality and the Sex Ratio of Intimate Killing." *Criminology* 34, no. 4: 577–600.

Giddings, Paula. 1992. "The Last Taboo." Pp. 441–469 in *Race-ing Justice, Engendering Power: Essays on Anita Hill, Clarence Thomas and the Construction of Social Reality,* edited by Toni Morrison. New York: Pantheon.

Giordano, Peggy, Toni Milhollin, Stephen Cernkovich, M. D. Pugh, and Jennifer Rudolph. 1999. "Delinquency, Identity and Women's Involvement in Relationship Violence." *Criminology* 37, no. 1 (February): 17–40.

Goddard, H. H. 1914. *Feeble-mindedness.* New York: Macmillan.

Goldstein, Paul, Henry Brownstein, Patrick J. Ryan, and Patricia Belluci. 1997. "Crack and Homicide in New York City: A Case Study in the Epidemiology of Violence." Pp. 113–130 in *Crack in America,* edited by Craig Reinarman and Harry Levine. Berkeley: University of California Press.

Golub, Andrew, and Bruce Johnson. 1997. "Crack's Decline: Some Surprises across US Cities." Research in Brief. Washington, DC: US Department of Justice, National Institute of Justice, July 1997.

Greenberg, David. 1977. "Delinquency and the Age Structure of Society." *Contemporary Crises* 1: 66–86.

Greene, Wade. 1970 "The Militants Who Play with Dynamite." *New York Times,* October 25.

Guerrero, Ed. 1993. *Framing Blackness: The African American Image in Film.* Philadelphia: Temple University Press.

———. 1993a. "The Black Image in Protective Custody: Hollywood's Biracial Buddy Films of the 1980s." Pp. 237–246 in *Black American Cinema,* edited by Manthia Diawara. New York: Routledge.

Gurr, Ted Robert. 1979. "Political Protest and Rebellion in the 1960s: The United States in World Perspective." Pp. 49–76 in *Violence in America,* edited by Hugh Davis Graham and Ted Robert Gurr. Beverly Hills, CA: Sage.

Harris, Anthony, and Lisa Meidlinger. 1995. "Criminal Behavior: Race and Class." Pp.114–143 in *Criminology: A Contemporary Handbook.* Belmont, CA: Wadsworth.

Harris, Anthony, and James Shaw. 2000. "Looking for Patterns: Race, Class and Crime." Pp. 129–163 in *Criminology: A Contemporary Handbook,* edited by Joseph Sheley. Belmont, CA: Wadsworth.

Hawkins, Darnell, John Laub, Janet Lauritsen, and Lynn Cothern. 2000. "Race, Ethnicity and Serious and Violent Juvenile Offending." Juvenile Justice Bulletin (June). Washington, D.C.: U.S. Department of Justice, Office of Juvenile Justice and Delinquency Prevention.

Healey, Joseph. 1997. *Race, Ethnicity and Gender in the United States: Inequality, Group Conflict and Power.* Thousand Oaks, CA: Pine Forge.

Heimer, Karen, and Stacy De Coster. 1999. "The Gendering of Violent Delinquency." *Criminology* 37, no. 2 (May): 277–318.

Herbert, Bob. 2007. "Harassed in the Classroom." *New York Times,* July 3.

Higginbotham, Elizabeth. 2005. "Women and Work: Exploring Race, Ethnicity and Class." Pp. 345–354 in *Great Divides: Readings in Social Inequality in the United States,* edited by Thomas Shapiro. New York: McGraw-Hill.

Hines, Revathi. 2006. "The Silent Voices: 2000 Presidential Election and the Minority Vote in Florida." Pp. 206–212 in *Race and Ethnicity in Society: The Changing Landscape,* edited by Elizabeth Higginbotham and Margaret Anderson. Belmont, CA: Wadsworth.

Hoffman, Bruce. 1993. "Terrorism in the United States: Recent Trends and Future Prospects." Pp. 220–225 in *Violence and Terrorism,* edited by Bernard Schechterman and Martin Slann. Guilford, CT: Dushkin.

Holmes, Steven. 2000. "Race Analysis cites Disparity in Sentencing for Narcotics. *New York Times,* June 8.

hooks, bell. 1993. "The Oppositional Gaze: Black Female Spectators." Pp. 288–302 in *Black American Cinema,* edited by Manthia Diawara. Los Angeles: The American Film Institute.

——. 1992. *Black Looks: Race and Representation.* Boston, MA: South End Press.

——. 1981. *Ain't I a Woman: Black Women and Feminism.* Boston, MA: South End Press.

Hooton, Ernest. 1939. *The American Criminal.* Cambridge: Harvard University Press.

Hoover, Kenneth, and Todd Donovan. 2004. *The Elements of Social Scientific Thinking.* Belmont, CA: Wadsworth.

Hsiao, Andrew. 2001. "Mothers of Invention: The Families of Police Brutality Victims and the Movement They've Built." Pp. 179–195 in *Zero Tolerance: Quality of Life and the New Police Brutality in New York City.* New York: New York University Press.

Hsu, Hsuan. 2006. "Racial Privacy, the L.A. Ensemble Film and Paul Haggis's *Crash.*" *Film Criticism* 31, nos. 1/2 (Fall/Winter): 132–156.

Humm, Maggie. 1997. *Feminism and Film.* Bloomington: Indiana University Press.

Inverarity, James. 1976. "Populism and Lynching in Louisiana, 1889–1896: A Test of Erikson's Theory of the Relationship between Boundary Crises and Repressive Justice." *American Sociological Review* 41(April): 262–280.

James, Jennifer. 1977. "Prostitutes and Prostitution." In *Deviants: Voluntary Actors in a Hostile World,* edited by Edward Sagarin and Fred Montanino. Morristown, NJ: General Learning Press.

Jewel, K. Sue. 1993. *From Mammy to Miss America and Beyond: Cultural Images & the Shaping of U.S. Social Policy.* New York: Routledge.

Johnson, Dirk. 2000. "Illinois Citing Faulty Verdicts, Bars Executions." *New York Times,* February 1.

Jones, D. Marvin. 2005. *Race, Sex and Suspicion: The Myth of the Black Male.* Westport, CT: Greenwood Press.

Jones, Jacquie. 1992. "The Accusatory Space." Pp. 95–105 in *Black Popular Culture,* edited by Gina Dent. Seattle: Bay Press.

Jones, Richard. 2007. "In Louisiana, a Tree, a Fight and a Question of Justice." *New York Times,* September 19.

Karmen, Andrew. 2000. *New York Murder Mystery: The True Story Behind the Crime Crash of the 1990s.* New York: New York University Press.

Katz, Jack. 1988. *Seductions of Crime: Moral and Sensual Attractions in Doing Evil.* New York: Basic Books.

Katz, Janet, and William Chambliss. 1995. "Biology and Crime." Pp. 274–303 in *Criminology: A Contemporary Handbook,* 2d ed., edited by Joseph Sheley. Belmont, CA: Wadsworth.

Kifner, John. 1970. "12 S.D.S. Militants Indicted in Chicago: Hoffman Gets Case." *New York Times,* April 3.

Kim, Suzin. 1996. "Gangs and Law Enforcement: The Necessity of Limiting the Use of Gang Profiles." *The Boston Public Interest Law Journal* (Winter).

Klein, Dorie. 1995. "The Etiology of Female Crime: A Review of the Literature." Pp. 30–53 in *The Criminal Justice System and Women.* 2d ed., edited by Barbara Raffel Price and Natalie Sokoloff. New York: McGraw-Hill.

Knowles, Louis, and Kenneth Prewitt. 1969. *Institutional Racism in America.* Englewood Cliffs, NJ: Prentice-Hall.

Krivio, Lauren, and Ruth D. Peterson. 2000. "The Structural Context of Homicide: Accounting for Racial Differences in Process." *American Sociological Review* 65 (August): 547–559.

Kuhl, Stefan. 1994. *The Nazi Connection: Eugenics, American Racism and German National Socialism.* New York: Oxford University Press.

Langer, Gary. 2008. "Obama's Candidacy Underscores Crosscurrents of Race and Politics." *ABC News,* June 22. http://abcnews.go.com/PollingUnit/Politics/Story.

Leadership Conference on Civil Rights. 2000. *Justice on Trial: Racial Disparities in the American Criminal Justice System.* http://www.civilrights.org/images/justice.pdf.

Lerner, Gerda, ed. 1972. *Black Women in White America: A Documentary History.* New York: Vintage Books.

Lipstyle, Robert. 1999. "Backtalk: The Entangled Web around Youth Sports." *New York Times,* May 23.

Lombroso-Ferrero, Gina. 1911. *Criminal Man, According to the Classification of Cesare Lombroso.* New York: G. P. Putnam's Sons.

Lopez, Mark Hugo, and Paul Taylor. 2009. "Dissecting the 2008 Electorate: Most Diverse in US History." Pew Hispanic Center. April 30.

Lubiano, Wahneema. 1992. "Black Ladies, Welfare Queens, and State Minstrels: Ideological War by Narrative Means." Pp. 323–361 in *Race-ing Justice, En-gendering Power: Essays on Anita Hill, Clarence Thomas and the Construction of Social Reality,* edited by Toni Morrison. New York: Pantheon.

Luckenbill, David, and David P. Doyle. 1989. "Structural Position and Violence: Developing a Cultural Explanation." *Criminology* 27, no. 3: 419–436.

Maguire, Kathleen, and Ann Pastore. 2007. *Sourcebook of Criminal Justice Statistics, 2007.* http://www.albany.edu/sourcebook.

Majors, Richard, and Janet Mancini-Billson. 1992. *Cool Pose: The Dilemmas of Black Manhood in America.* New York: Touchstone.

Manatu, Norma. 2003. *African American Women and Sexuality in the Cinema.* Jefferson, NC: McFarland & Company.

Mapp, Edward. 2003. *African Americans and the Oscar: Seven Decades of Struggle and Achievement.* Lanham, MD: Scarecrow Press.

Martin, Jonathan. 2008a. "McCain Alarms with Abortion Comment." *Politico.com,* August 14.

———. 2008b. "Ya Can't Make It Up." *Politico.com,* 13 July.

Massey, Douglas, and Nancy A. Denton. 1993. *American Apartheid: Segregation and the Making of the Underclass.* Cambridge, MA: Harvard University Press.

Matza, David. 1964. *Delinquency and Drift.* New York: Wiley.

Maxson, Cheryl. 1995. "Research in Brief: Street Gangs and Drug Sales in Two Suburban Cities." Pp. 228–235 in *The Modern Gang Reader,* edited by Malcolm Klein, Cheryl Maxson and Jody Miller. Los Angeles: Roxbury.

McArdle, Andrea. 2001. "No Justice, No Peace." Pp. 147–176 in *Zero Tolerance: Quality of Life and the New Police Brutality in New York City.* New York: New York University Press.

McArdle, Andrea, and Tanya Erzen. 2001. *Zero Tolerance: Quality of Life and the New Police Brutality in New York City.* New York: New York University Press.

McCaghy, Charles, and Timothy Capron. 1994. *Deviant Behavior: Crime, Conflict and Interest Groups.* New York: Macmillan.

McGrath, Charles. 2004. "Far Left Gathers for Weather Report." *New York Times,* June 12.

McKinley, James. 2000. "Sports Psychology: A Team is an Extension of the Fans." *New York Times,* August 11.

Meeks, Kenneth. 2000. *Driving While Black.* New York: Broadway Books.

Meier, August, and Elliott Rudwick. 1970. *From Plantation to Ghetto,* Revised Edition. New York: Hill and Wang.

Merton, Robert. 1938. "Social Structure and Anomie." *American Sociological Review* 3: 672–682.

Messerschmidt, James. 1993. *Masculinities and Crime: Critique and Reconceptualization of Theory.* Lanham, MD: Rowman & Littlefield.

Messner, Steven, and Reid Golden. 1992. "Racial Inequality and Racially Disaggregated Homicide Rates: An Assessment of Alternative Theoretical Explanations." *Criminology* 30, no. 3: 421–447.

Miami Herald Blog. 2008. "Christian Leader Calls Obama "Scary," Points to "Muslim Roots." September 10.

Miller, Jerome G. 1996. *Search and Destroy: African American Males in the Criminal Justice System.* Cambridge, UK: Cambridge University Press.

Miller, Jody, and Norman White. 2003. "Gender and Adolescent Relationship Violence." *Criminology* 41, no. 4 (November): 1207–1248.

Miller, Susan, and Michelle Meloy. 2006. "Women's Use of Force: Voices of Women Arrested for Domestic Violence." *Violence Against Women* 12, no. 1: 89–115.

Miller, Walter B. 1958. "Lower Class Culture as a Generating Milieu of Gang Delinquency." *Journal of Social Issues* 14, no. 4: 5–19.

Mitchell, Elvis. 2003. "Film Review: A Trip Back to the Contradictions of the Stormy 60s." *New York Times,* June 4.

Moffitt, Terrie. 1999. "Pathways in the Life Course to Crime." Pp. 41–58. in *Criminological Theory: Past to Present, Essential Readings,* edited by Francis Cullen and Robert Agnew. Los Angeles: Roxbury.

Moffitt, Terrie, Richard Robins, and Avshalom Caspi. 2001. "A Couples Analysis of Partner Abuse with Implications for Abuse Prevention Policy." *Criminology and Public Policy* 1, no. 1 (November): 5–36.

Moffitt, Terrie, Robert Krueger, Avshalom Caspi, and Jeff Fagan. 2000. "Partner Abuse and General Crime: How Are They the Same? How Are They Different?" *Criminology* 38, no. 1: 199–232.

Monster's Ball. 2001. "Special Features." DVD. Lions Gate Home Entertainment/ Signature Series.

Montgomery, David, and Aman Batheja. 2009. "Democrats will push to overturn Perry move to reject some stimulus funds." Star-Telegram.com, March 13.

Moore, Solomon. 2007. "Reporting While Black." *New York Times,* September 30.

Moran, Richard. 1997. "The New York Story: More Luck than Policing." *Washington Post National Weekly Edition.* February 17–23.

Morgan, John P., and Lynn Zimmer. 1997. "The Social Pharmacology of Smokeable Cocaine: Not All It's Cracked Up to Be." Pp. 131–170 in *Crack in America,* edited by Craig Reinarman and Harry Levine. Berkeley, CA: University of California Press.

Nagourney, Adam, and Elizabeth Bumiller. 2008. "McCain Leaps into a Thicket." *New York Times,* September 25.

National Institute on Drug Abuse. 1991. *National Household Survey on Drug Abuse: Population Estimates 1991.* Rockville, MD: National Institute on Drug Abuse.

New York Civil Liberties Union. 2009. *The School to Prison Pipeline: Fact Sheet.* http://www.nyclu.org/schooltoprison/factsheet (August).

———. 2007. *Criminalizing the Classroom—The NYCLU's Testimony Given Before NYC Council.* October 10.

———. 2007a. *Students, Educators and Advocates Call for an End to Aggressive, Excessive Police Presence in NYC Public Schools.* October 10.

New York Times. 2008. "National Exit Polls Table." November 5.

———. 2002. "College Football: Fan Violence Erupts During Victory Celebration." 25 November.

———. 1975. "3 Producers Back Film on Radicals." June 7.

Newman, Katherine S. 1999. *No Shame in My Game: The Working Poor in the Inner City.* New York: Alfred Knopf and the Russell Sage Foundation.

Newman, Maria. 2007. "Jena Update: Crowds, Activism and Outrage." *New York Times,* September 20.

Newsweek. 1992. "Special Report. Fire and Fury: America on Trial." May 11.

Nisbett, Richard E. 1993. "Violence and US Regional Culture." *American Psychologist* 48, no. 4 (April): 441–449.

Oliver, Melvin, James Johnson, Jr., and Walter Farrell, Jr. 1993. "Anatomy of a Rebellion: A Political-Economic Analysis." Pp. 117–141 in *Reading Rodney King, Reading Urban Uprising,* edited by Robert Gooding-Williams. New York: Routledge.

Oliver, William. 1994. *The Violent Social World of Black Men.* New York: Lexington Books.

Omi, Michael, and Howard Winant. 1994. *Racial Formation in the United States.* 2d ed. New York: Routledge.

Osthoff, Sue. 2002. "But Gertrude I Beg to Differ, A Hit Is Not a Hit Is Not a Hit: When Battered Women Are Arrested for Assaulting Their Partners." *Violence Against Women* 8: 1521–1544.

Pager, Devah. 2003. "The Mark of a Criminal Record." *American Journal of Sociology* 108: 937–975.

Paternoster, Raymond. 1984. "Prosecutorial Discretion in Requesting the Death Penalty: A Case of Victim-Based Racial Discrimination." *Law and Society Review* 18: 437–478.

Patterson, Orlando. 1997. *The Ordeal of Integration: Progress and Resentment in America's "Racial" Crisis.* Washington, DC: Civitas/Counterpoint.

Phillips, Julie. 2002. "White, Black and Latino Homicide Rates: Why the Difference?" *Social Problems* 49, no. 3 (August): 349–374.

Poussaint, Alvin. 1983. "Black-on-Black Homicide: A Psychological-Political Perspective." *Victimology* 8: 161–169.

Ptacek, James. 1997. "The Tactics and Strategies of Men Who Batter: Testimony from Women Seeking Restraining Orders." Pp. 104–123 in *Violence between Intimate Partners: Patterns, Causes and Effects*, edited by Albert Cardarelli. Needham Heights, MA: Allyn and Bacon.

Purdum, Todd. 1999. "A Police Shooting Death, A Study in Contrasts." *New York Times,* June 5.

Puzzanchera, C., and W. Kang. 2008. "Easy Access to the FBI's Supplementary Homicide Reports: 1980–2006." http://www.ojjdp.ncjrs.gov/ojstatbb/ezashr/asp/off-display.asp.

Rainwater, Lee, and William L. Yancey. 1967. *The Moynihan Report and the Politics of Controversy.* Cambridge, MA: The M.I.T. Press.

Raphael, Jody. 2006. "Compensating for Abuse: Women's Involvement in the Sex Trade in North America." Pp. 125–138 in *Rethinking Gender, Crime and Justice: Feminist Readings,* edited by Claire Renzetti, Lynne Goodstein and Susan Miller. Los Angeles: Roxbury.

Rebellon, Cesar. 2002. "Reconsidering the Broken Homes/Delinquency Relationship and Exploring Its Mediating Mechanisms." *Criminology* 40: 103–135.

Reinarman, Craig, and Harry G. Levine, eds. 1997. *Crack in America: Demon Drugs and Social Justice.* Berkeley: University of California Press.

Rennison, Callie Marie, and Sarah Welchans. 2000. *Intimate Partner Violence.* Bureau of Justice Statistics. Special Report, May.

Renzetti, Claire. 2006. "Gender and Violent Crime." Pp. 93–106 in *Rethinking Gender, Crime and Justice: Feminist Readings,* edited by Claire Renzetti, Lynne Goodstein and Susan Miller. Los Angeles: Roxbury.

Reskin, Barbara, and Irene Padavic. 2005. "Women, Men and Work in the Twenty-First Century." Pp. 366–377 in *Great Divides: Readings in Social Inequality in the United States,* 3d ed,, edited by Thomas Shapiro. New York: McGraw-Hill.

Risman, Barbara. 2005. "Gender as Structure." Pp. 292–299 in *Great Divides: Readings in Social Inequality in the United States,* edited by Thomas Shapiro. New York: McGraw-Hill.

Roane, Kit. 1999. "Uptown Block Opts Out of Intensive Police Program." *New York Times,* March 21.

Roberts, Sam. 2009. "No Racial Gap Seen in '08 Vote Turnout." *New York Times,* April 30.

Rocchio, Vincent. 2000. *Reel Racism: Confronting Hollywood's Construction of Afro-American Culture.* Boulder, CO: Westview.

Roncek, Dennis, and Pamela Maier. 1991. "Bars, Blocks and Crimes Revisited: Linking the Theory of Routine Activities to the Empiricism of 'Hot Spots.'" *Criminology* 29, no. 4: 725–753.

Royster, Deirdre. 2003. *Race and the Invisible Hand: How White Networks Exclude Black Men from Blue Collar Jobs.* Berkeley: University of California Press.

Russell, Katheryn. 1998. *The Color of Crime: Racial Hoaxes, White Fear, Black Protectionism and Police Harassment and Other Macroaggressions.* New York: New York University Press.

Ryan, William. 1976. *Blaming the Victim.* New York: Random House.

Sampson, Robert, and William Julius Wilson. 1995. "Toward a Theory of Race, Crime and Urban Inequality." Pp. 37–54 in *Crime and Inequality,* edited by John Hagan and Ruth Peterson. Stanford: Stanford University Press.

Saulny, Susan. 2008. "Obama-Inspired Black Voters Warm to Politics." *New York Times,* November 1.

Shapiro, Thomas. 2005. "Introduction." Pp. 1–7 in *Great Divides: Readings in Social Inequality in the United States.* 3d ed., edited by Thomas Shapiro. New York: McGraw-Hill.

Shaw, Clifford, and Henry McKay. 1942. *Juvenile Delinquency and Urban Areas.* Chicago: University of Chicago Press.

Siegel, Larry. 2008. *Criminology: The Core.* Belmont, CA: Thomson Wadsworth.

Siegel, Loren. 1997. "The Pregnancy Police Fight the War on Drugs." Pp. 249–259 in *Crack in America,* edited by Craig Reinarman and Harry Levine. Berkeley: University of California Press.

Sigelman, Lee, and Susan Welch. 1994. *Black Americans' Views of Racial Inequality.* Cambridge: Cambridge University Press.

Silberman, Charles. 1978. *Criminal Violence, Criminal Justice.* New York: Random House.

Sinker, Daniel. 2008. "Goodnight, Vietnam: Tuesday Night Will Finally Put to Rest the Ghost of a War That Ended 35 Years Ago." *Huffington Post,* November 2.

Smith, Dinitia. 2001. "No Regrets for a Love of Explosives; In a Memoir of Sorts, A War Protester Talks of Life with the Weathermen." *New York Times,* September 11.

Smith, M. Dwayne. 2000. "Capital Punishment in America." Pp. 621–643 in *Criminology—A Contemporary Handbook,* 3d ed., edited by Joseph Sheley. Belmont, CA: Wadsworth.

Sorenson, Jon, and Donald Wallace. 1999. "Prosecutorial Discretion in Seeking Death: An Analysis of Racial Disparity in the Pretrial Stages of Case Processing in a Midwestern County." *Justice Quarterly* 16: 559–578.

Spear, Allan. 1967. *Black Chicago: The Making of a Negro Ghetto, 1890–1920.* Chicago: University of Chicago Press.

Steffensmeier, Darrell, and Emilie Allan. 2000. "Looking for Patterns: Gender, Age and Crime." Pp. 85–127 in *Criminology: A Contemporary Handbook,* edited by Joseph Sheley. Belmont, CA: Wadsworth.

Steffensmeier, Darrell, Jennifer Schwartz, Hua Zhong, and Jeff Ackerman. 2005. "An Assessment of Recent Trends in Girls' Violence Using Diverse Longitudinal Sources: Is the Gender Gap Closing?" *Criminology* 43, no. 2 (May): 355–405.

Steinmetz, Suzanne. 1978. "The Battered Man Syndrome." *Victimology* 2, nos. 3/4: 499–509.

Stolberg, Sheryl Gay, and Adam Nagourney. 2009. "Partisan Fight Endures as Stimulus Bill Signed." *New York Times,* February 17.

Strauss, Murray, and Richard Gelles. 1990. "Societal Change and Change in Family Violence from 1975 to 1985 as Revealed by Two National Surveys. Pp. 114–136 in *Criminal Behavior: Text and Readings in Criminology,* 2d ed., edited by Delos H. Kelly. New York: St. Martin's.

Substance Abuse and Mental Health Services Administration. 1999. *National Household Survey on Drug Abuse: Population Estimates 1998.* Rockville, MD: SAMHSA.

———. 1996. *National Household Survey on Drug Abuse: Population Estimates, 1995.* Rockville, MD: SAMHSA.

Sullivan, Mercer. 1989. *"Getting Paid": Youth, Crime, and Work in the Inner City.* Ithaca: Cornell University Press.

Sutherland, Edwin. 1939. *Principles of Criminology,* 3d ed. Philadelphia: Lippincott.

Swarns, Christina. 2006. "The Uneven Scales of Capital Justice." Pp. 381–384 in *Race and Ethnicity in Society: The Changing Landscape,* edited by Elizabeth Higginbotham and Margaret Anderson. Belmont, CA: Wadsworth.

Tannen, Deborah. 1990. *You Just Don't Understand: Women and Men in Conversation.* New York: Ballantine.

Taylor, Ralph B., and Jeanette Covington. 1988. "Neighborhood Changes in Ecology and Violence." *Criminology* 26, no. 4: 553–589.

Thornton, Sarah. 1997. "General Introduction." Pp. 1–7 in *The Subcultures Reader,* edited by Ken Gelder and Sarah Thornton. London: Routledge.

Urbina, Ian. 2008. "Voters Find Long Lines, but No Catastrophes." *New York Times,* November 4.

U.S. Census Bureau. 2006. Current Population Survey, Annual Social and Economic Supplement, 2004 Racial Statistics Branch, Population Division.

———.2004. Current Population Survey Reports. The Black Population in the U.S., March 2004.

U.S. National Advisory Commission on Civil Disorders. 1968. *Report of the National Advisory Commission on Civil Disorders.* New York: E.P. Dutton & Company.

Valentine, Charles A. 1968. *Culture and Poverty: Critique and Counterproposals.* Chicago: University of Chicago Press.

Vandehei, Jim, and David Paul Kuhn. 2008. "Palin Reignites Culture Wars." *Politico. com,* September 2.

Vera, Hernan, and Andrew Gordon. 2003. *Screen Saviors: Hollywood Fictions of Whiteness.* Lanham, MD: Rowman & Littlefield.

Verniero, Peter, and Paul Zoubek. 1999. *Interim Report of the State Police Review Team Regarding Allegations of Racial Profiling.* New Jersey Department of Law and Public Safety Publication, April 20.

Visher, Christy. 1983. "Gender, Police Arrest Decisions and Notions of Chivalry." *Criminology* 21: 5–28.

Vold, George, Thomas Bernard, and Jeffrey Snipes. 2002. *Theoretical Criminology,* 5th ed. New York: Oxford University Press.

Wakin, Daniel. 2003. "Quieter Lives for 60s Militants, but Intensity of Beliefs Hasn't Faded." *New York Times,* August 24.

Waldorf, Dan, Craig Reinarman, and Sheigla Murphy. 1991. *Cocaine Changes.* Philadelphia: Temple University Press.

Walker, Alice, ed. 1979. *I Love Myself When I Am Laughing . . . and Then Again When I Am Looking Mean and Impressive: A Zora Neale Hurston Reader.* Old Westbury, NY: Feminist Press.

Walker, Samuel. 1990. "Reform Society: Provide Opportunity." Pp. 552–561 in *Criminal Behavior: Texts and Readings in Criminology,* 2d ed., edited by Delos H. Kelly. New York: St. Martin's Press.

Walker, Samuel, Cassia Spohn, and Miriam DeLone. 2004. *The Color of Justice: Race, Ethnicity and Crime in America.* 3d ed. Belmont, CA: Wadsworth.

Wallace, Harvey. 1996. *Family Violence: Legal, Medical and Social Perspectives.* Needham, MA: Allyn and Bacon.

Watkins, S. Craig. 1998. *Representing: Hip Hop Culture and the Production of Black Cinema.* Chicago: University of Chicago Press.

Weigel, David. 2009. "McCain Campaign Investigated, Dismissed Obama Citizenship Rumors." The Washington Independent.com, July 24.

Weiner, Rachel. 2008. "Voting Lines Stretch to Eight Hours." *The Huffington Post,* November 3.

Wells-Barnett, Ida. 1895. *A Red Record.* Chicago: Donohue & Henneberry.

Wicker, Tom. 1968. "Introduction." Pp. v–xi in *Report of the National Advisory Commission on Civil Disorders* by U.S. National Advisory Commission on Civil Disorders.

Williams, Monte. 2000. "Study Shows Rise in Number of Women Jailed for Drugs." *New York Times,* December 1.

Willis, Paul. 1990. *Common Culture.* Boulder, CO: Westview.

———. 1977. *Learning to Labor: How Working Class Kids Get Working Class Jobs.* New York: Columbia University Press.

Wilson, James Q., and Richard Herrnstein. 1985. *Crime & Human Nature: The Definitive Study of the Causes of Crime.* New York: Simon & Schuster.

Wilson, James Q., and George Kelling. 1982. "Broken Windows: The Police and Neighborhood Safety." *Atlantic Monthly* 249 (March): 29–38.

Wilson, William Julius. 1996. *When Work Disappears: The World of the New Urban Poor.* New York: Alfred A. Knopf.

Wolfgang, Marvin E., and Franco Ferracuti. 1967. *The Subculture of Violence.* London: Tavistock.

Wynn, Jennifer. 2001. "Can Zero Tolerance Last?: Voices from Inside the Precinct." Pp. 107–126 in *Zero Tolerance: Quality of Life and the New Police Brutality in New York City,* edited by Andrea McArdle and Tanya Erzen. New York: New York University Press.

Yablonsky, Lewis. 1970. *The Violent Gang.* Baltimore: Penguin Books.

Young, Jock. 1997. "The Subterranean World of Play." Pp. 71–80 in *The Subcultures Reader,* edited by Ken Gelder and Sarah Thornton. London: Routledge.

Zinn, Maxine Baca, and D. Stanley Eitzen. 2005. "Economic Restructuring and Systems of Inequality." Pp. 16–19 in *Great Divides: Readings in Social Inequality in the United States,* 3d, edited by Thomas Shapiro. Boston: McGraw-Hill.

Index

accusatory space, 217-218, 220

Anderson, Elijah, 137, 141, 242-245, 252, 258, 265-266, 242-243, 245, 252, 258, 265-267

angry aggression, 145-146, 149, 261

ascribed vs. achieved status, 143

The Associate, 49-50

authenticity in black movie characters, 40-42, 121-122; critique, 42-45, 47, 73, 75, 87n3, 303-306

Baby Boy, 87n1, 226-227, 232, 255

Bernard, Thomas, 135, 145-146

biological and psychological theories of crime: critique of, 235-237, 264-267, 267n1, 269n6; female violence and, 232-235, 264-267, 269n6; male violence and, 233-234; policy implications of, 235-237, 264-267; racial hierarchies and, 234, 236-237, 245-246, 249, 251-253, 265-267, 269n6; sexual symmetry and, 234, 264-267; similarities between life course theories and, 245-246, 249, 252-253, 257, 264-267, 269n6. *See also* life course theories of female violence

Birth of a Nation, 5, 6, 8, 15, 22, 198

black culture of poverty: academic constructions of, 11-12, 28-29, 54, 130-131; cinematic constructions of, 23-27, 67-68, 71, 72, 96-103, 126; conservative political agenda and, 11-14, 16, 19, 53-54, 97-99, 101; critique of, 11-12, 16-17, 55-59, 97-98, 126; definition of, 11-12, 53-54; media constructions of, 23-24, 25-27, 54; racialization and, 130-131

Black, Donald, 160-161, 162, 163-165

black female-headed households: academic constructions of, 176-178, 239-240, 268n3; cinematic constructions of, 26, 72, 96-101, 126-127, 215-218; conservative political agenda and, 16-17, 66-67, 96-101, 126; female violence and, 239-240, 268nn3-4; male violence and, 176-178; masculinization and, 239-240, 268n3; sexual symmetry and, 239-240; stigmatization of, 16-17; threats to nuclear family and, 17

black females and racial oppression: cinematic constructions of, 195-196, 222-223, 272-276, 283, 284, 290-294, 297-300, 302-304; disenfranchisement of, 304-306;

About the Author

Jeanette Covington is associate professor in the Department of Sociology at Rutgers University in New Brunswick where she teaches courses on crime, drugs, and drug policy. In earlier research, she wrote a number of articles on the impact of neighborhood change on crime and fear of crime as well as on drugs and crime. More recently, her published work has focused on how criminologists construct "race" in their analyses of race differences in crime. She received her B.A., M.A., and Ph.D. from the University of Chicago.

Breinigsville, PA USA
28 March 2010
235025BV00005B/1/P